ABOUT THE AUTHOR

John Snelling was born in Wales in 1943 and brought up there and in London and Canterbury. After graduation with honours degrees in both English and Philosophy, he lectured at Maidstone College of Art for a number of years before leaving to travel in the East, where began an interest in Oriental religion and philosophy. From 1980 until 1984 he was General Secretary of the Buddhist Society. He was also Editor of the Society's quarterly journal, *The Middle Way*, which is believed to be the most widely circulated Buddhist periodical in the West, perhaps in the world. John Snelling wrote many books for both adults and children and numerous articles as well as stories, plays and features for radio and scripts for television. He lived in the Sharpham North Community in Devon for a number of years before his death, in January 1992.

D1386346

The Buddhist Handbook

A Complete Guide to Buddhist Teaching and Practice

JOHN SNELLING

PROSPERO
B·O·O·K·S
A DIVISION OF CHAPTERS INC.

First published in the UK in 1987 by Rider

This revised edition first published in 1998 by Rider, an imprint of
Ebury Press, Random House UK Ltd.

This edition produced for Prospero Books, a division of Chapters Inc.

Papers used for this book are natural, recyclable products made
from wood grown in sustainable forests.

Printed and bound in Great Britain by
Mackays of Chatham plc, Chatham, Kent

ISBN 1 55 2678474

A Note on Language

The scriptural language of Theravāda Buddhism is Pali, that of Indian Mahāyāna Buddhism in Sanskrit – both dead Indian languages. In many cases, the spellings of names and terms in the two languages are similar: *bodhisatta/bodhisattva, kamma/ karma, Dhamma/Dharma, arahat/arhat, Gotama/Gautama.* I have not opted for a single standardized spelling throughout but generally have tended to use the appropriate spelling in the appropriate place, i.e. Pali when discussing Theravāda Buddhism, Sanskrit when discussing Indian Mahāyāna and Tantra. Variations of spelling will therefore occur in the text but should not prove an obstacle to understanding. Sometimes the appropriate alternative is given.

Caveat

Inclusion of any group or teacher in this Handbook does not imply endorsement of them by the author. This is in line with the traditions of Buddhism, which is not an authoritarian religion with a centralized authority that grants or with-holds the seal of approval. It is therefore up to the individual to test the ground for him- or herself, guided by common sense and the advice given by the Buddha himself, for example in the *Kalama Sutta* (see pp. 3–4).

Acknowledgements

I should like to sincerely thank the following for their kind help, advice, information, support, encouragement, etc.:

Geshe Wangchen, Phiroz Mehta, Francesca Fremantle, Robert Beer, Maurice O'C Walshe, Garry Thomson, Stephen Batchelor, Frances Wood (British Library), John Stevens, Eric Cheetham, Ven. Amaro Bhikkhu, Richard Hunn (Upāsaka Wen Shu), Arthur Burton-Stibbon, Rev. Jack Austin, Jim Pym, Nick Cook, Phuntsog Wangyal, Shenpen & Mike Hookham, U Ba Maw, Ken Wilber, Dr. Nina E. Coltart, Patrick Gaffney, Ven. Dr. H., Saddhatissa, Jim Belither, Ven Chushin Passmore, Dick St. Ruth, Nick Ribush, Brian Hickman (SOAS Library), Ven. Varapañño Bhikkhu, Michael Roach, Ven. Jagaro Bhikkhu, Victoria Forsyth – and all those who kindly supplied biographical details for the Who's Who section. Also my Editor, Oliver Caldecott, for his support.

In particular, Russell Webb's great kindness in substantially assisting with the compilation of the Who's Who section of the book in addition to his help and guidance in other areas must be specially mentioned, with gratitude.

Gill Farrer-Halls would like to thank Stephen Batchelor, Russell Webb and everyone else who kindly assisted in this work.

Contents

Part 1

Prologue

1   Why Buddhism?

Buddhism has gained enormous ground in the West during the past 30 years. Recently it was hailed as the fastest growing religion in Britain. There are well over 100 groups and centres established here by now, more in the United States and an ever-increasing number in Europe too. There is every indication that the interest in Buddhism will continue to grow, for it clearly supplies some deep spiritual need in the people of the Western world that their established religious traditions fail to fully supply. One might well ask, then: *'What does Buddhism possess that is especially valuable and helpful?'*

Freedom from dogma and finding the truth for oneself

Buddhism does not demand that anyone accepts its teachings on trust. The practitioner is instead invited to try them out, to experiment with them. If he finds that they work in practice, then by all means he can take them on board. But there is no compulsion; and if he happens to find the truth elsewhere or otherwise, all well and good. This essential freedom from dogma is enshrined in the Buddha's words to the Kālāmas, a people who lived in the vicinity of the town of Kesaputta:

> Come, Kālāmas, do not be satisfied with hearsay or with tradition or with legendary lore or with what has come down in your scriptures or with conjecture or with logical inference or with weighing evidence or with liking for a view after pondering it over or with someone else's ability or with the thought 'The monk is our teacher' *When you know in yourselves* 'These ideas are unprofitable, liable to censure, condemned by the wise, being adopted and put into effect they lead to harm and suffering', then you should abandon them. . . . (And conversely:) *When you know*

in yourselves 'These things are profitable...' then you should practise them and abide in them....[1]

Tolerance

If one reserves the right to find the truth for oneself, one must logically accord the same right to others – and also respect them if they arrive at different conclusions. From this comes that basic tolerance that the world so acutely needs today. There have inevitably been exceptions – some Buddhists have fallen short of the very high standards set by the Buddha himself – but on the whole Buddhism has kept its record remarkably clean of inquisitions, pogroms, religious wars and massacres, heresy-hunting and the burning of books or people.

A liberal tradition of free inquiry

If Buddhism is a non-dogmatic tradition, not founded on a book or articles of faith, what makes a Buddhist a Buddhist rather than nothing in particular? To start with, there is respect for the Buddha himself and for the manner in which he conducted his own search for spiritual truth. From this directly stems a sense of belonging to the tradition that the Buddha established: a liberal tradition of free inquiry into the nature of ultimate truth. Then too there is a sense of community with others of a similar (though not necessarily identical) outlook.

Practical methods

If the Buddhist emphasis is on finding out for oneself, this necessarily places primary emphasis upon *direct religious experience*, as opposed to belief or blind faith. However, one doesn't in the normal course of events just receive deep religious experience as manna from above. Though that can of course happen, one generally has to make a conscious effort. So Buddhism does not so much offer *things to believe* as *things to do:* a vast array of spiritual practices, ranging from moral precepts that one can apply in one's everyday life and virtues that one can cultivate, to meditative practices (a profusion of these) which help to develop untapped spiritual resources: faculties like profound wisdom or clear-seeing and an all-embracing, selfless compassion. Put in Western terms, the ultimate aim of Buddhist practice is to engineer mystical experience: to penetrate the great mystery at the heart of life and find the answers to the knotty problems that have perennially engaged the most developed minds of the human race. This implies a complete spiritual transformation of the person as well.

Healing and transformation

C. G. Jung once wrote: 'The whole world wants peace and the whole world prepares for war. Mankind is powerless against mankind. And the gods, as ever, show us the way of Fate....'

This is a succinct summary of our contemporary dilemma. The world today is beset by many grave problems, social, psychological, ecological, economic – and of course the threat of nuclear destruction casts its shadow over all. Our planet has now very literally become a great time-bomb – and it is five minutes to zero-hour. As the final seconds tick away we seem hopelessly in the grip of deep dark forces that we don't understand and over which we have no control.

Sometimes we project the evil outwards and lay the blame on other people and groups. Sometimes too politicians and social scientists claim to have solutions; but these are invariably partial and temporary, touching the surface and relieving superficial symptoms rather than getting down to the root causes. If we are honest, these root causes lie in the individual human heart, in *our* hearts, where a primitive but fanatical self-centredness holds sway. It is our own personal greed, hatred and delusion, collectivized and amplified on a massive scale, that cause our planet's grave problems. Yet just to see this is not enough. The dark forces within each of us must be acknowledged and brought up into the light. Then, through awareness and understanding, they can be transformed into the stuff of true wisdom and compassion. Buddhism offers us ways and means of doing this.

So we need Buddhism. And our world needs it too as never before.

2 The Heart of the Matter

What is the essence of Buddhism?

Quite simply, it is the great question of who or what we are, right here, now, at this very moment.

For you, the reader, this means nothing other than *who* or *what* is *right now* looking at *these* printed words on the page of *this* book.

Reflect on that for a moment. You see the letters of each word printed in clear black type on the bright white paper. As you stare they begin to vibrate a little, perhaps. The letters seem to stand out with super clarity for a second or two – and then go unstable....

But who is the reader that is looking at them?

Your initial reaction to this might be one of mild irritation. You have no doubt at all about the person who is reading these words. You call that person 'I' or 'me'. You have a name, a life-history, a profession or job, relationships, a nationality. If you were to turn away and seek out a friend or a member of your family, they'd know instantly who was confronting them.

But don't turn away. Continue to look at the words on the paper. If you're really concentrating on the book, your name isn't in your mind at the moment, nor your life-history; you're probably away from your job and your nationality isn't something of which you've been conscious since you last went abroad; and if you don't seek out anyone, you're not in a relationship. So what then is this 'I'? Right now, does it amount to anything more than a collection of thoughts and memories which are just transitory and insubstantial things that come and go in the mind like clouds in the sky?

So, if you really concentrate single-pointedly on what's before your eyes at this very moment, there are only the words on the paper. Thin black or flat white. As for who's reading them, that's after all not really so very easy to say, is it? Perhaps you're now beginning to feel a little uneasy. Things are not what you thought they were. Something that you always took to be self-evidently present has gone – or at least is not so solidly present. Or perhaps you feel a slight sense of amazement, as though you've touched upon the edges of a great mystery.

Actually, you've touched the deepest mystery of all. Scientists may send spacecraft to distant planets or probe remote quarters of space with radio-telescopes. They may investigate the mysteries of the sub-atomic world with electron microscopes. But the thing that in fact they know least about is this great mystery that is right here with each one of us all the time. For like everyone else, they subscribe to the consensus view and don't give the matter a second thought. Thus in a very real sense they fail to see what's right under their noses.

Buddhism, however, is centrally concerned with this mystery and how to unravel it. In the first instance it is necessary to see through the great delusion of 'I', of the so-called *person*. Then it's a matter of finding out what is *really* there. And now the plot thickens, for to penetrate this mystery is to penetrate the ultimate mystery, the mystery at the heart of all things, and confront what the Christians call *God*, the Hindus *Brahman* or *Atman* – and it goes by other names in other religions. Buddhists, however, hesitate to put a name to it or say anything at all about it. It is, they maintain, something that cannot be grasped by the intellect or described in words. It can only be seen directly; but that seeing brings about something truly miraculous: a total transformation, no less. The veils of delusion fall away and at last the world is perceived *as it really is*. At the same time a deep compassion also crystallizes: a pure, selfless kindliness and caring born of an understanding of the unity of all beings.

In essence, then, Buddhism is quite simple. But simple things are often hard to fully realize, so people need all kinds of aids and supports. A vast superstructure has therefore grown up around the basic heart-core of the Buddha's teaching: mountains of philosophical speculation, a voluminous literature, monastic codes and ethical systems, histories, cosmologies, different types of ritual and meditation practice, institutions and hierarchies. All or any of it may be helpful in enabling the sincere practitioner to zero in upon the central issue – who or what is here, now – and to keep doing so until that great mystery has been completely realized. But it can also become a massive hindrance, entangling the all-too-errant mind in a thick undergrowth of secondary accretions.

When Shūan Chinken wrote his Preface to the *Mumonkan*, a great textbook of the Ch'an (Zen) school of Buddhism produced in China in the early 13th century, he complained that he had been practically forced to take up his brush. *'Don't use it, don't use it, for it will be yet another drop in the great lake'*, he urged,[2] implying that the true practice of Buddhism is about getting rid of thoughts and other mental bric-à-brac and confronting the central matter starkly and squarely; books, however, just contain more potential clutter for the attics of the mind.

This should be borne in mind when reading the present book. When the reader's mind begins to bulge and ache with useful facts, perhaps it might then be as well to let them all go for the time being and just return to the present moment and the great mystery of what is here, now. When we are fully aware and awake to this, then we confront the very heart of the matter.

Part 2

The Buddha

3 The Indian Background

Buddhism is a child of India, a uniquely spiritual country. A concern for truth and a respect for that basic instinct in us that, if we heed it, urges us to reach for the highest spiritually – these have been and remain aspects of the Indian scene since time immemorial. Fundamental to the Indian religious outlook at its best[3] is a basic liberalism that comes from an understanding that there are many paths by which the great mystery of Ultimate Reality may be approached. Allied to this is a fundamental tolerance: a willingness to listen, to learn, to change and to coexist with others with whom one may not necessarily agree. Mahatma Gandhi, the father of modern independent India, exhibited these noble qualities in his own life and work.

About 1500 BC, a race of nomadic herders who had long since migrated from the Central Asian steppe thrust their way into north-west India. They spoke an Indo-European language – an early form of Sanskrit – and for this reason are popularly known as Aryans. In the valley of the River Indus, which lies in present-day Pakistan, these Aryans found the remains of what had once been a civilization as advanced for its day as those of Egypt and Mesopotamia. Great cities – Mohenjodaro, Harappa – had stood here but had sadly long since begun to crumble into the dust. The Aryans were well-armed warriors. They thus had little difficulty in dominating north-west India and establishing supremacy over the people they found there. These included the once proud creators of the Indus Valley Civilization, who were probably of predominantly Mediterranean stock. It was the age-old story of energetic, patriarchal barbarians colliding with a more sophisticated but essentially decadent, matriarchal people. But the Aryans did not destroy pre-existing culture; they learned from it, and they no doubt reinvigorated it. The civilization that afterwards developed and spread throughout

13

India is therefore the result of the dynamic interaction of the Aryans with the other peoples of India.

The period of Indian history ushered in by the coming of the Aryans is known as the Vedic Age (*c.* 1500–500 BC), after a series of literary compositions of great antiquity known as the *Vedas* (*Veda* = 'knowledge').[4] The oldest is the *Rig Veda*, a collection of 1028 poetic hymns. Of it Phiroz Mehta has written:

> What is the Rig Veda? A collection of hymns, the earliest document of the human mind, representing, according to most scholars, the religion of an unsophisticated age, the creation of inspired poets and seers. Many of the hymns, it is said, are simple and naïve, in praise of nature gods and goddesses; some deal with formal ritual; and others, especially the last book ... present the results of conscious reflections on the origin of the world and on the Supreme Being.... They embody penetrating intuitions. But no system of philosophy is presented at this stage, for mythology and poetry precede philosophy and science....[5]

Three other Vedas later came into being:

1 The *Yajur Veda* – concerned with sacrificial formulae.
2 The *Sama Veda* – which is purely liturgical.
3 The *Atharva Veda* (the last) – mainly a book of spells.

At the centre of religious life during the Vedic Age lay the ritual of sacrifice. The world had been created by sacrifice and was maintained by sacrifice, it was thought. This was, however, completely controlled by the hereditary brahmin priesthood, who claimed that they alone were fitted by birth to perform sacrifice and jealously guarded the secrets of its rituals. The most elaborate sacrifice was the *Ashvamedha* or 'Horse Sacrifice', which went on for about a year, involved a small army of specialist brahmins and the ritual slaughter of a large number of animals. It was an exceedingly costly affair.

At the social centre of the new culture, on the other hand, there developed a caste system, which divided the population up into various hierarchical groups: the brahmin priesthood (*brāhmana*); the warriors and aristocrats (*kshatriya*); the traders and other professionals (*vaishya*); and the cultivators (*shūdra*).

Later a sub-caste appeared: the Untouchables, who were probably of aboriginal stock and who strictly speaking did not have any caste at all. Caste probably existed in the Indus Valley Civilization and rested on a racial basis – the Aryans merely adapted it to their own purposes, taking care to reserve the higher echelons for themselves!

The caste system was a closed system; once born into a caste, there was no leaving it. Upward or downward mobility was unknown. And underpinning the whole thing was the notion of *Dharma*, a word with a range of meanings. Used in its widest, impersonal sense it can have connotations of universal law. Related to people, on the other hand, it can imply duty to family, to the surrounding sociopolitical matrix and religious duty. If a person lived dharmically, then, in his next incarnation, he might receive the reward of birth into a higher caste. This of course implies acceptance of the notion of personal rebirth or reincarnation.

The caste system has survived to a large extent to the present time, and has had its critics and its apologists. In its favour, it has been said that it helped establish a stable and well-organized society and fostered the virtues of patience, respect and responsibility. On the other hand, it is often criticized as being rigid, inhumane, unjust and the root cause of that pernicious malaise known as oriental fatalism.

The spiritual health and richness of India owe rather less to brahminism than to an alternative tradition that had its roots in pre-Aryan culture. This was essentially an ascetic tradition and its exponents were not brahmins as a rule but rather kshatriyas of the warrior or aristocratic caste. They would renounce the world and go off singly or in small groups into the solitude of forest and mountain fastnesses. It has been suggested that some were merely drop-outs, casualties who had failed to adapt successfully to conventional social life. Others may have been in search of supernormal powers – the forerunners of the legendary fakirs who later astonished European travellers in India by magically charming snakes, levitating and performing the Indian Rope Trick. The best of them, however, certainly withdrew from their social duties for only the highest spiritual purposes. They no doubt practised meditation and other mystical disciplines, including forms of yoga. Such practices may date back to pre-Vedic times, for images of figures sitting cross-legged in yogic posture have been unearthed by archaeologists working in the remains of the lost cities of the Indus Valley. It has also been suggested that the shamanistic influences transported by the Aryans from their northern homelands may also have been at work here. By means of such practices, the ascetics were able to gain direct knowledge of exalted spiritual states (*jhānas* in Pāli; Sanskrit, *dhyānas*). An élite few came to know *Brahman*.

Brahman was Ultimate Reality, no less. It was said to be One and all-pervading, but formless and ineffable: a great mystery. Thus it was often referred to in negative terms: '*Neti, neti*' – 'Not this, not this'. It was identical, however, with the great mystery at the heart of every human being, so if a man asked what his true nature was, he might receive the classic answer: '*Tat tvam asi*' – 'You are That'. In this, its immanent aspect, Brahman was known as *Ātman*.

These noble teachings, which really touched the spiritual heights, were recorded, though not in systematic form, in the 200 or so *Upanishads*, which were composed between about 800 and 400 BC. The most important are the *Iśā, Kena, Katha, Praśna, Mundaka, Mandūkya, Svetāśvatara, Chāndogya, Brihad-āranyaka* and *Taittirīya*. Like the Vedas, the Upanishads are the work of great poets but ones whose lyrical inspiration was fully informed by profound insight.

Some of the ascetics who had gained direct knowledge of Brahman must have left their mountain caves and forest hermitages to return to the world to share their wisdom with their fellow men. They must have impressed the ordinary people very much – and made the brahmin priests look little better than self-serving traffickers in mumbo-jumbo. The brahmins were sensible, however. They may have scorned these ascetics and discouraged the ordinary people from listening to them, but they did not launch any kind of violent campaign against them – rather the brahmins sought to incorporate aspects of the alternative wisdom into their own teachings. Also, alarmed at the number of young men who were throwing up their family duties to take to the homeless ascetic life, the brahmins began to propound the notion of Four Stages of Life. Firstly one is a student, then a householder, later one retires and gradually loosens the bonds that tie one to the world, and finally, only when one has discharged all one's other dharmic debts fully, can one become a renunciate or *sanyassin* and go off in search of religious truth.

Unfortunately, even the highest teachings seem invariably to undergo a fall when they are packaged for popular consumption by a professional priestly class. Thus it was with the Upanishads. The formless Brahman became formalized and eventually came to wear an anthropomorphic face, that of the great god Brahma. And the equally elusive Ātman that once great sages had hesitated to mention save in negative terms, that too congealed into a permanent personal entity or immortal soul – the *jivatman*. It was part of the Buddha's project to point out these debasements of the once noble teachings of the Upanishads, which in their original and highest forms were quite consistent with his own teachings.

By the time that the Vedic Age was drawing towards its close, Vedic culture had spread down the plain of the River Ganges and the restless Aryan invader had been long since transformed from a pastoral nomad into a settled agriculturist. He had also integrated, insofar as the caste system facilitated integration, with the other peoples of the area. The clearing of the great Gangetic Plain for agriculture had also unleashed a vast untapped economic potential. The population grew and prosperity burgeoned, great trading cities emerged and with them a sophisticated urban culture and a new individualism. New forms of political organization developed too as the old tribes began to be replaced by more highly organized groupings. Tribal republics appeared, ruled by elected aristocracies drawn from the kshatriya caste, and these may have been less well disposed towards the prevailing brahmin orthodoxy than the kingdoms that also appeared at this time. These were more expansionistic than the republics and two of them, Magadha and Kosala, vied for domination of 'Middle Country', the central heartland of the Ganges Plain, which by the time of the Buddha's birth (563 BC) was the main centre of civilization in India.

Wealth and social change generate stress, and from stress come psychological and spiritual problems. At the same time the necessary leisure and surplus resources are also available for

solutions to those problems to be sought. Thus the changes
outlined above probably increased the numbers of people taking
to the homeless life as followers of the alternative spiritual
tradition. But as life became more organized it also became
expedient for those ascetics to abandon their old anarchic ways
and become more organized themselves. They had also to
demonstrate their seriousness and usefulness to society. Thus we
find identifiable sects emerging, each with its own philosophy
and practices, and centred around a *shramana* or teacher. The
ascetics themselves were at first called *ājīvakas* or *parivajakas*
('homeless ones'; 'ones who had gone forth'). Five main sects
can be determined:

1   *Ajivakas.*   (As well as referring to ascetics generally, the term
    also referred to the followers of this particular sect.) The root
    teacher was Makkhali Gosāla and he seems to have taught a
    philosophy of utter determinism: the universe was a
    totally closed causal system but it was inexorably moving
    each person towards ultimate perfection, though the process
    would take untold aeons of time.

2   *Lokayatas.*   (The Materialists.) As propounded by Ajita
    Keshakambalin, a contemporary of the Buddha, the philosophy
    of this sect held that a human being was composed of
    the four elements and into those his constituent parts were
    resolved at death, which was an utter finality – 'When the
    body dies both the fool and the wise alike are cut off and
    perish.' In life then a man should seek the maximum of
    pleasure possible.

3   *The Sceptics.*   These held that the brahminical doctrines
    were mutually contradictory and that truth was utterly
    unattainable. They are said to have wriggled like eels out of
    every question put to them, but believed in cultivating
    friendliness and peace of mind.

4   *The Jains.*   The Jains held life to be an extremely painful
    business and aspired to attain *moksha* or liberation from the
    painful cycles of endless rebirth by withdrawing to a high,
    rarefied spiritual state. To do so they sought to amass the
    necessary karmic merit by the practice of extreme forms of
    austerity and impeccably moral conduct. They were par-
    ticularly preoccupied with the karmic consequences of killing

or causing suffering to living beings, even microscopic ones. They thus took the virtue of *ahimsā* (harmlessness) to extreme lengths and some would sweep the ground ahead of them when they walked and wear gauze masks over their faces. The Jain philosophy, which was systematized around the time of the Buddha by Mahāvira, has followers in India to this day, though few of them are extreme ascetics.

The fifth sect, which was in time to spread so widely that for a time it became the predominant religion of all Asia, was founded by Siddhārtha Gautama, the Buddha, whose life and work we will look at in the next two chapters.

4 The Buddha: The Early Years

Biographies of the Buddha were comparatively late arrivals.
There is no biography as such in the earliest Pali scriptures, but a
skeletal one might be pieced together from scattered references.
The Venerable Ñānamoli Thera (Osbert Moore) did just this in
his *Life of the Buddha* (Kandy, Sri Lanka, 1972). One of the
first true biographies was the *Buddhacarita* ('Acts of the
Buddha') of the 1st or 2nd century AD by the Sanskrit poet
Ashvaghosha. A condensed translation of this appears in Dr.
Edward Conze's anthology, *Buddhist Scriptures* (Harmonds-
worth, 1959 – a Penguin Classic). Various other versions of the
Life were subsequently produced – many of them contain
additions and embellishments not found in the earliest sources.

A brief outline of the Life

The man who was to become the Buddha was born about 563
BC of kshatriya stock at a place called Lumbini. This is situated
in the Terai region of what today is the kingdom of Nepal,
immediately below the Himalayan foothills on the northern
edge of the plain of the River Ganges, due north of the holy city
of Benares. He was given the name Siddhārtha and took the
clan-name Gautama. His father, Suddhodana, has been
variously described as the king or leader of a local people known
as the Shakyas – or even just as a prominent citizen of
Kapilavatthu, the Shakyan capital. The Shakyas were in fact
just one of a number of more or less independent peoples then
inhabiting this part of northern India who were politically
organized into tribal republics ruled by elected aristocracies.
    A remarkable man is deemed to require a remarkable birth.
So it is said that prophetic dreams heralded the great event; that

the Buddha-to-be was not conceived in the usual way but descended from the Tushita Heaven and entered his mother's womb in the form of a white elephant; that she carried him for ten months and then gave birth to him from her side and standing up; that he was born clean, unstained in any way but that nevertheless streams of water poured from the sky to wash both mother and child; and finally:

> As soon as born, the Bodhisatta (Buddha-to-be) firmly standing with even feet goes firmly to the north with seven long steps, a white parasol being held over him (by the gods). He surveys all the quarters, and in a lordly voice says, 'I am the chief in the world, I am the best in the world, I am the first in the world. This is my last birth. There is now no existence again'.[6]

Unfortunately, Siddhārtha's mother, Mahāmāyā, died a week after giving birth to him, and her place in his life was taken by her sister, Mahāpajāpatī, who in the polygamous society of the day was probably also one of Suddhodana's wives.

Not long after the birth, a wise sage named Asita came to Kapilavatthu. He gasped with wonder and smiled when the infant was laid before him, for he at once noticed that there

were 32 special signs on his tiny body. But then Asita began to
weep and when asked why replied that he was not weeping for
Siddhārtha but for himself. Siddhārtha would certainly grow up
to be a fully Enlightened buddha, a Teacher of Men and Gods,
but he, Asita, was old and would not live long enough to hear
Siddhārtha's profound teaching.

Suddhodana was far from delighted when he heard this. He
therefore determined to do whatever he could to prevent Asita's
prediction coming true. Reflecting that it would be experience
of the hard, ugly and painful things of life that would turn
Siddhārtha's mind towards religion, Suddhodana decided that
he would create a hermetic environment of comfort, beauty and
pleasure for Siddhārtha. The real world would be utterly shut
out.

Probably while Siddhārtha was still a boy it was sufficient
for Suddhodana to see to it that he was just closely chaperoned.
As he grew towards manhood and more disposed to take
independent action, more elaborate security arrangements
became necessary. So Suddhodana ordered three splendid
marble palaces to be built: one for the hot season, one for the
cool season and one for the rainy season. Siddhārtha was
confined in the upper storeys of these and every kind of pleasure
and luxury was laid on to make sure that he would not become
bored. He lolled around in splendid robes of Benares silk,
anointed by oils of the finest quality. He ate the most delicious
foods, and armies of musicians, dancing girls and the most
sensuous courtesans were on hand to amuse him.

One might have thought that such an environment would
have produced a decadent hot-house plant, but by all accounts
Siddhārtha grew up to be a splendid young man. He was good at
his studies, very handsome, just and kind, and he also excelled
at all kinds of sports and martial arts. Those last talents helped
him to win the hand of Yasodharā, his beautiful young cousin,
who was desired as a wife by many young noblemen and
princelings. Siddhārtha trounced all these other suitors easily in
a series of contests and he and Yasodharā were married when
he was still only 16. However, the mores of the day would no
doubt have allowed him to enjoy the pleasures of numerous
concubines as well. One child resulted from Siddhārtha's
marriage to Yasodharā – a son, Rāhula, born when Siddhārtha
was about 29.

No doubt information about life in the world beyond the walls of his pleasure palaces filtered through to Siddhārtha and aroused his natural curiosity. He was probably getting restless anyway. So a trip to the outside world was arranged, either with his father's knowledge or without it.

Siddhārtha made four fateful trips to the outside world, driven each time by his groom, Channa. On the first they encountered an old man, on the second a sick man and on the third a corpse being carried away to be cremated on the burning ghat. Having lived in pleasure palaces, completely insulated from such sights for nearly 30 years, the effect of these three encounters upon Siddhārtha was traumatic. Here were the true facts of the human condition: that men are susceptible to sickness, old age and death – all men: *even Siddhārtha himself....*

In order that life be tenable, most people suppress the reality and inevitability of death. Those who have been forced to confront it, however, will bear witness to the profound effect that it can have. A vital shock it always is, but one that can also bring about a sudden maturing of the whole personality by summarily clearing the mind of its usual clutter of trivial preoccupations and bringing into focus that which is of real importance.

The cloistered Siddhārtha received such a vital shock and at once all the pleasures and delights of palace life lost their charm.

But he also made a fourth visit to the outside world with Channa. On that occasion they saw a *sadhu*, a wandering holy man such as one can see on the highways and byways of India even today. It is also significant that this man, who was to awaken Siddhārtha's dormant spirituality, was not a brahmin priest but a follower of the alternative *shramana* tradition. He was alone and dressed in rags, and clearly possessed nothing; yet there was a quality about his whole demeanour that deeply impressed Siddhārtha – a tranquillity that other men, for all their possessions and family connections, clearly lacked. *Perhaps*, Siddhārtha wondered, *he has discovered some secret; perhaps old age, sickness and death are no longer frightening for him....*

And now the conflict within Siddhārtha's heart became really intense. He had been awakened to the central problem of human existence, the problem of suffering, and also shown a potential way of finding a solution to it. This would, however, mean not only giving up all the material riches that he enjoyed but also walking out on his family: his father, who expected him to do his duty, and his wife and son, whom he loved deeply. His heart was wrenched this way and that. A large part of him longed to stay, and yet at the same time there was a powerful force within him, a force that *could not* be gainsaid, that was pushing him out into the unknown.

This conflict eventually reached its inevitable climax. Around midnight on the very night that his son, Ràhula, was born, Siddhàrtha rose from his bed and dressed. Waking up Channa, Siddhàrtha asked him to saddle up his horse, Kanthaka. Then they rode through the night until they came to the River Anoma, which divided the land of the Shakyas from the neighbouring kingdom of Magadha. On the far bank of the river a poignant ritual took place. Siddhàrtha hacked off all his handsome jet-black hair, exchanged his silken robe for the ragged yellow one of a wandering holy man and took off all his rings and ornaments. Handing these to Channa, he asked him to take them back to Kapilavatthu along with the horse. Then the two of them said their farewells and Siddhàrtha walked off alone. His great spiritual quest for the solution to the problem of suffering had begun.

Siddhàrtha went and sought out the most distinguished *shramana* teachers of the day: Alàra Kàlàma and Uddaka Ràmaputta. Both taught him all that they knew and he for his part studied and practised assiduously. But though he obtained a great deal of intellectual knowledge and became proficient in the attainment of *dhyànas* (Pali, *jhànas)* he was still unsatisfied, for a complete solution to his spiritual problem still eluded him.

So then Siddhàrtha took himself off into the jungle near Uruvelà and began to submit himself to the most gruelling forms of asceticism. The rationale for this was that by mortifying the body, subjecting it to the most extreme forms of privation and suffering, suffering itself could be finally overcome. He spent long periods living alone and naked in eerie forests and in charnel grounds. He slept on beds of thorns. He burned in the heat of the midday sun and suffered cold at night. At the same time he tried to burn and crush all thoughts from his mind, and experimented with holding his breath for long

periods until there were violent pains in his head and he lapsed
into unconsciousness. He also starved himself into a state of
extreme emaciation:

> All my limbs became like the knotted joints of withered creepers,
> my buttocks like a bullock's hoof, my protruding backbone like a
> string of balls, my gaunt ribs like the crazy rafters of a tumble-
> down shed. My eyes lay deep in their sockets, their pupils sparkling
> like water in a deep well. As an unripe gourd shrivels and shrinks in
> a hot wind, so became my scalp. If I thought, 'I will touch the skin
> of my belly', it was the skin of my backbone that I also took hold
> of, since the skin of my belly and back met. The hairs, rotting at the
> roots, fell away from my body when I stroked my limbs.[7]

It is a gruesome picture, but it also portrays a virtuoso
performance of its kind and it impressed five other ascetics,
who asked if they could join him. However, in the long run
Siddhārtha had to admit to himself that it had not provided
him with a fully satisfying answer to his problem – and he
realized that if he went on abusing his body in that way he
would die before finding one. He therefore took a little food in
order to give himself enough strength to make a new start.
Witnessing this, his five fellow ascetics walked off in disgust,
declaring, 'Gautama has taken to the easy life!' This in itself
gives a hint of the spiritual one-upmanship that so often
underlies that sort of ascetic athleticism.

Siddhārtha was now a man *in extremis*. He had renounced
social role, material support, family – everything. Now even his
fellow ascetics had rejected him. He had also experienced the
extremes of sensual indulgence and of self-mortification – and
found that both ultimately led nowhere.

There was one thing that he had not really tried, however – a
middle way between the luxurious and the ascetical ways. He
also recalled an incident during a Ploughing Festival when as a
child he had sat beneath the rose-apple tree and entered a state of
meditation. He thought: 'Might that be the way to
Enlightenment?'

At a place nowadays called Bodh Gāya in the modern Indian
state of Bihar, Siddhārtha made himself a cushion of grass
beneath the spreading branches of the famous Bodhi Tree, a tree
of the species *ficus religiosa*. He determined to sit in meditation

here until he found an answer to the problem of suffering – or die in the attempt.

What next took place is sometimes recounted in high dramatic form. Besides Siddhārtha, the other protagonist is Māra, supported by his demonic hordes. Māra is a kind of Buddhist Satan, a Tempter whose role within the scheme of things is to maintain delusion and desire and all those wisdom-inhibiting factors that keep *Samsāra*, the world of illusion, in endless cyclic motion. When Māra saw what Siddhārtha was trying to do, he naturally became very perturbed. The last thing he wanted was that a way out of suffering and *Samsāra* be discovered. He had in fact been keeping a close eye on Siddhārtha's activities right from the time he had embarked on the homeless life six years before and had already tried to tempt him to give up his quest. He had whispered insinuations into Siddhārtha's ear, suggesting, for instance, that his energy would be better spent earning merit for himself by doing good works. Now that he saw that Siddhārtha was getting perilously close to success, however, he decided to launch an all-out attack with his army of hideous demons, supported by elephants, horses, chariots, infantry, auxiliaries and all – and he himself cheered them on with *'Sieze him, drag him, slay him...!'* But Siddhārtha was quite unshaken by all this and the attack collapsed. Poor Māra, knowing that he was beaten, slunk away, 'pained, dejected, depressed and sorrowful'. Still, he was to keep up his watch on Siddhārtha for another year and made further attempts to undo him, on one occasion deploying his ultimate weapon: his superseductive daughters!

We might interpret all this to mean that there were times during Siddhārtha's quest when he was tempted to give up. He may have felt at times that he had done enough and should go home and discharge his social duty. At other times perhaps powerful fears rose up within him. He may have become worried that he might go mad, that what he was doing might project him into some outlandish psychic state. Fear of the supernatural may also have hit him, or fear of death – or even an *angst* more frightful than that of death: a kind of existential terror of utter annihilation or non-being. We can take it, however, that he did not succumb to any of these. Sexual desire also reasserted itself with great force from time to time.

Other accounts of the final push for Enlightenment are less mythological and more informative. It would firstly appear from them that Siddhārtha went into *samadhi*, a state of meditative concentration in which he attained various *dhyānas*. It was proficiency in this that he had learned with his first teachers, Alāra Kālāma and Uddaka Rāmaputta. But then, with a mind fully clear and concentrated, he began to practise *vipassanā* or insight meditation and thereby gained certain special kinds of knowledge:

1 He 'remembered many former existences'.

2 He gained knowledge of the workings of karma: how those who acquire bad karma by performing evil actions are reborn in miserable states, while those who acquire good karma by performing meritorious actions are reborn in happy states.

3 He gained knowledge of the destruction of the *āsavas*, the 'cankers' or 'taints'. Three *āsavas* are often identified: sensual desire, desire for existence and ignorance. Later a fourth was added: addiction to views – or even to holding any views at all.

Garry Thomson has pointed out how thin this account seems of what to Buddhists is regarded as the greatest event of human history. But we must remember that at its core lies a radical transformation of perception, indeed of being itself, that cannot be adequately grasped by the intellect or described in words. It is truly ineffable. Yet we might propose certain pointers, understanding that these can only be tentative and provisional until we can gain direct insight into these things for ourselves.

We might suggest that Siddhārtha now finally *saw through* his 'I' or ego, saw that in an ultimate sense it was an illusion, a creation of thought rather than anything with a more solid existence. Moreover, with 'I' removed from the centre of the arena, there was no identifiable *subject* perceiving the world in a dualistic (subject–object) manner. Consequently 'the world' became a unity.

Siddhārtha must also have become aware that the world of manifestation was an apparent outpouring of energy from a mysterious, unlimited source. During deep meditation, his mind perfectly still and quiet, he could feel the presence of this source, *in totality*, in his own heart-core. It was similarly in all other beings. Thus it was the true nature of all things, the basic ground of being itself. Never having been born, however, it was not subject to suffering or death; thus it could be called *The Deathless*. It was also fully conscious; it was 'the one who knows' – though paradoxically it cannot know itself.

So, abandoning identification with the illusion of 'I' (there is no reason to believe that a conventional sense of ego identity did not to some extent persist), Siddhārtha from then on identified himself primarily with his true nature and sought to rest in that mysterious centre.

At dawn following the night of the full moon of May, this great spiritual hero looked up and saw the morning star rise. As he did so he saw the world for the first time with undeluded eyes. He felt like a man who had just woken up from a long and confusing dream. He was Siddhārtha no more, but the *Buddha – The Awakened One*. Touching the earth, he called upon it to bear witness to his great achievement.

5 The Buddha: The Teaching Career

Following his great breakthrough to Enlightenment, the Buddha is said to have remained in meditation under the Bodhi Tree for a while (seven days, four weeks, seven weeks – accounts vary), enjoying the supreme bliss of his great spiritual liberation. As for trying to communicate his great discovery, however, he felt that it would be a waste of energy even to try. Human beings were simply too deeply caught up in worldly attachments and pursuits to want to hear about it. But then the great god Brahmā Sahampati appealed to him, saying that there were some people with 'just a little dust in their eyes' who could be released from the coils of suffering if he would consent to teach. The Buddha's deep compassion was aroused and he agreed to the idea.

But who was he to teach? Alāra Kālāma and Uddaka Rāmaputta had died by this time and the only other potentially interested people still alive that he could think of were the five ascetics who had spurned him earlier. It would therefore have to be them and he located them in a deer park at Isipatana (modern Sarnath, near Benares). Recalling his earlier lapse, they decided to give him a cool reception, but then they noticed that his whole appearance had changed. He possessed a new spiritual radiance. This won them over in spite of themselves and made them receptive to his teaching.

So at Isipatana the Buddha preached his first sermon to the five ascetics on the subject of the Four Noble Truths; he also told them about the Middle Way that he had found between the extremes of sensual-indulgence and self-mortification. One of the five ascetics, Kondañña, understood at once.

'Kondañña knows!' the Buddha exclaimed, and immediately ordained him the first Buddhist monk (*bhikkhu*). This was done according to a very simple formula. Kondañña's four

29

companions followed suit shortly afterwards. And so, in Buddhist parlance, the Buddha began to *turn the Wheel of the Dhamma*; and so too was born the Sangha, the community of Buddhist monks – to which later nuns were also admitted.

The Buddha was about 35 when he became Enlightened. He lived until he was about 80, and those last 45 years of his life were given over to teaching. He walked the hot and dusty roads of central-northern India, going from village to town to city, addressing himself to all who wanted to hear what he had to say, regardless of distinctions of sex, caste, vocation or religion. He was a truly liberal and generous teacher.

He was also apparently a very inspiring teacher, for right from the start large numbers of people were ready to give everything up in order to follow him and devote themselves wholeheartedly to the practice of his teachings. There was Yasa, the worldweary son of a well-to-do Benares business family, four of Yasa's friends, and later 50 more, all young men of good social connections. Yasa's mother and wife became the first female lay followers, while his father became a lay follower too.

Another early convert was the fire-worshipping ascetic Uruvelā Kassapa. The Buddha so impressed him with a series of virtuoso demonstrations of supernormal powers that Kassapa and his 500 followers, matted-haired ascetics to a man, all entered the Buddhist fold. Kassapa's two ascetic brothers, Nādi Kassapa and Gayā Kassapa, joined the Sangha soon afterwards too, bringing with them 300 and 200 followers respectively.

Two important new additions to the early Sangha were Moggallāna and Sāriputta, who became the Buddha's chief disciples. They had formerly been disciples of another spiritual teacher, Sañjaya (the leader of the Sceptics?), but had not gained complete understanding through his teachings. On hearing a brief summary of the Buddha's *Dhamma*, however – 'All that is subject to arising is subject to cessation' – all their difficulties were resolved. They also brought with them 200 followers. In time Sāriputta was to become highly respected for wisdom, Moggallāna for supernormal powers.

These mass conversions led to certain misgivings in the kingdom of Magadha, where they took place – which is not to be wondered at since families were being broken up: husbands were leaving wives, sons were leaving parents – and disciples were also leaving their gurus. These misgivings soon evaporated, however – as the Buddha predicted.

The Buddha eventually decided to introduce a more formal ordination ceremony for his monks, which consisted of shaving the hair and beard, donning the yellow robe and reciting the Refuge three times: 'I go for refuge to the Buddha; I go for refuge to the *Dhamma*; I go for Refuge to the Sangha. . . .' Later a more complicated formula evolved.

A code of monastic rules *(Pātimokkha)* was not set up straight away. Apparently, in the early days, the Sangha was so strong and true that there was no need to do so. As all things mortal are subject to degeneration, however, the Buddha was eventually obliged to establish one.

The monks of this rapidly-growing Sangha lived the homeless life, wandering from place to place, carrying the Buddha's teachings out into the world 'for the welfare and happiness of the many folk'. During the Monsoon, however, the rainy season in India, they were allowed to go into retreat. This was not least because the Rains are a time of new growth and to walk abroad then would have meant trampling green shoots and other forms of new life underfoot.

If the Buddha himself was impressive and inspirational to a wide spectrum of people, it is clear that the *bhikkhus* of his Sangha were so too. On one occasion King Pasénadi of Kósala contrasted them with other monks and brahmins, who appeared to be 'lean, wretched, unsightly, jaundiced' and so forth. The Buddhists, on the other hand, were 'smiling and cheerful, sincerely joyful, plainly delighting, their faculties fresh, unexcited, unruffled . . . dwelling with minds like the wild deer' (Ñānamoli, 1972, p. 285).

The Buddha's early wanderings in the kingdom of Magadha eventually brought him to the capital, Rājagaha. Here the king, Bimbisāra[8], came to see him accompanied by a large number of citizens. The Buddha gave them teachings, which they all understood, and then they too all became lay followers. King Bimbisāra was particularly moved by the experience of receiving teachings from a buddha as it fulfilled a lifelong wish. He himself waited on the Buddha and his *bhikkhus* at the next day's alms meal; and afterwards, with truly regal largesse, he donated the Bamboo Grove, a pleasure-garden lying just outside the city, to the Sangha. A rich merchant later put up shelters there and so created the first proper Buddhist monastery. The Buddha spent his second and third Rains Retreats there, the first having been spent at Benares. Up until its foundation the *bhikkhus* had lived 'in the woods, at the roots of trees, under overhanging rocks, in ravines, in hillside caves, in charnel grounds, in jungle thickets' – or just out in the open on heaps of straw.

Other generous donations were to follow. One came from Anāthapindika, a layman so renowned for his generosity that he had been given the title 'Feeder of the Poor'. He first heard the Buddha preach the *Dhamma* in Rajāgaha. Inspired by what he heard, he invited him to spend the next (fourth) Rains Retreat at his own city of Sāvatthi, the capital of the neighbouring kingdom of Kosala, which was then ruled by King Pasénadi. Returning there in advance, Anāthapindika looked around for a suitable place nearby where the *bhikkhus* could stay. He lighted upon a pleasure-garden owned by a certain nobleman named Jeta and accordingly known as the Jetavana or 'Jeta's Grove'. On being asked to sell, however – perhaps half in jest, not really wanting to let the property go – Jeta named a preposterous price: the entire grove was to be covered with gold pieces. Anāthapindika held Jeta to his price, however, and cartloads of gold pieces were brought; they covered all but a tiny space. Impressed by Anāthapindika's piety, Jeta said, 'Enough, do not cover that space. It shall be my gift'. In due course another monastery was built here; and later, also near Sāvatthi, a third monastery: the Pubbarāma or 'Eastern Park'. This was donated by a generous laywoman named Visākhā. When the Buddha settled permanently at Sāvatthi, he spent alternate Rains Retreats at the Jetavāna and the Pubbarāma.

These generous bequests demonstrate how, from the very start, the Sangha was supported by a sympathetic lay community. In return the Buddha gave discourses to lay people and, the general monastic bias of early Buddhism notwithstanding, certainly encouraged them to practise to as great an extent as they were able. His qualified *bhikkhus* of course gave teachings too. This reciprocal relationship, which so clearly illustrates the Buddhist virtue of *dāna* or giving, survives in many Buddhist countries to this day. Besides food and shelter, the laity may donate cloth for robes, medicines and other requisites to the Sangha.

It was only natural that the Buddha should one day pay a visit to his own people at Kapilavatthu – and they for their part must have been very excited and curious to see this native son of theirs who had made such a great name for himself in the wider world. At Kapilavatthu, he stayed with a large number of *bhikkhus* at Nigrōdha's Park and gave talks on *Dhamma*, which had the usual profound effect. Even his father, Suddhodana, was established on the Path, though the visit was not without its heart-aches for Suddhodana. For one thing, the proud old kshatriya nobleman was deeply offended when he saw his son going out on alms round *(pindapāt)*.

'No-one in our family has ever lived by begging!' he protested.

'You belong to a noble line of kings,' the Buddha replied 'but I belong to the lineage of buddhas – and thousands of those have lived on alms food.'

Then plans to simultaneously install the Buddha's half-brother, Nanda (Mahāpajāpatī's son), as heir to the throne and marry him off as well were scotched at the last minute when the Buddha ordained him into the Sangha. And to cap that, when his own son, Rāhula, was sent along by Yasodharā to claim his inheritance, the Buddha simply turned to Sāriputta and said: 'Ordain him, Sāriputta.'

Quite understandably, Suddhodana complained bitterly to the Buddha about these ordinations. The bonds that tie father to son run deep; the loss of a son is painful beyond measure – but he, Suddhodana, had lost three sons: Siddhārtha, Nanda, and now Rāhula (who had become like a son after Siddhārtha's departure). He suggested that ordinations should not take place in future without parents' consent. The Buddha agreed to this.

It is also possible that Ānanda, the Buddha's cousin, who became his faithful personal attendant during the latter part of his life, was ordained about this time.

During the fifth year of the Buddha's ministry, Suddhodana died, though happily as he was by then an *Arahat* – a Worthy One. Later, his widow, Mahāpajāpatī, came to see the Buddha, who was again staying at Nigrōdha's Park, and begged him to ordain her as a nun. She repeated her entreaty three times, but each time the Buddha refused it. Such was her commitment, however, that she cut off her hair, donned the yellow robe and followed him when he travelled on to Vesālī, the capital of the adjacent state of Videha. At Vesālī, when Ananda saw Mahāpajāpatī and the other Shakyan ladies who had accompanied her, he was so moved by their tear-stained faces, dusty clothes and swollen feet that he spoke to the Buddha on their behalf. On being reminded of the motherly care that Mahāpajāpatī had selflessly lavished upon him when he was a child, the Buddha very reluctantly agreed to ordain her, but only if she would agree to submit to eight very stringent rules, one of which was that a nun (bhikkhuni) of 100 years seniority would still be junior to a bhikkhu who had only been ordained that very day and must accord him deference. Mahāpajāpatī gladly accepted these terms, so she was fully admitted into the Sangha; the ladies with her were also admitted in due course. Afterwards, however, the Buddha lamented to Ananda that the admission of women would seriously weaken his Dhamma: it would now only last 500 instead of 1000 years. This of course implies a certain prejudice against women, though it probably more closely reflects the prejudices current at that time and place than the Buddha's own views. After all, he had admitted to Ananda during their discussions about Mahāpajāpatī's admission that women possessed the same spiritual potential as men.

Another relative of the Buddha who later joined the Sangha was Yasodharā, his ex-wife, the mother of Rāhula. Indeed, it would appear from the records that she adopted an ascetic way of life from the time that the Buddha first left Kapilavatthu.

The crowds that were drawn to hear Buddha's teachings and the enormous moral and material support that the early Sangha attracted naturally aroused the jealousy of the other ascetic sects that existed in northern India at this time. The Buddha for his part never tried to win converts by demonstrations of low-grade magical tricks; in fact, he forbade the use of such gimmicks by his followers, though he did give a few remarkable demonstrations of supernormal powers himself when he felt that the particular situation justified them. He also never set out to poach devotees from other sects, as witness the case of the prominent Jain, Upāli, who had asked to join the order. As Upāli himself remarked, other religious leaders would have paraded him through the streets, boasting of having made an important convert, but the Buddha just urged him to think things over very carefully before transferring his loyalties.

But even though the Buddha himself always behaved according to the highest principles, there were others who were not so scrupulous and some were even prepared to restort to foul means to try to discredit both Buddha and Sangha.

The Buddha's attitude to the orthodox brahmin priesthood was characterized by his usual tolerance and liberality. Sometimes brahmins came to him for advice or teaching. He did not believe that ritual sacrifices involving the slaughter of animals served any useful spiritual purpose whatsoever, and he did not conceal the fact. Sometimes he expressed the view that sacrifice should be interpreted figuratively – that the real sacrifice was a giving up of selfishness, or a giving of donations to the Sangha and other ascetics. As regards Brahmā and his fellow gods, goddesses, demigods, demons and the other denizens of the Vedic pantheon, he did not so much deny their existence as hint more or less broadly that they were of little real importance.

(It should perhaps be noted by the way that modern Hindus do not regard the Buddha as an outsider to their tradition. In fact he is considered by them to be a manifestation of the great god Vishnu, one of the Hindu Trinity, who descends into the world in various forms at particularly difficult times to help set things right. The Hindu system certainly derived much from Buddha's teaching – and indeed Buddhism, during the more than 1500 years during which it was a significant part of the Indian spiritual scene, also derived much from Hinduism. Buddhist Tantra, for instance, has a great deal in common with the Shiva-Shakti tradition of Hindu Tantra).

The Buddha's problems were not solely from without, however. Quite early on the Sangha was rocked by dissension when the *bhikkhus* at Kosambi grew litigious with each other over a minor infraction of the monastic rules. The Buddha himself counselled a forgiving line but, being ignored, withdrew to the Pārilekkaya forest, where he was looked after by a lone bull elephant who, like himself, had retired into solitude to get away from the vexations of the herd. Eventually, the quarrelsome *bhikkhus* at Kosambi resolved their difficulties and harmony was restored.

Potentially more disastrous for the Buddha and the early Sangha were the machinations of the Buddha's unpleasant

cousin, Devadatta. At first Devadatta joined forces with
Ajātasattu, the son of King Bimbisāra of Magadha, in a double
plot that involved the murder of both King Bimbisāra and the
Buddha as a prelude to the seizure of their respective roles and
prerogatives. The plan misfired, however, so Devadatta resorted
to various direct methods of dispatching the Buddha: he hurled
boulders down onto him as he was preaching at Vulture Peak
Mountain; and later he loosed a savage elephant in his path.
Both stratagems of course failed utterly.

Finally, Devadatta managed to engineer an open schism and
lured 500 new *bhikkhus* away. Moggallāna and Sāriputta
followed them, and Devadatta in his triumph thought that they
had come to join his cause as well, so he invited them to sit
down. He then embarked on a long discourse that lasted most of
the night. When his back eventually began to pain him, he asked
Sāriputta to take over and settled down for a nap. Needless to
say, Sāriputta and his friend Moggallāna used this opportunity
to advise the schismatic *bhikkhus* of the error of their ways; they
also preached true *Dhamma* to them. Therefore when
Devadatta woke up he learnt to his considerable chagrin that he
had lost his following. Hot blood then gushed from his mouth,
we are told.

Obviously Devadatta's crimes had piled up a great stock of
black points in his karmic account, which he inexorably had to
suffer out in the hell realms, where he languished until the end
of the age. The Buddha himself proclaimed, however, that he
would eventually regenerate spiritually and become a buddha
himself, for eternal damnation is a concept unknown in
Buddhism, where every being is ultimately destined for Nirvāna,
even the most foul-hearted reprobate.

This forgiving aspect of Buddhism also comes out in the story
of a desperado named Angulimāla – or 'Finger Necklace'. It was
his habit to sever the fingers of his victims and wear them on a
string around his neck, hence his gruesome nickname. One day
down a lonely stretch of road he gave chase to the Buddha.
However, he found that he simply could not catch up with the
Buddha. He therefore shouted, '*Hey! Stop, monk!*', whereupon
the Buddha replied, 'But I have stopped, Angulimāla. Isn't it
time that you stopped too?' – and went on to explain that he
meant *stopped using violence*. This somehow touched a tiny

residual spark of decency in Angulimāla's black heart and, throwing away his sword, he begged to be allowed to become a follower of the Buddha.

The story of Kisa Gotami, on the other hand, well illustrates the Buddha's sensitivity as a teacher. She turned up one day with a dead child in her arms and begged the Buddha for medicine to bring him back to life. The Buddha saw at once that she simply could not accept her child's death, so he told her, 'Yes, I can help you. First you must bring me a mustard seed – but it must come from a house in which no death has ever taken place....' Of course, Kisa Gotami searched all day but could not find such a house, so in the evening when she came back to the Buddha she had learnt a deep lesson. 'I know now,' she told him, 'that I am not alone in my great grief. Death is common to all people....'

The Buddha's kindness also comes out very strongly in the incident of a *bhikkhu* who was suffering from dysentery. The poor man was lying in his own mess with no-one at all looking after him. The Buddha himself, assisted by Ananda, washed him and laid him out on a bed. Afterwards the Buddha admonished the other *bhikkhus* there in terms very reminiscent of Jesus Christ:

'*Bhikkhus*, you have neither mother nor father to look after you. If you do not look after each other, who will look after you? Let him who would look after me look after one who is sick....'

The Buddha was also a skilful peacemaker. One day he settled a dispute between the Shakyas and the Koliyas over water rights on the River Rohini. Tempers had apparently risen to such great heat by the time that he appeared on the scene that hardly anyone could remember the root cause of the quarrel. Then someone remembered: it was water.

'But how much is water worth?' asked the Buddha.

'Very little.' came the reply.

'And how much are the lives of people worth?'

'They are beyond price.'

In this way sense was made to prevail and the two armies which had been brought up were sent away.

On another occasion, the Buddha managed to dissuade King Ajātasattu of Magadha, king Bimbisāra's son, from attacking a peaceful neighbouring people called the Vajjians. At the same

time he held up the enlightened social and political practices of
the Vajjians as a model for the Sangha if it was 'to prosper and
not decline'.

This last incident took place in the final year of the Buddha's
life, of which a comparatively detailed chronology exists. He
was then about 80 and the long ministry of 45 years had begun
to take its toll. He still, however, wandered from one place to
another, waited on by the faithful Ananda.

He apparently started out from Rājagaha and went to
Ambalatthikā, and thence to Nālandā, where later a great
Buddhist university was built. At Nālandā, Sāriputta uttered a
'lion's roar' and proclaimed that the Buddha was the greatest
spiritual teacher ever – only to be admonished by the Buddha on
the grounds that he really didn't have the necessary breadth of
direct knowledge to be able to make such a sweeping statement.
Then it was on to Pātaligāma, where the Buddha foresaw the
building of the great city of Pātaliputra (modern Patna).

The Buddha and Ananda proceeded via Kotigāma and
Nādika to Vesālī, where they received alms food from the
courtesan Ambapāl, who also donated a park to the Sangha.
After that it was on to Beluvā, where the Buddha planned to
pass the Rains Retreat. Here, however, he was overtaken by
'violent and deadly pains', but he suppressed these symptoms
because it was not fitting that he should die without having
taken proper leave of the Sangha. Recovering temporarily, he
spoke to Ananda, stressing that it was not his intention that the
community should become dependent upon him personally.
Each *bhikkhu* should try to be as self-reliant as possible and
when in need of guidance should turn to the *Dhamma*. He, the
Buddha, had in fact taught them everything that they needed to
know; there were no secret or esoteric dimensions; he had not
maintained any 'teacher's clenched fist'. By the latter he was
possibly referring to devious teachers who kept their students in
a dependent state by withholding certain vital teachings.

The Buddha's next port of call was Savatthi, where he stayed
at Jeta's Grove. Here he heard of the death of Sāriputta;
Moggallāna died at about the same time. Addressing the
bhikkhus at Ukkacela shortly afterwards he used their passing as
an object lesson in his teaching that everything that is born must
die.

Shortly afterwards the Buddha was at Vesāli again. There, he and Ananda sat in the Capāla Shrine after going out on alms round together. Now the Buddha hinted to Ananda that, if asked directly, it was possible for him to prolong his life more or less indefinitely. Ananda, however, failed to seize the opportunity – a slip for which he was later sternly reprimanded by the Sangha, for the Buddha now let go of the will to live and the death process was set irreversibly in motion. Thus when Ananda did ask the Buddha to prolong his life, his request was greeted with a fateful, 'Too late. . . .' This is certainly an apocryphal touch and does poor justice to Ananda, whom the Buddha himself praised as being exemplary in his devotion: 'Your acts of love and kindness have been invariable and are beyond measure.'

Having spent some time at Vesāli, the Buddha cast a last – sad? – look at the city and proceeded to Bhandagāma. Thence he made his way to Pāvā by way of Hatthigāma, Ambagāma, Jambugāma and Bhoganāgara, giving teachings as he went. It was at Pāvā that Cunda the smith gave him the meal that was to precipitate his final and fatal illness. Scholars have debated the precise nature of the dish – *sūkaramaddava* – that poisoned him: minced pork has been suggested, also mushrooms. It caused sickness, bleeding and great pain, but still the Buddha was able to set out with Ananda for Kusinārā, an insignificant wattle-and-daub village in the country of the Mallas. He managed to reach the outskirts of Kusinārā but then his suffering became so intense that he had to lie down in a grove of sāla trees.

The final scene has been encrusted with mythological accretions – and understandably so, for the Buddha was an exceptional person; but he was also very much a *human* being, not any kind of god or superman, so at the heart of it there is a very human and touching drama. Thus while the sāla trees rain blossom even though it is out of season and the gods of the ten world-systems crowd round so densely that a hair could not be slipped between them, Ananda also goes away and weeps – and indeed there is a great grief in every sphere of existence, even among the animals, for a buddha, a Fully Enlightened One, is born into the world only very, very rarely. The local people also arrive in large numbers to pay their last respects, and even though he is nearing the end Buddha still carries on teaching. He agrees to see an ascetic named Subhadda – and converts him. And of course he gives advice to his Sangha. Indeed his very last words are ones of advice and encouragement to them:

'Impermanent are all created things. Strive on mindfully.'

Then he passes into meditation and, having traversed the hierarchy of trance states, arrives at Ultimate Nirvāna or *Parinirvāna*. If the true nature of that which he discovered beneath the Bodhi Tree at Bodh Gāya some 45 years before is a great mystery that cannot be conceived in conventional terms, how much more so this final fulfilment:

> *As a flame blown out by the wind*
> *Goes to rest and cannot be defined,*
> *So the wise man freed from individuality*
> *Goes to rest and cannot be defined.*
> *Gone beyond all images –*
> *Gone beyond the power of words.*[9]

Part 3

The Basic
Teachings and
Practices

6   The Buddhist World View

Before we set out to explore the Buddha's teaching in greater detail, it is important at the outset to get a picture of his view of the world. By 'world' we do not merely mean the physical world but the psychological and spiritual worlds as well, which in traditional Buddhist cosmology are all regarded as interlocking.

The Buddhist view of the material world is an undeniably primitive one, pretty well superceded by that which modern science with its more sophisticated methods of investigation has given us. What is really of interest here, therefore, are the spiritual and psychological aspects, and the underlying outlook.

In Buddhist cosmology, innumerable world-systems similar to our own are thought to float in infinite empty space, each one founded on a two-layered basis of air and water. Our world-system can be divided into three main layers:

1   *Kāmadhātu* – the Realm of Desire.
2   *Rūpadhātu* – the Realm of Form.
3   *Arūpadhātu* – the Realm of No-Form.

Within this three-tier system there are broadly six 'destinations', two 'good' and four 'bad', into which it is possible to be born:

1   Gods *(devas)*.
2   Humans.
3   Animals (including birds, fish, reptiles, insects, etc.).
4   Titans *(asuras)*.
5   Hungry ghosts *(pretas)*.
6   The denizens of the hell realms.

The *pretas* or hungry ghosts are disembodied spirits, who are often shown in Buddhist pictures as having hugely bloated

43

The Buddhist World View: A Chinese Version

bellies and tiny mouth-openings, signifying their enormous but essentially insatiable desires.

At the core of the world-system rises the massive bulk of Mount Meru, the axial mountain, from which seven concentric ranges of golden mountains radiate outwards, each separated from the next by an intervening sea. Between the last range and the outer boundary wall of iron mountains *(Chakravāla)*, there is a great ocean in which four great continents are situated, one at each of the points of the compass. These are the abodes of human beings and the southern continent, Jambudvipa, is clearly identical with India as we know it. Later Buddhist cosmologists moved the four great continents closer to Meru, probably so that people should not be exiled so far away from the vital centre.

In the human sphere there are periods of progress and decay; virtue advances and declines too, and life expectancy can vary from 80,000 years at the beginning of a new age *(kalpa)* down to 10 years on the eve of nemesis. Of all the ages into which one might be born, the most fortunate is a *Bhadra Kalpa*. No less than 1000 buddhas will appear during the 320,000,000 years of such an age. Each will rediscover the *Dhamma*, teach it and the Way will remain fully open for a time (500, 1000 or 5000 years); then a period of decline will set in and finally a dark age will descend when the teaching, hopelessly undermined by corruption, is lost completely. The doors to the Deathless then remain closed until another buddha appears on the scene to open them again. We of course currently live in a *Bhadra Kalpa* and Shakyamuni Buddha is the buddha of our time. We would appear to be in the kind of phase when the *Dhamma* is in decline. The buddha of the previous age was Dipankara and the next buddha will be Maitreya.

Mount Meru was thought to rise for a mind-boggling height above the terrestrial zone and to penetrate to the even greater depth beneath it. Down in the bowels of this subterranean world various hot and cold hells are disposed in tiers, rather as in Dante's *Inferno*, the lowest and hottest being the Avīci Hell. The torments of the Buddhist hells equal if not exceed anything conceived by Hieronymous Bosch and other Western inferno-logists. The human imagination seems to become unusually inspired when it comes to devising extreme forms of horror and torment – and the early Buddhists were no exception. However, the ultimate release of Nirvāna is possible even for the most perverted miscreant, even though it may take inconceivable aeons.

Above the hell realms, at the top of the subterranean zone, are to be found the caves in which the titans or *asuras* dwell. They are hot-tempered individuals, congenitally prone to jealousy, who periodically sally out of their dark labyrinths to do battle with the gods *(devas)* who inhabit the upper portions of Meru. The cause of this ongoing feud is the Great Wish-fulfilling Tree that grows half-way up the mountain.

The first three of the four upper terraces on Mount Meru are inhabited by different kinds of powerful spirits known as *yakshas*. On the fourth dwell the Four Great Kings, the guardians of the four quarters, who rank as gods. They keep a watch on goings-on below on earth and send in periodic reports to the superior gods that live above on the summit, who rejoice or lament accordingly.

The realm of the superior gods, who are headed by Sakra, is called the Heaven of the Thirty-Three *(Trāyastrimsha)* and among its delightful features are a beautiful city of palaces and jewelled parks. Every kind of pleasure and luxury is at the disposal of the gods who live here; in particular they enjoy the services of heavenly nymphs *(apsarāses)*, who are highly skilled in the arts of love and music. The lives of the gods are exceedingly long – reputedly 1000 years, and each day is equal to 100 human years. The bitter pill, however, is that even so the day will inexorably dawn when the floral garlands they wear begin to wither and their bodies give off an odour that makes them unattractive to their fun-loving consorts. Then they know that they must go into change and be recycled through the other realms of existence. In short: they die.

Above the summit of Meru there are four aerial heavens. These, with the lower realms already described, together make up the Sphere of Desire, which is only the first of the three tiers that comprise a Buddhist world-system. The other two tiers, the Sphere of Form and the Sphere of No-Form, which are again sub-divided into various hierarchical levels, rise overhead. These give a key to the whole system for they are clearly models of graded states of psychospiritual experience. As such they would have been explored by yogis engaged in meditation practice and all except the topmost five correspond to the various *jhānas (Skt. dhyānas)* or trance states. It was these that the Buddha explored with Alāra Kālāma and Uddaka Rāmaputta. Unfortunately, existence (if it can be called such) in these increasingly rarefied states, though stupendously long, is nevertheless still of limited duration.

Each world-system is subject to cycles of development and decay, and is moreover periodically either partially or totally destroyed by fire, wind or water, then recreated. Images of massive cosmic cataclysm thus occur in Buddhist literature:

> Worlds clash with worlds, Himalaya Mountains with Himalaya Mountains, and Mount Sinerus with Mount Sinerus, until they have ground each other to powder and perished.[10]

The Buddhist world-view is therefore one of a mind-boggling range of possible states, most of them fraught with terrible forms of suffering, in a universe of equally mind-boggling spatial and temporal dimensions. All is in a constant state of flux and every now and then undergoes more or less catastrophic convulsions.

And now for the especially bad news: the beings that inhabit the system are trapped in it. They cannot escape, not even into Keats's 'easeful death', for they are subject to continual rebirth – on and on and on through beginningless and endless time. If the bones of all the bodies that a person's consciousness-continuum has inhabited during one age alone were piled up, they would form a cairn higher than Vulture Peak Mountain, where the Buddha was wont to teach. All the tears of sorrow that have been shed during the long journey would exceed the waters of the four oceans; and the same might be said of all the mothers' milk that each has drunk.

Nor are these endless rounds of rebirth confined to one destination alone. It is quite possible, if one has accumulated the necessary bad karma, to regress from, say, the human realm to that of the animals, or even to become a hungry ghost or a denizen of one of the hells. On the other hand, the best that can be hoped for is to sojourn for a few aeons in some relatively peaceful or blissful state. In particular, by long practice of spiritual disciplines, one might be able to project oneself into the *deva* realms, the realms of the gods. But long though one's stay there might be, it is still a mixed blessing, for sooner or later one is certain to be rudely snatched away and recycled through the system, undergoing all the pangs of severance and insecurity in the process, often (usually?) with other more or less extreme forms of suffering thrown in as well. In Buddhist terminology, this is *Samsāra*, the churning sea of life in which beings are ceaselessly thrown about like tide-wrack.

But now for the good news: there is an Exit. This is precisely what the Buddha himself discovered as he sat beneath the Bodhi Tree on the night of the full moon of May – or rather rediscovered, for other buddhas had blazed that particular trail before him. As we saw, he had previously mastered the *jhānas* (absorbtions), but he saw that they merely led to temporary godlike forms of existence. What he discovered was a Way Out of the system, one that did not lead to a temporary resting place.

The nature of that escape and the method by which it may be achieved will be dealt with later, but it is important to note at this stage that it is only possible from one of the destinations in a world-system: that of human beings. The gods in their way are as much trapped in the system as the damned, the *asuras*, the *pretas* and the animals. Men and women do, however, have a chance of meeting with the teachings of a buddha, studying and practising them and achieving release.

So from the Buddhist point of view, the human realm is the centre of the action. It is the stage upon which the spotlights are trained and upon which all eyes are concentrated. The performers come on and play their parts. Afterwards, according to how they have done, they are led off to other destinations. Some will be taken up to join the gods in the boxes, galleries and stalls. Many will be cast into the pit, or dragged down into the grim labyrinth of cellars beneath the stage. A few, however, will go into the wings to make new entrances, and one or two will so refine their performances that they reach buddhahood. Then the gods will break into rapturous applause, for something truly marvellous has happened – something that is not really a personal achievement so much as a great step forward for the Totality.

The Buddha once told a story about a one-eyed turtle swimming in a great ocean. It comes up for air once every 100 years. Floating on the surface of the ocean there is a yoke, a board with a hole in it. The possibility of achieving a human birth after having fallen into the lower destinations is statistically less than that the turtle should rise to the surface of the ocean and put its neck cleanly through the hole in the yoke.

What are we to make of all this? Is it merely the product of dark and superstitious minds that we, children of a more 'advanced' age illuminated by the light of modern science, might safely cast away?

The truth is that it is very hard to say, for there is much here that, unless we have the vision of a buddha, we cannot know directly.

That having been said, many people find that the notion of being caught up in vast cycles of painful coming-into-being and ceasing-to-be across untold aeons evokes a strange resonance within the psyche. And is this really so surprising? It has taken the evolutionary process millions of years to create human beings, and we carry in our genes the imprint of all the struggles that organic life has undergone in the process. We have in a sense known the agony of the first fish to take to dry land; we have died with the dinosaurs; we have struggled to get up from four feet onto two; we have preyed and been preyed upon, struggled and failed, and succeeded too – but the weariness!

And in the contexts of our own present lives, have we all not experienced innumerable forms of suffering: loss of fortune, separation from loved ones, sickness, betrayal, disillusionment, confusion? Perhaps too, at moments of extreme distress, we have known what it is to be in hell? And have we not been repeatedly overtaken by painful change: snatched from pleasurable situations and had others collapse around us or turn irredeemably sour? Pleasure there has been too, happiness and other good things, but we know they do not last and that really there is no safe resting place, no lasting haven of security. The idea, then, of bringing the whole painful round to a proper conclusion in a Nirvāna that represents both the full flowering of the potentials of consciousness and ultimate unalloyed peace – this seems to the millions of people who over the past two and a half millennia have gravitated to the Way of the Buddha as convincing a goal as any on offer; and one that lends true meaning and purpose to life.

7 The Basic Teachings and Practices

Buddhism is not a fundamentalist religion. Its teachings are not dogmas or articles of faith that have to be blindly accepted at the cost of suspending reason, critical judgement, common sense or experience. Quite the contrary, in fact; their basic aim is to help us gain direct insight into the truth for ourselves. We are therefore invited to try these teachings out in our everyday lives. If they work, then we will naturally want to take them on board. If they don't work for us, then we can cast them aside with no qualms.

The nature of the direct experiential knowledge towards which the Buddhist teachings point came out very well many years ago in the interview that John Freeman made with C.G. Jung on the 'Face to Face' series on BBC Television. Freeman asked Jung directly if he believed in God. Jung baulked a little. 'The word "believe" is difficult for me', he explained. 'You see – I know....' In short, knowledge is direct, first-hand experience about which there can be no argument. Belief, on the other hand, arises when you have to take someone else's word for something about which, quite frankly, you know nothing. Of course, knowing may at times imply knowing that one does not know.

The Four Noble Truths

Buddhism does not take its starting-point on grand metaphysical questions like *Who made the world?*, *What is the meaning of Life?* and *What happens to us after death?* It is not concerned with proving the existence of a God or gods. Rather its root focus is on the down-to-earth fact that all existence, including human existence, is imperfect in a very deep way.

51

'Suffering I teach – and the way out of suffering', the Buddha declared.

The Buddha's teaching on this is set out in the doctrine of the Four Noble Truths, which, along with the principle of the Middle Way, was the subject-matter of the First Sermon that he preached to his original core of disciples in the Deer Park at Isipatana. It follows a medical pattern: a disease is identified, its cause diagnosed, a remedy is declared to exist and then that remedy is prescribed:

1 *Dukkha* exists.
2 *Dukkha* has an identifiable cause.
3 That cause may be terminated; and
4 The means by which that cause may be terminated.

The Pali term *dukkha* is traditionally translated into English as 'suffering' but, though it certainly includes this concept, it possesses a wide spectrum of connotations besides. At one extreme it takes in the most dire forms of mental and physical pain: the agonies of cancer, for instance, and the anguish of someone who falls prey to total despair. It covers our everyday aches and pains, our petty dislikes and frustrations too; and it extends to very subtle feelings of malaise: that life is never quite right.

Notice, however, that the Buddha is not saying here that there is *only dukkha,* or the dark side of life. He certainly does not deny that there is a light side: *sukha,* consisting of pleasure, happiness, etc. He stresses *dukkha* because it is *problematical*, whereas *sukha* is not. At the same time, there is no such thing as *perfect*, unalloyed happiness or pleasure. Even the most beautiful experience has a melancholy undertone simply because we know that it can't last. So *dukkha* touches everything that exists.

Strangely, however, there is something in us that staunchly resists facing the dark side of life. We have a dogged determination to continue in pursuit of worldly satisfactions even though enormous discouragements are put in our way. Our feeling is that, with a few modifications and adjustments here and there, we can overcome our problems, realize all our dreams and enjoy heaven on earth. Bad times are always provisional and

sooner or later we're going to get over the hump and then . . .
it'll be downhill all the way. . . .

In a way this shows spirit and could be regarded as entirely
commendable – except that there's a quality of wilful blindness
about it: a refusal to squarely face the true facts of the human
condition. The results of this can also be very destructive. How
many times have we hurt ourselves and others in the crass
pursuit of our own fantasies? Good things do come to us in the
course of events and should be accepted and enjoyed while they
last, but we tend to want *only* the good and, resisting all else,
pursue it exclusively and cling to it desperately if we do get it.

So the beginning of the road to wisdom begins with a realistic
(not pessimistic) recognition of the fact of *dukkha*. Life usually
has to have bitten us quite deeply, and often many times over,
before we reach this stage. But when we do reach it, we have in a
very real sense come of age as human beings, for an immature,
butterfly existence in pursuit of mere happiness is unsatisfying
in the final analysis. When we face up to the dark side of life, on
the other hand, we begin to appreciate the full grandeur and
challenge of human existence. Now too we can start to do
something about changing our lives and putting them on a
deeper, more authentic footing.

The second Noble Truth informs us that *dukkha* has an
identifiable cause. This is *tanhā*, which is literally translated as
'thirst', but in fact possesses the same kind of spectrum of
connotations as *dukkha*. There are gross forms of *tanhā*, like
obsessive lust for money and sensual pleasures; and there are
exceedingly subtle forms, like a desire to do good or to know the
truth. And of course there is a whole gamut of middling
connotations in between.

Basically *tanhā* can be reduced to a fundamental ache that is
implanted in everything that exists: a gnawing dissatisfaction
with what is and a concomitant reaching out for something else.
So we can never be at rest but are always grasping for something
outside ourselves. This is what powers the endless cycle-
wheeling motion of the Wheel of Life, driving us on from one
moment to the next, one life to the next. Here too resides our
native clinging to existence.

Tanhā is not an aberration. It is entirely natural. But if we
want to get off the Wheel of Life and thereby liberate ourselves

from *dukkha*, we must do something about it. This brings us to the third Noble Truth. This tells us that there is a method: a way or path that can be travelled to ultimate freedom.

Freedom from *tanhā* is known in Pali as *Nibbāna*, the Sanskrit equivalent of which, Nirvāna, has now entered English parlance. There are two kinds of Nirvāna:

1 That which has a residual basis.
2 That which has no residual basis.

The first arose in Shakyamuni Buddha as he sat beneath the Bodhi Tree at Bodh Gāyā on the fateful night of the full moon of May; the second arose when he finally passed away at Kusinārā. In the first case a living being continued to pursue an earthly life; in the second, there was complete extinction *(Parinirvāna)*: nothing tangible remained behind.

What is Nirvāna? Invariably it is stressed that it cannot be grasped via sense experience or by the mind operating in terms of its usual conceptual categories. And it certainly cannot be described in words. To do so would be like trying to describe the colour red to a blind person. As it lies wholly outside our normal field of experience, we can and must come to it through direct insight – and this indeed is basically what the Buddha's way is all about. However, bearing in mind that any description must be more or less inaccurate, a few tentative pointers may be given to guide us in the right general direction. The word 'Nirvāna' itself possesses connotations of 'blowing out' or 'extinguishing', as a flame may be blown out or extinguished once the fuel that feeds it has been exhausted. It is cool and peaceful. *Dukkha* doesn't touch it, nor the passions of greed, hatred and ignorance. In the Buddha's own words:

> Monks, there is an unborn, unoriginated, unmade and un-conditioned. Were there not the unborn, unoriginated, umade and unconditioned, there would be no escape from the born, originated, made and conditioned. Since there is the unborn, unoriginated, unmade and unconditioned, there is escape from the born, originated, made and conditioned.

Finally, even though Nirvāna is usually described in negative terms – it is obviously easier to say what it is *not* than what it *is*

– it is nevertheless lavishly praised in the Buddhist scriptures as amounting to supreme bliss, no less.

At once, of course, the mind starts to create speculative pictures – and stumbles into mistaken views. One classic howler is to see Nirvāna as some kind of nothingness. This is to fall prey to the mistaken view of annihilationism (complete non-existence), which is twinned with the equally mistaken view of eternalism (that something may exist forever). Nirvāna lies beyond both existence and non-existence. Another howler is to imagine Nirvāna as a heaven where all good Buddhists go. It is definitely not a place, nor is it 'somewhere else'. Paradoxically, though unconditioned itself, it only arises amid worldly conditions, and in the case of human beings, within the human body:

> In this fathom-long body, with all its perceptions and thoughts, do I proclaim the world, the origin of the world, the cessation of the world and the path leading to the cessation of the world.

The fourth Noble Truth defines this path to liberation by telling us what practical steps we have to take in order to root out *tanhā* and thereby create the fertile ground in which Nirvāna may arise. These steps are laid out in the teaching of the Noble Eightfold Path.

The Noble Eightfold Path

1	Right Understanding	*Sammā ditthi*
2	Right Thought	*Sammā sankappa*
3	Right Speech	*Sammā vācā*
4	Right Action	*Sammā kammanta*
5	Right Livelihood	*Sammā ājīva*
6	Right Effort	*Sammā vāyāma*
7	Right Mindfulness	*Sammā sati*
8	Right Concentration	*Sammā samādhi*

The Path can be further subdivided into three main elements: Wisdom, Morality and Meditation.

Although this kind of numerical, hierarchic structure – which was very much the traditional Indian way of presenting teachings – gives the impression that every step must be approached in due sequence, the three main elements of wisdom, morality and meditation in practice need to be developed together. Without meditation, wisdom remains hollow and theoretical; at the same time, the insights that arise in meditation need the informed understanding of wisdom or else they may not be recognized for what they are. T.S. Eliot talks in the 'Dry Salvages' section of his *Four Quartets* of having 'had the experience but missed the meaning'. Also, it will be virtually impossible to practise the Path without the moral basis.

Wisdom (Pali, *Paññā*; Sanskrit, *Prajñā*)

The Wisdom element features in *Right Understanding,* which implies the obvious, but perhaps often missed, point that in order to practise we need to have heard (or read) the Buddha's teachings, notably that of the Four Noble Truths, and have not merely understood them theoretically but have actively penetrated their truth by testing them against experience. Our wish to pursue the Buddha's Way is therefore founded on informed confidence in the soundness of the teachings rather than on blind faith or misguided attraction to its superficial aspects.

Right Thought on the other hand, must include correct motivation. We need to realize that we are practising, not to acquire greater powers and more possessions for ourselves, but rather to move away from the basic egocentric orientation to a new, wider, more selfless one. In short: there is in the final analysis no pay-off for 'me' in practising Buddhism. That having been said, it has to be admitted that none of us have perfect understanding and motivation at the start. As we continue, however, practice will tend to uncover all sorts of blind spots and subtle forms of self-centredness. The Buddha's Way is an ever-deepening learning process.

An actual change in our thinking processes must begin to take place too. The unreformed (i.e. selfish) mind, like a mill in perpetual motion, is constantly devising plans, plots and strategies for advancing its own cause, outflanking rivals and undoing enemies. Or else it indulges itself in egoistic or hedonistic fantasies. *Right Thought* is about switching over to *other*-directed mental modes: ones that are more altruistic and benign. We should also become increasingly concerned to act responsibly towards the environment. We think too of religious questions with a view, not to promoting ourselves as gurus or pundits, but in order the better to be of service to the world.

Morality (*Sila*)

Buddhist ethics are not codified into a rigid moral code; nor are they about making judgements and arousing sin and guilt, though every willed action produces consequences, as we shall see in greater detail when we examine the concept of karma. Rather, Buddhists try to be aware of any particular failing to live up to an ethical principle and resolve to do better next time. They also note in such cases that they have still a long way to go towards finally overcoming their faults, which breeds a healthy humility. There have always been in every religion those self-righteous people who refuse to recognize their own faults but instead nurse delusions of moral superiority. We all fall into these traps at times. Christianity has its 'whited sepulchres' who praise the Lord that they are not sinful like other men; Buddhism has its 'whited *stu*pas' too. Clearly honesty and keen mindfulness of one's actions are of the essence as a foil to these snares.

Right Speech, the third item on the path, is about not telling lies, slandering and backbiting, swearing and using 'harsh' language, wasting one's own and other peoples" time with frivolous chatter, and generally not using one's speech faculties in harmful or unproductive ways. It is also about being truthful. This is in fact very important, especially as our modern Western culture has debased truth and facts are wantonly suppressed or twisted to suit self-interest or in order to generate sensation.

Right Action, on the other hand, is about decent behaviour generally. A lay person may, as a token of their commitment to the Buddha's Way, subscribe to Five Precepts – *Pañca Sila* – and accordingly undertake to train him/herself to:

1   Refrain from taking life.

2   Refrain from taking that 'which is not given.
3   Refrain from misuse of the senses.
4   Refrain from telling lies.
5   Refrain from self-intoxication with drink and drugs.

Taking life not only includes the murder of human beings, of course, but killing other living beings as well. This inevitably raises the question of whether meat-eating is permissible or not in Buddhism. The members of the original Sangha were mendicants and as such were supposed to accept whatever food they were given. Thus it was technically permissible for them to eat meat – but only if they knew that an animal, bird or fish had not been killed *specially* to provide them with food. Many find this rather permissive attitude unsatisfactory, for to eat meat is in a sense to connive at slaughter, albeit after the event. Later, when the Mahāyāna developed, strong calls for total vegetarianism were put out.

Under 'taking that which is not given' comes stealing and all manner of allied practices whereby money or property – or even more intangible things – are immorally appropriated.

Misuse of the senses embraces a spectrum of vices. There is over-indulgence in food, which not only causes the rich and powerful to gorge themselves at the expense of the under-privileged – in its global aspect, this results in the appalling malnutrition suffered in the Third World – but also leads to disease and torpor. The serious Buddhist practitioner is generally encouraged to moderate consumption if only in the interests of maintaining energy and alertness. Strictly observant Theravāda Buddhist monks eat only one meal a day and that before noon.

Then there is glutting the eye with beautiful sights and the ear with beautiful sounds, all of which can become highly addictive as well as unconducive to practice. Similarly, as the mind is also a sense organ in the Buddhist view, one can overindulge in intellectual pastimes with similarly negative results. And, of course, one can abuse the body – both one's own and others' – for selfish pleasure.

This brings us to the ever-interesting topic of sex, a matter that generally comes in for a bad press in early Buddhism. As a primary generator of passion, it was considered extremely dangerous by the Buddha. At first he made no training rule about it for his Sangha but when one of his monks, Sudinna, slept with his former wife in order to satisfy his family's heartfelt wish for an heir, the Buddha dressed him down in no uncertain terms: 'Misguided man, it were better for you that your member should enter the mouth of a hideous, venomous viper or cobra than that it should enter a woman...' – and he went on to make a training rule that those in the Sangha should henceforth totally refrain from sexual intercourse.

In modern Europe celibacy has become highly unpopular, and those who gravitate to it are popularly thought to be likely candidates for neurosis... or worse. Sigmund Freud and his psychoanalytic school, though in many ways they did much good, are much to blame for this, for they did help to instil the notion in the popular mind that regular discharge of the sexual function is essential to mental and physical wellbeing. Actually, misguided indulgence and overindulgence in sex are as likely to lead to psychological problems as non-indulgence. Celibacy is in fact a very healthy state if sexuality, though not expressed, is clearly recognized. It certainly helps to simplify life and, by freeing a person from the very large energy- and time-consuming duties of supporting and bringing up children, affords them the opportunity of devoting themselves wholeheartedly to spiritual practice.

Lay people, however, are not expected to be strictly celibate, but still their sexual activity should be contained within reasonable constraints. Of course, the vast panorama of sexual excesses that have developed in recent years did not exist in the Buddha's day. He merely had to contend with pretty tame things like adultery and prostitution. We can, however, infer certain basic principles that should be observed: we should firstly try not to hurt others; and secondly we should try to be moderate, for immoderate indulgence of sexual desire will only serve to feed the fires of passion and attachment, which cuts completely contrary to the direction and spirit of the Buddha's Way.

The precept to refrain from intoxicating oneself with drink and drugs was formulated because these dull our perceptions and sensitivities. People use them to escape, if only fleetingly, from themselves and from the world. Buddhist training, on the other hand, is directed towards increasing clarity and awareness of what is happening both within and without; it is also very much about facing the world as it is and developing the strength to deal squarely with it using one's own resources.

Novice monks and nuns observe all these precepts and five more besides: refraining from eating more than one meal and that before noon, from attending worldly shows and entertainments, from using perfumes and adornments, from sleeping on a high or luxurious bed, and from possessing money (including gold and silver). Fully-fledged monks observe 227 precepts.

Application of the next item on the Eightfold Path, *Right Livelihood*, has become especially difficult today. In the Buddha's time there were butchers, traffickers in poisons, weapons and intoxicants, and a few other dubious types, but these were few compared with the legions that contemporary Western society entertains – and often applauds. In our pragmatic society, inspired as it is by commercial advantage rather than ideals or ethics, almost anything goes so long as it makes a fast buck. The fundamental principle at play in *Right Livelihood* is the classic Indian virtue of *ahimsā*: harmlessness. The serious Buddhist does not wish to compromise his integrity by becoming involved in any activity that is going to cause harm to other people, animals or the environment – or even outer space. Rather, he/she will wish to use his productive energies in ways that at least cause no harm and hopefully do some good. Such an attitude is not only virtuous and beneficial in itself, but serious Buddhist practice itself becomes impossible if one is caught up in the ramifications, mental, emotional and/or practical, of corruption of any kind. To be an effective Buddhist, one needs that space and calmness that can only come from being on reasonably good terms with oneself and with the world at large.

Even though it extols gentleness and patience in practice, Buddhism also makes it clear that some energy has to be put out too. This brings us to the next, the sixth item on the Eightfold Path: *Right Effort*. Again, the word 'right' is important here, indicating that energy too should be strictly regulated. Too much can be as counterproductive as too little. Also it is not goal-directed energy in the usual sense. One is not trying to obtain anything. As the Ven. Ajahn Chah has said:

> Proper effort is not the effort to make something particular
> happen. It is the effort to be aware and awake in each moment, the
> effort to overcome laziness and defilement, the effort to make each
> activity of our day meditation.[11]

Meditation (*Samàdhi*)

The seventh and eighth items on the Eightfold Path, *Right
Mindfulness* and *Right Concentration*, bring us fully into the
ambit of meditation. Meditation is the specialized activity that
helps us to fully realize the Buddha's teachings – to make them
an integral part of our being rather than just a new set of ideas to
be entertained theoretically in the mind. It weans away from
our usual habit patterns, particularly our involvement with our
thoughts and their emotional sub-themes. At the same time it
sharpens and intensifies our powers of direct perception: it gives
us eyes to see into the true nature of things. The field of research
is ourselves, and for this reason the laser of attention is turned
and focused inwards.

Meditation is not something to be toyed with lightly. It
involves opening up the psyche and operating with it at depth.
Problems, more or less difficult to handle, may arise. Therefore,
to begin with at least, it should always be approached in
conducive circumstances and with the guidance of an
experienced and qualified teacher. The right motivation must
also be present. It is a misapplication of meditation to use it to
obtain personal benefits – like 'mind power' or 'peak
experiences'. It is also generally unwise to dabble with it from
books. What is offered here is therefore general orientational
information for further research, not instructions for experimentation.

The classic Buddhist meditation posture is a cross-legged one,
with one leg laid on top of the other (Single Lotus) or the two
legs interwoven (Double Lotus). Alternatively, if either of these
options give pain, an upright chair may be used. The important
thing is that the back should be straight and unsupported, and
lightly balanced on the pelvis. The head should be squarely

balanced on an upright neck. The eyelids are lowered, and the mouth is lightly closed. The hands are laid one above the other in the lap, thumb-tip to thumb-tip, or lightly clasped. There are also forms of walking meditation – and one can even, in extreme circumstances, meditate lying down, though as there is always the danger of falling asleep in the horizontal position, it is not recommended.

Firstly, all personal problems and preoccupations are laid aside; then specialized techniques are brought into play. In basic Buddhist meditation, two elements are usually identified:

1   *Samatha* – tranquillity.
2   *Vipassanā* – insight.

In *samatha,* concentration *(samādhi)* is brought to bear on a single object to the exclusion of all else. It may be the breath, or a coloured disc, or the sensations of the body. Many suitable objects are enumerated in the traditional texts; the important thing is that they should be neutral, unexciting and unevocative. If the breath is used, no attempt should be made to alter it: to make it deeper or more rhythmic; it serves merely as a focus for concentration.

Things rarely go swimmingly in meditation – especially at first. Attention slips and the mind wanders away on beguiling trains of thought and fantasy. When this happens, the fact should be noted and the attention returned to the object of concentration. It will probably have to be brought back time and time and time again. The most important thing is not to set ambitious goals or strive for results – that is more likely to frustrate rather than hasten the development of concentration – but to simply perform the practice patiently and aim first and foremost at remaining aware of what is going on in the Now. Sometimes the mind is in turmoil throughout a meditation session and cannot develop any degree of concentration; the practice then is to remain fully mindful of this.

As concentration develops, the mind becomes increasingly tranquil. There are traditionally said to be eight *jhānas* (Skt. *dhyānas)* or absorptions through which the virtuoso *samatha* practitioner may progress. These are increasingly refined or subtle states of consciousness. As delightful states, the *jhānas* correspond to the happy realms of the gods and their divine companions, but they are also strictly temporary abodes and do not in any case amount to Enlightenment. They also present a special danger: the meditator may become addicted and not want to leave them. The Buddha was enabled to reach the *jhānas* under the guidance of his Hindu teachers – but he found them unsatisfying, hence his search for something else. He finally found what he was looking for by means of *vipassanā*. However, interesting though it might be to explore these little known reaches of inner space, in modern Western situations few living outside monastic communities have the time for doing so. Therefore, *samatha* meditation is usually practised briefly in the initial stages of a lay meditation session in order to establish a workable degree of mental calm and concentration in preparation for *vipassanā*.

In *vipassanā*, the mind is opened and awareness is directed to all that enters its ambit. Often at first a great deal of hitherto submerged psychological material rises into consciousness. This is a very positive process; the darkness is becoming conscious. Old fears and phobias, traumas and repressions can now be hospitably entertained in full awareness. The meditator is neutral towards them, neither rejecting nor repressing – nor, on the other hand, identifying and hence becoming carried away. If merely treated to 'bare attention', they will pass away. This is a very real and effective form of psychotherapy.

Later, as the mind quietens down, attention may be directed in a more systematic way. Traditionally there are said to be four 'foundations' of mindfulness:

1 Bodily activity.
2 Feelings.
3 States of mind.
4 Mental contents.

Again, whatever enters the field of attention is observed and analysed. Invariably it will be found to be subject to three conditions or marks.

The Three Marks of Existence

1 *Dukkha* – unsatisfactoriness.
2 *Anicca* – impermanence.
3 *Anattā* – not self.

We have already looked closely at *dukkha*, the flawed nature of all that exists: its inability to give lasting satisfaction or provide us with an unshakable basis of stability and security. *Anicca*, on the other hand, points to the observable fact that the world is a flux; nothing ever stays the same for long and ultimately everything is unstoppably headed – though admittedly at different comparative rates of speed – towards dissolution. *What about the Buddha's Way – surely that is exempt?* we may protest. Unfortunately, as the Buddha himself foresaw, even the *Dhamma* itself is subject to change and degeneration.

The third of the marks of existence – *Anattā* – points to perhaps the most profound discovery that can be made in meditation: that, search as hard as we will, we can never point to anything in ourselves that we can definitely say is the self. Neither the body, nor the thoughts, nor the feelings can be self, for they are *dukkha* and *anicca*, unsatisfactory and impermanent. All this we can observe, while the observer, the one who knows, remains ever elusive, standing outside the field of sense perception, outside the world.

To sit in meditation, dredging the depths of the mind for the one who is looking, the one who sees and knows, is rather like searching for a salmon in the deep, dark-green pool of an old river. We know that the great fish is down there; we sometimes think we see his cold eye looking up at us, or the flicker of his shadow on the silt bed, or the flash of his underbelly as he glides away to a deeper, darker place; but in the end he always eludes us – always remains a great mystery. This is *anattā*.

The Ego or 'I'

If a person called Jill begins to analyse herself, looking for the core in which her Jillness resides, she will find a pattern of ever-changing phenomena – body, emotions, sensations, ideas, etc. – but none of these could be said to be the essential, eternal and unchanging Jill.   But even if in deep meditation Jill can find no solid basis for her idea of herself as a separate individual, the idea of 'Jill' still works in terms of the common-sense conventions of the everyday world. Her friends and workmates will call her 'Jill' and both they and she will know what is meant when she uses the words 'I' and 'me'. In fact Jill needs a reasonably steady 'I' or ego in order to be able to function effectively in this world. It is a necessary stage of development.

We erect the idea of 'I' as a central reference point around which the world appears to revolve. This is by definition an *ego-centric* view and unavoidably leads to selfishness and all its attendant evils. The world also neatly divides in two: there is the sphere of 'I' and the sphere of Not-'I'. 'I', which is really just a more or less unstable fiction anyway, is usually fighting a losing battle to hold its own against Not-'I' (i.e. the rest of the world), and this inevitably leads to suffering. 'I' can't hold my own for ever – or indeed for long.

The Buddha's Way points to a development that leads beyond 'I' to wider and larger horizons. It unlocks the door of the cell of individuality and offers freedom – Nirvāna.

Other Aspects of Meditation

Through *vipassanā* meditation, the mind arrives at the understanding that 'everything that arises passes away and is not self' – which is what buddhas know. But this, as we have already indicated, is not merely a negative insight: the discovery of a pure nothingness. Nor is it the uncovering of a mysterious 'something'. It is Nirvāna – ineffable, infinitely subtle, fleetingly glimpsed at first but returned to again and again until it is fully established as the fulcrum of one's being and lived out in action. 'Real' meditation is direct, formless contemplation of this reality.

Though pure formless contemplation would seem in itself to be simple, it is not easy. Therefore, as concessions to the errant mind, many types of meditation practice have been developed that use forms to a greater or lesser extent. There are, for instance, meditations involving emotional arousals and imaginative visualizations. One may perhaps try to feel *mettā*, loving-kindness, for oneself and for the whole world. Or one may picture a beautiful person and then, as an antidote to lust, visualize their bodies full of obnoxious secretions and by-products, as undergoing the processes of ageing, death and decay. One may contemplate the qualities of the Buddha, or the Four Noble Truths, or other doctrinal formulations. When in due course we examine Tantra, we will see how elaborate deities and *mandalas* are created in detail by internal visualization and then dissolved away again. A full survey would be very extensive.

The tendency throughout the history of Buddhism seems to have been for vast accumulations to pile up over the formless heart of the matter – not merely elaborations of meditation practice but complex philosophical systems; also ritual, devotional practice, etc., etc. At times it has all conspired to obscure the formless heart – towards which, in theory at least, it's all meant to point. However, counter-movements have also sprung up periodically that have sought to sweep all the accretions and superstructures aside and to zero back to the basic essentials of pure formless contemplation with a minimum of superfluous trappings. In Tibet (and in mediaeval India too) there was *Mahāmudrā* and *Dzogchen*, and in China *Ch'an*, which became known as *Zen* when it was propagated in Japan.

Meditators also occasionally encounter the *iddhis* (Skt. *rddhis*). These are paranormal powers, like clairvoyance and telepathy, the ability to multiply one's body or transform one's shape, to levitate or walk on water, to recall former lives and suchlike. Though magic has a place in Buddhism – and a very large place in some of its traditions (for instance, that of Tibet) – it is generally speaking thought to be in bad taste to boast of one's occult powers or to show them off, particularly for worldly gain. The special danger they present is that common to all forms of power: they are open to misuse, may inflate the ego and may also sidetrack the meditator and cause him/her to forget his main concern: Nirvāna. The usual advice given is that, if *iddhis* are encountered, the meditator should mindfully observe them – and pass on. They do not in any case indicate any especially high level of attainment and should certainly not be mistaken for true Wisdom or Enlightenment.

Mindfulness

The practice of mindfulness is not reserved for the meditation cushion. It should be brought to bear on what is happening at any and every moment. Needless to say, our usual condition is a kind of waking dream. We are almost totally distracted, lost in trains of unreflective thought and fantasy, which are interwoven with beguiling emotional sub-themes. These move us reactively through life according to conditioned habit-patterns. We may be habitual grumblers, for instance, who at every pretext launch into embittered diatribes with all the predictability of Pavlov's dogs.

If we are able to wake up, if only occasionally and for a few moments at first, stand back from the ongoing drama of our lives and take an objective look at the habit patterns in which we are caught, then their compulsive hold over us begins to loosen. We *dis*-identify from them; that is, we begin to see that those thoughts and feelings are not *us*. They come along accidentally. They are neither an organic part of us nor are we obliged to follow them.

There are the beginnings of a remarkable freedom here. Closely observed anger, for instance, need not erupt into disastrous outbursts; its energy may indeed be used for positive purposes. For this reason, mindfulness has been likened to the sun that sheds light where there is darkness and whose warming rays foster life and growth.

When people begin to observe themselves they are often shocked and complain that Buddhist practice is actually making them *worse* human beings. Actually they were that bad all along only they never paused to look! We tend to select data and construct an idealized self-image. Unpleasant characteristics are suppressed because they don't harmonize with this pretty fiction. Once awareness is brought to play, however, the dark, unconfronted side of ourselves has to be faced – and that is invariably painful. Mindfulness also brings us squarely up against the world as it is rather than as we would like it to be.

The Five Aggregates

This amounts to the Buddhist Theory of Man. The Buddha

once told a parable about a cart. If the cart were to be dismantled, one would have here a pair of wheels, there a shaft and axle, a body somewhere else – and so forth. But where would the original cart be? It would no longer exist. All that would remain would be the separate components.

It is much the same with a so-called 'person'. In Buddhism, the theory is advanced that a human being is composed of five 'heaps' or aggregates (Pali, *khandha*, Skt. *skandha*). These are:

1   *The aggregate of matter.*   This includes the body, which is analysed in terms of four elements (solidity, fluidity, heat and motion) and their derivatives, which include our five basic sense organs (eye, ear, nose, tongue, body).

2   *The aggregate of feeling or sensation.*   Feelings/sensations are of three kinds: pleasant, unpleasant and neutral, and arise out of contact between a sense organ and a sense object. One extra sense organ comes into play here: the mind, which apprehends mind-objects (ideas, mental images etc.).

3   *The aggregate of perception.*   Perception is the faculty that actually *recognizes* an object by picking up its distinctive features. Its data come via the interaction of the five sense organs and the mind with appropriate objects.

4   *The aggregate of mental formations.*   This encompasses all the willed activities of mind, plus a few others.

5   *The aggregate of consciousness.*   When a sense organ or the mind makes contact with an appropriate object, simple awareness but not actual recognition of that object is the function of consciousness, which arises in dependence on that object. Consciousness is certainly not a kind of pure omnipresent mind-substance that registers impressions while existing independently of them. This was a view held in the Buddha's own day by Sati the Fisherman's Son – who was severely rebuked by the Master for his faulty thinking. 'There is no arising of consciousness without conditions', the Buddha unequivocally declared – and he went on to illustrate how, when a suitable set of conditions have arisen, the appropriately tinctured consciousness coincidentally arises.

When all these aggregates come together, the fertile ground

exists for the arising of a notion of 'I'. When the aggregates break up at death, however, where will 'I' be then?

Karma

The Sanskrit term *karma* (Pali, *kamma*) has entered English parlance. When some villain receives his come-uppance, this sometimes elicits a retort like, 'That's his karma!' Actually, it is the *vipāka* (Pali), literally the 'ripening'; the *karma* was the seed from which this developed.

Linguistically karma means *action*; specifically it refers to willed actions of body, speech and mind. All such actions, barring alone those of a buddha or *arahat*, produce subtle seeds which in time will spawn further consequences. These will be wholesome, unwholesome or neutral according to the nature of the original action. Unwholesome actions like killing or stealing will produce unpleasant results; wholesome actions like giving alms to a beggar or upholding the truth will produce pleasant ones. As the very first verse of the *Dhammapāda* puts it: '. . . . if a person speaks or acts with unwholesome mind, pain pursues him, even as the wheel follows the hoof of the ox that draws the cart.'

Karma is used to explain the differing conditions of people in the world. Some are healthy, strong and enjoy pleasant circumstances. This is the result of good deeds either performed in the present but more likely in a previous life, for karma is a force that can overleap death. In the same way the condition of the wretched of the earth can be put down to bad past deeds. In the East, where the notion of karma is general and by no means confined to Buddhist circles, this can result in extreme political *laissez-faire*. After all, rich and poor alike are receiving their just deserts, so why redistribute wealth? In any case, if the unprivileged are virtuous, they will receive their rewards in a future life.

However, these things can be complicated by the fact that various different types of karmic formations may come into play. For instance, a person may be born into a rich, aristocratic family; but due to the influence of a secondary or tertiary strain of negative karmic formations, they may not be able to enjoy the pleasures available in such circumstances. They may perhaps suffer physical disability and be in constant pain. Likewise, someone born into adverse conditions may be blessed with a contented disposition that allows them to be happy anywhere.

While it is very difficult to check the accuracy of such complicated and long-term ramifications, we can observe in our own lives how particular actions affect the way we subsequently feel and what happens to us. A sudden outburst of anger may sour relations in a particular context for hours, days or weeks. On a more sensational level, a momentary moral lapse can leave a fortune or a brilliant career in ruins.

Wise reflection on the *consequences* of actions, even small actions, may give us pause before we plunge ahead on some new course.

According to the traditional view, the kinds of repercussions that can await us for heedless actions may be dire indeed. We can be reborn as poor or sickly people; or we can regress to the animal or even the insect level of existence in a future life; we might find ourselves embroiled in one of the Buddhist hells for several aeons. However, this retributive aspect of karma can be overstressed. It can generate unnecessary guilt and fear of life – even terror. Ajahn Sumedho has a lighter, more balanced approach to the subject:

> We worry: 'I've done so many bad things in the past; what kind of result will I get from all that?' Well, all you can know is that what you've done in the past is a memory now. The most awful, disgusting thing that you've ever done, that you wouldn't want anyone to know about; the one that, whenever anyone talks about kamma and rebirth, makes you think, 'I'm really going to get it for having done that' – that is a memory, and that memory is the kammic result. The additions to that like fearing, worrying, speculating – these are the kammic result of unenlightened behaviour. What you do, you remember; it's as simple as that. If you do something kind, generous or compassionate, the memory makes you feel happy; and if you do something mean and nasty, you have to remember *that*. You try to repress it, run away from it, get caught up in all kinds of frantic behaviour – that's the kammic result.[12]

How to deal with karmic formations? Ajahn Sumedho

maintains that they 'will cease through recognition'. Thus in mindfulness practice, karmic formations are allowed to rise into the mind and then to pass into cessation – *without being acted upon*. It is the acting out of karmic formation that increases their strength, creating habit and causative patterns that go on and on, continually strengthening themselves.

There is also talk in Buddhist circles occasionally of 'burning out one's karma'. Some practitioners even welcome painful experiences and bear them willingly and patiently because they know that in so doing they are paying off old karmic accounts. I once asked a monk who was engaged in this kind of exercise how he found it. He said that it produced a deep sense of calming down: the old compulsive impulses to action were getting weaker and fainter. However, it is not necessary to burn out all one's karma in order to become Enlightened. But even then, if the psychophysical organism persists, it still can't escape the ripening of past karma. Even the Buddha himself was subject to this. When his nasty cousin Devadatta tried to kill him by dropping a boulder onto him from Vulture Peak, though the boulder was deflected, a splinter wounded his foot – the karmic pay-off for an attempt to kill and steal the property of a step-brother in a previous life.

Various objections can be raised against the notion of karma. For instance, if a million people die in a nuclear bomb-strike on a certain city, could they all be said to be equally guilty of unwholesome past-deeds? Statistically, isn't it inevitable that there will be at least a few extremely virtuous people among them – perhaps a saint or two? One answer that may be given is that what is in play here is collective karma. Presumably then, collective karma can at times override individual karma. But if we are to be rigorous and apply basic Buddhist doctrine, who is the karmically-afflicted individual anyway? Haven't we already heard that the notion of an 'I', an individual entity, is, in ultimate terms, a false view?

Here indeed lies the nub of the matter. As the *Visuddhimagga* asserts: 'No doer of the deeds is found/ No-one ever reaps their fruit;/ Empty phenomena roll on:/ This view alone is right and true. . . .'

Rebirth

Closely linked to the notion of karma is that of rebirth. This should not be confused with reincarnation, which is the view that there is a soul or subtle essence imprinted with an enduring personal stamp that transmigrates or commutes from body to body down through the aeons. Buddhism of course rejects that view. What it does admit, however, is *causal connection* between one life and another. Thus the karmic accumulations, good and bad, of a particular life (itself the culmination of an endless series of causally-connected past lives) will condition a new birth. Sequences of such interconnected lives form a continuum. Nothing is handed on, however, but the conditioning: the influences, the karmic charge.

To clarify this notion various standard illustrations have been developed. There is the example of the flame that is passed from one candle to others. It is not exactly the same flame that carries on down the line, but it is not a different one either. Another is the cannoning of billiard balls. One ball strikes another; on impact it stops dead; but the other ball moves on, strikes another ball and itself stops dead; then a third ball continues the process.... It is a single movement, passed on through a sequence of temporary vehicles.

It must be stressed that rebirth isn't just something that bridges the abyss of death between one physical life and another. It is something that is happening all the time. As we've already noted, our bodies are undergoing minute cellular changes from moment to moment; our feelings and thoughts change too. What appear then to be our continuous, flowing lives are in reality sequences of essentially separate life-moments, each a death and a rebirth. Take the analogy of a film. It is made up of individual frames, each slightly different from the next. As the film is run through a projector, however, the frames blend into each other and the illusion of flow is created. Our fascination with the ongoing drama obscures the true nature of what is happening.

Death

The exact way in which at physical death karmic accumulations condition a new life is a complex matter, though it is treated in the usual detail in the traditional texts. What is considered to be of vital importance is a person's state of mind in their final moments.

The science of death was pursued to considerable depth within the Tibetan Buddhist tradition. According to this tradition, when a person dies their consciousness-continuum leaves the body and moves into an intermediate or *bardo* state that is full of a bewildering phantasmagoria of powerful apparitions – ghosts, gods, demons, wrathful deities. Ability to stay cool and aware enough to deal with these phenemona depends very· much on the amount of spiritual practice performed in the past life. Now, therefore, the diligent meditator (or rather, his karmic inheritance) reaps the fruit of all the years of patient sitting. Help may also be given by friends, who can read the *Tibetan Book of the Dead (Bardo Thödröl)* over the corpse.

Firstly, there is a glimpse of a marvellous luminosity. This is none other than the Enlightened State itself. If the disembodied consciousness-continuum can see this for what it is and stay with it, then liberation is assured. But if the force of negative karma is too strong, all kinds of confusion may rise up, particularly terror. This of course is terror of something untoward happening to an individual entity, to the delusory 'I' that contaminates the particular consciousness-continuum. As that sense of 'I' has no definite form with which to identify itself, there is also a desperate reaching out for a new body in which to be reborn. Thus the deluded consciousness-continuum is swept along. Other lights will subsequently appear, offering other chances of liberation, but these too may be lost.

The disembodied consciousness-continuum may spend up to 49 days in the *bardo* state. If liberation is not achieved, terror and desire will eventually draw it into a new birth. If it is to be a human one, the future mother and father are seen lying together. In the case of a male birth, attraction for the mother is aroused; vice-versa in the case of a female birth. Heated by lust, the deluded consciousness approaches with a view to intercourse –

but is foiled. This generates anger, which seals a connection with the father's semen and the mother's blood. The new life is thereupon initiated.

Dependent Origination

If Buddhism makes no appeal to the idea of a creator God and if things are not self-creating, how do phenomena arise? The answer is that they do so as the result of preceding causes and in turn become the causes of future phenomena themselves. All phenomena are thus strictly dependent, conditioned and relative. The doctrine of *Paticcasamuppāda* (Pali), 'Dependent Origination', elaborates the Buddha's teaching on this matter. It shows that in the case of humans – and other sentient beings – a circular chain-reaction consisting of 12 conditioned and conditioning 'links' generates one complete life-cycle:

1 *Ignorance* gives rise to
2 *Volitional action*, which in turn gives rise to
3 *Conditioned consciousness*, which in turn gives rise to
4 *Name-and-form*, which in turn gives rise to
5 *The Six Bases*, i.e. the five senses and mind, which in turn give rise to
6 *Sense-impressions* (contact), which in turn give rise to
7 *Feelings*, which in turn give rise to
8 *Desire or craving (tanhā)*, which in turn give rise to
9 *Attachment*, which in turn gives rise to
10 *Becoming*, (the life- or rebirth process), which in turn gives rise to
11 *Birth* (or rebirth), which gives rise to
12 *Old age, death* – grief, lamentation, illness, sorrow and despair.

The final link is circularly connected with a new beginning, thus one life-cycle leads inexorably to another – and so on and on. . . . This is *Samsāra* as depicted in the Buddhist world-view: the fearful cosmic roundabout upon which myriads of suffering beings are trapped for vast aeons of time.

Dependent Origination is very central to basic Buddhist Teaching, but it is by no means easily grasped in its full implications. When the Buddha's favourite disciple, Ananda, was unwise enough to declare to the Master that he felt he had understood it, the Buddha rebuked him soundly, saying:

> 'Say not so, Ananda, say not so! Deep is this doctrine of events as arising from causes.... It is through not understanding this doctrine, through not penetrating it, that this generation has become a tangled skein, a matted ball of thread, like to munja-grass and rushes, unable to overpass the doom of the Waste, the Woeful Way, the Downfall, the Constant Round of (Transmigration).[13]

The Wheel of Life

The way in which beings are locked into endless cycles is graphically depicted in the great Buddhist image of the Wheel of Life (Skt. *Bhàvachakra*, see p. 76). The Wheel itself is held by Yama, the terrifying Lord of Death, who is actually devouring it with his fangs, leaving us in no doubt that in the Buddhist view to be caught on this vicious circle is a supremely wretched plight. The various links in the chain of Dependent Origination are symbolically represented by 12 small images set along the outer rim. Moving in a clockwise direction from the top, they are:

1 A *blind man* – Ignorance: the inability to see the truth.
2 A *potter* – Action. With the raw materials of clay and water, the potter creates a new pot on his particular kind of wheel.
3 A *monkey* – Conditioned consciousness. A monkey is skittish, wayward, virtually impossible to control. It blindly grasps one branch after another as it swings through the trees. So is a consciousness restless with karmic urges.
4 *Three men in a boat* – The boat is the vehicle that carries the men across the stream; similarly, the body is the vehicle that carries us – or more precisely, our karmic inheritance – through the world.
5 *Houses with doors and windows* – The openings are the 'sense-doors' through which sense-data passes.
6 *Lovers* – They signify the contact of sense-organ and sense-data that creates sense-impression.
7 A *man whose eye is pierced by an arrow* – The feelings that arise from sense impressions are so strong that they partially blind us. We thus cannot see the true way but stumble on into desire.

The Wheel of Life

8   A *man drinking* – Desire is a kind of insatiable thirst. If the thirst is for alcoholic drink, then it leads to intoxication: i.e. it seems to promise all kinds of delights and fulfilments, though in actual fact it must move us on one more notch around the Wheel.

9   A *monkey clinging to a fruit tree* – The monkey, symbol of the wayward, desire-ridden mind, has here found a suitable object of desire and has latched on to it. Actually it doesn't look too happy; nor is it apparently enjoying the fruit; it is just clinging on.

10   A *pregnant woman* – The clinging has clearly created an embryo: a new life is on the way.

11   *Woman giving birth* – The new life arrives, but in due course of time it will inexorably lead to –

12   *An old man* – He carries a burden, the weight of all the ills that beset human life; and he seems to be walking towards that lake – signifying death, dissolution – from which the blind man in the next panel (the first of the sequence) just seems to have emerged.

Thus the gyres roll on....

But there are wheels within wheels. Inside the outer frieze and comprising the main body of the Wheel, are five sections (in some versions six) in which are depicted the various realms into which rebirth is possible. Below there are the lower realms: those of the hungry ghosts *(pretas)*, of animals and the hell realm where the damned languish. Above, on the other hand, are the realms of human beings, of titans *(asuras)* and of the gods *(devas)*.

Inside this cosmic section of the Wheel of Life is a smaller ring in which beings can be seen falling into lower births and then climbing up into higher ones, only to fall again – and again – and again....

The Three Fires (or Poisons)

At the very centre of the Wheel we see three animals: a cock, a pig and a snake. These represent a teaching known as The Three Fires (or alternatively The Three Poisons). The animals symbolize three fundamental vices that keep the Wheel in spin:

The pig – *ignorance* (delusion, wilful blindness, etc.)
The snake – *hatred* (anger, aggression, etc.)
The cock – *greed* (lust, craving, etc.)

All three are shown either eating each other or vomiting each other up, illustrating the endless cycles of blind compulsion in which those under their power are caught. In a sense, therefore, greed, hatred and delusion 'power' the Wheel of Life. Also the Three Fires can initiate each other. For instance, ignorance of the way the world works leads us to desire, for we fondly believe that the attainment of some longed-for object will produce lasting satisfaction and entail no significant karmic cost. Then again, unfulfilled desire often produces frustration, anger and sometimes violence – consequences which those concerned, with whipping up the general public's appetite for consumer goods, entertainment and pleasure for profit, never seem to wish to recognize.

And so the world goes on, beginninglessly, endlessly, governed it would seem by a rigid determinism. The only logical response would appear to be a surrender to utter fatalism – were it not for one thing: *there is a Way Out.* In the top right-hand corner of the Wheel of Life stands Shakyamuni Buddha, gloriously free from these wheels within wheels. He stands there as a lasting testament to the fact that the power of ignorance, desire and attachment can be broken by *awareness*: by seeing what is really going on, rather than being compulsively caught up in the endless beguiling shadow-play of it all.

The Five Hindrances

The following are regarded as major obstructions to the development of concentration and so to progress on the Buddha's Path:

1 Sensual desire – *kāmacchanda.*
2 Ill will (or aversion) – *vyāpāda.*
3 Sloth/Torpor – *thīna-middha.*
4 Restlessness and worry – *uddhacca-kukkacca.*
5 Doubt – *vicikicchā.*

The study of the *Dhamma*, its practice, cultivation of the company of the wise and profitable discussion all tend to diminish these hindrances, which will gradually fade out as progress is made. Also, specific antidotes may be applied. For instance, to counteract sensual desire one may meditate upon the repulsive aspects of the body; and to counteract ill will, one may consciously direct good will towards an enemy or other particular object of aversion. Cutting down on food intake and taking outdoor exercise may help to diminish sloth/torpor.

Restlessness and worry are said to arise from an uneasy conscience and may be counteracted by repentance of past wrong deeds and a resolve not to repeat them. Moreover, as any Catholic priest or psychoanalyst would no doubt readily confirm, confession can be very helpful in easing the pangs of conscience.

We today are of course familiar with the neurotic form of worry, or chronic anxiety, that expresses itself in a deepseated and persistent sense of insecurity. This would seem very often to rise from the lack of a sound spiritual or philosophical orientation (not necessarily a Buddhist one) that endows life with meaning and points a way beyond exclusive identification with the illusion of 'I'. Without such an orientation, the individual ego stands alone, bewildered and under threat; an obsessive concern for self develops in the absence of anything more substantial, and with it a desperate search for a personal security that is not in the very nature of things available. In the modern world, where this unhappy condition has become generalized, there is talk of deep *angst* or unease haunting our culture. The antidote to this is obvious.

Finally, the confused form of doubt (rather than healthy scepticism) displays itself in a general inability to decide on any course of action and see it through. Instead there is uncertainty, vacillation, mixed motivation and muddled thinking. Specifically there may be lack of certainty about the Buddha's teaching, its practice and related matters. This hindrance may be resolved by the increasing clarity that comes from the study and practice of the *Dhamma*, and from discussions with spiritual friends. Buddhism places very strong emphasis on the importance of spiritual friends and the general company one keeps. After all, the earliest followers of the Buddha consciously grouped themselves into a community, the Sangha, thus affirming the benefits to be obtained from consorting with like-minded people. The option of joining the Sangha is still available, and lay people too can gain support from establishing relationships with the Sangha; they may also join groups and centres.

The Ten Fetters

This teaching enumerates those factors that bind individuals to samsaric existence:

1 Belief in personality – *sakkāya-ditthi*.
2 Doubt – *vicikicchā*.
3 Attachment to rules and rituals – *sīlabbata-parāmāsa*.
4 Sensuous craving – *kāma-rāga*.
5 Ill will – *vyāpāda*.
6 Craving for fine material existence – *rūpa-rāga*.
7 Craving for formless existence – *arūpa-rāga*.
8 Conceit – *māna*.
9 Restlessness – *uddhacca*.
10 Ignorance – *avijjā*.

Of special note here is that craving for *any* form of existence whatsoever, even existence in one of the subtle formless levels of the higher *jhānas*, is an impediment to liberation, as is attachment to rules and rituals. Rules and rituals certainly have their uses – and they are considerable. But essentially they are *means* for furthering spiritual development. They can, however, become ends in themselves. Every religion has its legalists, formalists, fundamentalists and dogmatists. They are quite ready to fight and even kill to defend the 'true way'. What they are really defending are empty vessels: pious forms of words and actions from which the living spirit has flown. In such cases, a particularly strong form of attachment has probably been forged, one that is not easily recognized as detrimental because its object is ostensibly so worthy. Fear, ignorance and a simultaneous grasping for security are more or less certain to be present too.

These 'mind-forged manacles' must be broken if development is to take place and freedom be won. Even the *Dhamma* must be laid aside once its purpose is served. The Buddha himself likened it to a raft that can be used for crossing the river of *Samsāra* to the further bank of Enlightenment. Just as a traveller, once he has crossed a river, will not hoist the boat onto his back and go on carrying it, so a person who has achieved the goal will lay the *Dhamma* aside. The person of the Way travels light – and lets no opportunity for further lightening his luggage slip by.

Arahat, Bodhisatta, etc.

As, through concerted and protracted effort, the fetters are progressively overcome, the practitioner is at last afforded a first fleeting glimpse of Nirvāna. Then he/she is an ordinary worldling no more but a stream-enterer or *sotāpanna*. Now there are at most only seven more rebirths before full and complete Enlightenment. As the final stages of the Path are undergone, he/she becomes a once-returner *(sakadāgāmi)*, then a never-returner *(anāgāmī)* and finally an *arahat* (lit. 'worthy one').

The *arahat* is the ordinary hero of the Buddha's Way as it was first enunciated. He/she is the person who has fully transcended all passion and desire to at last enjoy the cool bliss of Nirvāna. They do not manufacture any new karmic formations, but old ones still have to be worked out and through their momentum mundane life persists, though they put their remaining time in the world to good effect by teaching the *Dhamma*. To achieve arahantship, the help of an enlightened teacher is necessary; no such help is required by a *pacceka buddha*, a species of solitary practitioner who attains Nirvāna alone and unaided. He/she does not teach the *Dhamma*, however, though they might provide moral example.

Above *arahat* and *pacceka buddha* are fully-fledged buddhas, who are exponents of Supreme Enlightenment *(Sammā Sambodhi)*, In Basic Buddhist Teaching, a single buddha appears only once about every 320,000 years and restores the *Dhamma* after it has been completely lost during an immensely extended dark age. Shakyamuni is the buddha of our particular buddha-age. He combined the qualities of *arahat* and *pacceka buddha* insofar as he both won Enlightenment by his own efforts alone and then proclaimed the *Dhamma*.

The qualities of a buddha take an immense number of rebirths to forge once the initial resolve to become one has been affirmed. A buddha-in-the-making is a *bodhisatta* (Skt. *bodhisattva*), literally an 'enlightenment being'. A *bodhisatta* remains in the world, not due to the momentum of undischarged karmic debts, but due to the momentum of the initial compassionate resolve to help free all beings from the coils of suffering. Later, with the rise of the Mahāyāna, the Bodhisattva Ideal was to become generalized.

The Ten Perfections

1   Generosity – *dāna*.
2   Morality – *sīla*,
3   Renunciation – *nekkhamma*.
4   Wisdom – *paññā*.
5   Energy – *viriya*.
6   Patience – *khānti*.
7   Truthfulness – *sacca*.
8   Determination – *adhitthāna*.
9   Loving-kindness – *mettā*.
10   Equanimity – *upekkhā*.

These perfections or *pāramitā* are cultivated by a *bodhisatta* in his protracted pursuit of the ideal of buddhahood. Sound reason guides him, and always his motivation is utterly pure: free from all desire, conceit or misguided views. Thus in the perfection of giving, for instance, he seeks no return for himself and is impartial, like the sun, that casts its radiance over all without hint of favour; he moreover knows that, in ultimate terms, there is no giver, no recipient and nothing is given – yet he still gives.

These are also positive virtues that we can try to apply in our own lives. Generosity at least is something one can practise even when the time is not available for study or meditation. It is a very good way of promoting a shift away from a basically ego-centric orientation, for the ego is always trying to expand its province by accumulating, whereas to freely give is to reverse this 'I'-building process so that for once the energy flows the other way. Of course one may derive merit from giving, but even this can be given away so that there remains 'nothing for oneself'. Many who start practising generosity report the sense of joy it brings.

Renunciation is also an important feature of the Buddhist Path. Our many possessions are great sources of attachment and also serve to build up our sense that we are something special and have something to protect. They are also an enormous practical burden. Getting rid of things on the other hand, often produces a powerful sense of relief. It moreover frees resources so that they can be put to spiritual purposes. The simplicity of the monastic life – as 'homeless ones', the members of the Sangha are quite literally 'portionless' – is precisely the result of everything not essential to survival having been rigorously cut away.

Impatience is almost invariably the ego's response to adverse experiences or suffering, or indeed to anything that frustrates the fulfilment of its projects and programmes. Its contrary, therefore, *patience*, represents a will to accept and bear conditions that may be painful, unpleasant or simply not in conformity with what one wants. Actually, life is very often if not usually out of synchronization with what one would ideally like.

Finally, equanimity is that ability to accept the vicissitudes of life calmly and dispassionately. Kipling had the same idea when in his poem *If* he talked of meeting success and failure – and treating those 'two imposters' just the same. This is not a numbed indifference or, still less, a neurotic dissociation from life. Rather it arises from seeing that intrinsically all events are neutral and that it is desire that picks and chooses, grades this as good and that as bad. The *bodhisatta* sits comfortably in any set of conditions; he is immovably at home in the world whatever befalls.

The Brahma Vihàras

1   Loving-kindness – *mettà*.

2   Compassion – *karunā*.
3   Sympathetic joy – *muditā*.
4   Equanimity – *upekkhā*.

These are the four 'Sublime States'. 'These virtues tend to elevate man', Nārada Māhathera has written.

Loving-kindness represents a warm-hearted concern for the well-being of others. It is not sentimentally or erotically based, nor is it selectively applied to congenial people or one's nearest and dearest. Not that it is wrong to love one's friends and family – though even so attachment always ends in sorrow. However, that love should ideally be extended outwards in ever-increasing circles to ultimately embrace Totality. *Mettā* almost always expresses itself locally, however, in small and unsensational acts of kindness. As though to emphasize the centrality of *mettā*, HH the Dalai Lama has declared: 'My religion is kindness . . .'

Ajahn Sumedho has in his practical way pointed out that it is unrealistic to expect to be able to actually *like* every person who happens into our ambit. We can, however, control our impulses to reject or do them harm; and it may be possible to do them some good, even though we don't feel particularly inspired by their presence.

As time went by, compassion (*karunā*) was to become an increasingly highly-regarded virtue in Buddhism, for it is the motivating quality of the *bodhisatta*. As the hard carapace of 'I' breaks down, the division between self and others weakens and eventually their sufferings come to be regarded as one's own. Ven. Buddharakkhita, a Bengali *bhikkhu* who runs the Arogya Institute, a charitable organization that, among other good works, provides artificial limbs for the disabled in Bangalore, south India, believes that mere *dhammic* study and meditation do not necessarily effect profound spiritual change in themselves; in fact they can conduce to egoistic inflation if not combined with some form of altruistic service. He has put this belief into practice in his own life.

Sympathetic joy (*muditā*) is the very antithesis of that hard-hearted competitiveness that is so prevalent today – and which indeed is actively encouraged as an incentive to economic growth. The 'normal' view is to experience others as dangerous rivals threatening one's own 'legitimate interests'; hence feelings of hostility arise and jealousy at their successes and achievements. Anything that puts another ahead creates a sick, sinking feeling in the gut: a sense of being overtaken, left behind, of becoming 'past it' and hence a 'has-been'. Conversely, sympathetic joy celebrates the successes and achievements of others; they become one's own, just as through compassion their sufferings become one's own.

Conclusion

The basic Buddhist teachings therefore inform us that our own and the world's ills derive from the fact that, constituted as we are, our perception of the world is distorted. We seek permanence and security where they are not available; and rather than remain open and unattached, we postulate a fictitious central reference-point, an 'I', and contract around it, whereupon heaven and earth are set asunder and all manner of disjunctions set in motion. The antidote is to watch and understand how these problems arise in the first place; then to proceed to try and cure them by means of morality, meditation and wisdom. If properly done, the scales should fall from our eyes, we should see things as they really are and a complete reorientation should take place.

During the last two millennia or so, Buddhism has not remained static. There have been many new developments, changes of emphasis, restatements and modifications; but a fundamental concern to follow in the Buddha's footsteps to his goal of Enlightenment has remained constant. Moreover, the basic teachings are still transmitted in the living Theravāda tradition in forms probably reasonably close to the original. We therefore have, amidst so much change, an enduring touchstone against which all other developments may be compared and contrasted.

Part 4

The Development of
Buddhism in India

8 Four Councils and Eighteen Schools

Indian Buddhism was dealt the coup de grâce by the armies of the prophet Muhammad between the 10th and the 13th centuries AD, and had indeed been in decline for a long time before that. However, for more than a millennium after the Buddha's Parinirvàna it was a very active force in the land east of the Indus (and indeed in lands to the west of the great river too) and went through remarkable cycles of development there – far more indeed than anywhere else.

The major features of Indian Buddhism can be broken down as follows:

1   The establishment of the Word of the Buddha (Buddhavacana) as an oral tradition; its much later commitment to writing.
2   The holding of various councils or assemblies of the Sangha, some of which may be apocryphal. These were:

   i   The First Council, held at Ràjagaha immediately after the Parinirvàna.
   ii   The Second Council, held at Vesàli about 100 years after the Parinirvàna.
   iii   The Third Council, held at Patalipùtra (modern Patna) under the patronage of the Emperor Ashoka about 200 years after the Parinirvàna.
   iv   The Fourth Council, held under the patronage of King Kanishka at Jalandhar or in Kashmir around 100 AD. This is not recognized by the Theravàdins.

3   The division and sub-division of the Sangha into numerous schools, traditionally numbered as 18.
4   The emergence of a highly developed Abhidhamma, or commentarial tradition.

5   *The popularization of Buddhism, especially under the patronage of the Emperor Ashoka.*

6   *The emergence of the Mahàyàna, and the consequent major division into Mahàyàna and Hīnayàna. The development of the Màdhyamika and Yogàcàra schools of Buddhist philosophy.*

7   *The emergence of Tantra.*

After the *Parinirvàna* (Pali, *Parinibbàna*), the Buddha's mortal remains were cremated and the bones and ashes distributed to a number of places, where they were enshrined in monumental reliquaries (*stūpa*). How would his followers fare now that the Buddha was gone? It would seem likely that they fared quite well. The Buddha had, after all, always encouraged self-reliance. He had not tried to make himself indispensable by promoting himself as a personal leader; and in the same spirit he had not appointed a successor. He did, however, let it be known that after his passing the Sangha would still have his teaching, his *Dhamma* to guide it. Soon after the Rains Retreat following the *Parinirvàna*, therefore, 500 senior monks (said to be *arahats*) met together at Ràjagaha under the presidency of Mahàkàshyapa to recollect the Word of the Buddha. Upali recited the monastic code of conduct or Vinaya as he remembered the Buddha expounding it; and Ananda recited the teachings themselves, the *Sutta*. These renderings were debated and a definitive version agreed (though not unanimously).

For a variety of reasons, the Word of the Buddha remained an oral tradition for more than four centuries. This accounts for certain stylistic devices – repetitions, poetic flourishes, etc. – which made for easier memorization.

The teachings that had been agreed at the First Council were therefore carried away from Ràjagaha in memorized form to the various farflung districts where the scattered Sangha had established itself. The next step was their translation from the language used at Ràjagaha, which was probably Màgadhī, the language of Màgadha, into various local languages. Then in each locality they would have been broken up into convenient parts and one monk would become responsible for memorizing a particular part and handing it on by word of mouth.

Not everyone who attended the First Council at Ràjagaha

agreed that what had been recited there was the authentic Word of the Buddha; other members of the Sangha had been absent and, declining to adopt the authorized version, preserved and handed on their own versions of what the Buddha had taught. All this, added to the long oral phase when changes must inevitably have crept in, means that we cannot say with certainty of anything that, 'These are the precise words of the Buddha. . . .' Buddhism cannot therefore be a 'book' religion in the sense that, say, Islam or Judaism claim to be. It possesses no divinely revealed and hence 'infallible' and ultimately authoritative canons.

Nor has Buddhism ever been a centralized religion with a Vatican or Caliphate to regulate its affairs and ensure orthodoxy. The scattered communities of *bhikkhus* and *bhikkhunis* were thus allowed a healthy latitude to grow organically and creatively, untramelled by authoritarian constraints and pressures. Basically all would have been united in veneration of the Buddha, and would have been concerned to practise his Way, at the apogee of which lay the ideal of Enlightenment, or liberation from the painful rounds of cyclic existence. But inevitably in this liberal setting variations of discipline, practice and philosophical orientation began to creep in after the passage of a few decades – which could be construed as rich diversification... or dangerous deviation; even degeneration.

About 100 years after the *Parinirvāna* it became mooted that the monks in the Vajjian country were becoming lax about the rules. In particular, they were said to be accepting gold and silver from the laity. This led to the summoning of a Second Council at Vesālī where, after a great deal of difficulty and debate, the Vajjian minority were outvoted – but not outmanoeuvred. Unrepentant, they seceded from the orthodox line of the Elders or *Sthaviras*, whose school later became known as the Sthaviravāda, 'The Way of the Elders'. The schismatics, on the other hand, called themselves the Mahāsangha, 'The Great Sangha'. They differed philosophically from the Sthaviravādins in that they favoured the arguments propounded by one Mahādeva (or Bhadra), which set the standards for *arahats* at a rather less exalted level than the Sthaviravādins. Five points were enunciated:

1   An *arahat* could be seduced by another person.
2   An *arahat* could be ignorant of some matters.
3   An *arahat* might be in doubt.
4   An *arahat* might receive information from (or be instructed by) another person.
5   A person might enter the Way as a result of spoken words.

In addition, the Mahāsanghikas tended to play down the human aspects of the Buddha and to promote the concept of his being the magical manifestation of a transcendental principle. Conze describes the Mahāsanghikas as 'taking the side of the people against the saints, thus becoming the channel through which popular aspirations entered into Buddhism'. Conze also credits the Mahāsanghikas with paving the way for the foundation of the Mahāyāna, the Great Vehicle, of which more later.

This process of fragmentation was to continue. Excluding the Mahāyāna and tantric schools, within the Hinayāna, the so-called 'Little Vehicle'[14] or basic tradition of Buddhism, eighteen schools are traditionally said to have arisen in India, though it is in fact possible to trace more than that number. Each had its own version of what the Buddha had taught and different views on how that should be interpreted. How deeply felt these differences were is of course hard to tell at this remove in time. There do seem to have been occasional instances of acrimony when putative heretics were evicted from the Order. Warder also maintains that 'in certain cases rivalries of a more personal nature may have been involved, at least in bringing matters to a head'.[15] One would of course hope, however, that basic Buddhist tolerance mostly prevailed!

The Buddha had taught in a practical, *ad hoc* sort of way, giving teachings as and when the need arose. He did not propound a philosophical system, and indeed he seems to have regarded intellectual speculation as something of a red herring, irrelevant to the attainment of liberation. However, attempts began to be made within the various schools to extract certain topics from the basic teachings, to subject them to rigorous analysis and build them into coherent and integrated philosophical systems. These systematizations constitute an extensive philosophical tradition, Abhidhamma or 'Higher Dhamma'. At the heart of this lies the theory of *dhammas* (plural with a small *d*). Just as the modern physicist analyses the world into its basic constituent atoms, molecules, etc., so the Abhidhammist analyses it in terms of *dhammas*, which are successions of impersonal momentary events. The various schools spawned Abhidhamma systems of their own with different classifications and listings of *dhammas*.

The second group to secede from the Sthaviravāda became known as the Puggalavādins or 'Personalists', for they challenged the hallowed implications of the *anattā* doctrine by maintaining that the *puggala* (Skt. *pudgala*) or person does possess ultimate reality: that indeed there is a very subtle transcendental Self discernible only by buddhas but definitely not to be confused with the false self identified by ignorant people.

Later the Sarvāstivādins parted company from the Sthaviravādins too. They are described as realistic in tendency because, while not denying the hallowed *anattā* doctrine or asserting any sort of naïve materialism, they affirmed that things do exist in a real sense – hence the name 'All-things-exist School'. Past and future also possess real existence, because they are in continuity with the present. They also felt that *arahats* could undergo a fall from grace – a view they shared with the Puggalavādins.

About 200 years after the Buddha's *Parinirvāna*, during the 3rd century BC, Buddhism received a tremendous boost in India when it came under the patronage of the great Ashoka Maurya, the grandson of Chandragupta Maurya, who had by force of arms created a mighty empire in India. Ashoka himself seems initially to have followed in the family tradition of ruthlessness, winning the throne in 268 BC in a bloody power struggle, and then in the eighth year of his reign he dispatched his armies to deal with the Kalingas, a subject people living in the eastern part of India (modern Orissa) who had rebelled against his authority. The resulting carnage, destruction and suffering were appalling and affected Ashoka deeply. This experience prepared the ground for a dramatic conversion. A chance meeting with a Buddhist monk named Nigrōdha alerted Ashoka to the possibility of using his vast powers for purposes other than waging bloody war – he could in fact use them to promote peace and virtue. In an effort to arouse nonviolence, compassion and other moral virtues in his people, he ordered exhortations to be carved on rocks and pillars all over his empire – his famous Rock Edicts:

> Do not perform sacrifices or do anything else that might hurt animals.... Be generous to your friends.... Do not get involved in quarrels and arguments.... Try to be pure of heart, humble and faithful.... Do not think only of your good points; remember also your faults as well and try to put them right....

He also performed copious good works, setting up hospitals for both humans and animals, causing wells to be dug, and, as an alternative to military conquest, he applied himself to spiritual conquest. His new 'soldiers' were missionaries armed with the good news of the *Dhamma*. They went in many directions. Some even came to the West: to Egypt, Syria, Macedonia, Epirus and Cyrene (in north Africa). These efforts do not appear to have been very effective in the long-run; on the other hand, his mission to Sri Lanka was a lasting success.

With good Buddhist open-mindedness, Ashoka showed great interest in all the religions of his empire and conferred gifts upon them. He also went on religious tours and held discussions with holy men of all sorts. But the special liberality of his gifts to the Buddhists, including the founding of many monasteries, attracted hordes of bogus devotees – men lacking a sincere vocation for the *Dhamma* and on the lookout for an easy option. The infiltration of the Sangha by such charlatans led to great degeneration in the practice of Buddhism, a situation that concerned Ashoka very deeply. An assembly of *bhikkhus* was therefore called at his behest and a mass purge of some 60,000 bogus and heretical ones was carried out. Then a Third Council is said to have been held at Pātaliputra, Ashoka's capital, consisting of the 1000 genuine *bhikkhus* that remained after the purge. Some believe this Council to be apocryphal, but others assert that it did take place under the presidency of Tissa Moggaliputta, and that a new, purified compilation of the teachings was also made. Plans for dispatching missionaries abroad were drawn up as well.

The patronage of Ashoka, who came close to realizing the classical Indian ideal of a *Chakravartin*, a great enlightened

World Ruler, did much to advance Buddhism as a popular religion, whereas formerly it had been mainly restricted to the urban educated and privileged classes. Its subsequent strength at the grass roots level enabled it to withstand loss of patronage and even perhaps persecution under the Shungas, who ousted and succeeded the Maurya dynasty.

As an aid to promoting Buddhism on the popular level, the *Jataka Tales* were evolved. A collection of well over 500 of them has come down to us. Basically they are moral or cautionary tales, or they convey a simple aspect of Buddhist teaching.

After Ashoka, Buddhism became adopted by the Greeks in the north of India, and one of their kings, Menandros (Pali name, Milinda; reigned *c*. 155–130 BC), was a great champion of the *Dhamma*. His debate with a *bhikkhu* named Nāgasena that led to his becoming a lay disciple is preserved in a celebrated post-canonical dialogue, *The Questions of King Milinda (Milinda-Pañha)*. Royal patronage was also extended to Buddhism by Kanishka, a Scythian king who ruled a wide tract of land in north-west India, probably around the 1st century AD. It was under his auspices that a Fourth Council, the last in India, was convoked, though the Theravādins do not accept it. It was reputedly held either at Jalandhar or in Kashmir around 100 AD and its purpose again was to resolve differences within the Order. A monastery was built for 500 monks, and they wrote commentaries on the basic scriptures. A legend survives that the entire canon was engraved on copper sheets and deposited in a *stūpa*, but these have never been traced.

Of this entire tradition of Eighteen Schools, only one school survives today. This is the Theravāda, which is derived from that branch of the Sthaviravāda that was established in Sri Lanka by missionaries sent to the island by Ashoka around 240 BC.

According to the Theravāda view, a Fourth Council was held in the Aloka Cave near the village of Matale in Sri Lanka during the 1st century BC. The entire scriptural canon of the school was then rehearsed, revised and committed to writing on palm leaves (35–32 BC), so it comes down to us intact whereas the variant canons of the other schools have been lost to varying degrees. We call it the Pali Canon because it is written in Pali, one of the ancient dead languages of India, akin to Sanskrit. Pali became the scriptural and liturgical language of Theravāda Buddhism, but it was not the language in which the Buddha taught, which was probably Magadhi (the language of the kingdom of Magadha). An alternative name for the Pali Canon is the *Tipitaka* (Skt. *Tripitaka*), signifying its basic division into the three *pitaka* or 'baskets' of Vinaya, Sutta and Abhidhamma.

The following is a simplified analysis of the Theravāda Pali Canon:

1   *VINAYA PITAKA.* This consists of three main sections:

   i   *Suttavibhanga* – which explains the 227 rules or precepts listed in the *Pātimokkha* which are applicable to monks, followed by a section for nuns.
   ii   *Khandhaka* (lit. 'Chapters') – which details the rules; it subdivides into:
     (a) *Mahāvagga* – The 'Greater Section'; and
     (b) *Culavagga* – the 'Lesser Section'.
   iii   *Parivāra* – an appendix added at a later date.

2   *SUTTA PITAKA.* This consists of five main sections of collected discourses or *suttas:*

   i   *Digha Nikāya* – made up of 34 longer *suttas.*
   ii   *Majjhima Nikāya* – 152 medium length *suttas.*
   iii *Samyutta Nikāya* – 2875 (or 2889 – listings vary) 'connected' *suttas* arranged in 52 groups.
   iv *Anguttara Nikāya* – 2198 (or 2308) *suttas* arranged in an 11-fold numerical categorization.
   v   *Khuddaka Nikāya* – 15 separate works including, notably, the *Dhammapāda.*

3   *ABHIDHAMMA PITAKA.* This was a later addition; it consists of seven texts composed at different periods:

   i   *Dhammasangani* – Ennumeration of *dhammas.*
   ii *Vibhanga* – Further analysis of *dhammas.*
   iii *Dhātukathā* – Discussion of elements.
   iv *Puggalapaññatti* – Description of individuals.
   v   *Kathāvatthu* – Discussion of the points of controversy between the Hīnayāna sects; defence of the Theravāda view. (Probably the latest addition).
   vi   *Yamaka* – 'Book of Pairs'.

vii *Patthāna* – 'Book of Relations'.

A vast post-canonical literature also arose consisting of further commentaries, biographies of the Buddha and other edifying works.

9   Mahāyāna

Around the dawn of the common era, a highly significant new wave of development began to assert itself within the liberal spiritual tradition that the Buddha had set in motion. Its followers called it the *Mahāyāna* or 'Great Vehicle', in contrast to what had gone before, which was dubbed *Hīnayāna:* 'Lesser Vehicle'.

The Mahāyāna represented a great creative flowering of various potentials that had hitherto lain latent in the Buddha's basic teachings. South India is generally thought to have been where it originated, though Conze maintains that the north-west was another focal area. He stresses the importance of non-Indian influences – from both the Mediterranean and Iranian worlds – on the development of the Mahāyāna, and it was in the south and the north-west that those influences were generally most prominent. Non-Buddhist Indian influences must also have played a part too, however.

The main trends of the Mahāyāna may be summarized as follows:

The Bodhisattva Ideal

A new type of spiritual hero appears. Instead of the *arhat* (Pali, *arahat*), who seeks release from the painful rounds of rebirth for himself alone, and the *pratyeka* (Pali, *pacceka*) *buddha*, who wins it privately and never seeks to impart the Dharma to others, we have the *bodhisattva*, an individual to whom both these highly desirable options are available but who rejects them and instead throws himself back time and time again into the raging sea of *Samsāra* in order to help others. In other words, the preceding kind of spiritual individualism was replaced by a more altruistic orientation.

Those who aspire to become *bodhisattvas* themselves seek to generate *Bodhicitta* or 'Wisdom-heart'. This, with its inherent resolution to seek rebirth for purely compassionate reasons, will bring them back into the samsàric world after death, so they are in a sense voluntarily reborn, whereas ordinary unregenerate mortals who are reborn due to the force of bad karma decidedly do so entirely *in*voluntarily.

All this implies too a very basic difference in attitude to the world. The *arhat* and *pratyeka buddha* reject the world and seek quiescence in cessation: a kind of ineffable 'beyond'. The *bodhisattva*, on the other hand, maintains an Enlightened quiescence amid the hurly-burly of life.

The Six Perfections and the Bodhisattva Path

The aspiring *bodhisattva* practises six 'perfections' (*pàramità*): giving, morality, patience, vigour, meditation and wisdom. He also passes through ten stages *(bhùmi)* on his way to buddhahood. The first six stages correspond to the Six Perfections. At the higher four stages, however, he might become a kind of supernatural being, a celestial *bodhisattva*, to the class of which belong Avalokiteshvara, who symbolizes compassion, and Manjushri, who wields the sword of wisdom.

Compassion and Skill in Means

At the same time, compassion *(karunà)* was elevated alongside wisdom *(prajñà)* at the forefront of the virtues. The two, working together were thought to be a supreme combination. Buddhist compassion has connotations of being able to feel the sufferings of others as if they were one's own – which, indeed, from a high point that transcends distinctions of self, they really are. Unlike more popular forms of love, this compassion is not selective but goes out to all who suffer. Skill in means *(upàya)* was also emphasized, for the mere wish to help all living beings, each of whom is after all unique, would not by itself be very effective. The aspiring *bodhisattva* therefore needs to be able to come up with the most appropriate methods for each individual case.

Buddhahood as Transcendental Principle

As heirs to the Mahāsanghikas, the followers of the Mahāyāna played down the Buddha's historical aspect as Siddhārtha Gautama, the man who was born at Lumbini, and advanced the notion of buddhahood as a transcendental principle which has manifested over untold aeons in innumerable forms and in innumerable places. Various mythical 'buddhas' also emerged, supernatural beings who held sway in their own kingdoms – like Amitābha, the Buddha of Infinite Light, who resides in the Western Paradise, *Sukhāvatī*, where followers of the Pure Land sect hope to merit rebirth.

The Trikāya Doctrine

As a development of pre-existing notions, the Mahāyāna accorded the Buddha three bodies:

1 *Nirmānakāya* – his 'Transformation (or Appearance) body'. This is the body in which he appears in the world for the benefit of suffering beings. It is not, however, a real physical body; more of a phantom-like appearance assumed by –

2 *Dharmakāya* – his 'Dharma body', wherein he is one with the eternal Dharma that lies beyond all dualities and conceptions. There is also –

3 *Sambhogakāya* – his 'Enjoyment (or Bliss) body'. This is the 'body' that 'appears' to *bodhisattvas* in the celestial realm where they commune with the Truth of the Mahāyāna.

Faith and Devotion

The emergence of celestial *bodhisattvas* like Avalokiteshvara and mythical buddhas like Amitābha gave rise to devotional cults. Formerly, the tendency in Buddhism had been distinctly heroic – spiritual progress was possible only through intensive personal effort. Now it became possible to direct prayers for help to godlike beings who could intercede on one's behalf. They could also be effectively worshipped through *pūjā* and other devotional practices. There are similarities here with the *bhakti* cults of Hinduism.

A New Role for the Laity

Hitherto the bias in Buddhism had been distinctly monastic. The monks were considered to be the only ones with real spiritual potential and hence real spiritual status. This of course represented a kind of one-sidedness and begged to be redressed. The emergence of devotional cults was one way in which the aspirations of the laity for a fuller share in the religious life were met. In addition, one new Mahāyāna *sūtra,* the *Vimalakīrti-nirdeśa*, centred around an enlightened householder. Though not by any stretch of the imagination the average man-in-the-street in contemporary Vesālī, Vimalakirti represents a kind of ideal conspicuously lacking in Buddhism hitherto.

(There have in fact been various attempts to move the focus of Buddhism away from the monastery over the centuries, but these have achieved little success. Buddhism has always gravitated towards the monastic side of the spectrum of orientations.)

New Bearings in Philosophy

At the core of Mahāyāna philosphy lies the notion of Emptiness: *Shunyatā.* This is very much in the spirit of *anattā* (Skt. *anātman*) as first taught by the Buddha. It is often used to imply, not mere or sheer nothingness (that would be the nihilistic view), but 'emptiness of *inherent existence*'; that is, the absence of any kind of enduring or self-sustaining essence. There is also a sense in which it has connotations of 'conceptual emptiness': absence of thoughts. It could be regarded too as a non-term signifying the ineffable understanding arising within the practice of meditation. Although seemingly negative, it also has its positive uses – and of course ultimately points beyond the positive/negative dichotomy.

Another key term is *tathata*: 'thusness' or 'suchness', which signifies Emptiness in its immanent aspect: as it appears in the world of form. The Buddha is sometimes called the *Tathagata*: 'He who is thus gone'. The *Tathagata-garbha* (*garbha* = 'germ') doctrine, on the other hand, proposes the notion of an immanent Absolute: the manifestation in form of a transcendental principle.

Two Levels of Truth

The structure of our everyday language doesn't allow us to describe things as they really are. It carves the world up into separate bits and pieces and so distorts reality, which isn't in itself fragmented in that way. Out of this dilemma arose the notion of two levels of truth:

1 *Conventional Truth* – everyday 'common-sense' truth, basically distorted but open to skilful manipulation to point to:–
2 *Absolute truth* – the way things really are, as buddhas behold them with Enlightened eyes: empty, beyond thought and description.

Identity of Nirvana and Samsara

The uncompromising spirit of the Mahayana logic tears down all forms of separation, even that which distinguishes *Nirvana* from *Samsara*. In terms of Absolute Truth, *Nirvana* is *Samsara*; there is no split. This throws the ordinary world into a new light.

New Scriptures

The new Mahayana ideas, ideals and orientations were

proclaimed in a body of new *sutras*, which Conze has described as 'one of the most magnificent outbursts of creative energy known to human history and it was sustained for about four to five centuries'.[16] Often the historical Buddha, Shakyamuni, is cited as author and fictions have to be advanced to explain why the works in question took so long to come to light. It might be claimed, for instance, that the Buddha had decreed that a particular *sutra* be hidden away until such a time as the Buddhist world was ready to receive the unusually deep teachings that it contained.[17]

Possibly the Mahāyānists actually believed that these *sutras* came from the same mystical source as the original ones; i.e. from the transpersonal Dharmakāya. They are usually much longer and less immediately accessible than their counterparts in the Pali Canon, more elaborate and mystical, poetic and often encrusted with rich imagery and other ornate stylistic devices. 'Spiritual truths are conveyed, not through the medium of words alone but symbolically by means of gorgeous phantasmagoria'.[18] Philosophically, the point of view taken is often very high, that of full Enlightenment, no less; thus:

> They are the Sacred Word which, uttered everlastingly on the heights of existence, reverberates through limitless space and unending time.[19]

The *Saddharma-pundarīka* ('White Lotus of the True Dharma'), the *Vimalakīrtī-nirdeśa* ('Exposition of Vimalakīrtī') and the vast *Prajñāpāramitā* ('Perfection of Wisdom') literature are early examples of the new *sutras*.

The word *Mahāyāna* was coined by the Mahāyānists to distinguish themselves from their predecessors, whom they dubbed followers of the *Hinayāna* or 'Lesser Vehicle'. This of course implies a value judgement and indeed it does appear that rivalry did occasionally creep into the relations between the followers of the two traditions. Hinayānists were sometimes said to have coldly and selfishly opted for a lesser spiritual goal (i.e. Arhatship); that even if successful, they had not 'finished what they had to do'. The Hinayāna teachings were sometimes dismissed as low-grade Dharma strictly for beginners and people of limited spiritual understanding and potential; in short, the Mahāyāna was supreme.

Competitive sectarianism must have been more apparent than real, however, for the more sensitive and sincere would have been immediately aware that it was very much out of keeping with the kindly, tolerant and humble spirit set by the Buddha himself. Conze in fact maintains that Mahāyānists and Hinayānists lived together in the same monasteries and shared much else in common. He also quotes the Chinese pilgrim I-tsing, who visited India around the 8th century:

> The adherents of the Mahāyāna and Hinayāna both practise the same Vinaya, recognize the same five categories of faults, are attached to the same four truths. Those who worship the Bodhisattvas and who read the Mahāyāna *sūtras* get the name of Mahāyānists; those who do not are Hinayānists.[20]

Certainly the Hinayānists remained in the majority until possibly as late as the 8th century AD. They probably did not view the new *sūtras* with much favour but on the whole they maintained a noble silence about Mahāyāna developments, which must inevitably have influenced them to some extent. Philosophically, they went on quietly developing their own Abhidhamma, which reached its apogee around the 4th century AD.

Conze distinguishes two phases in the development of the Mahāyāna:

1 An *unsystematic phase; c.* 100 BC to 500 AD
2 A *systematic phase; after c.* 150 AD

The preceding outline broadly covers the unsystematic phase. The systematic phase, on the other hand, encompasses the emergence of the two major philosophical schools: the *Mādhyamīka* and the *Yogācāra.* Of these two schools, Conze has written:

> They differ in that they approach salvation by different roads. To the Mādhyamīkas, 'wisdom' is everything and they have very little to say about *dhyāna*, whereas the Yogācārins give more

weight to the experiences of trance (i.e. meditation). The first annihilate the world by a ruthless analysis which develops from the Abhidhamma tradition. The second effect an equally ruthless withdrawal from everything by the traditional method of trance.[21]

The Mādhyamīka School

This was founded by Nāgārjuna (c. 150 AD), a South Indian philosopher of genius whose birth was, according to some, predicted by the Buddha himself and who is also reputed to have received instruction from the Nāgas (serpent kings) in the Dragons' Palace beneath the sea. His major work is the Mūla Mādhyamīka-kārikā. In the fine tradition set by the Buddha, Nāgārjuna devised new ways for driving us into the arms of the Inconceivable. His method, dialectic, aims at pointing to Shūnyatā by ruthlessly negating all pairs of opposites. Shūnyatā is thus a Middle Path (madhya means 'middle') dynamically generated by the mutual negation of dualities like production and extinction, annihilation and permanence, unity and diversity, coming and going, etc., etc.

The right teaching is the Middle Path devoid of name and character where no speech or thought can reach. It transcends all points of dispute such as 'the four forms of argument and the hundred negations', thus even going further than Yajñavalkya's famous theory of 'neti, neti' (not this! not this!) in the Upanishads.[22]

Insofar as Shūnyatā depends on the opposites which are negated, Nāgārjuna's philosophy is said, for example by Professor Stcherbatsky, to put forward a theory of universal relativity. Nāgārjuna also distinguished two forms of truth: (1) worldly truth and, (2) higher truth. In terms of worldly truth, the Law of Dependent Origination asserts that the things of the world come into being through causation; in terms of higher truth, however, all is universal relativity – hence Shūnyatā. Worldly truth is not without its uses, however, for higher truth can only be reached by going through it.

In the early part of the 5th century AD, the Mādhyamika sub-divided into two sub-schools:

1   *Prāsangika*, founded by Buddhapālita; and
2   *Svātantrika*, founded by Bhāvaviveka.

The Yogācāra (or Vijñānavāda) School

This, on the other hand, flowered in the 4th century AD and its principal exponents were Asanga (*c*. 310–390) and his younger brother Vasubandhu (*c*. 320–400), who hailed from north-west India. The Yogācārins took a more positivistic line of approach than the Mādhyamīkas. All is mind or consciousness, they maintained, hence their central doctrine of *citta-mātra*: 'mind only' or 'nothing but consciousness'. According to this view, the objects of the world do not exist *per se* but are created from and by mind. To explain how this is done, they put forward the idea of a store consciousness (*ālaya-vijñāna*), a kind of collective unconscious in which the seeds of all potential phenomena are stored and from which they ceaselessly pour into manifestation. Delusion (itself a creation of mind) consists in taking these for real, whereas they are in truth just evanescent projections of mind. The cure for this sickness is seeing through the illusion and, by means of the practice of meditation (from which the whole orientation of both schools undoubtedly sprang), establishing pure consciousness devoid of all content, hence beyond the subject-object dualism.

The Yogācārins are also credited with perfecting the *Trikāya Doctrine*, the theory of the Three Bodies of the Buddha, and with having taken Buddhist Logic to a high pitch of development. Their greatest logician was Dignāga (second half of the 4th century BC), a pupil of Vasubandhu. Logic was particularly useful in philosophical debate, then very popular in India. Buddhists had in fact debated with each other since the earliest times, and this in itself may have contributed to the subdivision into so many schools. Public debating has survived in the Tibetan Buddhist tradition to this day; it involves highly mannered procedures, including dramatic physical gestures.

The highly sophisticated philosophical ideas summarized here demonstrate how far Buddhism had developed from being the simple path of homeless ascetics living in caves and beneath the roots of trees. Monasteries had of course originated during the

Buddha's own time, and as the centuries progressed they became large and splendid establishments with facilities for scholarly activities. The greatest of them grew into monastic universities like Nàlandà, Vilabhi, Vikramashilà, Jagaddala and Odantapuri.

The Chinese pilgrims I-tsing and Hsüan-tsang both visited Nàlandà and have left descriptions. Nàlandà was apparently vast and architecturally very fine, graced with beautiful sculpture and grounds, its 'rows of monasteries with their series of turrets licking the clouds'. Its campus included schools of study, lecture-halls, residential quarters and numerous many-storied library buildings to accommodate its wealth of manuscripts. All this was properly administered and subject to regulation, fixed penalties being prescribed for any breach of the rules. The working day, run strictly by the water-clock, went on for about eight hours. The students not only studied Mahàyàna subjects, but the teachings of the Eighteen Schools as well; also the Vedas and other aspects of Brahminism, and secular subjects (logic, grammar, mathematics, medicine, etc.). Degrees were granted to successful students. Nàlandà was extremely well-endowed and its monks were not only well fed but, according to Hsüan-tsang, waited on by two lay servants apiece; moreover, if they went outside they were provided with elephant or litter transport. Nagàrjuna is said to have worked at Nàlandà.

Sadly, this great establishment and the wealth of learning that it once housed were ruthlessly destroyed during the Muslim depradations. When a Tibetan pilgrim visited its site in 1235, he found only one ancient monk teaching Sanskrit grammar to some students amongst the burnt-out rubble. Word then came that another raiding party of Turks was on its way, whereupon monk and students wisely made themselves scarce until the marauders had gone again. The Tibetan could find none of the books for which he was looking.

10   Tantra

The Mahāyāna was not the only creative innovation to arise within Indian Buddhism. New dispositions soon began to stir within the Mahāyāna itself and between the 3rd and the 7th centuries AD these constellated into a distinctive new phase of Buddhism: a 'third turning of the Wheel of the Dharma. 'Tantra' is the term usually applied to it by modern commentators, but 'Mantrayāna' (or 'Secret Mantra Vehicle') and 'Vajrayāna' (or 'Diamond Vehicle') were more usual in the past, though specialists would insist that all these terms are not strictly interchangeable.

Traditionally, the usual kind of explanation is given for the origin of Tantra: that it was originally taught by the Buddha himself but, because of its highly specialized nature, not for general application. Hence it is sometimes labelled 'Esoteric Buddhism'. Linguistically a *tantra* is a kind of scripture in which teachings of the kind that have come to be described as 'tantric' are set out. Thus the tantric scriptures are a kind of late-arriving fourth addition to the original three *pitaka* of Vinaya, Sūtra and Abhidhamma.

In common with all other forms of Buddhism, Tantra is primarily concerned with the attainment of buddhahood. Doctrinally it is founded squarely on a classic Buddhist basis and philosophically its debt is mainly to the Mahāyāna, notably for the Mādhyamīka teaching on Emptiness *(Shūnyatā)*. What is original and distinctive is what it has to offer in terms of *methods*. Tantra is in fact about transforming the gross body, speech and mind into those of a buddha by means of special practices, some of which involve working consciously with extremely subtle processes beyond the range of normal awareness. This must moreover be done within the context of a special relationship with a guru. If the ideal of the Hinayāna is the *arahat* and that of the Mahāyāna the *bodhisattva*, the spiritual hero of Tantra is the *siddha* or adept.

This has brought us into the field of Yoga, a phenomenon that is as old as Indian civilization itself. There are indeed varieties of Hindu Tantra, notably those which centre around the cult of the great god Shiva. In his aspect as 'Great Ascetic', Shiva is the prototype of the dedicated yogi who, in his ardent pursuit of his spiritual ideal, subjects mind and body to the most extreme austerities. But Shiva also has an antithetical erotic aspect and iconographically he is often depicted as coupling with his consort or *Shakti*.²³ Indeed sexual symbolism plays a conspicuous part in Tantra – and understandably so, for it is the self-division of the primal unity into a bipolar dualism and the subsequent dynamic interaction of the two poles that generates the creation of the 10,000 things; and of course that very process of creation can itself be reversed and a conscious return to unity achieved.

Specialists and partisans have hotly debated whether Buddhist Tantra emerged from its Hindu counterpart or was an independent development. Perhaps the most useful approach would be to regard both as outpourings from the general melting-pot of Indian religious creativity. Certainly Buddhist Tantra flourished in India for several centuries before the eclipse of Buddhism in that land and achieved a high state of development. What we know of it comes mainly from Tibet, however, where it was preserved down to modern times in forms far closer to the Indian originals than is generally supposed. The information given in this chapter is therefore based almost entirely on Tibetan sources, in particular the Gelugpa school. This line of transmission was not only to take root in Tibet itself but throughout the Himalayan region and to reach far up into Mongolia and Siberia as well. Another separate and less important line of transmission ran northwards through China to Japan, where Tantra survives today in the Shingon school.

As Tantra involves a great deal of symbolism and ritual, certain specialist terms need to be clarified before we proceed:

Yidam. The tantric pantheon is composed of a phantasmagoria of incredible deities *(yidam)*, both male and female, who are graphically and colourfully depicted in Tibetan religious art replete with all manner of powerful symbolism. Some are benign, wear beatific smiles and hold up their hands in gentle gestures of benediction. Tara and Avalokiteshvara are examples of these. Others are extremely fearsome: snarling, befanged, wreathed in flames and wielding skulls, severed heads, daggers and other gruesome impedimenta – like Mahākāla, Yamāntaka, Guhyasamāja and Chakrasamvāra. All are archetypal images of primordial energies; they are the passions transformed and personified – or, more precisely, they are emanations of one supreme tantric buddha sometimes represented in the form of Vajradhāra or Ādi-Buddha.

Dhyāni-Buddhas. Some of the deities of the tantric pantheon are grouped together in families. Important among these are the families of the Five *Tathāgatas* or so-called *Dhyāni-Buddhas,* Vairocana, Akshobhya, Ratnasambhava, Amitābha and Amoghasiddhi. These are again invested with dense symbolism and represent five primary energies to whose activity all created phenomena may be attributed.

Mandala. This is a *temenos*, a sacred space. It is also a model of both the cosmos and of the total human being, for there is an equivalence between the two: they are macrocosm and microcosm. Just as the Buddhist cosmos revolves around the axial mountain, Meru, so too in man there is a heart-centre where the mystery of ultimate reality is enshrined. Formally, *mandala* thus consist of series of concentric precincts converging on a focal sanctum or palace, guarded by dread guards, where the presiding *yidam* or some other potent symbol of Ultimate Reality resides. In a sense, therefore, *mandala* are maps of the spiritual journey itself and contemplation of them assists in the accomplishment of that journey by awakening latent spiritual potentials buried deep in the psyche of the practitioner. Carl Gustav Jung observed that mandalic patterns arose spontaneously in the thoughts and dreams of many people, himself included, and saw them as a token of spiritual ripening.

Mantra. These are highly-compressed, power-pack formulae, usually of Sanskrit origin, which are charged with deep meaning and magical potency. They may be recited verbally, visualized or written down. The most famous of course is *Om Mani Padme Hūm* (see pp 212). The essence of each tantric deity is encapsulated in his/her own *mantra*, which may have both long and short forms. Recitation of a *mantra* represents a kind of practice that can be readily carried on in everyday situations. It purifies the speech and 'protects the mind' by maintaining a constant spiritual connection; and of course it helps disperse mental chatter. Short verbal formulae called *dhārani* and *paritta* (blessings) were used from early Buddhist times.

Bīja (or Seed) Mantra. This is a vowel or consonant which embodies the heart essence of a particular tantric deity. It may be visualized in luminous form, and the deity then emerges from it.

Mudrā.   Literally, a 'seal' or 'symbol'; this is a ritual gesture of the hands imbued with deep symbolic significance. In tantric contexts the significance again relates to an aspect of a particular tantric deity. (see p 213)

Mahāmudrā.   Literally, 'The Great Seal', this signifies more than just the subjective realization of Emptiness. 'It is the Buddha nature, the basic mind within all sentient beings' (Khenpo Könchog Gyaltsen); it is 'voidness itself . . . the ultimate nature of every single phenomenon' (Geshe Rabten); it is 'non-dual awareness that transcends intellect; it is non-conceptual, lucid, like all-pervading space' (Maitripa). In short, it is the very apogee of the tantric path.

Vajra (Tib. Dorje, lit. 'lord of stones') and Ghanta (Bell).   These are the most important ritual objects in Tantra. Formally the *vajra* is a single or double sceptre and is derived from the thunderbolt of the Hindu god Indra. It symbolizes skilful means and the adamantine or diamond-like quality of *Shūnyatā* – its indestructible, changeless character – when skilful means are allied to wisdom, which is symbolized by the *ghanta* or bell. Other ritual objects include dagger *(phurba)*, skull-cup (symbolizing impermanence), thigh-bone trumpet, etc., etc. (see p 118)

Generally Tantra is divided into four main categories:

Action Tantra *(Kriyātantra)*.
Performance Tantra *(Caryātantra)*.
Yoga Tantra *(Yogatantra)*.
Highest (or Supreme) Yoga Tantra *(Anuttarayogatantra)*.

The old school of Tibetan Buddhism, the Nyingma, opted for a sixfold classification divided into two main groupings: Inner Tantra and Outer Tantra. Outer Tantra incorporates Action, Performance and Yoga Tantras; Inner Tantra replaces Highest Yoga Tantra with three new categories: *Mahā Yoga, Anu Yoga* and *Ati Yoga*.[24]

According to most commentators, these different categories exist because of the differing spiritual abilities of human beings. Highest Yoga Tantra is, in tantric eyes at any rate, the apogee of the Buddhist Path; but it is not for everyone. Each person must therefore find which level is appropriate to them. It may indeed be that they are suited to no tantric path at all, in which case they would be advised to practise a Sūtra path. (The Tibetans divided all Buddhist teachings into Sūtra and Tantra. Sūtra includes both Mahāyāna and Hīnāyāna.)

Who are the favoured people who are qualified to pursue a tantric path? Basically it is those who have already advanced far upon the Sūtra Path in both present and previous lives. This means that they have achieved a high degree of mastery over the passions through the exercise of moral restraint, patience and so on, thus being able to transform the powerful emotions that may arise in ordinary life situations instead of needing to resort to ascetic withdrawal from worldly involvements, which is the classic Hinayāna method of dealing with these difficult and dangerous manifestations. They will also have attained an equally high degree of stability and concentration through the practice of *samatha* meditation; a clear understanding of Emptiness should have arisen too. But perhaps most important of all, they must be totally committed to practise, not for egocentric gains, but in order to achieve Enlightenment for the benefit of others. This compassionate orientation, *Bodhicitta*, which was of course taken over directly from the Mahāyāna, is of particularly crucial importance.

The tantric path has its dangers: this is repeatedly stressed in the traditional texts. Improper dabbling may cause psychic damage, perhaps blighting not merely this but many future lives. Therefore, to prevent fools from rushing in, all manner of safety precautions have been set up.

For a start there is the veil of secrecy that traditionally enshrouds all tantric matters – hence the name 'Secret Mantra'. Tantric texts are written in an enigmatic 'opaque' or 'twilight' language that renders their contents meaningless to the uninitiated; also those initiated into tantric cults have to uphold grave vows *(samaya)*. Such measures are not merely designed to protect the unwary from getting burnt; they also protect the teachings themselves, for malpractice weakens their effectiveness: the spiritual equivalent of debasing the coinage.

Then it is emphasized that the would-be practitioner should enjoy the guidance of a guru who possesses at least the minimal qualifications as set out in the traditional texts. These qualifications vary according to the category of Tantra involved. To teach at the lower categories, the guru need not actually be a fully Enlightened practitioner himself, but he must have mastered an extensive range of expertise. He will, moreover, have the discernment necessary to see how far the disciple *(chela)* has progressed along the path and whether he is ready for Tantra; he will also be able to steer him past all the pitfalls and point him towards those particular practices that will be most effective in his unique case. Finally, a special compatibility must exist between guru and *chela* for an effective 'dharmic connection' to be forged.

In view of its many problematic aspects as well as the fact that buddhahood can be won by other means, what reasons are there for taking the Path of Tantra?

Apparently there are some people for whom it is a uniquely suitable Way. It also has the distinct advantage of being a very quick one. Those who pursue Sūtra paths may take many, many lifetimes to reach the ultimate goal; the tantric practitioner may do so in a single lifetime if he follows Highest Yoga Tantra.

When the *chela* is ready to begin serious practice, his guru will initiate him into the *mandala* of his chosen deity. The ritual itself is known as *abhisheka* and possesses connotations of *empowerment* insofar as it not only authorizes practice but also endows it with special potency. Tantric initiations are often large public events. Many thousands of people have flocked to the Kālachakra Initiations that His Holiness the Dalai Lama has given at Bodh Gàya and in the West in recent years. Most of these will not embark upon serious practice under a guru; for them attendance at the initiation represents a way of gathering blessings and of establishing a strong karmic connection with the particular tantra that may ripen in a future lifetime.

The seriously committed *chela*, on the other hand, will receive teachings and begin the preliminary practices that are essential for establishing the correct foundation of purity, correct view and sound motivation. Ethical and other restraints have to be observed, and he will have to perform such strenuous and enhumbling feats as the legendary 100,000 prostrations and similar permutations of *mantra* recitations, offerings and other devotional actions.

His Holiness the Dalai Lama gives this advice to those

wishing to be initiated into a tantric path:

Initially, you should take refuge in the Three Jewels from the round orb of your heart, then take a vow of individual emancipation, and after that generate the aspirational and practical minds of enlightenment. Then, when you arrive at the point where it is suitable to hear Tantra, you should receive teachings on Ashvaghosha's *Twenty Stanzas on the Bodhisattva Vow (Bodhisattvasamvaravimshaka)* and *Fifty Stanzas on the Guru (Gurupañchashika)*. Then you may receive initiation.'[25]

Vitally important at this stage is Guru Yoga, which involves practices concerned with developing faith in and devotion towards the lama-guide and with generally deepening the dharmic connection with him. For the guru is not just a kindly spiritual chaperone. He must be regarded as identical with the Buddha and with the chosen *yidam*. Tantric practices are moreover actually stated to be quite ineffectual if performed without his empowering blessing. The special nature of the relationship with him can in fact hardly be understated. It is extremely dynamic and powerful.

Another important part of tantric practice is Deity Yoga. This involves the development of a relationship with the particular *yidam* and the realization of his/her enlightened qualities. The proximity and intensity of the relationship that the *chela* will attempt to achieve will vary according to the level of Tantra at which he is working. At the Action Tantra level, for instance, the deity is conceived as the Lord and the practitioner as his devotee, so the relationship is essentially a separate one and the practices performed are external: the *chela* recites *mantras* and prayers, performs *mudras* and prostrations, makes offerings and so forth. Actual meditation on the deity is not so important at this stage, but becomes increasingly more so as one ascends the tantric ladder.

At the topmost level, that of Highest Yoga Tantra, there are two main stages: the *Generation Stage* and the *Completion Stage*.

The Generation Stage is essentially preparatory. Here the practitioner learns to conjure the deity and his *mandala* out of the primal Emptiness of his mind or out of a seed syllable *(bija)*, to visualize the deity in fine detail and to dissolve him/her back into Emptiness.

The Completion Stage is about actualization – specifically the achievement of full buddhahood by special yogic means. A very specialized view of the human organism comes into play here, which sees the gross human body as containing two other bodies of increasing subtlety. These three bodies correspond to the Mahāyāna classification of the Three Bodies of the Buddha: Dharmakāya, Nirmānakāya and Sambhogakāya. The most subtle body consists of fine channels called *nadi* along which a number of plexus points or *chakras* are disposed. A so-called 'wind energy' circulates through this system, which is basically inseparable from consciousness, but in its most gross forms manifests as passions like anger and lust. In the unregenerate individual, the *nādi* are knotted up, so the movement of the wind energy is vitiated. Using the virtuoso powers of concentration perfected by means of intensive practice at the Generation Stage, the tantric yogi seeks to direct and dissolve the wind energy into the minute *bindu* or 'droplet' situated in the heart *chakra*. If this is achieved, conceptual thought automatically and instantaneously ceases and what remains is nothing less than the primordial state itself: *Mahāmudrā*.

Controversy surrounds Buddhist Tantra – and indeed seems to have done so from its earliest phases – on account of its apparently unconventional methods and symbolism. In a recent conversation, a Western student was discussing the demise of Buddhism in India with a learned Indian *bhikkhu*.

'The reason can be summed up in one word', the *bhikkhu* announced.

'Islam?' ventured the Westerner.

'No – Tantra!' came the unequivocal reply.

Sexual symbolism, which certainly abounds in Tantra, is no doubt largely responsible for such attitudes. Many tantric deities are shown in passionate union with their consorts. This has different connotations from its Hindu counterpart, for here the masculine denotes the active force of skilful means *(Upāya)* and the feminine the passive quality of wisdom *(prajñā)*. Enlightenment results from their union. The four stages of relationship between men and women (looking, smiling, touching and physical union) are also used as analogies for the kinds of relationship that are possible with one's chosen deity.

As for sexual yoga, there is a tradition that this may be

practised in certain very special and closely controlled circumstances during the Completion Stage of Highest Yoga Tantra – but only by advanced practitioners who have transcended egotism and generated perfect *Bodhicitta.*

Recently a Western student asked her guru whether such practices were still used.

'They're secret practices,' the learned *khenpo* replied 'so how can I know ...?'

Finally, what is the modern Westerner to make of Tantra?

Its vast pantheon of deities, its rituals, symbolism and yogic practices together indicate that we are dealing to a very great extent here with what in the West is generally classed as magic. But this is not to say that it is primitive superstition. It is in fact highly developed methodologically and reconciled with the most sophisticated metaphysical notions and the loftiest spiritual aspirations. But it works extensively with levels of consciousness that developed back in the mists of history long before the emergence of rationalism and the dualistic view of the world that currently holds sway. These ancient residues still actively exist in our multidimensional consciousness. Basically, they operate like dream consciousness. There is no distinction between inner and outer. Thoughts and imaginings, feelings, impressions, experiences – all flow freely in and out of each other. This being so, a deity conjured up in the mind is as 'real' as a person encountered in the so-called 'outside world'; and in the same way, a picture or a string of words (spells) can possess immense effective power.

Unfortunately, in the West we have tried to cut ourselves off from these dimensions; we fear and repress them. In the East, however, they were rather more humane and sensible. As Buddhism developed – and this is very particularly clearly brought out in its Tibetan phase – though it engaged in rivalry with the pre-existing traditions that it encountered, it did not attempt to expunge and obliterate them. Rather it was wisely prepared to assimilate them. Thus the old animistic gods became 'guardians of the Dharma' and their power was thereby harnessed to the cause of Enlightenment.

This, therefore, we tentatively suggest, explains the particular power of Tantra. It embodies all the strengths of all the forms of Buddhism that developed hitherto, and to them it

adds the magical dimension. So it could be said to be a logical
culmination and completion of the process of development of
Buddhism: all aspects of the human being are here mobilized in
the great adventure of Enlightenment. This also explains the
immense popularity currently enjoyed by Tantra among
Westerners, for it fulfils a need that is not really met in any of
the serious Western traditions. 'Magic', as it survived in this
hemisphere is a somewhat dishevelled remnant and usually
attracts the wrong kind of practitioner for the wrong reasons.
Tantra, on the other hand, offers people ways and means of
integrating the magical into their lives and applying it to
authentic spiritual purposes.

Dorje, Ghanta (Bell) and Phurba (Dagger) drawn by Robert Beer

Part 5

The Spread of Buddhism

11 The Southern Transmission Sri Lanka, Burma, Thailand, Laos, Kampuchea and Indonesia

Fortunately, the fire and fury of the Muslim invasions which by the 13th century had all but expunged Buddhism from the land of its origin did not totally obliterate the religion from the face of the earth, for by that time it was already firmly implanted in the soil of other countries.

Two thousand years ago, Indian influences spread throughout south and south-east Asia, and these included all forms of Buddhism as well as aspects of Hinduism. Today we find three southern Asian countries, Sri Lanka, Burma and Thailand, which may still be called *Buddhist* countries in the full sense of the term. What is locally regarded as a pure form of Theravāda has established itself strongly in all of them on a firm monastic basis, with Pali as the canonical and liturgical language. In Indonesia, however, rather different developments have taken place.

Different groups lived in this general area 2000 years ago and their distribution did not conform to the national boundary lines on any modern map. Later they were supplânted by other racial groups and gradually, over the centuries, a more settled picture more closely resembling the present-day one began to evolve. Of course, being an island, the first country we will look at is an exception to this general rule.

Sri Lanka

Around 240 BC, the Emperor Ashoka dispatched his *bhikkhu* son, Mahinda, to the beautiful tropical island of Sri Lanka (or Ceylon), which lies in the Indian Ocean just off the southern tip

of India. Mahinda was very well received by King Devanampiyatissa and entertained at the royal capital of Anurādhapura. Crowds flocked to hear him preach the Dhamma and it was early on predicted that, 'These *bhikkhus* will be lords upon this island'. And so indeed it proved to be. Devanampiyatissa donated a tract of land outside Anurādhapura, the former Mahāmegha Park, to them, and here a great *vihāra*, the Mahāvihāra, was founded, which in time became the headquarters of Buddhism upon the island.

Seeing the enthusiastic reception that Mahinda evoked everywhere, King Devanampiyatissa asked him whether Buddhism had yet truly taken root upon the island.

'Not yet, Your Majesty', Mahinda is reputed to have replied. 'It has certainly sprung roots but they have not yet grown deep into the soil. Only when a *Sīmā*[26] has been established and when a son born in Sri Lanka of Sri Lankan parents becomes a monk in Sri Lanka, only then will it be true to say that the roots of the Dhamma are deeply embedded here.'

Those conditions were fulfilled soon afterwards.

Mahinda's nun sister, Sanghamitta, was also brought over from India to establish an order of nuns. With her came a branch of the Bodhi Tree, which was duly planted in the grounds of the Mahāvihāra; later saplings were transplanted to other sites on the island. These living connections with the basic origins of Buddhism are still to be seen.

It was in Sri Lanka during the reign of King Vattagāmani (89–77 BC) that the Pali scriptures were first committed to writing on prepared palm leaves at the Aloka Vihāra. Another scholarly achievement in Sri Lanka was the translation into Pali of the old Sinhalese commentaries in the 5th century AD. One of the scholars involved, Buddhaghosa, also produced an important work called the *Visuddhimagga* ('Path of Purification'), of which Conze has written:

The book is a compendium of the Tipitaka and one of the great masterpieces of Buddhist literature which describes authoritatively, lucidly and in great detail the principal meditational practices of the Buddhist Yogin.[27]

Sri Lanka did not escape schism during the following

centuries, and some of its dissenting schools were influenced by Mahàyàna and tantric developments. A major controversy broke out which resulted in a secession from the Mahàvihàra and the establishment of the Abhayagirivihàra, the monks of the latter taking a more progressive line than the orthodox Sthaviravàdins. Thereafter royal patronage flowed now to one side, now to the other, but in the long run the more conservative disposition triumphed. A council held at Anuràdhapura in 1160 finally settled the matter by suppressing all non-Theravàda schools.

The progress and well-being of Buddhism on the island was inevitably affected by political upheavals, including invasion from South India and, later, European colonialism. From the 16th century onwards the Sinhalese suffered the intrusions firstly of the Portuguese, then of the Dutch and finally of the British. Efforts at conversion to Christianity were made and Buddhism was often persecuted to the extent that its very survival on the island was at times jeopardized. *Bhikkhus* had even to be imported from other Theravàdin countries, notably Thailand and Burma, to ensure continuity.

The revival of Buddhism got fully under way in Sri Lanka towards the end of the last century. Ven. Sri Sumangala and Ven. Dharmànanda established two Buddhist monastic colleges, the Vidyodaya and the Vidyolankara Pirivenas (monastic colleges), in 1873 and 1875 respectively. Here traditional education in Buddhism, Pali, Sanskrit, Sinhalese history and related subjects could be obtained. At about the same time a brilliant young monk named Ven. Mohottivattè Gunànanda challenged the Christians to open religious debate. The Christians took up the challenge, most notably at Pandura in 1873, when they bandied arguments rather unsuccessfully with Ven. Gunànanda in public for about a week. Reports of these debates got into the foreign newspapers and so reached the attention of the distinguished pioneer Theosophist, Colonel Henry Steel Olcott, in the USA. He came to Sri Lanka with the leader of the Theosophical Society, Madame H.P. Blavatsky, and both of them 'took Pansil' (i.e. the Five Precepts) at Galle in 1880. Thereafter the Theosophists worked alongside native Buddhist idealists like Ven. Sri Sumangala and Anagàrika Dharmapàla (David Hewavitarne, 1864–1933), to regenerate

Sinhalese Buddhism. The movement was very successful. In 1887, after 12 years of effort, there were 46 schools on the island providing Buddhist education whereas formerly there had been only Christian schools. By 1903 there were 174 Buddhist schools.

During the present century numerous Europeans have received ordination and/or Buddhist training in Sri Lanka, notably the German-born *bhikkhus* Ven. Nyànatiloka, Ven. Nyànaponika, and the British-born Ven. Ñànamoli. The island hermitage at Dodanduwa (Galle district) has been a notable centre for training European *bhikkhus*. Meanwhile the Buddhist Publication Society, founded by Ven. Nyànaponika, has done much useful Buddhist literary propaganda work in the English language. Its headquarters are in Kandy.

Mention must be made of the noble efforts made by the Sri Lankans themselves to help bring knowledge of Buddhism to the West. A Sri Lankan Buddhist *vihàra* was established in London in 1926 by Anagàrika Dharmapàla, and though closed in 1940, was reopened in 1954 by Ven Nàrada Mahàthera, who also performed valuable *Dhammaduta* (or Buddhist missionary) work elsewhere, notably in Indonesia and Vietnam. Many important *bhikkhu* teachers have resided at the London *vihàra*. Meanwhile, Dr. G.P. Malalasekera, the professional diplomat and scholar, was also a notable ambassador for Buddhism in the West. He became the first Editor-in-Chief of the Sri Lankan Government-sponsored *Encyclopaedia of Buddhism* (1966–).

Buddhist monks have enjoyed a high measure of social influence, even of political power, right from the early days of Buddhism upon the island. They have also been rich and powerful landowners. Since national independence was won in 1947, the role of the monk as a political animal has been a matter of keen controversy. Ven. Walpola Rahula played a conspicuous part in the debate as an apologist for the politically engaged monk. By contrast, however, there are and ever have been purist monks who have rejected social and political status and withdrawn to the seclusion of the forest in search of that ascetic simplicity of lifestyle that they see as essential to the proper practice of the Buddha's Way.

A significant modern development in Sri Lanka has been the Sarvodaya movement ('The Awakening and Welfare of All') of

A.T. Ariyatana, which has sought to apply Buddhist principles to social and economic development at the grass roots level. As Ken Jones wrote in *The Middle Way* (Vol. 59. No. 1, pp 52–3):

> It emphasises self-realisation through compassionate social action in creating a simple, egalitarian co-operative commonwealth. The purpose of material well-being is to support individual spiritual growth, with cultural diversity and creativity, local community development, environmental harmony and appropriate technology all directed to the same end.

Sri Lanka is associated with two important relics of the Buddha. In the early days of Mahinda and Sanghamitta, a collar-bone was reputedly brought from India and in 371 AD a tooth arrived. The Portuguese claimed to have seized and destroyed the tooth – but the Sri Lankans counter that only a fake was destroyed and that the real one survives to this day. Each year it is paraded with great festivity through the streets of Kandy during the Esala Perahera – a fine and fitting celebration of a religious tradition that goes back such a very long way.

Claiming to be the guardians of the longest surviving continuous tradition of Buddhism, the Theravāda Buddhists of Sri Lanka are conscious of having the special role of preserving the original teachings of the Buddha in a pure form. This inevitably implies conservatism and orthodoxy – but it is a conservatism and an orthodoxy that have had the vigour to remain a living force for over 2,000 years. Today there are about 20,000 monks on the island.

Burma

Lying immediately to the east of India, Burma is carved from north to south by the great river Irrawaddy. The original inhabitants were the Mon people, who also occupied parts of what is today Thailand. The Burmese themselves came down from the mountainous regions to the east of Tibet and established kingdoms in central Burma by about the 3rd century AD.

It seems that Buddhism did not strongly establish itself here until the 5th or 6th centuries BC. Afterwards there is evidence of both Hinayana and Mahāyāna activity. Tantrism, also filtered down from the north and one particularly scandalous sect known as the Aris (after *arya* = 'noble') is known to have existed.

An important event for the Theravāda cause was the conversion of King Anawrahta of Pagan (1044–77) by a certain Shin Arahan, who was a Mon. Anawrahta attempted to suppress the Aris and then petitioned Manuka, the Mon King of Thaton, for scriptures. When he received an unenthusiastic response, Anawrahta reacted in a somewhat unBuddhist fashion by sending in his troops to simply appropriate what he wanted by force. Manuka was led back to Pagan in chains, and 32 elephants carried away his wealth, Buddhist relics, images and scriptures. His monks, artists and craftsmen were appropriated as well.

Anawrahta's dynasty was to hold sway for two centuries and during that time a great Buddhist culture blossomed at Pagan. Literally thousands of temples (including the famous Ananda Temple) and pagodas were built in a relatively small area, which has caused descriptive images like 'a forest of stone' to be coined. Unfortunately, Pagan was attacked by Mongol invaders in 1287.

A turbulent period ensued when Burma was dismembered into warring states. Buddhism of both the Hinayāna and Mahāyāna varieties persisted, however, and great temples and pagodas continued to be built. The most famous Burmese pagoda is the gilded Shwedagon in Rangoon, 326 feet high, started in the 14th century as a monumental reliquary for some of the Buddha's hair.

During this period there was dissension within the ranks of the Theravāda fraternity. One party, which traced its lineage back to a Singhalese monk named Capata (12th century), disputed the validity of ordinations dispensed by other lineages. The matter was resolved towards the end of the 15th century when King Dhammaceti of Pegu (1472–92) introduced a 'canonically valid monastic succession' from Sri Lanka. Since then Sri Lankan Theravāda has predominated, though a folk religious tradition venerating popular deities known as *nats* continues to exert a hold over the ordinary Burmese.

Burma was united as a single country in the 18th century and during the reign of King Mindon (1853–78) Buddhism once more enjoyed royal patronage. Between 1868 and 1871, a Council was held at Mandalay, King Mindon's capital, when the text of the Tipitaka was revised prior to being formally inscribed on some 729 marble slabs. These were erected in the precincts of the Kuthodaw Pagoda.

The British came to Burma in 1885 during the reign of the last king, Thibaw (1878–85), and governed the country as a province of their prized Indian Empire. During this colonial period, Buddhism was closely identified with the Burmese national identity: 'To be a Burmese is to be a Buddhist'. Buddhist monks and groupings like the YMBA (Young Men's Buddhist Association) played an important part in nationalist agitation against colonial power. During this period the so-called 'Shoe Question' became charged with symbolic significance for the Burmese. This arose from the insensitive British habit of disdaining to remove footwear within the hallowed precincts of Buddhist shrines.

Following Independence from the British in 1948, Burma has been a socialist state and presently it is a secular one too. Its Buddhist traditions have survived, however, and still exert a strong hold over the people. Ordination into the Sangha is greatly respected, and most men will shave their heads and enter the robe, if only for a short, token period. Another Council was held in Rangoon in 1954–6, when the Tipitaka was again put under close scrutiny by wise Mahātheras. Traditional Buddhist festivals – Thingyan, Thadingyut, Tazaungdine, Tabaung – are still celebrated enthusiastically in all parts of the country. Pagodas continue to be built and embellished: the latest, the Mahāvijaya Pagoda, in the vicinity of the Shwedagon, was formally completed in 1986.

In modern times thousands of people, including Westerners, have derived much benefit from the intensive meditation practices developed by masters like Mahāsi Sayadaw and U Ba Khin. Mahāsi Sayadaw (1904–82) was an ordained monk who began teaching meditation in Rangoon at the request of the first post-Independence Prime Minister, U Nu, who himself strove hard though not always successfully to establish the new Burma on a sound Buddhist footing. Centres teaching Mahāsi Sayadaw's method have sprung up all over the world. U Ba Khin

(1899–1971), on the other hand, was a remarkable layman who managed to combine serious Buddhist practice with a highly active life involving government service at Cabinet level. He had studied *vipassanā* meditation under Saya Thet Gyi, a well-known lay teacher who had been a pupil of Ledi Sayadaw. Ba Khin's method involves sweeping the body with the attention, noting the evanescent play of sensations. Many U Ba Khin centres have been set up around the world too, and the method has also been vigourously propagated by S.N. Goenka.

Other important modern Burmese masters include Sunlun Sayadaw, Taungpulu Sayadaw, U Pandita, Mohnyin Sayadaw and Mogok Sayadaw. Rene Sircar is a former nun who has taught in the West. Mention must also be made of the good work of the scholarly Sayadaw U Thittila, who spent some years in London, and was for a time Librarian at the Buddhist Society.

Thailand

Thailand, formerly Siam, is a beautiful country about the size of France situated in south-east Asia. Elephants still haul teak in its northern mountains; the central plains, on the other hand, are one of the world's most fertile rice-growing areas; lush tropical beaches abound in the south.

Buddhism is traditionally said to have first appeared among the Mon people, the original inhabitants, in the 3rd century BC, brought by missionaries sent from India by the Emperor Ashoka. What exactly took place historically is unclear, though a fine Buddhist art evolved in Dvaravati, a Mon kingdom that flourished from about the 6th century AD. A few centuries later, however, the land fell under the sway of the Khmers of Kampuchea and its religious life was influenced accordingly. There are traces of both Mahāyāna and Hindu influences from this time.

The Thai people, though not themselves racially Chinese, originated in southern China, and it is therefore highly likely that their first encounter with Buddhism was with one of its Chinese forms. By the 14th century, however, having ousted the hitherto dominant Khmers and established themselves both as masters of parts of present-day Thailand as well as of neighbouring Laos, they promoted the Sri Lankan brand of Theravàda Buddhism. About 1361 BC, *bhikkhus*, including one Mahàsami Sangharàja, were brought over from Sri Lanka to 'purify' local Buddhism, and Pali was established as the religious language. The Thais were able to return the compliment when in the mid-18th century they sent monks to Sri Lanka to revivify the ailing Sinhalese Sangha. This strong Theravàda tradition has survived in Thailand down to the present time.

Today Buddhism is the state religion of Thailand and over 92 per cent of the population adhere to it. The king has to be a Buddhist, though his mandate as Defender of Religion means that his formal protection is extended to all persuasions: Hindu, Muslim, Christian, Confucian and whatever else, even the Communist Party.

The custom of most young men to spend a period of time during the *Vassa* (the Rainy Season) in a *wat* (Buddhist monastery) survives to the present. They learn what it is like to be a monk, rising early to chant and meditate, refraining from eating after noon and abiding by the Vinaya. If the life suits them, they will stay on for a few years – or for life. Young boys also become temporary novices. According to custom, they are given a big send-off and ride away magnificently costumed as little Prince Siddhàrthas; later their finery is removed, their heads are shaven and they too don the yellow robe.

The present King of Thailand himself spent a fortnight in the robe at the royal Wat Bovornives. His ancestor, King Rama IV (or Mongkut; 1851–68), the inspiration for the musical *The King and I*, also entered the order for a short time – and stayed for some 27 years, becoming a renowned Pali scholar and reformer of the Sangha. When the King, Mongkut's elder half-brother, died, he harkened to the call of duty and duly ascended the throne. Both he and his son, King Chulalongkorn (1868–1910) did much to modernize the country while respecting its ancient traditions.

Buddhism is highly organized in modern Thailand and subject to a degree of state control. There is a Supreme Patriarch, appointed by the King, who is therefore nominally head of the Buddhist 'church'; below ranges a pyramid of ecclesiastical hierarchy radiating outwards into the regions. As a result of King Mongkut's reforms, there is also a basic division of the Buddhist 'church' into the Mahānikāya and Dhammayuttika Nikāya 'denominations', though the differences between them are very minor today.

In recent years, in common with other south-east Asian countries, Thailand has been launched through an accelerating pattern of disturbing change that has thrown up many complex social and political problems. The role of Buddhist monks within these changing patterns is obviously subject to different interpretations. The conservative Sangha has in fact come in for some criticism for its opposition to change and reform. Meanwhile, more radical elements in the Sangha have argued for a more activist stance.

Many Westerners have derived a great deal of benefit from the living Buddhist traditions of Thailand, especially from the ascetic Forest Tradition that flourishes in the north-east of the country. Here a strong tradition of highly effective meditation and Vinaya practice has been preserved. Of particular importance has been the influence of Ajahn Cha, a disciple of Ajahn Mun, who has been responsible for training many notable Western *bhikkhus* at Wat Nong Pah Pong in Ubon province. Ajahn Cha's foremost Western disciple is the American-born Ajahn Sumedho Thera, who firstly helped to establish the international Wat Pah Nanachat under Ajahn Cha's auspices and later Chithurst Forest Monastery in rural West Sussex, the first of a number of highly successful monasteries and centres in Britain. Branch centres are also now springing up in other parts of the world too. All these centres derive a high level of support from both Thailand itself and from expatriate Thais. Thai temples have also been established in the West: for example, the Buddhapadipa Temple in London, where a Thai *bot* (meeting hall) has been recently constructed in traditional style.

Other influential modern Thai teachers have been the scholarly Buddhadāsa Bhikkhu and Ajahn Mahā Boowa. Also Dhiravamsa, who first came to Britain in the robe in 1964 as Chao Khun Dhammasudhi, but later resigned monk status to become a lay meditation teacher. He now works mainly in the United States.

Laos

Laos is a tiny landlocked country sandwiched between powerful neighbours: China, Burma, Thailand, Kampuchea, Vietnam. Small wonder then that its history has been much marked by strife and foreign domination. During its early period, it fell under the power of the Khmers, who probably introduced Buddhism – and Brahminism. Later it became virtually a province of Thailand and in consequence the Thai form of Sri Lankan Theravāda became dominant among the Laotians and survived until modern times.

A Communist revolution of the familiar south-east Asian variety took place in 1975, whereupon thousands of monks fled the country, including the Supreme Patriarch of Laos. A few *bhikkhus* who supported the Communist Pathet Lao, however, chose to remain behind. Though the Communist government initially attempted to destroy the Sangha as an active force in Laotian life, it failed and subsequently, becoming more pragmatic, tried to utilize the monks as teachers of the Marxist creed. The residual Sangha have attempted to adapt to the changed situation, but fundamental contradictions existing between the Marxist and Buddhist philosophies have yet to be fully resolved. In the long run, therefore, it is still to be seen whether an authentic form of Buddhism will be able to survive on Laos.

Kampuchea

Kampuchea, formerly Cambodia, is situated in the Mekong valley between Thailand and Vietnam, though unlike Laos it enjoys access to the sea. The Khmer people are the dominant group there. During its early history, which is poorly documented, the area fell, like Burma and Thailand, under Indian cultural and religious influences. Both Brahminism and Mahāyāna Buddhism certainly enjoyed favour, and the Sanskrit language was used.

Then, around the 9th century, a great civilization blossomed. It centred on the Angkor region and over the following centuries the Khmer kings glorified themselves by building numbers of

marvellous temples, each an intricately carved stone Mount
Meru surrounded by walls and terraces and moats; some of the
larger ones even have palaces and offices within their precincts.
The most famous is Angkor Wat itself. Here syncretistic
Mahāyāna-Brahminical rituals were performed with elaborate
ceremonial; there were also facilities for scholarship. But the
cost of building and maintenance bore heavily on the backs of
the people and both the inevitable internal unrest and attack
from outside weakened the dynasty. Finally, Angkor was
abandoned to the ministrations of the jungle in the 15th
century.

It is thought that Theravāda Buddhism had meanwhile come
into ascendency around the 13th century, possibly as the result
of Thai influence. It established itself strongly, however, but
was totally destroyed during the depradations of the
Communist Khmer Rouge, who took over the country in 1975,
intent upon creating a new order by literally exterminating all
representatives of the old, which unfortunately included the
Buddhist Sangha. The Vietnamese invasion of 1979 ousted the
Khmer Rouge and religious life was sanctioned again to a
limited degree. The present situation is uncertain.

Indonesia

That Buddhism penetrated the Indonesian archipelago long ago
and thrived there is palpably borne out by the fact that
Borobodur, the largest Buddhist monument in southern Asia, is
situated on the island of Java. Borobodur, which dates from the
mid-19th century AD, is a massive stone replica of the cosmic
mandala. Firstly there is a series of five terraces, the area of the
base terrace being some 403 square feet. Above there are three
ascending rings of *stūpas*, with a tall *stūpa*, symbol of Mount
Meru, in the very centre; its tip touches a height of 108 feet. The
whole edifice is prodigally decorated with some 27,000 square
feet of carvings and over 500 stone Buddhas.

Buddhism probably came to the archipelago along with other
Indian influences around the 5th century AD. The Theravāda
may have been favoured by the King of Srivijaya, a kingdom on
Sumatra. Tantra, however, was later to become very popular on

the large island of Java, where it enjoyed the patronage of the Shailendra dynasty. Borobodur is one of its artistic products. Later a cult evolved that combined Buddhist and Shaivite tantrism and this persists in Bali and elsewhere to the present time, though on account of the dominance of the Hindu components the Buddhist contribution is often overlooked. That this survived the coming of Islam to the islands from the 15th century onwards bears evidence of its vigour and the favourableness of local conditions.

In recent years, Buddhism has begun to re-emerge as a separate religion in Indonesia. This process has been stimulated by Chinese immigrants, by missions sent from Thailand and Sri Lanka, and by the energy of monks like Ven. Jinarakkhita Thera, who was at one time a pupil of Mahāsi Sayadaw. Both the Theravāda and Mahāyāna traditions are therefore now again represented in this part of the world.

12 The Northern Transmission: North-Western Springboard and the Silk Road

A different thrust took Buddhism northwards from India into Central Asia, China, Tibet, Mongolia, Korea, and Japan, as well as into the kingdoms straddling the Himalayan chain: Bhutan, Sikkim, Nepal, Ladakh. Both Theravāda and Mahāyāna teachings were disseminated in the process; but in the long run the Mahāyāna was to prevail – and indeed to undergo exciting new phases of development. Today, however, if not entirely extinguished in places like China and Tibet, where it once flourished, only a drastically truncated remnant of Buddhism survives. We can in fact call none of these northern countries *Buddhist* countries as we applied the term to Sri Lanka, Burma and Thailand.

The North-Western Springboard

One area played a vital role in the transmission of Buddhism to China and other parts of east Asia. This lay to the north-west of the Indian heartland and encompassed parts of Kashmir and the Punjab, extensive portions of the modern state of Pakistan and neighbouring Afghanistan, and even extended through into eastern Iran and the southernmost part of what today is Soviet Central Asia (formerly Russian Turkestan). At its heart lay Gandhāra, a district of profoundly evocative associations for Buddhists which once lay in eastern Afghanistan/western Pakistan, centering on Purushapura, which in its modern manifestation as Peshawar is the first major township that the weary overland traveller to India encounters once he has crossed the Khyber Pass.

This general area lies at what was once one of the world's

great crossroads. Here East met West: rich and powerful influences from India converged and mingled with others coming from Iran, western Asia and the Greco-Roman world, from central and northern Asia, from China and the Far East. Small wonder then that this was to become one of the breeding grounds of the Mahāyāna as well as the springboard from which Buddhism was launched on its northward and eastward journeys.

Trade routes passed this way, and along them sometimes tramped the feet of conquering armies as well as those of successive waves of migrants. Notable were the Aryans, who had such a profound effect upon Indian civilization. Then around 327 BC came Alexander the Great, who cut a swathe through the power of the Persians, then dominant in the area. His dreams of glory fizzled out in the Punjab, however, when his weary troops downed their arms and refused to proceed. Alexander returned home but he left influential pockets of Greeks behind him. Scythians, Parthians, Kushāns and Huns all came afterwards – and much later of course, the armies of the Prophet Muhammad, who were to dispense such violence in India.

Buddhist missionaries are reputed to have been sent to Gandhāra not long after the *Parinirvāna* of the Buddha, but the religion did not take firm root in the north-west until the time of the Emperor Ashoka, whose grandfather, Chandragupta Maurya, had extended imperial power in this direction. Ashoka himself had in his youth served as Viceroy in Taxila, a great centre of learning and trade that once flourished near Gandhāra, and when he came to power he placed great importance upon Buddhist missionary efforts in this corner of his great empire.

After the decline of the Maurya dynasty in the 2nd century BC, the Greco-Bactrians reasserted their power and pushed their conquests as far as the Punjab. They were Greeks who had settled in Bactria, a fertile region lying between the Oxus river and the Hindu Kush mountains in northern Afghanistan. During this period Buddhism was favourably regarded by one Greek king, Menandros, who apparently was afflicted by some dire spiritual crisis for which he could find no relief until he met a certain Buddhist monk named Nagasena. Menandros's discussions with Nagasena are recorded in the *Milinda-pañha*, an important non-canonical Pali text. They revolved around the problem of how the Buddha could have believed in rebirth without at the same time believing in a reincarnating 'I' or ego. Nagasena was able to masterfully resolve the king's difficulties and as a result Buddhism gained a powerful patron; indeed, Menandros is reputed to have died a member of the Sangha.

Later the Greeks were supplanted by other people, including the Scythians and the Parthians. Afterwards came the Kushāns, a nomadic people who had originated in China (where they were known as the *Yueh-chih*), and thence migrated by a roundabout route through Central Asia that took them to Bactria, the Oxus and the Kabul valleys, and eventually on to the plains of India. The Kushāns (who are also sometimes called the Indo-Scythians) established a great empire which extended across northern India, up into parts of Chinese Turkestan, westwards into Afghanistan and on almost as far as the Sea of Aral in present-day Russia. Though they began by attacking Buddhism, they later became dedicated patrons of the religion and enthusiastic builders of monasteries and *stūpas*. Thus between the 1st and the 3rd centuries AD, Buddhism blossomed in this vital part of the world. Its greatest patron was Kanishka (*c.* 78–101 AD). Bharat Singh Upadhyaya has written:

> Kanishka's reign . . . marked a turning point in the history of Buddhism and Buddhist literature. It witnessed the rise of Mahāyāna Buddhism and the magnificent literary activity started by Pārśva, Aśvagosa, Vasumitra, and others. It was in this age that Pāli gave place to Sanskrit. In the field of art, Gandhāra sculptures developed and the figures of the Buddha and Bodhisattvas began to appear. It was during Kaniska's reign and largely through his efforts that Buddhism was successfully introduced into central and eastern Asia. There was ceaseless literary activity throughout his vast empire. . . . A truly integrated Asian culture came into existence at this time, based as it was on the highest purposes of life for which Buddhism stood.[28]

Apparently Kanishka started out as a bellicose young potentate of the usual sort but later underwent an Ashoka-like conversion to Buddhism after witnessing the appalling slaughter caused by his campaigns in Kashgar, Yarkand and Khotan (modern Chinese Sinkiang). He is reputed to have convened a

Fourth Buddhist Council, when the scriptures and commentaries of the Sarvàstivàdin school were compiled and committed to writing under the presidency of Vasumitra; this, however, is dismissed as a pure myth by many scholars. He is also credited with building numerous monasteries and *stūpas*.

The Kushàna dynasty was ousted by the Sassanids, who came from Iran and professed the fire-worshipping creed of Zarathushtra. They, and the rulers of the petty kingdoms that supplanted the Kushāna empire, seem to have been generally tolerant towards Buddhism, however, and the religion continued to flourish between the 3rd and 5th centuries. It was during this period that the cave monasteries at Bamiyan in northern Afghanistan were dug out. Bamiyan also boasts the largest stone statue in the world: a standing Buddha 177 feet high.

Buddhism had reached its apogee in this region by the 5th century; thereafter it declined, hit by the depradations of the White Huns (Hephthalites), by general economic decline and a resurgence of Hinduism. When the Chinese pilgrim, Hsüan-tsang, passed through en route for India in the 7th century, he encountered much devastation – even in once glorious Gandhara. Only one corner of Peshawar was still inhabited and most of the numerous monasteries were ruined and deserted.

The Silk Road

If the part of Central Asia we have just been looking at was the springboard from which Buddhism was launched into China, then its trajectories followed the courses of the Silk Road, that great international mercantile artery along which from time immemorial the fine silks of far Cathay were transported by caravan to the eager markets of the West. For along with their goods, the merchants carried ideas of all sorts, including religious ideas, and Buddhist missionaries originating in Central Asia – Parthians, Soghdians, Bactrians, Kushàns, and perhaps a salting of Indians too – also tramped the same dusty routes.

The first leg of the Silk Road ran through the Tarim Basin, an extremely inhospitable corridor occupied by great sand-dune deserts, notably the Taklamakan, and bounded by soaring mountain ranges (the Tien Shan and the Kun Lun). Nowadays this lies in Chinese Sinkiang (formerly Turkestan) but in ancient times it lay beyond Jade Gate, the entrance to China proper, though the Chinese attempted to assert control here in order to protect their valuable trading connection. Beyond Tun-huang (spelt *Dunhuang* nowadays), the Silk Road divided into two routes: one spur ran northwards through Turfan, Kucha and Kashgar, the other south through Khotan.

The importance of the ancient communities of this region was not merely as staging-posts on the route along which the Dharma was transmitted to China. A great Buddhist civilization, now called *Serindian* or *Sino-Indian*, once flourished here, brought no doubt by Buddhist missionaries from the Central Asian Springboard and consolidated by Kanishka's conquests in the area. It had its own art too, in which Greco-Roman and Iranian as well as Indian influences were strongly reflected, and of course there were traces of Chinese influence too. Little was known about this Buddhist civilization, however, until the closing years of the last century.

In 1888, a brutal Afghan named Daud Mohammed hacked down a young Scotsman named Andrew Dalgleish in the Karakorams. A redoubtable British agent, Lieutenant Hamilton Bower, who happened to be in Sinkiang at the time, was detailed to track down Dalgleish's killer. This he did, but during the course of his investigations Bower visited Kucha and there was able to purchase an ancient Sanskrit medical text written in Brahmi characters. This was only the beginning; soon the sands of the deserts of Sinkiang were yielding up a wealth of hitherto unsuspected texts in a variety of languages (Sanskrit, Prakrit, Gandharan, Tokharian, Soghdian, Khotanese, etc.) as well as works of art of a very high order – and all remarkably well-preserved on account of the extreme aridity of the local climate.

When news of this reached the West and Japan, an archaeological scramble was set in motion. Large expeditions were mounted to plunder the lost cities of the Silk Road for their treasures. Sir Aurel Stein went in for Britain, Professor Paul Pelliot for France, Count Kozui Ohtani for Japan, Professor Albert von le Coq for Germany – and many more besides. Vast hoards of texts and artefacts – sometimes whole walls containing valuable frescoes – were crated up and transported out to foreign museums. The hoard in the British Museum alone is reputed to be so large that much of it still remains in the vaults of the building, unstudied and even uncatalogued.

The greatest find of all, made by Aurel Stein, was at Tunhuang. Over 1000 temples and shrine rooms had been hollowed out of a cliff here forming a great monastery complex which had not only served as a settled community and haven for weary Buddhist monks plying the long trail between India and China, but had also in its day been a highly important translation centre. Stein found wonderful paintings here and, in a sealed chamber, a stupendous cache of texts and paintings on silk that had been hidden since the 10th century.

In recent times this area has been staunchly Muslim – and, despite the counter-religious efforts of the Chinese Communists who now control it, still remains so. Apparently, however, many of the ancient Buddhist centres in Sinkiang were abandoned before the Muslim incursions reached their height. The cause was probably the drying up of the glaciers in the high mountains, which rendered irrigation and hence life impossible in that harsh terrain. And so for 1000 years and more the sands of the deserts wafted over those sequestered outposts of Buddhism.

13   The Northern Transmission: China

Later Han Dynasty (25–220 AD)

In the 1st century AD, because of a prophetic dream in which a great figure 16 feet high and radiant like the sun appeared to the Emperor Ming Ti, agents were dispatched to the west. Somewhere in the wastes of Tokharistan they met two '*bodhisattvas*' who had with them a white horse, a picture of Shakyamuni Buddha and a copy of the *Sūtra in 42 Sections*, a summary of basic Buddhist doctrines (with Mahāyāna interpolations) that still exists. The *bodhisattvas*, Kāshyapa Matanga and Dharmaratna, agreed to return to the Han capital, Loyang. There they set about translating the *sūtra* at a place called White Horse Temple (Pai-ma-ssu), which still exists though the present buildings are more recent.

In factual terms, however, what probably really happened was rather more prosaic. Around the turn of the common era, Buddhism simply began to filter into China from Central Asia. It was brought down the Silk Road by merchants, envoys, monks and other travellers, and nurtured in the expatriate communities in Loyang and a few other northern cities. Down to the end of the Han period, during which China enjoyed a fairly stable centralized government, its progress among the native Chinese themselves was probably fairly slow because a number of important factors stood in the way of its acceptance. There was the deep-seated xenophobia of the Chinese themselves. Self-consciously regarding themselves as citizens of a great empire – the centre of the world, no less – with a long and glorious history, a sublime culture and noble traditions, what use then could they have for an alien cult? Buddhism was also in many ways inimical to the prevailing ideology, which derived from the sayings of the sage Confucius (551–479 BC).

This upheld the ideal of a stable, harmonious social order in which every human unit, from the Emperor or Empress down to the humblest peasant, played their part according to hallowed custom. Confucianism is very much a *this*-worldly creed and as such its devotees could only look with disfavour on any religion that seemed to encourage the abandonment of all worldly ties in favour of the pursuit of a remote and vague spiritual ideal. Also the fact that the Buddhist Sangha did not work but looked to other people to support them cut totally against established Chinese values.

Gradually, however, the barriers began to break down – and this process was probably aided by one particular factor: the presence in China of a homegrown mystical tradition called *Taoism*. This was traditionally said to derive from the teachings of the mythical Yellow Emperor, Huang Ti (2698–2597 BC), but it was reformed and revived by the great sage Lao Tzu, author of the classic *Tao Te Ching*. The Taoists were very un-Confucian in their dislike of the social world, which they thought artificial and corrupt. They advocated a return to simplicity and harmony with nature, and their ideal was *wu wei*, a kind of uncontrived mode of being that flowed with all the effortless suppleness of water out of the darkness of the ultimate unknowable mystery and adapted itself to whatever it encountered. The Chinese seem to have found certain points of similarity between the teachings and practices of the Taoists and those of the Buddhists, and this opened up an avenue whereby Buddhism was able to penetrate their culture. In Arthur Waley's words, they could regard Buddhism as 'a sort of foreign Taoism'.

The existence of a serious Buddhist community in Loyang emerges into the light of history in 148 AD, when a Parthian missionary named An Shih-kao made his appearance. Other foreigners from Central Asia and India followed in the succeeding years, notably a Kushān named Lokaksema. These are credited with bringing the Mahāyāna teachings. That they imparted them not only to members of expatriate communities but to local Chinese is borne out by the fact that the task of translating the Buddhist scriptures into Chinese was now begun with some energy.

As An Shih-kao and his colleagues were not fluent in Chinese, they used 'translation teams' that included not only people conversant with the various relevant languages but also with the subtleties of Chinese literary style. A text would probably have been recited from memory, roughly translated and then subjected to a process of progressive refinement. Furthermore, a new vocabulary had to be evolved to provide correlatives for specialist Buddhist terms, and though at first crude Taoist equivalents were employed, precise Chinese neologisms were later coined. For convenience, brief texts were chosen in the pioneering stages and often paraphrases were made of longer works. The early appearance of 'meditation handbooks' proves that from the earliest times there was deep interest in this form of practice.

The Period of Disunity (220–589)

Latterly plagued by revolt and court intrigue, the Han dynasty finally expired in 220 AD and for more than 350 years the Middle Kingdom was riven apart. At first it was divided into three competing kingdoms ruled by independent warlords; there followed a short-lived and precarious period of unity under Western Chin (265–316) before war and chaos were again unleashed and eventually 'barbarian' tribes took control of the north. The most powerful, the Toba, who originated in Mongolia, established the Northern Wei dynasty and in time became thoroughly sinicized. Meanwhile, successions of native Chinese rulers held sway in the south.

Ironically, it was the decline and fall of the centralized Han empire that created the right conditions for Buddhism to gain popularity and spread to other parts of China.

For one thing, the offical Confucianism lost prestige and credibility, and in particular the intellectual and aristocratic élite began to look elsewhere for spiritual inspiration. Taoism and a new mystical metaphysic called the *Dark Learning* engaged their interest, but Buddhism with its profound teachings on suffering and impermanence had something particularly pertinent to offer amidst the prevailing chaos. The sophistication of its schools of thought probably also attracted many cultured people, as did the notion of withdrawing from the world to the seclusion of a remote temple (preferably set in idyllic pastoral surroundings) in order to quietly contemplate the deepest spiritual mysteries.

Thus was born the gentlemanly scholar-devotee that is so characteristic of Chinese Buddhism. Many of these fled from the north as it was overrun by foreign invaders and found sanctuary in the Yangtse basin and in the south, thus opening up those parts of the country. Gradually distinctive northern and southern types of Chinese Buddhism began to emerge from the resulting cleavage.

Buddhism also now began to infiltrate court circles in many parts of the fragmented empire. Once it had fallen under the patronage of the mighty of the land its success was assured. It even found favour with some of the barbarian dynasties in the north. The reasons were not entirely spiritual. These very much wanted to undermine traditional Chinese culture and its dominant Confucianism; to advance a foreign religion was a good way of doing this. They may also have felt that the gentle teachings of the Buddha would produce a more tractable kind of subject – the Taoists, on the other hand, were always stirring up trouble. Most importantly, however, they welcomed Buddhist monks at first because of the magical benefits they thought them able to bestow. Later, however, these monks assumed more dignified roles as wise counsellors. Under the Northern Wei dynasty, patronage of Buddhism soared and colossal schemes for building monasteries, temples, pagodas, and *stūpas* were initiated. The impressive Yun-kang and Lung-men cave temples were begun at this time and still exist to bear witness to the vigour and dedication of the dynasty.

Buddhism was also taken up by native Chinese rulers in the south, notably by the early 6th century Emperor Wu, who tried to make himself into a kind of Chinese Ashoka by suppressing Taoism and squeezing his nobility for substantial contributions towards the cost of building temples and monasteries. One enterprising fund-raising scheme that he devised was to reduce himself to the level of a temple servant ... and then have his subjects 'ransom' him. Needless to say, though acclaimed in Buddhist literature, the Confucians wrote him off as a feckless fanatic.

One important result of this general success was the

emergence of a native Sangha by the middle of the 3rd century, when a Chinese version of the Vinaya (monastic code of discipline) was produced. Formerly monks and nuns had probably existed on a more *ad hoc* basis. As the period progressed and Buddhism attracted increasing patronage, the numbers of monasteries and temples as well as of ordained monks and nuns fairly soared. Zürcher quotes the following figures for the Northern Wei empire alone:

477 AD: 6,500 monasteries; 77,000 monks and nuns
c 514 AD: 30,000 monasteries; 2 million monks and nuns[29]

Unfortunately, as so often with organized religion, power and prosperity led to worldliness and a fall from the high standards originally professed. The jealousy of the Confucians and Taoists was also aroused, and they were able to exploit the inevitable distrust of Buddhist success felt in official circles to foment trouble. The result was anti-Buddhist backlash, notably in 446 and 574.

Buddhism also gained ground on the popular level. Sections of the much-abused peasantry were quite ready to seek refuge from the oppressive burdens of taxation, conscription and forced labour by retreating to Buddhist monasteries, or else to find spiritual consolation in simple acts of humble piety, like making offerings at temples or going on pilgrimage. They also liked to pray for help and protection to benign *bodhisattvas* and buddhas like Akshobhya, Maitreya or – most popular of all – Amitàbha.

Chinese Buddhism therefore developed into very much a two-class system, with the sophisticated brand of the gentry contrasting strongly with the popular variety in which there was a strong element of superstition. Even at the height of its prestige, Buddhism was never the sole religion of China, however. It always had to co-exist alongside Confucianism, Taoism and the folk religions. It underwent considerable modification as a result. This, plus the interaction of the teachings brought from India with the Chinese character itself, ultimately produced distinctively Chinese forms of the religion. But that took time – several centuries, in fact.

During the period of Disunity, northern China remained in

close contact with Central Asia via the Silk Road. A whole new wave of teachers arrived, initiating a fresh burst of activity on the translation front. Among these may be counted Dharmaraksha, 'a sinicized Indo-Scythian from Tun-huang' (late 3rd century), who translated the *Saddharma-pundarīka Sūtra* or '*White Lotus of the True Dharma Sūtra*', a highly influential Mahàyàna scripture that was to become the basic text of the indiginous T'ien T'ai school. The other four most influential Mahàyàna *sutras* in China were the *Prajñaparamitā*, the *Vimalakīrti-nirdeśa*, the *Surāngama-samādhi* and the *Sukhāvati-vyuha*. All had been translated by Dharmaraksha's time. Arguably most popular among sections of the Buddhist élite was the *Vimalakīrti-nirdeśa*, which was admired for its fine literary qualities as well as its sublime philosophy. It held a special appeal for lay-people because it centred around a certain enlightened layman of Valiśàli who, out of deep compassion, had taken the sickness of the world upon himself. Such was the perfection of his wisdom, however, that Manjushri, Subhuti and other of the highest luminaries of the Buddhist firmament were afraid to visit him for fear of the philosophical put-downs that might be inflicted upon them.

The *Vimalakīrti-nirdeśa* was retranslated by the doyen of all the translators, Kumàrajiva, who was active in the north about a century after Dharmaraksha. He was born around 350 (some place his birth as early as 344), either at Kucha or at Karashahr. His mother, who ordained as a nun while he was yet young, took him to Kashmir to get him a good Buddhist education. There, among other things, he imbibed Sarvàstivàdin teachings. He later discovered the Mahàyàna and his particular penchant, Màdhyamīka philosophy, while on a visit to Kashgar. He afterwards spent many years at Kucha and his great reputation for piety spread far and wide. It even reached China.

In 384, Kucha was taken by a Chinese general, Lü Kuang, who thereby acquired the now famous master as one of the spoils of war. Though not a Buddhist himself, Lü Kuang bore Kumàrajiva off to his domains in Kansu. Nothing is known of the next 17 years, but in 401 the fortunes of war again caused Kumàrajiva to change hands. This time he passed to a Tibetan potentate named Yao Hsing, who transferred him to his capital at Ch'ang-an. His new master being an ardent Buddhist,

Kumārajiva was given every encouragement and assistance, including a translation bureau with a reputed personnel of 800. Ten concubines were also allotted to him in the hope that his exceptional talents might be perpetuated. This would of course mean that he would have had to resign monk status. Offspring did apparently appear, but none matched their sire's accomplishments.

In the matter of translations, however, Yao Hsing would have had no cause for disappointment. Kumārajiva was perfectly equipped to be a great translator. Equally at home in both Chinese and Sanskrit, he was also endowed with literary gifts of a very high order. His translations are said by Arthur Waley to be 'rather free' but 'infinitely more agreeable to read' than the more exact versions of other translators. Besides the Vimalakirti-nirdeśa, among the numerous sūtras that Kumāraja and his team translated or retranslated were the Saddharma-pundarika, the Sukhāvati-vyūha, the 'Diamond Sūtra' (Vajracchedikā Sūtra), etc. He is also credited with having introduced Mādhyamika philosophy to China.

Two of Kumārajiva's assistants are important. Seng-Chao (c 384–414) is said to have literally 'held the brush' for the Kuchan Master, for he had been a copyist of Confucian and Taoist texts in lay life and so was possessed of polished literary skills. His own text, Chao Lun, in which he tried to put across the Buddhist view of Emptiness, was highly influential in awakening the Chinese to Buddhism. He employed Taoist terminology extensively – what the Chinese called ko-yi: 'extending the meaning' or 'borrowing the idea'. His colleague Tao-Sheng (360–434), on the other hand, wrote an essay on 'sudden enlightenment' long before the advent of the Ch'an school. He also wrote a text to the effect that 'a good act entails no retribution' – that is, in terms of karma.

One of the few important translators working in the south was Fa-hsien, who distinguished himself by actually travelling to India (399–414) to obtain texts, particularly Vinaya texts. He practically walked the whole way, crossing the Gobi desert and the Hindu Kush mountains in the process and successfully negotiating all kinds of physical and spiritual perils. The outward journey took him six years; he then spent six years in India and finally returned to China by sea via Ceylon and Java –

an equally adventurous undertaking that took a further three years.

Sui and T'ang Dynasties (581–907)

Though Buddhism advanced enormously in China during the Period of Disunity, it is generally thought to have enjoyed its golden age during the T'ang dynasty (618–907), which followed the Sui dynasty (581–618), when the great empire was once again united under a single imperial régime. Having reached it apogee by the 9th century, Chinese Buddhism then began the slow, 1000-year decline that has continued to the present.

During the preceding periods, the ground-work had been thoroughly laid; conditions were therefore ripe for a fully-realized *Chinese* Buddhism to burgeon. In particular, a number of highly developed schools emerged, nearly all of them Indian in origin but to a greater or lesser degree modified and taken on to new heights of development by the Chinese genius. These schools were subsequently transmitted to Korea and Japan, where they underwent further development. Some of them are now being transmitted yet again, this time to the West.

The following are the principal Chinese schools of Buddhism:

The Vinaya School (Lü-tsung)

Principal text: The Vinaya in Four Parts, translated by Buddhayashas and Chu Fo-nien.

Mainly concerned with the Vinaya (monastic code of discipline) and the strict observance of both its positive and negative aspects (do's and don'ts), this school played a useful part in raising monastic standards in China. Its foundation is credited to Tao-hsüan (596–667)

The Realistic School (Chü-shê)

Principal text: The Abhidharma-kosha of Vasubandhu

This derived its inspiration from an early text written by
Vasubandhu (c 316–396), the brother of Asanga and a native
of Purushapura (Peshawar) who, before his conversion to the
Mahàyàna, was an ordained member of the Sarvastivàda (or
'All-things-exist') school, one of the Eighteen Schools of the
Hinayàna, the teachings of which he studied in Kashmir. The
Abdhidharma-kosha, which represents a critical outline of
the Abdhidharma system of the Vaibàshika, a group of
Sarvàstivada philosophers, was translated into Chinese firstly
by Paramàrtha (563–567), Vasubandhu's biographer, and later
by Hsüan-tsang. The school that arose in China eventually
became an appendage of the Idealist School (*Fa-hsiang* – see
below).

The Three Treatises School (San-lun)

*Principal texts; The Màdhyamika-shàstra and the Dvàdasha-
dvàra ('Twelve Gates') of Nàgàrjuna; also the Shata Shàstra
('One Hundred Verse Treaties') of Aryadeva.*

This was based on the Màdhyàmika or 'Middle Way' teachings
of Nagàrjuna and his followers (see pp 105–6), who sought to
advance the perfect wisdom of absolute Emptiness by the use of
a 'transcendental dialect' negating all views. Introduced by
Kumarajiva, these teachings were refined by Chih-tsang
(549–623), the master of Chia-hsiang monastery and a prolific
writer of commentaries. In his 'Essay on the Double Truth'
(*Erh-ti Chang*), Chih-tsang argues that the transcendental can
only be discussed in antithetical language, but this does not
result in mere negation; in fact, as the dialectic is pushed
forward, our usual notions of being and non-being are gradually
refined and an increasingly inclusive, totalistic vision begins to
unfold. The school declined after the rise of the Idealist School
(*Fa-hsiang*), but was later revived by Suryaprabhasa, an Indian
monk who arrived in China in 679.

The Idealist School (Fa-hsiang)

Principal texts: The Vimśatikā-kārikā or 'Twenty Stanzas' and other texts by Vasubandhu and his followers.

This is the Chinese development of the Indian Yogācāra school founded by Vasubandhu and his brother Asanga (see pp. 106), which propounded the doctrine of *citta-mātra* or 'mind only'. Its great champion in China was Hsüan-tsang (596–664), a kind of saintly innocent of heroic stature who emerges as arguably the most engaging figure in the history of Buddhism in the great empire. His interesting life-story warrants a digression.

Remarkable from an early age for his purity, Hsüan-tsang ordained as a monk and applied himself to assiduous study. He eventually decided to travel to India himself. He slipped out of China without official permission, and journeyed overland via the Silk Road. That his travels were rich in the stuff of high romance is demonstrated by the fact that they formed the basis for the novel *Monkey* by Wu Ch'ên-ên, which exists in a classic English translation by Arthur Waley. Waley also summarized Hsüan-tsang's life in *The Real Tripitaka*, a book which incidentally gives us a vivid portrait of Buddhism in both China and India during the 7th century.

At the very start of his monumental pilgrimage, the 'Great Traveller', as he became called, nearly came to grief at the hands of a spurious guide; then in the great deserts he was harrassed by spectral horsemen. In both these and other tight corners he was saved by divine intercession. Then at Turfan the local king was loth to let one of his prowess slip through his fingers and was prepared to forcibly detain him to enjoy the benefits of his edifying company. Men of wisdom were in those days revered and accorded the kind of celebrity currently reserved for TV soap-opera and sports stars. By threatening to go on hunger strike, Hsüan-tsang was able to recover his liberty. He then crossed the T'ien Shan mountains, visited Samarkand, looped south into what today is Iran, proceeded on to Afghanistan and eventually descended onto the plains of India in the vicinity of Gandhāra.

In India Hsüan-tsang visited most of the major Buddhist centres and pilgrimage-places, studying both widely and deeply as he went. He stayed twice at Nàlandà and on the first occasion was able to study Yogàcàra philosophy under an ancient master named Silabhadra, who was reputed to have mastered all the books in the world. He also studied logic, which stood him in good stead in a great public debate in which he triumphantly championed the Mahàyàna against all-comers. The patron on that occasion was Harsha, then Emperor of India, who had jealously snatched Hsüan-tsang from the court of Assam, where he had gone in the hope of reforming the errant king. The favour that he enjoyed with Harsha and the largesse that was heaped on his head were, however, something of a mixed blessing for they delayed Hsüan-tsang's return to China.

Eventually, feted and acclaimed, Hsüan-tsang re-entered Ch'ang-an in 645. He had been away for 16 years and had brought back numerous Buddha relics and images; also some 657 texts. Famous by now, he enjoyed the favour of the emperor, who earnestly wished him to surrender the robe and enter public service. Hsüan-tsang tactfully declined, however, for he wished to devote himself to the translation of his collection of texts.

It was Arthur Waley's considered opinion that, while Hsüan-tsang's translations affected a revolution in method and managed a closeness to their originals that earlier translations had failed to achieve, they were nevertheless marred by mistakes, misleading interpolations and other flaws. They also lacked the literary qualities that had graced Kumàrajiva's renderings.

The Mantra or Tantric School (Mi-tsung or Chen-yen)

Principal text: The Mahàvairocana ('Great Brilliance') Sùtra.

This is the Chinese manifestation of Tantra with all its esoteric paraphernalia of yogas, *mantras, mandalas, mudràs, dharanis,* initiations and secret doctrines. It was introduced from India during the T'ang dynasty by Subhakarasimha (637–735), who arrived in the Middle Kingdom in 716 and translated the *Mahàvairocana Sùtra* nine years later. In 720, another Indian, Vajrabodhi (670–741), arrived and began to expound the teachings and initiate neophytes into practice. Special

sanctuaries had to be built for the performance of the necessary
rituals, which involved the use of complex *mandala*. A third
Indian, Amoghavajra (705–774), reinterpreted the tantric
teachings in terms of the Chinese classics; he was also active at
the imperial court and is credited with initiating three T'ang
emperors. Tantric rites were thought to give magical protection
to the empire against catastrophe; they could also influence
developments in the after-death state and confer other occult
benefits. The School flourished for less than a century and was
eventually supplanted by Lamaism. It was taken to Japan by
Kūkai, where it became known as Shingon.

The Avatamsaka or 'Flower Adornment' School (Hua-yen)

Principal text: The Avatamsaka Sūtra.

Although the *Avatamsaka Sūtra* originated in India, a fully
fledged system developed from its teachings emerged in China
and was later transmitted to Japan, where it became known as
Kegon.

The plethora of translated texts and commentaries that had
become available in China, all collectively propounding an
apparent cacophany of differing views, begged for some kind of
system of classification that would lend them some measure of
coherence. The Hua-yen was one of the schools that responded
to this need. It put forward the notion that immediately after
his Enlightenment the Buddha had preached the Avatamsaka
teachings but had met with only blank incomprehension from
his listeners. Seeing them standing as if 'deaf and dumb', he
realized that he would have to compromise and so evolved the
simpler Hinayāna teachings. In time, as the level of
understanding among his followers progressed, he was able to
give out increasingly advanced teachings, but the *Avatamsaka*
remained the summation and apogee of his system. Dr. D.T.
Suzuki was echoing this to his classes in New York as late as
1951: 'Kegon is believed to have been the expression given by
the Buddha in his Enlightenment,' he maintained. 'All other
teachings were given by the Buddha to his disciples after he had
come out of the Enlightenment. In Kegon he made no

accommodation to his hearers. . . .'30

Hua-yen is a creation of cosmic vision on the grandest scale. It evokes a Universe where everything freely interpenetrates everything else, where Totality may be contemplated and Ultimate Truth realized in even the tiniest speck of dust. It reinforces its imaginative philosophical arguments with rich poetic images like that of the *Jewel Net of Indra*: a vast web or network of gems, each of which reflects every other – and also the reflections in every other – and so on *ad infinitum*. . . .

Edward Conze described Hua-yen as a link between Yogācāra and Tantra. While providing a 'cosmic interpretation to the ontological ideas of the Yogācārins'31 it shared with Tantra a fascination with the play of cosmic forces. Unlike Tantra, however, Hua-yen was not concerned with the attainment of liberation by means of the magical manipulation of those forces; its practical bias was rather towards contemplation and aesthetic appreciation of them. By doing this, the devotee would eventually be led to repose in ultimate quiescence.

The outstanding figure in the early history of Hua-yen is Fa-tsang (643–712/3), a fully sinicized Soghdian monk who was born in Ch'ang-an. He was at one time a member of Hsüan-tsang's translation bureau but became disenchanted with Idealist philosophy after reading the *Avatamsaka Sūtra*.

Hua-yen philosophy attracted the interest of the Empress Wu (ruled 690–705 – the only female 'Son of Heaven') and various emperors, perhaps, it has been suggested, because its all-embracing system appealed to their totalitarian cast of mind. Despite her notorious ruthlessness, Empress Wu was an enthusiastic supporter of Buddhism and even claimed, perhaps to justify her own seizure of power, to be an incarnation of Maitreya. In 704, she commanded Fa-tsang to lecture to her on the *Avatamsaka Sūtra*. The master noticed a golden lion in the throne room and cleverly used it to elucidate Hua-yen philosophy. The gold of the lion symbolized *li* or ultimate principle (numenal aspect), he maintained, while the lion-form symbolized *shih* or causally-determined characteristics (phenomenal aspect). On the basis of the fact that every distinct part of the lion was made of gold, each phenomenon could be said to embrace every other phenomenon while at the same time being a perfect manifestation of numenon.

Tu-shun (557–640) was the first patriarch of the Hua-yen school; his 'Contemplating the Dharmadhātu' (*Ha-Chieh Kuan*) is thought to have set the pattern for subsequent commentaries, its 'round view' reflecting the totalistic vision of its subject. Commentaries also flowed from his successor, Chih-yen (602–668); for instance, the *Hua-yen Chin Shou Hsuan Chi*: 'A Search for the Profound Mysteries of the *Hua-yen Sūtra*'. The third patriarch was Fa-tsang, and the fourth Ch'eng-kuan (Master Ch'ing-liang, 738–838), a giant of a man who was heaped with honours and titles – 'Master of the Purple Robe', 'National Preceptor', etc., etc. – by his great patron, Emperor Te-tsung. The next patriarch, Kuei-feng Tsung-mi (780–841), benefitted from similar imperial largesse.

Finally, when a general decline of Buddhism set in in the 9th century, the Hua-yen School also went into eclipse, having flourished for over 200 years.

The T'ien-t'ai or White Lotus School (Fa–hua)

Principal text: The Saddharma-pundarīka Sūtra.

Although sometimes called the 'Lotus' school because of its veneration of the *Saddharma-pundarīka* or 'White Lotus of the True Law *Sūtra*', this school derives its principal name from the fact that its *true* founder and fourth patriarch, Chih-i (538–597), lived on Mount T'ien-t'ai in Chekiang. It too was a genuinely Chinese development.

Although accepting the myth that, following his failure to put across his advanced teachings, the Buddha had compromised and expounded simpler teachings, the T'ien-t'ai School differed from the Hua-yen in providing alternative classifications of Buddhist scriptures and teachings. These demonstrated, it was claimed, that the *Saddharma-pundarīka* was the real 'king of *sūtras*', for it alone was fully 'round' in the sense that it included the essence of all the other teachings. It was therefore the perfect packet that could ferry all men across the ocean of *Samsāra* to the far shore of Enlightenment, regardless of their level of understanding. Allied to this was the notion of a single vehicle (*ekayāna*) in which all other doctrines were united.

The T'ien-t'ai also put forward lofty philosophical doctrines, which owed a lot to those of the Hua-yen and Idealist Schools. Arguably most important was that of the Three Levels of Truth, which bears traces of the influence of Nāgārjuna. The three levels are; (1) Void or Emptiness; (2) Temporariness; and (3) Mean. The first signifies that no *dharma* can exist by itself alone but is causally generated and maintained in dependence. However, though *dharmas* are essentially void or empty, they do enjoy temporary existence as perceived by the senses; this constitutes the second level. The third level arises from the fact that emptiness and temporariness are two sides of a dualism that generates a higher third: a mean or middle. This should not be taken as lying between the other two, however; rather, as J. Takakusu puts it: 'It is over and above the two: nay, it is identical with the two, because the true state means that the middle is the very state of being void and temporary'.

Because they are perpetually united and harmonious, the Three Levels of Truth must therefore not be treated separately but always as 'all in one and one in all'. By the same token, phenomena are so interpenetrated by the numenal that the whole cosmos can be contained in a single instant of thought or in a follicle of hair. This confers a degree of spiritual stature on the ordinary and the every-day that had been largely absent from Buddhism hitherto: the apparently mundane *is* the spiritual; they are not two.

In terms of practice, this school advocated 'concentration and insight' (*chih* and *kuan*) as methods of obtaining Enlightenment. Concentration puts an end to erroneous thinking by making it clear that all *dharmas* are devoid of self-nature and hence exist without really existing. Insight, on the other hand, means to fully penetrate the phantasmagoric character of all *dharmas* and to become grounded in Absolute Mind. Incidentally, this Absolute Mind – or 'Womb of the Tathāgata', 'True and Genuine Suchness', etc., etc. – is the repository of all potentialities, both pure and impure, and in its synthetic totality is fully present in all things, whether sentient or insentient. Thus Buddha-nature and the possibility of Enlightenment are utterly unexclusive.

In 577, the reigning emperor dedicated the revenue of the district adjacent to Mount T'ien-t'ai to the upkeep of Chih-i and his community. The Master is said to have promoted nonviolence on his monastic domains and to have banned fishing. He went to Ch'ang-an to give discourses to two emperors. A prolific writer of commentaries and manuals, his *Pan-chiao* ('Classification of the Teachings') is very famous. It seeks to harmonize the seemingly contradictory aspects of the Buddha's teachings by dividing them into eight groups and evaluating them in terms of their relevant *upaya* or function. Chih-i also identified five major phases in Shakyamuni's life.

After Chih-i, the T'ien-t'ai transmission line runs: Kuan-ting, Fa-hua, T'ien-kung, Tso-ch'i, Ch'an-jan and Tao-sui – the latter being the teacher of Dengyō Daishi, who introduced the school into Japan in the 9th century, where it became known as Tendai.

The Pure Land School (Ching t'u)

Principal text: The Smaller and Larger Sukhāvatī-vyūha Sūtras.

The devotees of this school venerated Amitābha (the Buddha of Infinite Light) and sought, not outright Nirvāna, but rebirth in the Western Paradise or 'Pure Land' of Amitābha, also called Sukhāvatī. In that idyllic environment, no new negative karmic accumulations would be created and all existing ones would evaporate; Nirvāna would be therefore just a short step away.

At root, the school harked back to the notion expounded in early Buddhist cosmology that within a few hundred years of the Buddha's death a degenerate period would set in when Enlightenment would no longer be attainable by one's own efforts or 'self-power' (in Japanese: *jiriki*) alone. One would therefore have to depend on external grace: in this case, the benign intercession of Amitābha. This represented the opposite of 'self-power', namely 'other-power' (*tariki*). It was also felt that there was in any case an element of egoism in the very idea of 'self-power': that one could win Enlightenment by one's own efforts alone. As that was basically the Hinayāna outlook, Pure Land Buddhism reflected the Mahāyāna accommodation to devotional forms of practice. The mantric repetition of the name of Amitābha – '*O-mi-tō-fō*' (in Japanese: '*Namu-Amida-butsu*') – was the central practice developed here.

A former Taoist named Hui-yüan (334–416) promoted the cult of Amitābha in China during the Period of Disunity and in 402 founded the Fellowship of the White Lotus, from which the Pure Land School eventually developed. Other significant figures in its early history are T'an-luan (476–542), Tao-ch'o (c 645) and Shan-tao (613–681). Its teachings were transmitted to Korea and, more significantly, to Japan, where division into the Jōdo and Jōdo Shin sub-schools occurred. The Pure Land School in its various forms and derivatives is still very much in existence and today has a following in the West.

The Dhyāna School (Ch'an; Jap–Zen)

Principal texts: Ostensibly nil; actually the Lankāvatāra, Heart, Vimalakirti-nirdésa and Vajracchedikā Sūtras.

Ch'an represents the finest achievement of Chinese Buddhism: an original and highly creative re-expression of the essence of the Buddha's teaching in terms that are distinctively Chinese. As such it may also be regarded, alongside Abhidharma, Mahāyāna and Tantra, as one of the major creations of Buddhism as a whole. It was transmitted to Korea (where it became known as *Son*), to Vietnam, and to Japan (where it became known as *Zen*); also in more recent times to the West.

Ch'an is often described as a product of the down-to-earth, practical slant of the Chinese character. Indians, on the other hand, are said to be by nature more airy and metaphysical – and indeed the Chinese were quite fascinated with the marvellous intellectual creations of India for a long time. After the centuries of importation and absorbtion, however, their own native genius asserted itself resulting in the emergence of Ch'an, which is often described as the complete 'sinicization' of Buddhism.

Ch'an is about a return to essentials. All the teachings, texts, practices, codes of morality and behaviour, etc., etc., that sprang up around the basically simple teaching of the Buddha were intended as aids to progress *beyond*: to Enlightenment. But as the years went by, the diligent practitioner might become attached and trapped in them. Just as the *bodhisattva* Manjushri wields his Sword of Wisdom to summarily slice through the net of delusions, so the impulse behind Ch'an was to sweep all the training paraphernalia of Buddhism aside and to zero in on the heart of the matter: the direct insight that transformed Siddhārtha Gautama into the Buddha beneath the Bodhi Tree at Bodh Gāya.

The general thrust of Ch'an is typified by its rejection of book-learning and verbalization. Ch'an, it was claimed, was 'a special transmission outside the scriptures'; it placed 'no reliance on words and letters'. What was transmitted was buddhahood, Enlightenment itself, no less, which consisted in a 'direct pointing to the heart of man', in a 'seeing into one's own nature'. This was handed on from master to disciple, heart to heart. To authenticate their tradition, the followers of Ch'an traced lines of transmission which showed how, by a process similar to apostolic succession, the teachings had been handed down without interruption.

However, although they often expressed a contempt for the scriptures, the Ch'an masters frequently showed themselves well-versed in them – and indeed the *Lankāvatāra, Vimalakirti-nirdeśa* and *Vajracchedikā sūtras* were studied within the school; other texts as well. Furthermore, in time original Ch'an texts appeared, like the '*Platform Sūtra*' of the Sixth Patriarch, Hui-neng, the '*Records of Eminent Monks*', the '*Ching-te Record of the Transmission of the Lamp*', and the '*Record of the Finger Pointing at the Moon*'. The ostensible rejection of scriptures was therefore very much the posture of people well-versed in the traditional texts. One cannot give wealth away if one does not have it, or transcend the ego where no stable, mature ego exists; so too with book-learning.

This really goes for the whole of Ch'an: it is intended for practitioners saturated in all aspects of Buddhist teaching and practice. However, the anti-scriptural, unconventional and sometimes iconoclastic behaviour of many Ch'an masters is often mistaken by uninformed Westerners as a cue that the demands and formalities of traditional training can be dispensed with – that Ch'an offers an easy short-cut to Enlightenment. Nothing could be further from the case. The Ch'an Master who burned a Buddha-image was himself a deeply pious monk; and the Ch'an Master who declared that there was no such thing as Enlightenment was himself fully Enlightened!

The term 'Ch'an' is in fact a Chinese corruption of 'dhyāna', the Indian term for the absorption or high bliss states achieved through *samatha* meditation. Sitting meditation was always an important aspect of Ch'an practice as an aid to the development of inner stillness and the accumulation of vital energy or *chi* (a Taoist influence). But in the seminal days in China sitting was rather less important than it was subsequently to become in Japan, whence most of what we know of Ch'an/Zen in the West today has come. What the early Chinese Masters stressed rather was the 'non-abiding mind' – the mind that rests nowhere, beyond all thought and relativity. This is nothing other than our ordinary, 'everyday mind' – and the Ch'an practitioner would seek to remain with it in all situations, not just in sitting. It was to drive this point home that Huai-jang, seeing Ma-tsu sitting in meditation, siezed a tile and began frantically rubbing it. When asked what he was doing, he replied that he was trying to polish the stone into a mirror. 'Impossible!' cried Ma-tsu; whereupon Huai-jang retorted that it was equally impossible to forge a Buddha-mind through sitting alone.

Richard Hunn (Upāsaka Wen Shu), a former disciple of the late Charles Luk, has written:

From all the Chinese Ch'an records, it is easy to determine that at least 80% of the 'awakening experiences' in fact took place during apparently mundane activities... working in the fields, cooking rice, hearing one's name called, a slap, a kick! And there is reason for this. Continual introspection or 'turning back' of the mind arouses an 'inner potentiality' (*nei chih*), which eventually breaks through into 'ordinary' consciousness. One then sees that seemingly conditioned events... one's own self... all surroundings... arise in this marvellous emptiness....

Thus of old the teaching was simple and consisted in 'direct pointing'. To remove obstructions, the old masters 'probed' their disciples to see what their troubles were. If they clung to the 'worldly', they stripped that attachment away; if they clung to the 'saintly', on the other hand, the master would shout or give them a slap to snap them out of that.

Fa-yung lived in seclusion on Niu-t'ou Mountain. When Tao-hsin went there, Fa-yung offered to put him up in a spot behind his cave. On the way there, they spotted wild animals, whereupon Tao-hsin feigned fear. Fa-yung said, 'I see that this is still with you' – meaning the *kleshas* (defilements), in this case fear. Later, Tao-hsin approached the rock where Fa-yung spent all his time sitting in meditation. He motioned as if writing the character *fo* (Buddha) on the rock, saying, 'I see that this is still with you' – meaning deep attachment to the very idea of the saintly Buddha-state. Fa-yung got the message, changed his practice, opened a temple and freely interacted with the world.

Initially, however, most disciples withdrew their attention from the play of events in the 'world' in order to disentangle themselves from false thinking. But once sure about the underlying (birthless and deathless) nature, they were obliged to harmonize this with their everyday activities. Thus the Ch'an masters used the terms 'host' and 'guest' for the 'numenal' and the 'phenomenal', and the terms *ti* and *yung* (principle and activity) in order to make clear both sides of the business ... Another term coined within Ch'an was *yeh shih* or the 'initial consciousness' i.e. the primordial mind that underlies all actions and which mirrors the surface play of phenomena.

(*Letter to the author dated 11/6/87. Edited.*)

In a book on Rebirth, the Indian sage Sri Aurobindo lamented that Buddhism was just about Enlightenment in quiescence. He failed to take account of Ch'an, where the Enlightenment attained in quiescence must be brought and tested where the action is. In the classic *Ten Ox-herding Pictures*, which symbolically depict the Ch'an/Zen path, the final picture shows the Master coming into the market-place 'with bliss-bestowing hands'.

The seminal figure in early Ch'an is Bodhidharma, a south Indian Master who is said to have arrived in China around 520. His historicity is often challenged, particularly in the West. Though he was honoured as the First Patriarch of Chinese Ch'an, 27 other Indian patriarchs were identified, the first being Mahàkàshyapa, who reputedly received transmission directly from the Buddha. The way this happened is quite precisely documented. Right from the time of his Enlightenment, the Buddha had been unhappy about the capacity of other people to understand his subtle teaching. Usually he compromised and produced verbal teachings, but on one particular occasion he had said nothing but merely held up a flower. Of all the disciples present, only Mahàkàshyapa got the message. A smile and an answering smile registered that transmission had taken place – and so it went on. ...

Bodhidharma is depicted in Ch'an and Zen paintings as a grim and glowering figure with huge, bulbous eyes. Legend has it that he sliced off his own eyelids in order to keep awake and aware. Shortly after arriving in China, he visited Emperor Wu of Liang.

'What is the meaning of the Dharma?' the Emperor asked.

'Vast emptiness without holiness', Bodhidharma replied.

'Who is standing before me now?'

'I don't know....'

Evidently neither the Master nor the Emperor were particularly impressed with the other. The interview ended and Bodhidharma departed for the adjacent state of Wei, where he is alleged to have spent nine years sitting facing a wall in the Shaolin temple. Then one day a monk visited him in search of teaching. Bodhidharma did not gratify his wish, so eventually, as proof of his earnestness, the student chopped off his left arm with a sword. That impressed the Master.

'My soul isn't at peace', the student complained. 'Please pacify it, master.'

'Bring your soul here and I'll pacify it', came the reply.

'I've been looking for it for years but haven't been able to find a trace of it', the student had to admit.

'There!' Bodhidharma declared. 'It's pacified once and for all.'

The history of the Ch'an School begins in earnest, however, with the Sixth Patriarch, Hui-neng (638–713). He was an unlettered woodcutter who one day happened to hear the *Vajracchedikā Sūtra* being recited. Captivated, he longed to study the *Sūtra* under the guidance of a Master. He therefore travelled to see the Fifth Patriarch, Hung-jen (601–674), who allowed him to enter his monastery as a lay menial. When the time came for the patriarch to nominate his successor, he announced that this supreme honour would be conferred upon the author of the verse which demonstrated the best understanding of the teaching. His foremost disciple, Shen-hsui (*c* 600–706), wrote a very penetrating piece, but this offering was capped by another from the lowly skivvy in the kitchen. This is traditionally cited as the cause of a split in the Ch'an school.

The account that has become prevalent in the contemporary

West is that two rival schools subsequently emerged: a Southern School led by Hui-neng and a Northern School led by Shen-hsiu. Doctrinally the bone of contention was whether enlightenment was gradual, as Shen-hsiu claimed, or sudden – Hui-neng's view. Hui-neng's outlook was, it is usually claimed, the more radical and uncompromising. In his poem, Shen-hsiu had likened the mind to a mirror that had to be continually polished to be kept free of dust. 'The mirror bright is nowhere shining'. Hui-neng had countered; 'As there is nothing from the first/Where can the dust collect?'

Hui-neng's Southern School was eventually to triumph, leaving its rival to go the way of all flesh. Some commentators, however, feel on the evidence of contemporary texts that the significance of the split has been exaggerated and that little of the animosity that is usually described really existed between the two schools. Rather Hui-neng happened to come along at a time when social and historical conditions were right for the reception and a full flowering of Ch'an, and his school attracted the necessary support, notably in pertinent political quarters.

Later there were further sub-divisions and traditionally 'Five Houses' (and Seven Sects) are said to have arisen between the 9th and 11th centuries, including the *Fa-yen*, *Yun-men* and *Kuei-yang*. These all died out, however, but two others survived: the *Lin-chi* (Jap. *Rinzai*) and the *Ts'ao-tung* (Jap. *Sōtō*). In their later Japanese forms, both schools place primarily stress on sitting practice (Jap. *zazen*) and the Lin-chi/Rinzai school is popularly distinguished from the Ts'ao-tung/Sōtō by its use of *kung-an* (Jap. *kōan*), a term which possesses connotations of a legal case or precedent. In China, however, *kung-an* were employed within all Five Houses and arose well before the time of Master Lin-chi (d. 867). Their origin quite probably lay in the favourite trick of the early masters of suddenly calling out to a student. When the student's head automatically turned, they followed with an urgent, '*What is it???*' Richard Hunn explains:

> In this they were very skilful, for at such moments one is already
> 'half way there' in the sense of the mind being emptied of surface
> activity. Techniques of this kind are very subtle; they 'steal the
> pearl from under the dragon's chin', sieze the 'still point' right in
> the midst of movement.

(ibid)

Ch'an monks acquired the reputation of being great travellers; even after 'breaking through', they might go on foot from Master to Master, testing the depth of their insight. They also differed from their confrères in other Buddhist schools in that they were not loth to turn their hands to manual labour. Hui-hai (720–814) is credited with having introduced this innovation. The maxim, 'a day without work is a day without food', is attributed to him. He also formulated other monastic rules aimed at restoring the ascetic way of life practised by the original Buddhists.

In breaking down the dichotomy between the sacred and the profane, Ch'an also paved the way for lay practice, and indeed a few – though admittedly not many – enlightened laymen and laywomen do grace its annals: for instance, Layman P'ang, who discerned the numenous in the simple tasks of his everyday life:

How wonderful, how miraculous!
I fetch wood, I carry water.

In a similar spirit, some Ch'an masters were disposed to announce that there was nothing special about any of Buddhism. Even Enlightenment was no big deal. It was all just a matter of eating when hungry, sleeping when tired and answering the call of nature.

'Smoothly functioning in response to the moment – what are you lacking?' Master Lin-chi demanded of his followers. And later: 'I tell you: There is no Buddha, no Dharma, no training and no realization. . . .'

There is undeniably something very attractive about Ch'an for all its legendary severity. Its qualities can perhaps be most immediately appreciated in the art that it inspired. Here simplicity, naturalness and spontaneity are of the essence. A few deft strokes of the brush, executed (hopefully) without conscious contrivance, evoke an image, say, of bamboos bending in a gentle breeze. This will radiate all the unique magic of the fleeting moment and at the same time indicate the character of the artist – perhaps even, to the cognoscenti, the depth of his insight. Such subtle creations are deceptive, however. Their manifest freedom is not to be confused with the merely anarchic; it is the *informed* freedom that comes of long and arduous training.

There was generally a great flowering of Buddhist art during the T'ang period, notably of sculpture. In the visual arts, the dominant influence was the style evolved in India during the Gupta period (320–535), which was characterized by 'restrained sensuousness, with smooth, soft surfaces, and facial expressions exhibiting a certain sweetness.'[32] This tempered the austerity that is apparent in images fashioned in the Wei and Sui periods.

The picture that emerges of Buddhism in T'ang dynasty China is a very impressive one. Thousands of temples and monasteries were scattered about the empire, inhabited by a flourishing Sangha of monks and nuns, among them some of the finest talents of the age. The temples and monasteries ranged from humble provincial establishments or ones situated in remote mountain regions, to truly gigantic and magnificent complexes that were repositories of great wealth and fine art. There were even 'official' temples, funded by the state for the purpose of invoking spiritual protection against danger from within or without.

The non-official establishments were of course primarily dedicated to ministering in various ways to the spiritual needs of the lay people to whom most of them looked for their support; but they were also social, cultural and educational centres. Temple festivals, like the Lantern Festival, the Festival of the Buddha's Birthday and All Soul's Festival, were great occasions for collective celebration in which all strata of society took part, as were processions, pilgrimages and vegetarian feasts. Often the Sangha used these occasions to give talks to the laity, and a popular literature consisting of edifying tales with entertaining and 'miraculous' embellishments developed.

Inspired by the Mahāyāna ideal of compassion, which in China often took practical forms, the Sangha was very much involved in performing good works – like looking after the old and the sick, helping the poor and distributing food in times of shortage. This public-spiritedness overflowed into the field of useful works: the building of roads and bridges, rest-houses and bath-houses, the sinking of wells, tree-planting and so forth.

Religious societies also flourished, some of which were secret societies. Both Sangha and laity participated, and their activities included devotional projects (like copying *sūtras* or carving statues) and the provision of various forms of mutual aid.

As a cultural contribution, on the other hand, the invention of printing by Chinese Buddhists is of enormous significance. The earliest example of printing extant is in fact a copy of *The Diamond Sūtra* dated 868. As this is no crude effort, it is clear that printing had been used as a cheap way of reproducing texts and simple images and charms for some time before that date.

Buddhist temples and monasteries also developed into powerful centres of commerce. In fact, Buddhism has been credited (or blamed) for pioneering modern-style capitalism and banking in China. The larger establishments were very rich foundations, often endowed with extensive lands which, as only Ch'an monks performed manual labour, were commercially farmed with the use of slave labour; otherwise a share-cropping system was employed. In addition, the Sangha owned rolling mills, oil presses and hostelries, all operated for monetary gain. The profits from these activities, at least some of which may have been tax-exempt, augmented by donations, led to the accumulation of great wealth – the so-called 'Inexhaustible Treasury' – which was used for money-lending and pawn-brokerage. The hoarding of vast quantities of useful and precious metals in the form of images also took place.

Though most T'ang emperors patronized it, the imperial government inevitably felt compelled to exert its control over this affluent, enterprising, extensive and influential Buddhist 'church'. In characteristic style – bureaucracy was pioneered in China – it placed it under the overall supervision of a government ministry staffed by an army of civil servants. Bowing to expediency, the Buddhist 'church' in its turn seems to have come to accept the supremacy of the worldly authority and to acquiesce in a high degree of bureaucratic interference in its internal affairs. Census of the Sangha, the control of monastic examinations and the issuing of certificates of ordination were all matters eventually supervised by lay bureaucrats.

Still, church/state tensions persisted and became acute when towards the middle of the 9th century the dynasty was ravaged by civil war. With its coffers sorely depleted, the state naturally looked with envy at the vast wealth hoarded up in the monastic treasuries. The temptation to seize it became great – and whatever scruples might have stood in the way were weakened by a return to classical Confucian values that again stigmatized

Buddhism as an alien cult.

In 845, during the reign of Emperor Wu-tsung (reigned 841–7), an order was promulgated to the effect that all Buddhist establishments should be destroyed, their lands and wealth seized, their slaves freed, and that all monks and nuns should return to lay life. Buddhism itself was not outlawed, nor was any move made against the laity; moreover the order was quickly lifted. Nevertheless, serious damage was done – damage which, allied to other unfavourable developments, initiated a decline of Chinese Buddhism that sadly has never been effectively reversed.

From the Wu-tai and Sung Dynasties to the People's Republic (907 – date)

Aside from the Communists, most of the rulers of China during this very long period were by no means unsympathetic to Buddhism. In fact some were very sympathetic, particularly the foreign dynasties who, as we have seen before, had their own reasons for favouring a non-indigenous religion. As a consequence, the material base of Buddhism did revive and a Sangha did re-form – temporarily. But the creative spark had gone. During that final millennium the Chinese Buddhist 'church' mainly lived on the achievements of its past and underwent a steady process of decline.

What were the immediate reasons for this?

Firstly there was the resurgence of Confucianism. This was not the old Confucianism either, but a new and improved variety equipped, among other things, with a sophisticated metaphysic that owed not a little to Buddhist philosophy. This neo-Confucianism had the intellectual cachet that its precursor had lacked and in consequence Buddhism began to lose its grip on the minds and hearts of the intellectual élite, who in the more settled social climate were anyway more likely to seek a niche for themselves in the imperial service than in a Buddhist monastery. As a result, Buddhism was left to cater for popular spiritual needs, which was not conducive to the expression of its highest potentials. The religion was furthermore diluted by the syncretism that became fashionable.

Another blow was the destruction of Buddhism in India, which meant that no new inspirational impulses came from that direction. At the same time there was a deterioration in the quality and behaviour of the Chinese Sangha, caused in part by the practice inaugurated by the Sung dynasty (960–1279) of trafficking in monk certificates in order to raise funds for the relief of its financial embarrassments. These certificates granted the bearers useful exemptions; they could also be purchased by undesirables – even by criminals intent on escaping from justice. 'Monks' with wives and children became by no means rare. No doubt sincere monks and nuns still existed, but the prestige of the Sangha suffered.

This decline was of course quite in keeping with the Buddha's teaching on impermanence as well as with his prediction that the Dharma would go through repeated cycles of decadence and destruction after every initial period of vitality. In short, the great pitch of creativity and excellence that had been achieved during the T'ang period could not have been expected to have lasted. Of the various schools, those that weathered the decline best were Ch'an and Pure Land. Pure Land was fortified by the undeniable strength of its popular appeal. It spawned numerous societies, some of them claiming membership running into thousands. The very simplicity advocated by Ch'an, on the other hand, lent it a good measure of resilience; also the fact that its monks and nuns were prepared to work. It also enjoyed favour in high places. The prevalent syncretism also touched Ch'an. For instance, some practitioners employed Pure Land practices, like repeating the name of Amitābha.

In many ways, the Sung period was a glorious one for Ch'an. In terms of its art and general cultural importance, this was indeed its golden age; but internally there was impoverishment as the initial unconventional vigour and spontaneity gave way to increasing formalization and institutionalization. There was indeed a tendency to look back nostalgically to the times of the early Masters, and the *kung-an* collections made at this time which anecdotally record their sayings and doings reflect this. Two classic collections appeared, the '*Blue Cliff Record*, (*Pi-yen-lu*; Jap. *Hekiganroku*), compiled by Hsueh Tou Ch'ung Hsien (980–1152), and the '*Gateless Gate*' (*Wu-men-kuan*; Jap. *Mumonkan*), compiled by Wu-men Hui-kai (1184–1260), which were commented upon and assiduously studied. Sadly, the *kung-an* lost their original freshness too and, though used as an affective practice aid within the Lin-chi/Rinzai tradition, there was a tendency for them to become mere stock answers to stock questions.

Of the original Five Houses of Zen, only Lin-chi/Rinzai and the Ts'ao-tung/Sōtō remained by the Sung dynasty. There was some measure of rivalry and mutual criticism between the two, the devotees of the Lin-chi castigating the others for being quietists; that is, taking refuge from the problems of life in sitting stillness. The Ts'ao-tung fraternity retaliated with the criticism that the Lin-chi were hung up on words and concepts – a snipe at the *kung-an*. Nevertheless, the degree of rivalry may have been exaggerated.

A minor but perhaps indicative popular development during the Sung period was the transformation of the dignified Maitreya, the Buddha-to-be, into Pu-tai, the 'Hemp Sack Monk', often known as the 'Laughing Buddha'. As Pu-tai is depicted as a grinning, pot-bellied hedonist, he suggests the celebration of worldly rather than spiritual values; there is also a hint of decadence about him.

The Mongols established the Yüan dynasty in China in 1280. They made Buddhism their state religion – for the final time. In particular they favoured Lamaism, or the Buddhism of Tibet (see Chapter 16), and thereafter that exotic form of Buddhism was also a part of the Chinese scene and was patronized by the succeeding dynasties. The Lamaist 'Cathedral', the Yung-ho-kung, is still one of the tourist sights of Peking. However, Lamaism never caught on to any appreciable extent among the mass of the people, though on China's western peripheries, where the empire once blurred into Tibet (now, alas, forcibly incorporated into the Chinese state, but formerly independent), it was strongly in evidence until comparatively recent times.

Subversive or secret societies – not to be confused with the genuine religious societies – claiming Buddhist connections were active during this period. They often had a strong messianic element: perhaps proclaiming the advent of some Maitreya who would set the world to rights – according to their own blueprints, of course. The Maitreya Society and the White Lotus Society (no connection with Pure Land) were prominent among them and were responsible for fomenting revolts and rebellions. The popular legacy these groups have left to contemporary Western culture is the myth of the fighting *kung-fu* monks. These are supposed to have practised the martial arts with superhuman skill and to have been able to defeat all comers brilliantly – and often in droves. Such skills, while they may be feasible given the required training, do not of course indicate any measure of spiritual attainment. Indeed some might argue that no serious Buddhist would engage in martial arts training (excepting perhaps in its gentlest forms, like Aikido, and then strictly for therapeutic purposes) as to do so would cut directly against basic ethical principles, non-violence being the most obvious.

Latterly, towards the end of the last century, both China and its Buddhism were in a parlous state. The great empire itself was falling apart and this left the door open for foreign intrusion. Christian missionaries now became active and, while promoting their own creed in a highly organized and energetic way, they singled Buddhism out as the principal target for their attacks. At the same time the modern secular scientific outlook, itself thoroughly inimical to Buddhism, also began to make its presence felt.

These challenges had a positive effect in that they galvanized some sections of the Chinese Buddhist community into action. The initiative had by now passed from the Sangha to the educated laity, and it was mainly laymen who, around the turn of this century, made a brave attempt to revive Chinese Buddhism and its decadent Sangha. Influenced in part by the methods of the Christians, Buddhist organizations, some of them active in missionary and educational work, were set up. Contacts were also made with foreign Buddhists and this allowed new and stimulating influences to flow in. Chinese Buddhists also went abroad to study. For instance, around 1930, Wong Mou-lam, who translated *The Platform Sūtra* into English and also founded the journal *Chinese Buddhism*, went to Sri Lanka to study Pali and Sanskrit. After Wong's departure, *Chinese Buddhism* was taken over by a 'Mr Chen', who has informed the present writer in correspondence of his numerous sympathetic foreign friends in Shanghai in the early 1930s, including 'Mr Goddard, an American, founder of the

Followers of the Buddha in the USA.' This would appear to be Dwight Goddard, compiler of A *Buddhist Bible*.

However, the tide of history was flowing ever more strongly against Buddhism as this century advanced. Buddhism now encountered its most formidable adversary in Marxism. Though looking with disfavour on Buddhism, as on all religion, the Communists did not initially feel that it needed to be destroyed. The establishment of an ideologically correct state would cause it to wither away naturally, they thought – with a little help in the form of anti-religious propaganda. In the meantime, attempts were made to bring Buddhism under control by organizing it under a central umbrella – the Chinese Buddhist Association. On the face of it, this displays a distinctly fellow-travelling complexion, though that might be merely pragmatic: a mask worn in the interests of survival.

The situation deteriorated considerably during the era of the so-called Cultural Revolution (1965–75). Buddhist temples and monasteries were then sacked and in some cases destroyed and the already weakened Sangha was further depleted. The excesses of this time have since been regretted, however, and a new, more liberal policy introduced.

Certainly the omens do not look particularly promising for Chinese Buddhism; yet, writing in 1986, John Blofeld found cause for optimism. Reflecting on his experiences during a visit to Shanghai that year, he felt that, while the percentage of Buddhists among the population must at present be tiny and though 'knowledge of Buddhism among the masses is almost nil', yet 'old values and beliefs persist'; thus 'there must be a considerable reservoir of potential Buddhists awaiting the advent of teachers able to put the Buddha Dharma across to audiences already somewhat favourably disposed towards it'. Finally, reiterating his hopes for a 'widespread resurgence' that he could vividly picture if not hope to live to see, he concluded: 'I possess very little evidence on which to build that dream of the future, but have not the smallest doubt that it will be fulfilled'.[33]

The Chinese part in the transmission of Buddhism to the West has not been great. A few pioneering Westerners, like John Blofeld himself, were able to study in China before the Communist Revolution and have handed on their knowledge.

Since 1949, of course, visits for the purpose of study and obtaining training in Buddhism have not been possible. A few Chinese teachers have managed to come to the West, mainly to America. Buddhist activity takes place in Hong Kong and Taiwan, as well as in expatriate communities elsewhere in Asia and the United States. Lu K'uan Yü (Charles Luk) has been arguably the most influential writer and teacher living in Hong Kong.

14 The Northern Transmission: Vietnam and Korea

Vietnam

Vietnam, a long thin sliver of territory lying along the extreme eastern edge of the Indo-Chinese peninsula, has indelibly impressed itself on modern consciousness as the quintessential war-torn south-east Asian country. Though now under a Communist régime, it was a place where Buddhism flourished – and indeed one of the unforgettable images of recent times is of Vietnamese Buddhist monks publicly burning themselves as a protest against the corruption of the Roman Catholic élite left behind by the colonial French after their withdrawal.

In ancient times the northern region, Annam, was for many centuries a province of the Chinese empire. To the south lay the Indianized states of Funan and Champā, which then overflowed beyond the present-day frontiers. The Vietnamese themselves originated in the north and in time came to dominate the whole land. Independence from China was gained in the 10th century, but Chinese influences continued to exert a powerful effect and in the long run this meant that the standard brand of Sri Lankan Theravāda that triumphed elsewhere in south-east Asia did not do so here; instead Chinese forms of Mahāyāna Buddhism, notably a successful amalgam of Ch'an and Pure Land, prevailed until the country fell to the Communists in 1975. Since then Buddhism has declined enormously and from time to time we hear reports of active persecution.

Many Vietnamese Buddhists now live as refugees in the West. One monk, Thich Nhat Hanh, who currently resides at Plum Village in France, has achieved international fame as a proponent of 'Engaged Buddhism'. In the early 1960s Nhat

Hanh was recalled from his studies at Columbia University in the United States to help with the so-called Third Way of Reconciliation: a brave attempt to provide a viable alternative to the corruption of Saigon and the Communism of Hanoi, then bloodily battling for supremacy. He established Van Hanh University and set up the School of Youth for Social Service, which sent people out into the rural areas where the fighting was taking place to help the peasantry who were caught in the crossfire. Nhat Hanh coined the phrase 'Engaged Buddhism' in his book, *Vietnam: Lotus in a Sea of Fire*.

Korea

The Korean peninsula is a curving thrust of land reaching down from the north-east corner of China towards the southern tip of Japan. Though its people have staunchly fought for independence over the centuries, they have inevitably come strongly under the influence of the massive neighbouring presence of China. The positioning of their small country, moreover, has naturally made it a kind of bridge whereby Chinese influences have been transmitted to Japan. At times too the traffic has flowed in the opposite direction.

It appears that Buddhism was introduced into Korea from China around the 4th century AD. The transmission continued subsequently and many of the principal Chinese schools were introduced. In terms of development, Korean Buddhism tended broadly to follow the Chinese pattern – with one important difference. Being a small and politically vulnerable nation, the Koreans could not tolerate the same diversity of schools that proliferated in China. Various attempts, none entirely successful, were therefore made to syncretize and harmonize the teachings of the Buddhist schools, though in time the local form of Ch'an/Zen, called *Son* in Korea, was to prevail and has persisted to the present time despite the general rush towards Western-type modernization that has produced a concomitant explosion of Christianity.

Korean Buddhism enjoyed its golden age during the Silla (668–935) and Koryo (935–1392) periods. It was then favoured by the intellectual élite and honoured with royal patronage;

pilgrims went to China to obtain texts and teachings; monasteries and temples were constructed and a thriving Sangha established. Five doctrinal schools came to the fore, four of them – the Vinaya, Nirvāna, Avatamsaka and Yogācāra schools – broadly emulating Chinese prototypes. The fifth, the Popsong, on the other hand, was an early attempt at syncretism by Wonhyo (617–86). Later the Ch'an/Zen school was introduced, traditionally around 630 and, mirroring the Chinese pattern, it came into conflict with the doctrinal schools on account of its iconoclastic character.

Zen proved too vital to be stifled, however, so efforts to reconcile it with the doctrinal schools were initiated during the Koryo period. An ordained monk of the royal house, Uich'on (1055–1101), attempted a harmonization on the T'ien-t'ai pattern but his anti-Zen bias hindered his success. A more successful attempt in the same direction was undertaken by Chinul (*aka* National Master Pojo; 1158–1210), a somewhat independent figure who had evolved a personal practice that combined both study and meditation. Chinul's advantage was that he had obtained direct insight into the spiritual authenticity of *both* paths. He founded the Chogye Zen sect, which was plumbed into the main Chinese Ch'an lines of transmission by the monk T'aego (1301–82), who spent many years receiving Lin-chi (Rinzai) training in China.

Following the Chinese model, from the 13th century onwards the growth of neo-Confucianism and other un-sympathetic developments led to an anti-Buddhist reaction and concomitant stagnation and decline. Attempts were made to stem the slide but by the beginning of the present century Korean Buddhism was in a parlous state.

Between 1910 and 1945, the Japanese occupied Korea and attempted to introduce their brands of Buddhism as part of their programme of domination. This aroused nationalistic feeling and spurred the Korean Buddhist community into action with the result that the Zen and doctrinal streams were eventually united into a unified Chogye order. This has maintained its pre-eminent position to the present time in South Korea, which was severed from the north by the Korean War (1945–53). North Korea is now of course a Communist state.

The modern revival traces its roots back to Kyongho Sunim

(1849–1912) who, after his major breakthrough at the age of 32, spent 20 years teaching in an orthodox manner and won widespread renown. His career adopted a more eccentric course during the last nine years of his life, however, when he returned to a secluded village, grew his hair long and adopted layman's dress. He had numerous disciples, notably Mangong Sunim (1871–1946), who was active during the 'dark age' of the Japanese occupation. In more recent times, Kusan Sunim (1909–83), a disciple of Hyobong Sunim (1888–1966), has attracted a certain amount of attention in the West. He established a centre for training Western students at his monastery, Songgwang Sa. Master Kusan also visited the USA and Europe and inaugurated Korean Zen temples there. Meanwhile, a few Korean Zen masters have moved permanently to the West, notably Seung Sahn Sunim (*aka* Soen Sạ Nim, 1927–), founder of the Providence Zen Center, and Samu Sunim (1941–) of the Zen Lotus Society, Toronto.

15 The Northern Transmission: Japan

The Early Period (538–1184)

Tradition has it that a political delegation arrived in Japan from Korea in the year 538. Among the gifts it brought for the Emperor were a bronze Buddha image, some *sūtras*, a few religious objects and a letter warmly praising the most excellent Dharma. Despite some initial reluctance, these gifts were accepted and a temple was duly built to house the image and accord it the appropriate respects. However, an epidemic of disease ravaged the land shortly afterwards, and this was interpreted as a sign that the indigenous deities (*kami*) were displeased at the veneration of a foreign deity. To appease them and secure remission of the plague, the Emperor ordered the new temple to be committed to the flames; the Buddharupa was meanwhile tossed into a canal.

But Buddhism was an unstoppable force. How could it be otherwise when the Buddha himself, so it was mooted, had predicted that it would 'spread to the East'? Despite the unpromising start, more scriptures and Sangha did reach Japan and, though some resistance still came from some of the conservative followers of Shintō, the native religious tradition, Buddhism began to take hold. Its success was mainly due to the fact that it won favour at court, where it was thought to possess occult powers capable, among other things, of protecting the state against disease and promoting social harmony. It was also flexible enough to be able to coexist with Shintō, eventually even to merge with it, and it moreover accorded the old *kami* an honourable place and purpose within its own pantheon.

Around the turn of the 7th century, steps began to be taken by the dominant clan towards organizing the country into a centralized state. The great empire of China provided a useful model, and Chinese culture and institutions began to be imported wholesale into Japan at this time. Chinese literary, artistic, architectural and technical forms were adopted, for example, and a governmental bureaucracy was set up on the lines of the Chinese pattern. The projected centralized state also needed a philosophical sub-structure to underpin it, and here Confucianism and Taoism had obvious advantages to offer. But most of all, Buddhism, which had been taken to a superlatively high pitch of development in T'ang dynasty China, enjoyed special favour at court. The Empress Suiko (reigned 592–628) was such a committed Buddhist that she retired to a nunnery shortly after her accession, and her nephew, the crown prince, Shōtoku (547–622), himself an enthusiastic Buddhist too, reigned as regent for more than 30 years, during which time the Buddhist cause was advanced considerably in the land.

The initial Korean connection having been largely superceded, increasing numbers of Japanese monastics and scholars now began to go to China to raid (in the nicest sense) its Buddhist riches. Initially six of the great Chinese schools were transplanted to Japanese soil in this early period and given Japanese names:

Japanese name	Chinese name	Indian name
Sanron	San-lun	Mādhyamika
Jōjitsu	Ch'êng-shih	Satyasiddhi
Hossō	Fa-hsiang	Yogācāra
Kusha	Chü-shê	Abhidharmakośa
Kegon	Hua-yen	Avatamsaka
Ritsu	Lü	Vinaya

The Ritsu school, which was imported into Japan in 754 by the Chinese monk Chien-chên, set procedures for the ordination of monks and nuns on a proper formal footing.

Buddhism tended to remain an élitist persuasion, however, and to be closely bound up with the offical state. The Emperor Shōmu (724–49), for instance, ordered state temples to be set up in every province and prayers for the peace and prosperity of the nation were to be offered in them. His capital of Nara meanwhile burgeoned into a splendid Buddhist capital replete with exquisite temples, sculpture and artefacts, created mainly at public expense and owing much to Chinese styles in art and architecture. The political power of the Sangha, many of whom were of the scholar-gentleman type, was considerable in Nara. Non-official and popular manifestations of Buddhism, on the other hand, tended to be frowned upon and were sometimes punished. Nevertheless so-called 'people's priests' did appear in the hinterland; they lived wandering and sometimes eremitical lives, dispensing popular religious services; a few of them won reputations for miraculous powers.

The Heian Period (794–1184)

The groundwork having been laid in the previous period, important changes and developments now began to take place that resulted in the emergence of a more characteristically Japanese form of Buddhism.

Firstly, the capital was shifted from Nara to other sites, eventually being fixed where Kyōto now stands. This effectively undermined the political power of the learned metropolitan Sangha (which it was fully intended to do) and thereafter the focus of Buddhism in Japan shifted from the political centre to the secluded mountain regions where the important new movements chose to establish their headquarters. The Tendai and Shingon Schools in particular came very much to the fore now, supplanting the other schools that had established themselves and laying the foundations for the future development of Buddhism in Japan. Esoteric ritualism became a particularly powerful force.

There was at the same time great rivalry between the various sects and, following the Chinese pattern, monasteries became centres of worldly wealth and power. Armies of so-called 'warrior monks' (sōhei) carried on internecine strife and even on occasion stormed the capital to assert their political will there. Buddhism nevertheless continued to enjoy court support, largely on account of its presumed occult powers, but more accessible forms of Buddhist belief and practice did begin to infiltrate other sections of society as well. Finally, Shintō and Buddhism managed to rise into a more or less harmonious unity that persisted until the 19th century.

The founding father of the Tendai School, the Japanese elaboration of the Chinese T'ien-t'ai, was Dengyō-daishi (or Saichō, 767–822), who established his headquarters at Mount Hiei, not far from the new capital – but not too near either. He had entered the Sangha at an early age and, after devoting himself to study and practice, eventually became especially partial to the teachings of the T'ien-t'ai School, which were based on the *Lotus Sūtra*. Dengyō enjoyed the favour of the Emperor Kammu who in 804 sent him to pursue his researches in China. He spent a few months on a 'wild scamper from monastery to monastery' (Arthur Waley), trying to pick up as much as he could of the different kinds of Chinese Buddhism – not only T'ien-t'ai.

Dengyō brought back many *sūtras* to Japan from China and an improved knowledge of various teachings and practices. Upon this basis he and his successors developed their school along lines that did not adhere inflexibly to the Chinese prototype; rather they enriched it with elements borrowed from Ch'an, Shingon, Pure Land and other forms of Buddhism; a modified Vinaya was also adopted. Dengyō continued to enjoy the favour of the emperor, but he largely succeeded in liberating his school from state interference and from the other schools. Dengyō's disciples further developed Tendai Buddhism and Mount Hiei eventually grew into one of the greatest monastic complexes of all time, with some 3000 temples and halls.

The founding father of the Shingon School, which burgeoned on the basis of Chinese Tantrism, on the other hand, was Kōbō-daishi (or Kūkai; 774–835), who occupies a particularly warm place in the hearts of the Japanese people. He was a man of many parts: scholar, ascetic, traveller, sculptor, calligrapher, educationalist, rainmaker. He too began his religious and philosophical studies young, became a monk at the age of 19 and was attracted to esoteric Buddhism. His chief textbooks became the *Mahāvairocana Sūtra* and the *Vajraśekhara Sūtra*. Though some seven years younger, he went to China in the same group as Dengyō-daishi and stayed until 806. He had the good fortune to study with Hui-kuo (known in Japan as Keika Ajari), who solved all his spiritual doubts and difficulties and also gave him formal transmission; therefore when Hui-kuo died, Kōbō-daishi became the Eighth Patriarch of the esoteric school.

Kôbô-daishi returned to Japan with many new skills and accomplishments to impart. He began his activities in Nara, the old capital, but later removed to the mountains and eventually founded his headquarters at Mount Kôya on the Kii peninsula –

Kôya is (or rather was) an almost inaccessible place compared to Hiei, but how many pilgrims congregated there every year! On the mountain a little town has come into existence.[34]

His career was a successful one and he too enjoyed imperial favour – to the extent that he was allowed to build a Shingon temple in the emperor's palace, where he performed esoteric rituals and ceremonies. He had a great reputation for occult powers, and was heaped with honours for his successful forays into the field of rainmaking. Shingon devotees do not believe him dead to this day but rather sitting in silent meditation behind the closed doors of his retreat at Mount Kôya.

Ritualistic Shingon practices were very influential during this period. Indeed no less an authority than Dr D.T. Suzuki unequivocally declared that 'the Buddhism of the Heian period was flooded with magic ritualism'.[35] Even the highly philosophical Tendai School adopted its own esoteric rituals, which perhaps helped make it more generally palatable.

Buddhism remained essentially an upper class preserve, however, as is palpably demonstrated by the aestheticism that grew around it. Gorgeous robes, sonorous chanting, dramatic rituals – these stimulated the eventual emergence of Nôh drama. Buddhism also influenced the arts of poetry, painting, sculpture and architecture. But the élitist tendency was also restrictive, for as Suzuki has declared: 'aristocracy is a one-eyed child; it sees the refined surface but lacks solidity and frequently sincerity. Real power must grow from life itself'[36]. In short, Buddhism had to reach the ordinary people.

A beginning was made in this direction during the latter stages of the Heian period. Certain teachers did begin to disseminate popular devotional forms of Buddhism, principally derived from the Pure Land cult of Amitâbha (*Amida* in Japan). These devotional cults propounded the notion that salvation was possible through the intercession of benign buddhas and *bodhisattvas*. This could be obtained by the repetition of a simple formula such as *Namu-Amida-butsu* (the *Nembutsu*). In this way, the minefields of philosophy and ascetic practice, both of which required special talents and conditions, were effectively bypassed and absolute faith was placed in 'other power': a redeeming action originating from beyond the self.

Two figures are especially important in the popularization of Amidism at this time: Kūya Shōnin (902–72) and Ryōnin (1072–1132). Kūya, who was also known as the Market Sage, quit the rarefied atmosphere of mountain retreat and lacquered temple to take Buddhism among the masses. He lived a peripatetic life and, in addition to his specifically spiritual efforts, was also involved in social welfare and good works. Ryōnin, on the other hand, brought Kegon (Avatamsaka) philosophy, with its central notion of universal interpretation, to Amidism. This in turn influenced the Tendai School.

The Kamakura Period (1185–1333)

This was a period of crisis, when Japan was both threatened from without and ravaged by internal disunity and violent change. In particular, power was wrested from the hands of the effete imperial aristocracy by the *samurai* or warrior class, and a *Shōgunate* (military governorship) was in 1185 established at Kamakura, well away from Kyōto, the capital, by the dominant Minamoto clan. This new climate did not favour the study of abstruse philosophy and the performance of elaborate rituals; rather, more robust and generally accessible teachings and practices became the order of the day. Consequently, the fortunes of the Tendai and Shingon Schools declined and more earthy, democratic movements advanced, notably the devotional schools and Zen; lay Buddhism also began to come into its own and the spiritual potential of women was recognized. Ultimately, for all its stresses, this was the most highly creative time for Japanese Buddhism – its golden age, no less.

The devotional cults in particular brought Buddhism within reach of the ordinary man and woman. In particular, two major Pure Land schools came to the fore: the *Jōdo-shū* ('Pure Land School') and the *Jōdo Shinshū* ('The True Pure Land School').

The seminal proponent of the Shin sub-school was Hōnen
Shōnin (1133–1212), who believed that the present state of the
world was so dark that few could practise the traditional
methods effectively; he therefore advocated as an alternative
'easy path' sincere faith in the beneficence of Amida coupled
with recitation of the *Nembutsu*.

This highly pared-down formula was taken to an ultimate of
economy by Hōnen's follower, Shinran Shōnin (1173–1262),
the founding father of the Jōdo Shinshū, who believed that there
still remained a vestige of self-power in the Shin doctrine. In his
view, the degenerate state of the age was such that the devotee
should forsake all hope that he could achieve anything
whatsoever himself, even by repeating the *Nembutsu*, and
should place his fate utterly in the hands of Amida. A dangerous
corollary to this was that morality was ineffectual; indeed sinful
people, if they fully acknowledged their hopelessness and
appealed wholeheartedly to Amida, might be more in line for
salvation than those who attempted to live ethically.
Ordination into the Sangha was likewise a vain step and
Shinran himself, though a monk initially, married and had
children, thus encouraging lay practice by his example. Shinran
was particularly active teaching among the common folk.

A highly controversial figure, on the other hand, was
Nichiren Shōnin (1222–82), who has attracted a bad press on
account of his apparently un-Buddhistic disposition. He in
many ways typifies a type often to be found in Buddhism:
active, energetic, passionate, even obsessive, and highly
aggressive – the sort of person who is drawn to the teaching of
the Buddha not so much because he exemplifies its gentle virtues
and peaceful ideals but, on the contrary, because, whether he
consciously knows it or not, he needs the gentling influence of
Buddhist practice to cool his hot nature. Still, the Dharma has
its uses for such people – and indeed Nichiren saw himself as the
manifestation of bodhisattvic energies vital to the times. The
son of a lowly fisherman, he trained in the Tendai School and
came to the conclusion that the *Lotus Sūtra* was the key to
salvation in the prevailing dark age. He did not advocate that
the *sūtra* be read and reflected upon, however, but argued that
the whole of its teaching was encapsulated in the title; therefore
all that was necessary by way of practice was to repeat the

formula *Namu-myōhō-renge-kyō* which could be roughly translated as 'Homage to *The Lotus Sutra*'. This would definitely not ensure rebirth in some kind of paradise; it would evoke the Enlightenment of Shakyamuni Buddha *here* and *now*. His creed was thus a trenchantly this-wordly one. It was moreover aggressively nationalistic, the more so as Nichiren was highly apprehensive of a Mongol invasion of Japan.

Unfortunately, Nichiren did not merely think the other schools completely incapable of saving Japan and the world from impending apocalypse; he considered them downright disastrous and pugnaciously demanded that the state suppress them and rally exclusively behind his own cause. This produced the inevitable counter-reaction and he was himself persecuted quite viciously – but that merely served to reinforce his conviction of his own rightness and galvanize his sense of mission. Although his school has been stigmatized as being the very antithesis of Buddhism (by Edward Conze and John Stevens), it did not finally end up in the graveyard of discarded cults and defunct fads but has survived as a powerful force in Japanese Buddhism to the present time.

Arguably more important than the development of popular devotional forms of Buddhism was the rise of the Zen School at this time. This placed supreme emphasis on self-power: on the active mobilization of all one's energies towards the realization of the ideal of Enlightenment. In its more austere forms, Zen also had no time for excrescences (like rituals or philosophical study) and embellishments but took a no-nonsense, down-to-earth stance. For all these reasons it found favour with the *samurai* class whose fortunes were now in the ascendent and whose members, men who lived constantly under the shadow of death, needed a spiritual way that would not merely reconcile them with their lot in life but make it an authentic path of spiritual development. Zen philosophy and training (especially that of the Rinzai branch) fulfilled their requirements admirably. It equipped the *samurai* to face death with equanimity, while its invocation of a mode of action originating beyond thought, and manifesting spontaneously and in perfect harmony with the spirit of the moment, could be applied with effect to military practices – swordsmanship, archery, wrestling, etc. – thereby transforming them into authentic martial arts. Thus in an actual combat situation, the Zen-trained swordsman could bypass concern for personal safety and intellectual planning, both of which could be crippling, and make his moves freely, guided by this mysterious power. On the other hand, the military ethos, with its tough dedication to training and discipline, itself contributed much to Japanese Zen. All of which might suggest that Japanese Zen lacked an aesthetic side. Not so. The Zen virtues of spontaneity, simplicity, tranquillity and alone-ness inspired the emergence of a very distinctive aesthetic. This is exemplified in the so-called Zen arts of calligraphy, ink painting, *haiku* poetry, pottery and flower arrangement (*ikebāna*); also in house and garden design and the tea ceremony (*cha-no yu*).

The two major surviving branches of the Chinese Ch'an School, the Lin-chi and the Ts'ao-tung, known in Japan as the Rinzai and Sōtō respectively, were introduced during the Kamakura period. Traditionally the Rinzai line is said to have been transmitted by Eisai (1141–1215) and the Sōtō by Dōgen (1200–1253). Both branches place primary emphasis on sitting meditation (*zazen*). There is a slight difference of attitude, however, summed up in the maxim, 'Rinzai is for the general, Sōtō for the farmer'. In other words, Rinzai is the more purposeful and militant. In addition to *zazen* practice, it employs the use of *kōan*: apparently illogical questions, concerted application to which will (hopefully) precipitate the practitioner beyond normal thinking processes. The Sōtō disposition, on the other hand, is less goal-orientated. Just to sit in *zazen* is to be in the Enlightened state; there is nothing more to be achieved, nowhere else to go.

Originally a Tendai monk, Eisai paid two short visits to China (1168 and 1187–91). On the first visit, an interest in Zen was awakened; the purpose of his second visit was to deepen his understanding of it. On his return to his homeland in 1191, he attempted to propagate Rinzai Zen in Kyōto but ran into opposition from the Tendai fraternity. He escaped to the martial atmosphere of Kamakura, where he was better received and where he established his first temple, Shōfukūji, in 1215. He later returned to Kyōto but had to compromise and, when he did eventually build a temple there, Kennin-ji, it was not exclusively a Zen centre of activities. Nevertheless, Eisai laid a basis upon which Daiō Kukushi (1235-1308 - not to be confused with his pupil Daitō) and other Japanese and Chinese Rinzai Zen masters could build. The Japanese masters tended to gravitate to the imperial capital, Kyōto, and were often active in worldly affairs; the Chinese masters, on the other hand, tended to find patronage under the military authorities at Kamakura. Prominent among the Chinese were Daikaku (1203-68) and Bukkō (1226-?), the founders of Kenchō-ji and Engaku-ji respectively, who evolved an 'on-the-instant' 'warrior Zen' adapted to the needs of the denizens of Kamakura. They improvised *kōan* out of the actual life-and-death situations in which their students were caught up.

Dōgen (1200-53), the seminal master of the Japanese Sōtō Zen School, came from an aristocratic background but lost his parents at an early age, a traumatic experience that forcefully impressed upon his mind the transitoriness of the things of this world. Intellectually brilliant from childhood, he entered the Sangha at the age of 13 and initially trained in the Tendai School. Unresolved questions drove him elsewhere, however, and he eventually gravitated to the Zen School. He spent four formative years studying in China under Master Ju-ching (1163-1228), the Abbot of T'ien-t'ung monastery. Then in 1227, having had his Enlightenment confirmed by his master, Dōgen returned to Japan, intending to propagate Sōtō Zen there but in Kyōto he also came under pressure from the devotees of the older schools. More doggedly independent than Eisai, he refused to compromise and eventually established a temple, Eihei-ji, in a remote province. This remains one of the two main temples of the Japanese Sōtō Zen School to this day (the other is Sōji-ji, founded by Keizan). Like the Pure Land masters, Dōgen was convinced of the degenerate nature of his times but nevertheless felt that it was necessary to struggle for the truth. He himself avoided honours and all the other worldly pitfalls to which so many of his contemporary monks had fallen victim. He did, however, believe that the state should be based on the ideas of Zen Buddhism and probably tried to impress that view upon the pious Emperor Gosaga.

Dōgen earnestly enjoined his own followers to forsake the pursuit of fame and fortune and, remaining ever keenly aware of death and the general unpredictability of things, to wholeheartedly apply themselves to the practice of sitting Zen. He was less averse to scriptural study than his Rinzai counterparts and in fact left various influential writings behind, notably his classic *Shōbōgenzō* ('Eye and Treasury of the True Dhama'), in which he wrote the following lines in characteristically terse and direct style:

> To study the way is to study the self. To study the self is to forget the self. To forget the self is to be enlightened by all things. To be enlightened by all things is to remove the barriers between one's self and others.[37]

At the age of 52, Dōgen became ill and died soon after arriving in Kyōto for medical treatment.

The monks involved in the transmission of Zen to Japan from China also transmitted neo-Confucian values and ideas. These found favour with the Kamakura authorities, whose military code of honour (*bushidō*) elevated loyalty to one's clan lord to the status of a high virtue. Chinese arts and sciences were also brought over in a similar way. Eisai, moreover, is credited with having introduced tea into Japan from China.

Ashikaga (or Muromachi) Period (1336–1573)

The demise of the Kamakura régime amid fighting and bloodshed inaugurated a new era of internal strife and instability that broadly lasted until the establishment of the Tokugawa Shōgunate (Shōgun = military ruler) in 1603. More and more power was wrested from the hands of the central government by provincial warlords. At the same time it was a period of economic growth that saw increased rural prosperity, the emergence of a merchant class and – something hitherto unseen in Japan – the blossoming of an urban culture.

But for Japanese Buddhism the truly creative phase was over. A slide into stagnation or 'long narcosis' (Suzuki) now began that was to broadly last until the end of the 19th century. According to Dr Suzuki, all the latent potential seemed to have been realized during the Kamakura period with the result that 'what followed was more or less the filling-in and working out of details'.[38]

Of the various Buddhist schools, the Rinzai Zen School fared best, especially during the 14th and 15th centuries, largely due to the favour it enjoyed with the military rulers. Much patronage was heaped upon it, with the result that many fine temples were built, replete with fine works of art, lavishly endowed and commanding large estates. In Kyōto the so-called 'Five Mountains' – five splendid temple complexes – came into being and here the arts or 'ways' (dō) of Japanese Zen Buddhist culture were developed to a high pitch of aesthetic excellence. In the strictly religious sphere, however, there was only increasing hierarchical institutionalization and formalization, but no doctrinal or methodological development.

During this period, all Buddhist schools increasingly sought followers among the ordinary folk. Provincial temples and local organizations were set up; peripatetic priests were also a feature of the times, like Zen Master Ikkyū (1394–1481), putatively sired by the Emperor Gokomatsu, who wandered extensively, mingling with all classes and practising a somewhat iconoclastic lifestyle which embraced many of the pleasures of the flesh. He was, on the other hand, strongly critical of the stuffy hypocrisy of those decadent monks who scrupulously observed the superficial outward forms but neglected inner practice. Ironically, by order of the Emperor, Ikkyū spent the last years of his long life in the highly respectable role of Abbot of the venerable Daitoku-ji monastery in Kyōto.

Towards the end of this period, which closed with a century of civil strife in which the important Buddhist schools took an active part, the first Japanese encounters with Christian missionaries took place.

The Azuchi-Momoyama and Edo Periods (1573–1868)

Ironically – and sadly – in order for Japan to be reunited and pacified, the political and military might of the Buddhist strongholds had to be broken. This task was vigorously undertaken by a ruthless and vengeful warlord named Oda Nubunaga (1534–1582), who was prepared to stop at nothing in order 'to bring the whole country under one sword'. He violently subdued the Kyōto region and broke the control that the Jōdō-Shinshū school exercised over the vital commercial port of Osaka. But his most devastating act was to destroy the Tendai centre in Mount Hiei with its 3000 temples, and slaughter most of its 20,000 inhabitants.

Nobunaga's reign was short-lived but his work was carried on by his less vengeful but no less ambitious protégé Toyotomi Hideyoshi (1536–1598) and finally brought to fulfilment by Hideyoshi's successor Tokugawa Ieyasu (1542–1616), who in 1603 established the Tokugawa Shōgunate which ruled Japan from its bastion at Edo (modern Tōkyō) for two and a half centuries – the longest period of peace and, for the most part, prosperity in the history of the country. This was achieved by closing the country to the outside world and establishing internally a régime of inflexible authoritarian control that created stability and order – but at the price of effectively stifling all creative change and innovation.

In the religious sphere, neo-Confucianism, which had been transmitted to Japan from China by Rinzai Zen monks, now became the offical creed for the simple reason that it promoted those feudal virtues that the new régime wished to inculcate into the subject masses. Buddhism, on the other hand, while not persecuted, was brought under strict state control. The state even interfered in matters of doctrine, invariably coming down on the side of orthodoxy. New teachings and practices were prohibited, nor was it permissible to found a new school or temple. Meanwhile existing major temples and sub-temples were classified according to tradition and all Japanese, regardless of whether they were Buddhist or not, were obliged to register at one of them, though more for demographic than for religious purposes. In the prevailing climate of peace and prosperity Buddhism benefitted materially – but spiritually the ongoing process of stagnation that had been inaugurated at the demise of the Kamakura régime was generally consolidated.

The closure of Japan to the outside world also meant that no new stimuli to fresh development were able to infiltrate the country from other Buddhist countries. The one exception was the arrival of Obaku Zen from China via the open port of Nagasaki in 1654. It was brought by Yin-yüan (1592–1673), a Chinese Rinzai Zen Master known in Japan as Ingen. While the Rinzai school had continued along traditional lines in Japan, in

China it had been modified. Most conspicuously it was prepared to make concessions to those not able to rise to the full rigours of the pure unalloyed Zen training. So it had adopted devotional practices from Pure Land and sanctioned *sūtra* study as a valid form of spiritual endeavour. While Yin-yüan came in the first place as a reformer of Rinzai Zen, he met with resistance and was ultimately obliged to found a separate school – but one which became very successful. He also introduced cultural innovations from Ming China: new styles of ritual, architecture, clothing and so forth.

Some of the devotional cults were viewed with disfavour by the new régime and were forced underground. Otherwise, as before, the Zen School survived best during this period and a few influential figures did emerge, notably the poet Bashō and the Rinzai Zen Masters Bankei and Hakuin, the latter being the most important.

Bankei Yōtaku (1622–93) was something of an iconoclast who challenged orthodox Zen teaching. He himself spent many years intensively pursuing Enlightenment. Then at last he realized that he had been in possession of what he had been seeking all along and decided that the term *the Un-born* best described it. This of course directly echoed the Buddha's pronouncement that there had to be an Unborn, Not-become, Not-made, Not-compounded for there to be release from what is born, become, made and compounded. At the same time Bankei concluded that all the sweat and tears of his years of searching had been so much waste of time. Consequently he advocated a simple formula, 'Awaken to the Un-born in the midst of everyday affairs', as an alternative to the long-drawn-out formal rigours of conventional Zen training. Obviously this was not designed to go down well with the Zen establishment, but Bankei had charisma and was able to attract a huge following, notably among the ordinary people. Imperial recognition eventually came but the school that he established did not survive for long after his death.

Matsuo Bashō (1644–94), on the other hand, was not a Zen monk but a poet who consciously transformed the practice of poetry into an authentic religious way. By nature prone to wanderlust, he loved the life of the open road that led him to where he could commune with unspoiled nature. From these lonely wanderings came his poems. His preference was for the highly economical 17-syllable *haiku* form, which he took to unparalleled heights of poetic subtlety. Many of his finest *haiku* are thought to succinctly catch the elusive, often melancholy magic of the passing moment and thereby express the true spirit of Zen.

Finally, Hakuin Zenji (1685–1768) not only reformed Rinzai Zen and restored the *kōan* system but laid the foundation for the future development of the whole Zen School down to present time. Consequently he is placed in the first rank of Japanese Zen luminaries, alongside Dōgen Zenji. He was also a notable painter, calligrapher and poet in the Zen manner.

Initially it was intense fear of Hellfire that drove the impressionable young Hakuin into the Buddhist Sangha at the age of 15. His doubts and fears were not allayed, however, and he considered quitting Buddhism in favour of poetry, for which he had a certain talent. Unclear as to what to do, he decided to consign his fate to chance. One day he opened a book that had been brought out to be aired. It happened to be a Zen text – and it inspired him to undertake intensive *zazen* practice. This led to his first break-through, which he believed to be the most significant in centuries. His pride in his achievement was unsentimentally smashed, however, when he subsequently came under the hammer of an exceedingly hard Master. Then after grappling with the *kōan Mu* for three years, he experienced another illumination after being hit on the head while out on alms round. 'You are through,' his Master told him.

Soon afterwards he was struck by a 'Zen sickness' as a result of his extreme spiritual exertions. Fortunately he was able to cure himself with the meditative practice for reviving the spirit-energy described in his text, *Yasenkanna*.[39] Afterwards he again applied himself intensively to meditation and *sūtra* study. He eventually returned to his run-down home temple of Shōin-ji in Hara (Shizuoka prefecture), where one night his mother appeared to him in a dream bearing a robe in which were concealed two mirrors, one bright, the other dull. Suddenly, however, the dull one blazed with a light a million times more bright than the other. Then Hakuin saw that to look at anything was to see his own face and that it is the Buddha-eye that beholds the Buddha-nature. An even more profound insight followed, hinged around a problem arising from the *Lotus Sūtra* and occasioned by his hearing the chirping of a cricket, but utterly devoid of any drama. Then he at last recognized the incompleteness of his earlier enlightenments, great and small and, weeping, declared: 'The practice of Zen is not easy!'

Hakuin lived to the advanced age of 84 and as his fame grew increasing numbers of disciples were attracted to him, with the result that rural Shōin-ji became the most influential centre of Zen of the period. Nor did he lack the common touch but was greatly concerned to help ordinary people;[40] he also left many influential writings, notably his *Orategama*. In his teaching he emphasized intensive *kōan* practice. He himself invented the famous *kōan* of 'The Sound of One Hand Clapping'. He also placed great importance on the generation of the so-called Great Doubt and on the Great Death, his term for the death of the 'I' or ego, beside which natural death is indeed trivial.

From the Meiji Restoration to the Present Time (1868–date)

As the 19th century progressed, it became increasingly clear that the hermetic feudal order established and maintained by the Tokugawa Shōgunate was both outmoded and redundant. As the outside world pressed Japan to reopen her doors, internal dissent grew; finally a coup d'état restored the imperial régime in 1868 and the modernization process began apace.

Ardent nationalism now asserted itself. The new order elevated the Meiji Emperor to the status of a god while Shintō, detatched from Buddhism, was made a state cult. At the same time Buddhism, a foreign religion, was subordinated and subjected to persecution. Estates and endowments were seized and Sangha evicted from temples, which were then either closed or destroyed. Buddhism had, however, established itself too deeply in the affections of the Japanese people for this policy to be sustained, so after a short while it was abandoned and religious freedom was promised.

The various pressures that were brought to bear upon Japanese Buddhism at this time – to which the advent of energetic missionary Christianity was later added – in the long run had the beneficial effect of snapping it out of its 'long narcosis' and spurring new development. For the first time in centuries contacts with other Buddhist countries, and indeed with Western ones as well, were made. This encouraged Buddhist scholarship, and various Buddhist universities – Ohtani, Ryukoku, Komazawa, etc. – were established in the first part of the present century. Much useful Buddhological work was undertaken and continues. Critical editions of Pali, Sanskrit, Chinese and Tibetan texts have been produced, translations made and in-depth studies carried out. Pioneers in this field include B. Nanjio and K. Kasahara, who studied Sanskrit under Max Müller, and J. Takakusu. In Nishida Kitarō, meanwhile, Japan produced a philosopher of world rank.

The influence of Nichiren played an important part in the militaristic nationalism that developed in the 1920s and 1930s. This caused devastation in Manchuria and Korea and led directly to Japanese entry into World War II. Nichiren devotees were also involved in political assassinations during the immediate pre-War period.

Nearly all the Buddhist schools, except for example the lay Nichiren movement, Soka Gakkai, acquiesced in the Japanese involvement in World War II. The *götterdämmerung* of 1945 left the country spiritually devastated, but since then it has of course rallied remarkably and, pouring all its energies into development along Western technological lines, has outstripped all its rivals to emerge as an economic power of the first rank.

A significant feature of the post-World War II period had been the enormous success of the so-called New Religions, which in fact represent new orchestrations of traditional themes. Prominent among the Buddhist New Religions are Risshō Kōsei-kai, and Sōka Gakkai (motto: 'Promotion of peace, culture and education through Buddhism'), both of which take their basic inspiration from Nichiren and the *Lotus Sūtra*, though in keeping with the climate of the times they tend to talk vociferously of 'peace'. Lay-oriented, they have recruited mass followings running into millions from among ordinary people, to whom they offer practical support, help with personal problems and a sense of meaning. Both stress this worldly-success and social involvement. Sōka Gakkai, the largest of the New Religions, has strong political connections.

In contemporary Japan, the traditional Buddhist schools,

which co-exist alongside the New Religions, have also tried to widen the scope of their appeal and generally regenerate themselves to meet the challenge of the modern world. As we have already noted, however, loyalty to a single religion is not a feature of Japanese religious life; but that life is undeniably rich and diverse – and Buddhism certainly continues to play a very significant part in it.

Japan has also played a large part in the transmission of Buddhism to the West. Japanese *rōshis* showed an interest in building bridges to the United States as early as the latter part of the 19th century. Some Zen has also been transmitted to Europe, as have the devotional schools of Jōdo and Jōdo Shin, while some of the Nichiren sects have attracted mass followings.

Bodhidharma, after Hakuin Zenji.

GURU RINPOCHE (PADMASAMBHAVA) drawn by Robert Beer

16   The Northern Transmission: Tibet

Situated mainly on a vast plateau in Central Asia at altitudes of 13,000 feet and more, Tibet – the 'Land of Snows' – is curtained on many sides by formidable mountain ranges, like the Himalayas and the Kun-Lun. In this naturally secluded situation a unique culture once flourished: one in which Buddhism, as the dominant factor, was harmoniously integrated into every aspect of life. Sadly, since 1959 that culture has been systematically destroyed by the Chinese Communists, who have taken over the country and sought to forcibly impose their own Marxist ideology upon it. Nowadays there are signs of a change of heart and a certain level of Buddhist observance is again permitted in the so-called 'Tibet Autonomous Region', but irreparable damage has nevertheless been done.

Although fertile valleys watered by great rivers do occur in Tibet, the country is largely arid, barren and sparsely populated. Nevertheless, travellers are almost unanimously agreed in finding the primaeval landscape compellingly beautiful, specially as the rarefied atmosphere allows colours to reach the eye with primary intensity and distant objects appear close. In such a setting, all kinds of strange, mystical and magical things – the stuff of Tibetan Buddhism itself – become believable.

The First Transmission (c. 640–838)

It seems that originally the Tibetans were a primitive, largely nomadic and pugnacious people whose warlike activities caused more than a few headaches for their neighbours. As their power and organization grew, they were able, for instance, to launch campaigns in China itself and on one occasion captured the capital, Sian. Spiritually they inclined to animism and other primitive magical beliefs and practices. A species of priest existed among them called *bön-po*, who are usually described as *shamans* though more specifically the name implies that they recited *mantras* which could be used for exorcism, invoking powerful spirits and so forth. The *bön-po* may also have been concerned with the death rituals of the early kings. In time, as we shall see, Bön was to emerge as an independent religious cult in its own right, deeply influenced by Buddhism but emphatically separate from it.

On the face of it, this does not look like very fertile ground for the lofty teachings of the Buddha – and indeed, the earliest attempts at propagating those teachings in Tibet in their more prosaic forms do not seem to have been overly successful. Tradition has it that it was only with the arrival of the tantric adept Padmasambhava (or Guru Rinpoche) towards the end of the 8th century AD that success was ensured. He alone possessed the occult know-how necessary to subdue the demonaic forces inimical to the transmission of Buddhism. He could counter magic with magic – and emerge victorious. One of his particular feats was to conquer the spirits that hitherto had been frustrating the building of Samyé (completed 787 AD), the first Buddhist monastery of Tibet.

It should be noted in passing that the old demons and spirits were not annihilated, as they would have been in the West, with all the grim paraphenalia of witch-hunts and inquisitions; rather they were obliged to submit to the Dharma. Thereafter they continued to play a tolerated if subordinate role as 'Dharma protectors'. Psychospiritually, this could be seen as the assimilation of the magical – mythical in the collective Tibetan psyche, whereas in the West it was ruthlessly repressed.

His seminal exploits won for Padmasambhava a deep and lasting place in the affections of the Tibetans. As regards his life, however, it is hard to disentangle truth from myth, and there have inevitably been those scholars who have questioned whether he visited Tibet at all, although innumerable sites in Tibet and the Himalayan region are mythically associated with him.

By the time of Padmasambhava, Buddhism had of course been flourishing in India for over a millennium. It had also been transmitted throughout south-east Asia and northwards, bypassing Tibet, to China, Korea and Japan. It is indeed strange that Tibet remained outside the Buddhist fold for so long, though the reasons for this are not hard to find. Once it did take root, however, those roots were to run exceedingly deep and to transform every aspect of Tibetan life. Commentators have often reflected upon the curious enigma that, once adopted – and then against all the apparent odds – Buddhism became for the Tibetan people the one pearl of great price for which they were ready to sacrifice almost anything.

The transmission of Buddhism to Tibet divides into two distinct phases. The first took place during the era of the so-called Three Great Religious (i.e. Buddhist) Kings: Songtsen Gampo (c. 609–649), Trisong Detsen (704–797) and Ralpachen (805–38).

Now, according to Tibetan hagiography, Songtsen Gampo was an incarnation of Avalokiteshvara, the Bodhisattva of Compassion, who in Tibet is known as Chenrezi. He took two wives, one Chinese, the other Nepalese; and these were not only Buddhists but incarnations of Tara (Tib. Drölma), Avalokiteshvara's consort. Thus the ideal *dramatis personae* was fortuitously assembled for the enactment of the great drama of the establishment of Buddhism as the state religion of Tibet. To do so, however, the resistance of the *bön-po* who exerted powerful influence among the nobility, had to be first overcome. Also the linguistic apparatus for the translation of Buddhist texts into Tibetan had to be set up. As Tibet had hitherto not developed a system of writing, one of Songtsen Gampo's ministers, Thönmi Sambhota, was dispatched to India. He subsequently evolved an alaphabet based on Sanskrit models and composed treatises on grammar. The rambling and magnificent Jokhang, the premier temple in Tibet, often called the 'Cathedral of Lhasa', also dates from Songtsen Gampo's reign.

Discarding the testimony of tradition, some modern scholars have doubted, not merely that Songtsen Gampo was a *bodhisattva*, but that he was a serious Buddhist at all. They credit him with the foundation of Tibetan power and see his importance – and his interest in Buddhism – as primarily political. It has also been disputed that pre-Buddhist Tibet was as benighted as is usually made out. Professor Namkhai Norbu, for instance, has argued that the early Tibetans possessed forms of writing and other cultural assets; also that *bön-po* sages were initiated into advanced spiritual teachings of the kind presently transmitted as *Dzogchen* (lit. *Great Perfection*).

All are agreed, however, that King Trisong Detsen was considerably more important than Songtsen Gampo. It was he who invited to Tibet the Indian master Shāntarakshita, who in turn inaugurated the building of Samyé, though as we have seen he ran into trouble and eventually had to be assisted by Padmasambhava. Other monasteries and temples were also established during Trisong Detsen's reign, and monks were favoured with royal patronage. Influential for the future too was the Great Debate held at Samyé between 792 and 794 under the sponsorship of the King himself. In this the Indian *pandit* Kamalashila defended his conventional Indian brand of gradualistic, ethically-orientated Buddhism against one Hva-shang Mahāyāna, a representative of the Chinese Ch'an (Zen) school of sudden enlightenment. According to Tibetan accounts, the verdict went in favour of the Indian party and the Chinese departed. Thereafter Tibet took its Buddhism exclusively from India, though some residual Chinese influence did remain – in Dzogchen, for instance.

The flow of Buddhist wisdom, tangibly represented by a two-way traffic of monks and masters passing between Tibet and India, continued as the period progressed. Meanwhile, the work of translating Indian texts went on apace – and indeed the Tibetans are credited with having achieved great clarity and exactness in their renderings. Teams including both Tibetan and Indian scholars were employed and a very precise system of equivalents for Sanskrit technical terms was worked out. During the reign of Ralpachen, the last of the Great Religious Kings, the translations hitherto made were revised and reworked.

The Dark Age (838–c. 1000)

Ralpachen was certainly a pious king – but he was also a weak one. He appears to have been content to leave affairs of state in the hands of chosen monks. Court intrigue eventually resulted in his murder along with that of his chief minister; then his brother, Langdarma, ascended the throne.

Langdarma's name is one that lives in infamy in the annals of Tibetan Buddhism, for he instigated a vicious repression of the Dharma that effectively terminated its first transmission. His reign was brief, only from 838 to 842, for he was himself soon murdered by a vengeful Buddhist monk. Langdarma's brief reign of terror ushered in a spiritual dark age that was to last until about the year 1000 AD.

This 150-year dark age is a period about which little is known. Centralized power was broken and Tibet disintegrated politically. Buddhism did not entirely die out, however; it continued to exist underground and among isolated hermits and communities. But the controlling influence of the Buddhist hierarchy and the monasteries was absent and, according to some accounts, this led to deviation from orthodoxy, in particular abuse of tantric practice.

The Second Transmission (c. 1000–1959)

According to tradition, an area of great importance in the second wave of transmission was western Tibet (Ngari Khorsum). Latterly this has been a remote and inhospitable wasteland, the domain of hardy nomads and freebooters. 1000 years ago, however, a number of prosperous independent kingdoms existed there, notably Gu-gé in the upper Sutlej valley, with its twin cities of Tsaparang and Thöling; also Purang, just south of the sacred lake Manasarovar. Though far from Lhasa and the Central Provinces, these kingdoms were well-placed to receive a fresh influx of teachers and teachings from India, Kashmir and the north-west.

Notable among these agents of regeneration was Rinchen Zangpo (958–1055), a great Tibetan *lotsava* (translator) and builder of temples, who made three trips to India and spent in all some 17 years there, studying, practising and collecting texts. Another was the Indian master Atisha (982–1054), a teacher at the great monastic university of Vikramashilā, who was persuaded to bring the precious Dharma across the formidable

Himalayan mountain barrier; as a token of their gratitude, the Tibetans heaped him with rich offerings – a king's ransom in gold, the story goes – which he donated to his old university. Atisha arrived in western Tibet in 1042 and later went on to the Central Provinces, finally settling at Netang, where he died.

Meanwhile, Buddhism was similarly being restored in eastern Tibet, where a Nepalese master named Smrti was active; and in the Central Provinces, from where Tibetan spiritual travellers like Drogmi (992–1072) and Marpa (1012–96) ventured down to the plains of India. The former, who received generous aristocratic sponsorship, spent many years studying with a tantric master named Shantipa at Vikramashilā. Marpa on the other hand, a less well-funded aspirant, served his spiritual apprenticeship mainly at the feet of a 'great adept' (*Mahāsiddha*) named Naropa (1016–1100) at his hermitage in Bihar.

Once the second transmission got fully under way, new monasteries were built and old ones were restored. Organizational and spiritual development then proceeded, with the result that a number of distinctive schools emerged, each favouring particular teachings or texts, tracing a lineage back to seminal masters, and having its own particular style and emphasis. With organization and development came cultural (as opposed to strictly spiritual) activity, wealth and worldly power. In time, Buddism came to dominate the political life of Tibet, and there evolved that distinctive theocratic, or more accurately, *buddhocratic* style of government that we have already noted.

Once Buddhism had been all but expunged in the land of its origin, the doors were closed to outside influence and the great plateau of Tibet became a time capsule in which the Mahāyāna Buddhism of mediaeval India was reverently preserved by diligent guardians. The teachings were laboriously analysed, systematized and codified in terms of graduated stages leading towards an ultimate goal of Enlightenment. By the 14th century a complete Buddhist canon in Tibetan had been standardized. This achievement, which was masterminded by a scholar named Butön, may be classed as an intellectual achievement of world rank. It divides into two parts:

1. The *Kangyur*, comprising the teachings (*sūtra*). 108 volumes.

2. The *Tengyur*, comprising the commentaries (*shastra*). 225 volumes.

The *Kangyur* was printed in Peking in 1410. Various other printings of these massive compilations, together comprising over 4500 works, were later produced.

The Tibetans also produced over the centuries a vast Buddhist literature of their own, including commentaries, histories, verses, biographies of great masters and so forth. This was not, however, creative or innovatory in the main but essentially exegetical. In Tibet, self-expression was always subjugated to the higher authority of tradition and the received word.

The principal schools of Tibetan Buddhism

The Kadam (lit. 'Bound by Command') School

This school traced its lineage back to Atisha, who had stressed the need to establish a solid basis of monastic discipline and guru devotion before undertaking the adventure of tantric practice. As the Dalai Lama has written:

> Their trademark was this synthesis of various vehicles (*yānas*), as expressed by their saying, 'The external practice is moral discipline (i.e. Hinayāna); the inner practice is the bodhi-mind (i.e. Mahāyāna); and, practised in secret, is the secret *mantra* (i.e. Vajrayāna).' In the Kadampa Order, these three were taken as interconnected, intersupportive aspects of training.[41]

Atisha's disciple, Dromtön (1008–64), who founded the monastery of Reting in 1056 and who shaped the school, seems to have been of a particularly reclusive and puritanical disposition. Kadampas were required to submit to four strict laws which demanded strict celibacy and abstension from intoxicants while at the same time prohibiting travel and the handling of money. Such an austere régime does not seem to have held much appeal for the Tibetans and the school did not survive long as an independent entity.

The Sakya School

This school was named after its principal monastery, situated to the west of Shigatse in southern Tibet, which was founded in 1073 by Konchog Gyalpo (1034–1102), a disciple of Drogmi. The latter translated one of the basic texts of the school, the *Hevajra Tantra*, and therefore ranks as one of its founding fathers. Another teaching favoured by the Sakyapa is 'The Way and its Fruit' (*Lam-dre*) by the 9th century Indian adept Virūpa, which integrates the teachings of *sūtra* and *tantra* into a course of training designed to induce Enlightenment in a single lifetime.

The school was subsequently developed by five great masters and was the first to rise to political power. This happened in the 13th century, during the period of the Mongol overlordship of Tibet, when Godan Khan made Sakya Pandita, the foremost lama of the day, his Viceregent in Tibet. The honour subsequently passed to Sakya Pandita's nephew, Pagpa, and his successors. The Mongols also held sway in China at this time, and the special priest – patron relationship that they established with the Tibetans was to form the basis of subsequent Chinese claims to hegemony over Tibet. The almost kingly status of the Sakyapa patriarchs was eclipsed when Mongol power declined in the 14th century. A little later the Sakya school itself subdivided into its Ngor and Tsar branches.

The succession of the heads of the school, who bear the title *Sakya Trizin*, is also distinctive. It is basically hereditory, but does not pass directly from father to son, rather obliquely from uncle to nephew across a bifurcated family line. The present *Sakya Trizin*, the 41st (born 1945), currently lives in exile. His school, whose noble traditions he strives to preserve, has been successfully transmitted to the West.

The Kagyu (lit. 'Transmitted Command') School

This school has separated into a number of branches, but all trace their lineage back to the Indian masters Naropa and Tilopa – and ultimately back to the buddha Vajradhara. These great masters were *Mahāsiddhas* – adepts skilled in various advanced yogic practices – and in fact the emphasis within the school had remained on practical mysticism rather than on, say, scholarship. Notable among its basic teachings are the so-called *Six Yogas of Naropa*, which include mystic heat yoga (*dumo*) and the yoga of the *bardo* or intermediate state between death and rebirth. These disciplines are famous as particularly fast routes to the attainment of buddhahood, but they have to be practised with great energy and under the guidance of a qualified guru.

Marpa the Translator studied and practised with Naropa in India. When he later returned to Tibet, Marpa married and ostensibly settled down to the life of an ordinary householder; at the same time, however, he discreetly continued to pursue his tantric path. This was highly significant. The Kagyu School, along with other tantric traditions, does not require strict celibacy or membership of a religious institution upon its followers, though it was later, like the other Tibetan schools, to spawn its own monasteries.

Marpa's foremost disciple was Milarepa (1052–1135), who is one of the best known and most popular figures in Tibetan Buddhism. He too never ordained or lived in monasteries but rather represents the type of independent Tibetan yogin who pursues his solitary austerities in mountain caves and other remote places. He started out as a student of the black arts, intent on wreaking horrible revenge on those who had done wrong to his widowed mother, but later saw the error of his ways and, in terror of grotesque karmic repercussions, embarked upon a crash course of authentic spiritual instruction under Marpa. His master gave Milarepa a very hard time, requiring him for instance to build, knock down and rebuild a tall tower several times. He persevered, however, and attained buddhahood. He also became famous for his miraculous powers and would cheerfully take on and subdue all-comers in contests of magic. In paintings, Milarepa is often shown with a green tinge to his body, apparently the result of subsisting on an unappetizing diet of nettles for a long time. Also he cups a hand to one ear, which indicates another of his talents: he was a poet as well as a great mystic.

Milarepa's most influential disciple was Gampopa (1079–1153), the 'Doctor of Takpo', who had originally studied medicine and also the teachings of the Kadampa tradition. He later built a monastery and engaged in literary activities, his most well-known text being *The Jewel Ornament of Liberation*. From Gampopa's disciples stem the various Kagyupa sub-schools, including the Karma, Drugpa and Drigungpa.

The Karma Kagyu sub-school used to have its headquarters at Tsurphu monastery (founded 1185) in the Central Provinces, but it enjoyed a considerable following in Kham and other eastern provinces, whence the head of the order, the Karmapa (sometimes called the Black Hat Lama), was frequently wont to go on great visitations accompanied by a large armed cavalcade (*Karmapa Garchen*). The headship of this sub-school passes, not by heredity, but according to a system unique to Tibet. This is based on the notion that a spiritually advanced being is able to consciously choose whether or not to return to the world after death. Thus when a Karmapa dies, he leaves behind a letter containing directions; a search is then begun after an appropriate lapse of time for the child in which the great compassionate spirit that expresses itself through all Karmapas has been reborn. A similar system operates in various other Karma Kagyu lineages and in other Tibetan Buddhist schools as well. Beings who have been identified as voluntary reincarnations are known as *tulku* and carry the title *rinpoche* (lit. 'precious one'), though these terms have other applications as well. It has been suggested that the system originated in India among a group of highly venerated adepts known as the Eighty-four *Mahāsiddhas*.

The late Karmapa, the 16th – he died in Chicago in 1981 – latterly set up a headquarters at Rumtek in Sikkim after quitting Tibet in 1959. He was one of the first to appreciate the importance of disseminating the teachings of his sub-school to Westerners, and very early on sent lamas to the West, notably Chögyam Trungpa Rinpoche (1939–87) and Chujé Akong Rinpoche, who together established the first Tibetan Buddhist centre in Scotland (Samyé Ling) before Trungpa Rinpoche's departure to North America.

The Drugpa sub-school, on the other hand, was introduced into Bhutan in the 17th century and today remains the principal school of Buddhism there and also in Ladakh and other parts of the Himalayan region.

The Nyingma (lit. 'Old Ones') School

This name was almost undoubtedly originally coined as a convenient umbrella term to describe all those various groups and individuals who, after the second transmission of Buddhism to Tibet, remained devoted to the teachings and practices propagated during the first transmission. As the 'Old Ones' they formed a natural contrast to the 'New Ones' (*Sarma*) who subscribed to the new teachings that had been brought by Rinchen Zangpo, Atisha and their colleagues.

Moreover, in the eyes of the Nyingmapa, Padmasambhava came to occupy a uniquely exalted position, being regarded not merely as a manifestation of Avalokiteshvara but as the spiritual equal of the Buddha himself. With his colourful robes, cavalier moustache and tantric wand upon which various gruesome severed heads and skulls are skewered, he figures very prominently in Nyingmapa iconography. Needless to say, the school is richly imbued with magical and mystical connotations.

As the new schools organized themselves and flourished in both spiritual and worldly terms, the Nyingmapa began to consciously regard themselves as a distinct school and to emulate them. They too built a few monasteries – Mindroling was the most important in Central Tibet – and began to ordain their own monks. They also codified their teachings, many of which, they claimed, had been cunningly hidden by Padmasambhava in caves and other secret places (some were even said to have been hidden in 'mind') in anticipation of a time when people would be ready for them. These texts were known as *terma* ('treasures') and those who discovered them as *tertöns*. The classification of Nyingmapa teachings distinguishes nine *yānas* or paths to Enlightenment, the first three being based on the *sūtras* and the remaining six on the *tantras*.

Despite efforts at organization, the Nyingmapa remained essentially individualistic, sometimes even anarchic, and their lamas tended to be married men who operated independently at the local level. Many of them supported themselves by dispensing those occult services – exorcism, rainmaking, divination, healing, etc. – that the ordinary, unsophisticated Tibetans required. These are known as *ngakpas*. Others who gained a reputation for proficiency in tantric practice might gather a few disciples informally around themselves. The school could never have been a match for its newer rivals, especially those with a strong monastic base, but it was generally tolerated and has survived down to the present. It has also produced many great adepts and masters. The last supreme head of the order, H.H. Dudjom Rinpoche, was considered an incarnation of Dudjom Lingpa (1835–1904), a notable yogi and *tertön*. Rinpoche settled in Darjeeling after quitting Tibet, and paid various visits to the West, where he established centres; he passed away in France in 1987.

The Gelug (lit. 'Virtuous') School

The seminal master of this school, which is sometimes called the 'Yellow Hat Order' in the West, was Tsongkhapa (Lobsang Drakpa; also known as Jé Rinpoche; 1357–1419), who is identified as a manifestation of Manjushri, *Bodhisattva* of Wisdom. He hailed from the region of the great Kokonor lake in north-east Tibet. After having travelled and studied widely, Tsongkhapa gravitated to the Kadam School. He earned a high reputation as a writer and teacher, and was later warmly received in the Lhasa region. In 1409 he founded his first monastery, Ganden, in a panoramic natural amphitheatre in the hills to the east of Lhasa. Two other great monasteries were later founded, Drepung in 1416 and Sera in 1419, which lay to the west and north of the holy city respectively. Because of their scholarly orientations and their division into colleges or *dratsang*, these are often described as monastic universities. They certainly grew vastly in size and population. In their heyday Drepung and Sera are said to have each housed upwards of 7700 monks each.

Tsongkhapa is also credited with having established the 'Great Prayer' Festival (*Mönlam Chenmo*), which used to be held over a three-week period in Lhasa immediately after the *Losar* (New Year) celebrations.

Such was Tsongkhapa's fame that during his heyday the Emperor of China was eager to meet him; the good monk could not go himself but sent a proxy. On his death, his body was duly embalmed and enshrined in a *stūpa* at Ganden. There it remained, venerated and inviolate, until the *stūpa* was (reputedly) recently opened by Chinese soldiers, who are said to have been shocked to find the body perfectly preserved with hair and fingernails still growing. The annual festival of Ngachö Chenmo, when thousands of butter-lamps are burned, commemorates Tsongkhapa's death.

Although he is sometimes characterized as a self-appointed reformer of Tibetan Buddhism, Tsongkhapa did not consciously set out to found a school of his own. He certainly uncompromisingly castigated what he deemed to be the dharmically incorrect views prevalent in certain schools, notably the Jonangpa, but his main importance was as an energizer and resynthesizer of existing teachings. In particular he reaffirmed Atisha's stress upon the monastic virtues and upon the need to establish a firm basis in the *sūtra* teachings before graduating to the *tantras*. He was also strongly scholastic in orientation and encouraged the study of the great Indian masters of philosophy and logic: Nāgārjuna, Asanga, Dignāga, *et al.* Tsongkhapa codified the path to Enlightenment in terms of graduated stages and expounded these in his *Lam.rim Chenmo*. Professor Tucci has described this as 'the *Summa* of Lamaist doctrine as he saw it'.

In the long run, however, Tsongkhapa's chief disciples were able to evolve a distinct school separate from the Kadam to which Tsongkhapa had originally adhered. From these disciples also came the line of Dalai Lamas, who are also thought to be emanations of Avalokiteshvara. Here again the *tulku* system of succession was employed. The word 'Dalai' itself is of Mongolian origin and means 'ocean', implying an ocean or vast repository of wisdom. The title of the first Dalai Lama was posthumously bestowed upon Gendun-drup (1391–1474), the disciple and putative nephew of Jé-Tsongkhapa. Another important reincarnating patriarch within the school is the Panchen Lama, whose seat is traditionally the great monastic complex of Tashilhunpo, near Shigatse in southern Tibet. Later there was to be considerable rivalry between these two grand lamas – or, more precisely, between their followers.

In the 16th century the Gelug School began its rise to political pre-eminence when it came to enjoy the favour of a new generation of Mongol Khans. In 1642, Gusri Khan installed

Ngawang Lobsang Gyatso (1617–1682), the Fifth Dalai Lama, as the virtual ruler of Tibet under overall Mongol protection, summarily quelling with the sword the ambitions of the other schools and the temporal powers who supported them, in particular the Karma Kagyupas, who were supported by the kings of Tsang province. After obtaining power, however, the Fifth Dalai Lama proved to be a highly effective and tolerant ruler. The other schools were reorganized and to an extent stripped of worldly wealth and power, but only the Jonang, a Kagyupa sub-school, was suppressed.

Over the ensuing centuries, the régime of the Dalai Lamas consolidated its temporal power over the whole country, and though at times it was necessary, on the basis of the old priest – patron relationship, to accept a measure of Chinese interference, it effectively held sway in Tibet right down to 1950. As the Dalai Lamas came to be regarded by general consensus as the spiritual as well as the temporal leaders of the country, they received teachings in various schools and are not technically heads of the Gelugpa order. That honour is reserved for the Abbot of Ganden monastery, the Tri Rinpoche (or Ganden Tripa).

Besides the Great Fifth, there have been two other outstanding Dalai Lamas. One was the Great Thirteenth (Thubten Gyatso; 1876–1933), who between 1913 and his death made Tibetan independence a full reality. He also attempted to reconcile his country with the realities of the modern world. In this he met with considerable resistance from the conservative monastic element in Tibetan society, which was opposed to all change, however moderate. The other is the present incumbent, the Fourteenth (Tenzin Gyatso; b. 1935), who has had to steer the Tibetans through the greatest crisis of their history: the appropriation of their country by the Chinese. Although now living in exile in the Indian hill station of Dharamsala, he continues to exert a pre-eminent hold over the hearts and minds of his people, both those in exile and those living under Communist rule in Tibet itself. He has also emerged as a spiritual leader of world rank. He would be the first to admit that latterly, prior to the Chinese takeover, Tibet had become socially and politically ossified, and that the old obsessively conservative régime was permeated with numerous faults and abuses. It remains an open question whether His Holiness will ever return to his homeland.

The Gelug was the final school of Buddhism to emerge in Tibet; in fact the only other development of note during the ensuing years was the emergence of the eclectic Ri-mé (lit. 'Not-biassed', 'non-partisan') movement among some scholarly Nyingma lamas in eastern Tibet during the 19th century. Notable figures in the movement were Jamgön Kongtrül the Great (1813–99), Jamyang Khyentse Wangpo (1820–92), his *tulku* Jamyang Khyentse Chökyi Lodrö *et al.*

Despite occasional rivalry, particularly for worldly power and influence, a greater degree of similarity rather than of difference maintains between these major schools. They are all basically compounded of the same raw materials: Indian Mahāyāna Buddhism plus an admixture of a few native Tibetan contributions. What lends each its own individual character, therefore, is the manner in which it organizes the raw material and the particular emphases that are stressed.

While these schools were developing, the *bön-po* tradition was emulating them and emerging as a conscious and, to some extent, organized religion in its own right. It, in fact, adopted and absorbed much from within the Buddhist tradition in terms of teaching, practice, iconography and so forth, either directly or in slightly ammended form. For instance, just as the Buddhists venerated Shakyamuni Buddha as the primal originator and inspiration of their tradition, so the *bön-po* elevated one Shenrab Miwo to a similar status. He is a shadowy figure, said to have originated vaguely in the west, whose life story was clearly modelled upon that of Shakyamuni. *Bön-po* teachings were also codified into the so-called *Nine Ways of Bön*, and a goal identical with Buddhist Enlightenment was held up as the ultimate fruit of their path. Buddhist influence also prompted the discontinuation of certain old *bön-po* practices, such as blood sacrifice. There were even a few Bön monasteries, though in general style the *bön-po* were closer to the *ad hoc* localism of the Nyingmapas with all its rich magical – mythical nuances, than to the newer schools with their relatively sophisticated organization and worldly interests. Also, a certain anti-Buddhist sentiment, perhaps a lingering resentment at having been displaced from spiritual primacy, can be occasionally detected in their outlook, though this did not erupt into active hostility and, quietly tolerated or simply overlooked, the Bön religion has been able to survive to modern times.

Finally a word should be said about Dzogchen (lit. 'Great Perfection'), which is currently enjoying a certain vogue among Westerners. Although it is transmitted as a tantric teaching within the Nyingma school – where indeed it is regarded as supreme – it is also propagated as a 'wholly self-sufficient path in its own right' by Professor Namkhai Norbu, a married lama from the Dérgé district of east Tibet who used to teach at Naples University and now informally guides Dzogchen groups in many Western countries. As presented by Prof. Norbu, Dzogchen seem to have a Zen-like directness,[42] cutting through the usual dense undergrowth of primary and secondary accretions to zero in on the spiritual core. Dzogchen, he says, 'is a teaching concerning the primordial state of being that is each individual's own intrinsic nature from the very beginning'. Once perceived, the object of practice is to remain unerringly focused in this state in every aspect of life:

> There was a very great master of Dzogchen living in Tibet and at one point a very learned scholar visited him, saying, 'You practitioners of Dzogchen are always meditating – that's it, isn't it?'
> 'What is it that I'm meditating on?' asked the master.
> The scholar then asked, 'Ah, so you don't meditate then?'
> The master replied; 'When am I ever distracted?'[43]

Prof. Norbu also characterizes Dzogchen as the essence of all other teachings and traces its origins back to pre-Buddhist times, when, he claims, it flourished among the *bön-po* of Zhang-zhung, the mythical original Tibet.

Some Special Aspects of Tibetan Buddhism

Important in Tibetan Buddhism is the figure of the lama. Basically the term is a Tibetan equivalent of the Indian *guru*: a spiritual teacher. As such, contrary to popular misconceptions, a lama does not necessarily have to be a celibate monk. But his guidance is essential if the disciple (*chela*) is to successfully negotiate the difficulties and dangers of the spiritual path – and especially those of its dizzy tantric heights. So importantly is this figure regarded in this context that, while classic Indian Buddhism speaks of Three Jewels, Buddha, Dharma and Sangha, Tibetan Buddhism sometimes speaks of Four Jewels, the additional one being the lama. In some cases, the lama should be more highly regarded than Shakyamuni Buddha; indeed he is Ultimate Enlightenment itself.

Naturally all this places a great deal of responsibility on the shoulders of any lama and requires that he behave impeccably. Consequently the conduct of certain lamas who have come to the West and fallen prey to the temptations abundant in this quarter have given cause for concern.

In 1984, His Holiness the Dalai Lama asked about Buddhist teachers who regularly broke certain precepts, replied unequivocally that it was a teacher's duty to completely practise what he taught to others and thus be a spiritual example. Therefore, if a teacher enjoined one course on his students and pursued another himself, 'this means that the spiritual guide does not have the proper qualifications.'[44] So it was very important for a student to know the requirements of a teacher and to thoroughly check him out before establishing a dharmic or guru–*chela* connection; likewise a teacher should also check out a prospective student. According to the *Mantra (Tantra)* System, however, the situation was slightly different. A teacher *could* engage in activities usually prohibited – but only if he had achieved stability; i.e. had the capacity to behave in that way without jarring the faith of others. His Holiness concluded:

> However, if a lama does not have this capacity and we think, 'Oh, these are the grand activities of a lama', then we are in a difficult position and must make up our own minds as to how to proceed.[45]

No member of the tantric Buddhist pantheon is held in greater regard by the Tibetans than Avalokiteshvara (Tib. Chenrezi), who in his various manifestations as *Bodhisattva* of Compassion embodies the highest ideal of Mahāyāna Buddhism, indeed its very 'driving force' (Stephen Batchelor): the setting aside of all self-regard in favour of a wholehearted dedication to free all other sentient beings from the coils of

Samsāra. His incarnate activities are also mythically woven into the fabric of Tibetan history. The origin of the Tibetan people themselves, for instance, is attributed to his union, in the form of a monkey, with an autochthonous demoness – a myth which neatly accounts for the latent receptivity of the Tibetans to the teachings of Mahāyāna Buddhism, and also for their fiery, passionate nature. Subsequently Avalokiteshvara was incarnate as both King Songtsen Gampo and Padmasambhava, as well as the Dalai Lamas. It was appropriate therefore that the Dalai Lama's majestic main palace in Lhasa should be called the *Potala* after the abode of the *bodhisattva* in south India.

Highly characteristic too of Tibetan Buddhism – and closely connected with the cult of Avalokiteshvara – is the *mantra*, '*Om-mani-padme-hum*', which is muttered by all classes of Tibetan Buddhists, inscribed on flags, painted on walls, twirled within prayer-wheels – and even carved on stones and wayside rocks. It is literally translated as 'Hail to the Jewel in the Lotus'. A volume could – and indeed has – been written on the infinity of meanings encompassed within these few words. As Stephen Batchelor has said, 'the *mantra*... functions as a symbolic and highly condensed expression of the entire path to enlightenment'.[46]

The Mantra, Om-mani-padme-hum

In recent years foreign travellers have again been able to enter Tibet. They have been horrified at what they have discovered. Of the more than 2000 monasteries that once adorned the land, treasure-houses of priceless ancient art as well as profound wisdom, only a handful remain standing. The rest have been wantonly destroyed, their precious sacred contents either destroyed as well, desecrated or dispersed, and their occupants humiliated, persecuted and secularized. It is testament to cultural vandalism on a par with the burning of the great library of Alexandria. Although the present political climate is less extreme, it remains to be seen whether Buddhism will ever again flourish in the Land of Snows. In the meantime, its traditions live on among exiled Tibetan communities and their ever increasing numbers of Western co-religionists. The modern lama is not the denizen of remote mountain solitudes any more; he may be a jet-setter ministering to an international body of students, a man familiar with the workings of modern hi-tech gadgetry as well as with the great mysteries of the spirit.

Mudras drawn by Robert Beer

17 The Northern Transmission: Mongolia, Russia, Himalayan Region, Nepal and Bhutan

Mongolia

Although the Mongols came in contact with Chinese Buddhism as early as the 4th century, it was the Tibetan variety that captured their imagination and long-term allegiance. As in Tibet, Buddhism here had to confront powerful local religious traditions of great antiquity, notably the native shamanism.

Mongolian Buddhism always remained spiritually and theologically dependent on Tibet and, aside from the incorporation of indigenous elements, no truly local development took place. This does not mean, however, that it is without historical significance. The Mongol Yüan dynasty established Lamaism in China, a fact to which the Lamaist Temple in Beijing remains a monument. As we have also seen, Mongol *khans* wielded great power in Tibet itself at various times and advanced the worldly fortunes of, firstly, the Sakya School, and later the Gelug School. After the 16th century, the Mongols remained devoted and enthusiastic Gelugpas, building thousands of monasteries and ordaining a high proportion of their male population as monks. Various *tulkus* appeared among them, the greatest being the so-called *Hutuktu (= tulku)* or 'Grand Lama of Urga' (modern Ulan Bator).

Nowadays Mongolia is split. Inner Mongolia comes under the aegis of China and Buddhism there has suffered much the same fate as in China itself and in Tibet. Outer Mongolia, on the other hand, established itself as an independent People's Republic with Russian help in the 1920s. Despite initial repression, the Marxist régime did not manage to expunge

Buddhism from the hearts and minds of the people, however, and it has survived as a living presence into the more tolerant climate and political changes of recent years.

Currently, the chief monastery is Gandenthekchenling in Ulan Bator, seat of the Khambo Lama KH. GAADAN (sic), who is President of the Asian Buddhists Conference for Peace. This worthy organization regularly dispatches its journal, *Buddhists for Peace* to the West. This is a prestigious publication for an impecunious nation, but its complexion is a distinctly fellow-travelling one, suggesting that the Buddhists of Outer Mongolia, in common with, for instance, their Orthodox Christian counterparts in Russia, have to at least appear to acquiesce in the prevailing political order in order to survive. His Holiness the Dalai Lama visited Mongolia in 1982 and performed the Yamāntaka Initiation for 140 lamas at Gandenthekchenling. A crowd of 20,000 people is said to have gathered outside. More recently, His Holiness gave Kalachakra Initiation in 1995; the first time this has been performed here since 1934.

Russia

Tibetan Buddhism was spread to other northern Asian nomadic peoples by the enthusiastic and energetic Mongols. One result of this is that today there are three residual pockets of lamaist Buddhists living in what was Soviet territory, but which are now independent republics since the demise of the Soviet Union in 1989.

One is to be found in Buryatia, which lies in the Lake Baikal region of eastern Siberia. Forty miles from the capital, Ulan Ude, there is a large monastery, the Ivolginsky, 'The Buddhist Centre of the USSR' (TASS). This and its fellow, the Aginsky (not strictly speaking in Buryatia but in the neighbouring Chita region of Siberia), are the only monasteries now remaining in the region. The chief lama of Buryatia and official head of the Buddhists in the USSR is the Bandido-Khambo Lama. Empassioned pleas for world peace also tend to emanate from this quarter; unfortunately, less congenial emanations filter through to the outside world as well. In the 1970s, groups monitoring the persecution of religion in the USSR reported the death in a local labour camp of a distinguished lama named Bidya Dandaron.

Another Tibetan Buddhist group living in this region are the Kalmuks, who originated in Asia but migrated to Europe and were resettled in the lower Volga region around 1630. They remained there until World War II, when they were expelled for collaborating with the Germans; some have since been allowed to return. Geshe Wangyal, a much-travelled Kalmuk lama of the Gelug School, latterly, from about 1955 until his death in 1983, ministered to a group of his fellow expatriates who had emigrated to the USA after World War II and established an exile community in Freewood Acres, New Jersey.

Geshe Wangyal's root guru was none other than the famous and much-maligned lama, Khampo Agvan Lovsang Dorjiev (1853–1938), whose journeys between Lhasa and Russia precipitated the Younghusband Expedition (1904), when British troops marched to Lhasa. Later Dorjiev returned to his native land and in the optimistic early phases of the Revolution, when such things seemed possible, actively pursued a vision of reconciling Buddhism and Communism. Sadly Dorjiev's hopes were not realized in the long term and he met his end in 1938, during the dark days of Stalinist repression.

The third Buddhist enclave is in Tuva, a buffer between China and Russia lying east of the Altai Mountains. There are very few temples here, two or three prayer houses and a small number of tantric lamas.

Russia has also produced some fine Buddhist scholars, notably Theodore Stcherbatsky, author of *Buddhist Logic* and *The Central Conception of Buddhism*. In 1923 the first centre for Buddhist Studies in Europe was established in St. Petersburg/Leningrad; it ceased to exist in 1938.

The first community of Western Buddhists also appeared in Russia in the 1890s under the inspiration of Karlis Alexis Tennisons (1873–1962), a Latvian who was declared Buddhist Archbishop of Lithuania, Estonia and Latvia by HH the Thirteenth Dalai Lama.

Finally, in 1907, with the permission of Tsar Nicholas II and the blessings of the Thirteenth Dalai Lama, the foundation stone of a Buddhist temple was laid in St. Petersburg. It was probably intended for use by visiting diplomats from Buddhist Countries like Siam (Thailand) and Japan. The construction was supervised by Tennisons, and the temple was finally opened in 1915. It still exists, but has latterly been used as a scientific laboratory. Latest reports suggest that it is to be turned into an 'anti-religious museum', specializing in Islam and Buddhism.

Rough estimates reckon that there are currently more than half a million Buddhists in these areas, and the numbers are growing now these people have religious freedom in the post Soviet-era.

Himalayan Region

That magnificent arc of hills and soaring mountains that dominates the northern edge of the sultry plains of India also contains pockets of Tibetan Buddhism. Small communities of Tibetan refugees live in the region too, notably at Dharamsala in the Indian state of Himachal Pradesh, where His Holiness the Dalai Lama conducts his government-in-exile.

To the west, Ladakh, once an independent Tibetan kingdom isolated in its mountainous domain, is now an integral part of India. The Gelug and Drugpa Kagyu Schools are dominant here; but while traditional monastic life goes on in great *gompa* (monasteries) like Hemis and Tikse, the ancient local Buddhist traditions are to a degree under threat, not from Marxist ideology as in Tibet itself, but from that equally insidious factor, modern development, which includes tourism of course. There is also a vigorous local Muslim population against which the local Buddhists are not always able to hold their own. Nearby Zanskar and Spiti are also Tibetan enclaves.

In the east, on the other hand, lies Sikkim, once an independent kingdom but annexed by India in 1975. In the 17th century, Tibetan migrants from Kham entered Sikkim and had little difficulty in subjugating the gentle indigenous animists, the Lepchas. They also established Tibetan Buddhism, so Sikkim became a natural haven for Tibetans fleeing from Chinese oppression during the 1950s, and the Karmapa, the supreme head of the Karma Kargyu sub-school, established his headquarters there at Rumtek.

Finally, further to the east there are many Buddhists in the Indian state of Arunachal Pradesh.

Nepal

Nepal can claim the supreme Buddhists accolade of being technically the Buddha's birthplace. Lumbini, which lies just inside its southern frontiers, is one of the four great pilgrimage-places for Buddhists. A millennium and a half after the Buddha's birth, when the Muslims overran northern India, this Himalayan kingdom became a sanctuary for fleeing Indian Buddhists, who brought texts, relics and sacred artefacts with them and established a Sangha in the Kathmandu Valley, which is still today dominated by the burnished Buddhist pinnacles of Svayambhunath, the famous Monkey Temple.

However, this Sangha did not hold its own very well in the local spiritual climate and in a comparatively short time its monks forsook the monastic Vinaya to marry and become a separate caste on their own. Though a Buddhist scholarly tradition centred around four schools of philosophy (Svabhāvika, Ashvarika, Karmika and Yatrika) did survive down to recent times, Buddhism and Hinduism have so blurred into each other in the colourful religious melting-pot of the Central Valley of Nepal that today it is often hard to disentangle the two.

In the second half of the present century, however, connections were established with Sri Lanka and attempts initiated to establish a sound Theravāda Sangha on Nepalese soil. Ven. Amritānanda Thera, who was trained in Sri Lanka and who founded a centre at Svayambhunath, worked energetically to this end. For one thing, he translated numerous Pali *suttas* into Nepalese, before his death in 1990.

Nepal's Buddhist connections with Tibet go back a long way too – at least to the 7th century when, according to tradition, a local king sent his daughter as a wife for King Songtsen Gampo. During the following centuries much Buddhist traffic passed through Nepal, for it was a major avenue whereby the religion was transmitted from India to Tibet. Newari craftsmen from the Kathmandu region also worked on many of the religious buildings on the great plateau and their influence on Tibetan art was considerable.

There have also been reverse moments when Tibetan Buddhism has spilled back over the Great Himalaya into Nepal. The Sherpa people of north-east Nepal are in fact a Tibetan people. They have built numerous modest *gompa* and *chörtens* in their mountainous domain and kept their Tibetan Buddhist traditions alive there. Then, in the 1950s, the Chinese invasion of Tibet brought over a new wave of refugees. Meanwhile, in the north west, Dolpo and Mustang are two ancient Tibetan kingdoms that, like Zanskar and Ladakh, have until very recently managed to almost totally avoid the intrusions of modernity and progress.

Bhutan

In the 17th century Shabdung Ngawang Namgyal of the Drugpa Kagyu sub-school of Tibetan Buddhism established a buddhocracy in this eastern Himalayan kingdom. Numerous imposing *dzongs* (forts) were built which served as both monastic and administrative centres. Succession passed from one *Shabdung* (or *Dharma Rāja*) to the next by means of the *tulku* system, though as few incumbents survived to their majority, the reins of power were usually in the hands of a succession of Regents, known as *Deb Rājas*. Earlier this century, these institutions were replaced by a monarchy.

Having observed the disastrous consequences of thoughtless development elsewhere, and appreciating the very real benefits that their spiritually rich traditions confer upon their citizens in terms of intangibles like psychological well-being, the modern political leaders of Bhutan have been very concerned to restrict material 'progress' and other modernizing trends at a level consistent with the preservation of their traditional Buddhist culture.

Part 6

Buddhism Comes West

18   Slow Beginnings

Buddhism in Europe to World War II

Sadly, Buddhism has drastically declined, or even in some cases been virtually driven out of existence, in many of the Asian countries where it once so magnificently flourished. Usually the opposing factor has been a form of materialism, either consumerism or Communism, the origins of which can invariably be traced back to Western sources. This is especially ironical, for as the light of Buddhism fades in the East we see it beginning to shine with increasing brightness in the West. A great new chapter in the history of Buddhism may be beginning: one that may, as it develops, be no less glorious than any that have gone before.

It is impossible to pinpoint exactly when Buddhism first impinged upon the Western consciousness. Back in ancient times, when the Greeks enjoyed connections with northern India and adjacent lands, Buddhist ideas no doubt travelled along the great arteries of trade, notably the Western reaches of the Silk Road, to the Mediterranean world. Theorists have even proposed that Buddhist ideas somehow got into the general melting-pot from which Christian doctrine was extracted. During the Dark Ages, the dominance of Islam in the Middle East effectively blocked European interest in the East, though Arab storytellers did infiltrate the Buddha into Christian legend as St. Josaphat (*Josaphat = Bodhisat or Bodhisattva*) of the Barlaam and Josaphat story. This tells the familiar tale of a young aristocrat who gives up wealth and privilege to search for spiritual truth, accompanied by a monk.

At the dawn of the modern era, a new expansive energy was unloosed that easily surmounted the Islamic barrier. Voyages and expeditions of exploration to the East got under way, and in their wake followed the traders, the colonialists and the Christian missionaries. Buddhism was encountered in Mongolia, Tibet, China, Japan, Ceylon (Sri Lanka), Siam (Thailand), Burma and other farflung and exotic places. Sadly, bigotry prevented most contemporary Westerners from seeing any good in any religious system other than the Christian one. Buddhism was therefore almost invariably dismissed as benighted idolatry and efforts were made to convert its misguided followers, or even at forcible suppression. When efforts were latterly made by missionaries – by Spence Hardy and Samuel Beal, for instance – to study the religion, it was usually with a view to finding ways of discrediting or undermining it.

The 19th Century

It was not until the 19th century that European scholars began to make a serious effort to collect Buddhist texts and, having mastered the languages in which they were written (Sanskrit, Pali, Tibetan, etc.), to subject their contents to dispassionate study. Only then did Westerners begin to have a clearer picture of what Buddhism was really about. The establishment of the Asiatic Society of Bengal in Calcutta in 1784 by, among others, Sir William Jones (1746–94), a judge in the employ of the East India Company and a Sanskritist himself, was a great catalyst. The Society assisted – albeit in a small way – the Hungarian Csoma de Körös (1784–1842), who had gone to the East in search of the mythical lost homeland of his people; he didn't locate that but instead became a great pioneer of Tibetan studies. Substantial Buddhological work was also done by the Frenchman Eugène Burnouf (1801–52), onetime incumbent of the Chair of Sanskrit at the Collège de France; and by German scholars like Max Müller (1823–1900), Hermann Oldenberg (1854–1920), et al. Then in 1881, the Pali Text Society was established by T.W. Rhys Davids (1843–1922), whose interest in that lost Indian language had been aroused when his previous work as a magistrate in the Ceylon Civil Service had produced a case involving a point of Buddhist ecclesiastical law that could only be resolved by reference to Pali texts. The PTS has continued its good work to the present time.

In addition, archaeological field work by Sir Alexander Cunningham and others led to the uncovering of long forgotten Buddhist sites in northern India and elsewhere. Various places mentioned in the texts as having been visited by Shakyamuni Buddha were located, including Lumbini, his birthplace. Such finds tended to confirm the historical accuracy of these old texts, and the Buddha himself could be accepted as a real person rather than dismissed as just a myth. Some appreciation too began to emerge of just how extensive and highly developed Buddhism had once been.

The 19th century was also the time when established religion – that is, the conventional brand of church (or chapel) Christianity – began to lose its grip over the hearts and minds of ordinary people. This created a spiritual vacuum. All kinds of phenomena rushed to fill it: occultism, spiritualism, science, the Religion of Art (Aestheticism, or Bohemianism). But some too, now that accurate information was available, began to look with less prejudiced eyes at Buddhism among the other religions of the East. The apocalyptic writer, Friedrich Nietzsche (1844–1900), author of *Thus Spoke Zarathustra*, who in his famous dictum 'God is dead' put into words what was already observable fact, also spoke sympathetically of Buddhism in his writings, as did the pessimistic German philosopher Arthur Schopenhauer (1788–1860), whose notion of 'the will', enunciated in his *The World as Will and Representation*, appears close to the Buddhist concept of *tanhā*:

> His general message is evidently close to that of the Buddha: that all life is pervaded by suffering, the cause of suffering is desire or craving, and the way to blessedness is by the extinction of craving. Both for him and the Buddha, the ultimate goal of life cannot satisfactorily be described in language.[47]

But soon Buddhism was to become more than a mere academic interest. In 1879, the journalist, Sir Edwin Arnold, published his famous epic poem, *The Light of Asia*. This, which Christmas Humphreys has proclaimed 'the "best seller" of all Buddhist books in the West', helped a wider lay public to appreciate that the Buddha's teachings contained spiritual ideas

of great depth and beauty. Arnold also drew attention to the
sorry state of the Buddhist holy places in northern India,
notably Bodh Gāya, and initiated a scheme for buying the site
from its (then) Hindu owner. This project was not fully realized
until 1949.

The year after *The Light of Asia* appeared, the founders of the
Theosophical Society, the formidable Russian lady, Madame
Helena Petrovna Blavatsky (1831–91), and her American
colleague, Colonel Henry Steel Olcott (1832–1906), declared
themselves Buddhists and confirmed it by 'taking Pansil' – i.e.
reciting the Five Precepts – at Galle in Sri Lanka.

Theosophy was one of the cults that sprang up in the vacuum
created by the decline of conventional Christianity in the West.
Its founders claimed that the known religions of the world
merely propagated a superficial spiritual message for mass
consumption. Behind this, however, lay a hidden or esoteric
dimension strictly reserved for the initiated. This was itself
derived from an 'Ancient Wisdom-Religion', antedating all the
known religions, of which Theosophy was the modern
exposition. The cult also – and this no doubt did no harm from
the point of view of attracting followers – contained stiff
admixtures of occultism and other exotic ingredients, and its
charismatic leaders regularly commuted to the occult plane to
receive guidance from *Mahātmas* or 'Masters of Wisdom'.
However, they at the same time claimed that Theosophy was
quite compatible with that other fashionable child of the age:
science.

The movement caught the mood of the times and won
considerable popularity among the spiritually undernourished
middle classes of Europe and America. It also caught on in the
East too, and its headquarters were eventually set up at Adyar,
just outside Madras. Its leaders particularly favoured Buddhism
because they considered it 'the noblest and least defiled'
remnant of the great Ancient Wisdom-Religion – hence the
gesture in Galle in 1880. Madame Blavatsky, Colonel Olcott
and their colleagues subsequently went on to work vigorously
for the revival of Buddhism generally and in Sri Lanka in
particular, where they were assisted by a native Ceylonese,
Anagārika Dharmapāla (David Hewavitarne; 1864–1933),
with whom they went to Japan in 1888. In 1891 Dharmapāla

founded the Māha Bodhi Society in Calcutta: an important step in the direction of reviving Buddhism on its native ground. He also became active in the agitation for the restoration of Bodh Gāya to Buddhist hands.

The 20th Century – To World War I

The pioneer Theosophists often come in for wry critical comment in modern Buddhist circles, and this is understandable, for Western Buddhists have with difficulty disentangled themselves from the subtle (and gross) distortions that Madame Blavatsky and her colleagues projected upon the Buddha's teachings. But, to their lasting credit, the Theosophists prepared the way for Westerners to go deeper into the study and, eventually, the practice of those teachings.

The first Westerner to accomplish the giant step of taking the yellow robe was Allan Bennett (1872–1923), an enigmatic figure whose enthusiasm for Buddhism was awakened by reading *The Light of Asia*, though previously, as a member of the Hermetic Society of the Golden Dawn, he had rubbed shoulders with dubious necromancers of the ilk of Aleister Crowley and MacGregor Mathers. Funded by Crowley, Bennett went to the East and first studied the *Dhamma* in Sri Lanka before going on to Burma, where he was ordained as a *sāmanera* at Akyab in 1901. *Bhikkhu* ordination came the following year, when he took the name Ananda Maitreya, which he later changed to Ananda Metteyya (the Pali form).

By now determined to lead a Buddhist mission to Europe, Ananda Metteyya set up an international organization in Rangoon. A support group was also set up at the British end: the Buddhist Society of Great Britain and Ireland (founded 1907). The pioneer *bhikkhu* arrived back in Britain in 1908, but he was plagued by ill health which obliged him to return to Burma after six months. Though apparently idealistic, high-minded and highly energetic in his missionary work, his oratory was not up to scratch and so he was not able to effectively move his audiences.

In 1914, ill health finally forced Ananda Metteyya to disrobe and return to England. He was by now a broken man. He survived until 1923, supported largely by Buddhist sympathizers but still active in his Buddhist propaganda work, which he attempted to finance by his inventions. Among his ambitious schemes were a machine for registering the power of thought and another for making oxygen out of fresh air. Success, it seems, ever eluded him.

One day in 1904 or 1905, a Scotsman named J.F. McKechni (1871–1951), picked up a copy of Ananda Metteyya's journal *Buddhism*. In it he saw an advertisement that changed his life. He sailed out to Rangoon to give editorial assistance to Ananda Metteyya, and it was there that in 1906 he was ordained into the Sangha as Bhikkhu Silacara. He too wore out his health with strenuous Buddhist missionary work and in 1925 he disrobed and returned to Britain, spending the last years of his life in an old peoples' home at Bury.

The first non-British Westerner to enter the Sangha was a German virtuoso musician named Anton Gueth (1878–1957), who ordained as Nyanatiloka Bhikkhu in Rangoon in 1903. He later moved to Sri Lanka, though he came to Europe in 1910–11 and ordained the first *sāmanera* on European soil. Returning to Sri Lanka, he lived at the Island Hermitage in Ratgama Lake, Dodanduwa, though being an enemy alien he was interned or otherwise uprooted during the two World Wars. His foremost disciple, Ven. Nyānaponika (Siegmund Feniger; 1901–94), also of German origin, was one of the major influences behind the founding of the Buddhist Publication Society. He, like his great German mentor Nyānatiloka, also produced influential books.

Interest was also gaining ground in Germany itself. In the early years of this century, Dr Paul Dahlke (1865–1928) built the first Buddhist *vihāra* in Western Europe in the grounds of his ascetic life, closely following the monastic Vinaya. Later George Grimm (1868–1945) founded the 'Old Buddhist Community' at Utting in Bavaria. This still exists and, dating its year of inception as 1923, claims to be by one year the oldest Buddhist organization in Europe.

Much significant – and forgotten – pioneering work was done in Russia, which of course has Lamaist Buddhists among its Buryat and Kalmuk peoples. The temples built by the Kalmuks in the lower Volga region must rank as the oldest

Buddhist foundations in Eastern Europe. Pioneering Buddhological studies were also carried out in Russia by fine scholars like Stcherbatsky, Obermiller *et al*. There was practical experimentation too in the community of European Buddhists that built up around the Latvian, Karlis Alexis Tennisons (1873–1962), as early as the 1890s. Tsar Nicholas II, the last of the Romanov line, and some high nobles like Prince Ukhtomsky were probably quite sympathetic to Buddhism. Influential too in Russian court circles was a healer named Badmaev, a Buryat who had studied Tibetan medicine at Chakpori, the Medical College near Lhasa. The Revolution was a setback, however, and later the Stalinist purges resulted in a vicious repression. Many lamas were put on show trial and executed, many monasteries were closed and the religious functionaries who escaped with their lives were forced to return to lay life. During World War II, however, the need to rouse national feeling against the invading Germans led to religious concessions; monasteries and temples were then reopened, monks returned to them and Buddhist life began again.

The 20th Century – the Inter-War Period

But Britain, with its close colonial connections with Buddhist countries, not to speak of its political stability, naturally generated the most significant Buddhist activity.

After the first Buddhist Society had been formed, local groups began to spring up, magazines were published and lectures were vigorously delivered by enthusiastic speakers. World War I interrupted activities, but afterwards the sight of so many women in black and the full realization of the horrors of trench warfare conspired to produce a climate favourable to a peaceful persuasion like Buddhism. Now the movement really started to get under way – and, as so often happens, a natural leader appeared as well. This was Travers Christmas Humphreys (1901–83), a young man with a quick mind, a poetic turn of phrase and a flair for dramatic oratory that he put to good effect in his professional calling as a barrister at London's Central Criminal Court, the Old Bailey. The same talents that made Toby Humphreys the star advocate in many a famous murder trial were also, ironically, put at the service of Buddhism. As a speaker, writer, organizer, energizer and general figurehead, he was to lead the British Buddhist movement for over half a century and to see it develop from an eccentric marginal interest to something that could be fairly counted among the religions of Britain.

But Humphreys himself was a product of Theosophy and his Buddhism was one with a distinctly Blavatskian slant. The first organization that he established with his future wife, Puck (Aileen Faulkner), was in fact an adjunct of the Theosophical Society. It was called the Buddhist Lodge; and so it remained from 1924 until 1943, when it became the Buddhist Society, London, and subsequently simply The Buddhist Society, though it had long since parted company with the TS due to philosophical differences. The Buddhist Lodge was active in organizing lectures and classes, and in publishing Buddhist books. It also produced its own journal, *Buddhism in England*, founded and edited by Arthur C. March, which later became *The Middle Way*.

In these early days, the sort of Buddhism prevalent was the Theravāda variety. With few translated texts available, little was yet known of the Mahāyāna – and still less of the Vajrayāna: the Buddhism of Tibet. However in 1922 a rather strange expedition set out from Britain. It was composed of a number of prominent British Buddhists, including G.E.O. Knight, Captain J.E. Ellam (Hon. Secretary of the original Buddhist Society of Gt. Britain and Ireland), Frederic Fletcher and G. Montgomery McGovern (onetime lecturer at London University's School of Oriental Studies). Their intention was to visit the Dalai Lama in Lhasa and obtain permission to study Tibetan Buddhism at first hand in the 'Forbidden Land' of Tibet itself. With them they took an imposing silver urn containing an impressive scroll on which the Buddhists of Britain saluted His Holiness, the emanation of Avalokiteshvara. In the event, though these enterprising stalwarts got as far as the southern Tibetan city of Shigatse, they were not allowed to proceed to Lhasa. Reluctantly obliged to return to British territory, they then decided in best British style that they weren't beaten yet. They therefore elected that one of their party, McGovern, should try to slip through to Lhasa in disguise. This he contrived to do, though not without appalling suffering. McGovern spent a short time in the Holy City and, though seriously ill, was able to meet the Great Thirteenth Dalai Lama. Eventually, however, when he was strong enough to travel, he was again requested to depart – and perhaps this time he was not too sorry to do so.

While in Shigatse, one of McGovern's colleagues, Frederic Fletcher (1877–51) became ordained as a novice of the Gelug school – the first Westerner to be so honoured. An Oxford graduate, Fletcher had also been inspired by *The Light of Asia*; he had travelled widely as well, to Sri Lanka and elsewhere; finally his experiences as a major in World War I convinced him of the futility of worldly life, hence his interest in going to Tibet. Subsequently, he received Theravāda *bhikkhu* ordination in Sri Lanka, travelled extensively in India and finally lived for many years in Burma. His religious name, Lama Dorje Prajñānanda, reflects his dual loyalties to both Vajrayāna and Theravāda.

Rather more well-known are the Tibetan adventures of the great French mystic, traveller and author, Alexandra David-Neel (1868–1969). Having worked as a singer for the Opéra Comique and as a journalist, it was the discovery of Oriental religion and philosophy in the Musée Guimet in 1903 that settled the course of her life. After a brief attempt at marriage, she departed for the East in 1904, intending to stay 18 months; instead she stayed nearly 20 years! She had an audience with the exiled Thirteenth Dalai Lama; then she went to Sikkim, where she met Lama Yongden, her future travelling companion and adopted son. For a time, the two of them lived in a cave-hermitage in the Himalayas, learning Tibetan Buddhist philosophy and Tibetan language from lama teachers. They also made three abortive attempts to get into Tibet at this time, which put Madame David-Neel in the bad books of the British. Much later, in 1924, though in her mid-50s and both ragged and exhausted, she became the first European woman to enter the 'Forbidden City' of Lhasa. To do so, she had secretly entered Tibet from the East and laboriously tramped for six months, on foot and in disguise, across some of the most inhospitable terrain in the world. The faithful Yongden had been her sole travelling companion. Later still, during World War II, she lived in China along the eastern marches of Tibet. The final phase of her life was lived out in her villa in Digne (Haute Provence). Remarkable to the last, she died at nearly 101 years of age.

Madame David-Neel caught the public's imagination with books like *With Mystics and Magicians in Tibet* and *My Journey to Lhasa*. But she was not alone. At this time almost every traveller to Tibet produced a book, and many of them attempted some kind of account of local religious 'beliefs' and practices. The first major pioneering study of Tibetan Buddhism, entitled *Lamaism, or the Buddhism of Tibet*, was made by Dr. L.A. Waddell, a British medical officer who began studying the subject in Darjeeling in the fading years of the 19th century, employing Tibetan servants and two 'very learned lamas' to assist him. He even fitted out a private temple for study purposes as well as visiting others in Sikkim and Bhutan. As Principal Medical Officer with the Younghusband Expedition to Lhasa (1904), Waddell had the opportunity of carrying on his studies at first hand in the Tibetan capital. Other pioneering works were produced by Sir Charles Bell, the Political Officer in Sikkim, who developed a friendship with the Thirteenth Dalai Lama when he was in exile in Darjeeling and in 1920/1 paid an official visit to Lhasa. Bell was a great enthusiast for all things Tibetan.

We have already mentioned the pioneering Tibetological work of Alexander Csoma de Körös. Better known are the early translations of Tibetan texts made by the American Dr. W.Y. Evans-Wentz (1875–1965) and Kazi Dawa-Samdup. Evans-Wentz was an academic folklorist who trained at the universities of Stanford, Oxford and Rennes. He was influenced by the Irish poet, W.B. Yeats, and his first book was entitled *Fairy Faith in Celtic Lands*. Subsequently, an interest in rebirth took him to the East, where in 1919 he met Kazi Dawa-Samdup, a Sikkimese schoolmaster who had at some time worked for the British Political Officer in Sikkim and also for the Tibetans as plenipotentiary in India and been a member of the political staff of the exiled Thirteenth Dalai Lama. Together, Evans-Wentz and Dawa-Samdup produced several useful translations, including ones of *The Tibetan Book of the Dead* and the biography of Milarepa.

In 1925, Anagārika Dharmapāla came to England with the intention of founding a branch of his Mahā Bodhi Society. Suitable premises were found the following year in the west London suburb of Ealing and opened with all the usual ceremony. The Buddhist flag designed by Col. H.S. Olcott was unfurled and speeches were delivered by the Anagārika, Christmas Humphreys, A.C. March and others. Two years later a more centrally situated house was obtained near Regent's Park, and three learned English-speaking *bhikkhus* from Sri Lanka took up residence there. This effectively created a branch of the Sangha, albeit not a native-born one, on British soil. There has been a Sri Lankan Vihāra here in London ever since, except for a hiatus between 1940 and 1954. Anagārika Dharmapāla passed away in India in 1933.

The Buddhist Lodge and the British Mahā Bodhi Society were the twin poles that sustained British Buddhism down to World War II. Despite occasional slight differences, they were in many ways complementary organizations and often got together to arrange joint functions, like the annual Wesak or Buddha Day celebration.

The Buddhist Society also hosted distinguished Buddhist visitors to London, like Ven Tai Hsü from China, and Dr. D.T. Suzuki from Japan. Dr. Suzuki (1870–1966) is nowadays revered as 'the Man who Brought Zen to the West'. He trained in Rinzai Zen under Imagita Kōsen Rōshi and Sōyen Shaku at Engaku-ji in Kamakura. Later he worked for the Open Court Publishing House of Dr. Paul Carus in LaSalle, Illinois, where he perfected his knowledge of the English language and of Western thought. A highly gifted writer, teacher and lecturer as well as a man of very profound spiritual insight, Suzuki in fact made available the hitherto undiscovered treasure-house of Mahāyāna Buddhism to Westerners, though he is more usually remembered as a great propagator of Zen. He first visited London in 1908, when he met Ananda Metteyya, and again in 1936 when he attended the World Congress of Faiths, which was held under the auspices of Sir Francis Younghusband. The climax of the Congress was a great public meeting when various distinguished speakers were billed to speak on 'The Supreme Spiritual Ideal'. Suzuki appeared to be dozing, but when he came to speak he dismissed all knowledge of this highfalutin' theme and instead went on to talk about his little house in Japan. His audience were fascinated; they realized that here was very subtle but profound teaching.

One person who was very impressed with Dr. Suzuki at the Congress was a sharp young man about town named Alan Watts (1915–73) who, as a protégé of Christmas Humphreys, had lately assumed the Editorship of *Buddhism in England*. Watts too possessed communications talents of an exceedingly high order and went on to make a big name for himself in the United States as a writer and talker on Zen and related matters.

These slow developments, over so many centuries, prepared the ground for what, following World War II, was to be an unprecedented and utterly unexpected flowering of Buddhism in Europe. The great veteran Dharma-spreader Toby Humphreys intuitively saw it coming. Proclaiming it, he loved to quote from Victor Hugo: '*There is one thing that is stronger than armies: an idea whose time has come. . . .*'

19   The Flowering of the Lotus

Buddhism in Europe from World War II to date

(Note: Addresses and further details of many of the groups and centres mentioned in this chapter can be found in the next.)

Up until World War II and for some years afterwards, Buddhism remained a largely middle class preserve. One of its twin pillars in London, the Buddhist Society, for instance, had very much the aura of a gentleman's club about it. Until well into the new era, its front door was kept firmly closed and anyone who rang the bell would be thoroughly looked over before being granted admittance.

But things were rapidly changing, and no more so than during the 1960s when a new generation came of age. Regardless of class, its members had been brought up in relative affluence and been given good educational opportunities. They also enjoyed new freedoms: to travel, to explore art, politics, sex and drugs, and to experiment with alternative lifestyles. Inevitably many began to encounter the perennial problems that beset those who have had everything yet still find themselves dissatisfied. In short, they were poised to probe more deeply into the mystery of things. The Western religions could not provide satisfactory answers, so there was a mass turning to the East. Many travelled to India, Nepal, Sri Lanka, Japan, Korea, Thailand and elsewhere, and spent time there, either enjoying the local venal pleasures or else exploring the religious traditions. Or both. Or each by turns. Vedānta attracted some but in the long-term Buddhism proved to be of more considerable influence.

Zen

Now at last the Mahāyāna traditions began to come into their
own. Springing directly from Dr Suzuki's pioneering work, Zen
became quite fashionable in Britain and other parts of Europe,
though it never caught on to the extent that it did in the United
States. For a while a kind of intellectual quasi-Zen held the
field. Monica Furlong has dubbed it 'Christmas Zen' after its
main exponent, Christmas Humphreys. Basically it was
recycled Dr Suzuki put over with verve and more than a little
showmanship. Christmas Humphreys' protégé, Alan Watts,
also did well with Christmas Zen in the United States, whither
he emigrated in 1938.

In 1953 Watts, returned for a brief visit to England. The
members of the Buddhist Society had of course read his
eminently readable books and heard all about his exploits across
the Atlantic, where he was 'setting America alight with his new
approach to Zen'. They therefore turned out in force to hear
him lecture at the Caxton Hall.

Watts, now sporting a crewcut, strode onto the podium,
stood stock still for a moment, then cried, *Wake up!'*

The audience was stunned – but made no special response.
Watts was therefore obliged to repeat the gambit. Again no
special response. 'Direct methods' having fallen rather flat, he
then went on to deliver a straight lecture on the theme that we
are all asleep to the 'zen' within us.

Of course, Humphreys and Watts, both highly gifted
communicators, did marvellous work in spreading knowledge
of Zen. But it was left to others to go more deeply into the
matter. This meant actually going to the East and submitting to
long and arduous *zazen* practice under an acknowledged master,
which by general agreement is the only viable avenue to genuine
Zen realization.

Among the adventurous souls that took this challenging
course was another of Christmas Humphreys' protégés, an
Austrian lady named Irmgard Schloegl, who went to Japan,
lived for many years in Kyōto and received Rinzai Zen training
at Daitoku-ji under Sesso Oda Rōshi, Gōtō Zuigan Rōshi and
Sōkō Morinaga Rōshi. Zen training is hard, and the Japanese –
at this time at least – were not noted for their liking of

foreigners, and women did not enjoy great standing in their eyes either. Dr Schloegl must therefore have needed a lot of determination to stay the course. She did, however, and eventually returned to London with authority to teach. Ever since she has guided the large and successful Zazen Class at the Buddhist Society, and has also established an independent organization, the Zen Centre, to which Christmas Humphreys with characteristic generosity left his villa in St. John's Wood when he died in 1983. In 1984 the house was renamed Shōbō-an, 'Hermitage of the True Dharma', and in the same year Dr. Schloegl was ordained as Ven. Myōkyō-ni by Sōkō Morinaga Rōshi in a traditional ceremony held at a Sussex monastery. Sōkō Rōshi occasionally visits London and the Buddhist Society Summer School.

The London Zen Society has also represented the Rinzai Zen tradition in Britain for many years. It developed from Hannyakai, a society founded by Kim Wall and others in 1966. Its Spiritual Director is Sochu Suzuki Rōshi (b. 1921), who succeeded Nakagawa Sōen Rōshi (1907–84) as Abbot of Ryutaku-ji, the famous Zen monastery in Mishima, Japan. Sōen Rōshi was a respected poet; he also made creative innovations in Zen ritual and took a keen interest in the development of Zen in the West. Another of Sōen Rōshi's pupils, Nakagawa Kyudo Rōshi, currently based in New York, also occasionally visits the London Zen Society, which is housed in north London.

All forms of Zen centre around the practice of *zazen*, or sitting meditation. In the Rinzai tradition, however, *kōan* are also employed. These are profound or enigmatic questions which serve as a focus, concentrating the mind on the central issue: the question of essential nature – of what is sitting here now, searching for itself. The progress – or lack of it – one has made, not merely towards understanding essential nature but in actually becoming it, is tested during the *dokusan* or *sanzen* interview with the Master or *rōshi*. In the Sōtō tradition, on the other hand, the emphasis is on just sitting (*shikan taza*). To sit is to be a Buddha: an enlightened person. In the words of Master Dōgen, the seminar teacher of the tradition in Japan:

This type of *Zazen* is not something that is done in stages of meditation; it is simply the lawful gateway to carefree peace. To train and enlighten ourselves is to become thoroughly wise; the *kōan* appears *naturally* in daily life. If you become utterly free you will be as the water wherein the dragon dwells or as the mountain whereon the tiger roams.[48]

Another lady graduate of Toby Humphreys' Zen Class also went East in search of Zen training. Peggy Kennett (1924–96), a music teacher by training, was in 1962 ordained into the Rinzai tradition by Ven. Seck Kim Seng, Abbot of Cheng Hoon Teng Temple in Malacca, Malaysia. She then went on to study Sōtō Zen under Chisan Kōhō Zenji (1879–1967) at Sōji-ji, a temple in Yokohama. With a licence to teach, Jiyu Kennett Rōshi (as she had now become) arrived on the West Coast of the USA in 1969, established the Zen Mission Society in 1970 and then went on to found an Abbey at Mount Shasta, California, where she was Abbess for many years. Today Shasta Abbey remains the headquarters of her Order of Buddhist Contemplatives of the Sōtō Zen Church (OBC), which propagates a form of traditional Sōtō Zen training adjusted to modern Western cultural norms. OBC monks, who may be of either sex and train together, tend to call themselves 'Reverend' rather than the usual 'Venerable'; their chanting (which is in English) is also formally based on Gregorian plain-chant.

In 1972, Throssel Hole Priory was set up amid 18 acres of fields and woodlands in the north of England under the auspices of Jiyu Kennett Rōshi's British Zen Mission Society. It has developed well down to the present and enjoys a good reputation as a well-run training monastery. Life there, as in all authentic Zen temples, is simple and disciplined, and centres around the meditation hall, where trainees meditate (it is called 'serene reflection' here), attend services and ceremonies, study, eat and sleep. There are also periods of work. Its Abbot at the present time is Rev. Daishin Morgan OBC (b. 1951).

Sōtō Zen has also been represented in Europe by Taisen Deshimaru (1914–82), a Japanese monk who trained under Kōdō Sawaki. Deshimaru lived the householder's life for many years, marrying and begetting children; but the call of Zen drew him away and, after his teacher's death, he travelled to Europe on the Trans-Siberian Railway. Settling in Paris in 1967, he taught for some 15 years and in 1970 founded L'Association Zen d'Europe; this spawned *dōjōs* and *zazen* centres in other parts of France, Belgium and West Germany, as well as in North and South America and North Africa. Besides his temple in Paris he also had a larger one in the Loire Valley. His student, Nancy Amphoux, has written: 'Deshimaru's personality was unique: blustery, sensitive, truculent, subtle and inimitable. Its greatest strength lay in the boundless universal energy that he transmitted. . . .'

The Rinzai and Sōtō approaches are blended in the teaching of Taizen Maezumi Rōshi (1931–95), founder of the influential Zen Center of Los Angeles. In recent years a branch of ZCLA, the Zen Practice Centre, has existed in south London under the auspices of Sumi and Colin Fukō Barber. Meanwhile, one of Maezumi Rōshi's Dharma heirs, Genpo Merzel Sensei (b. 1944), has started teaching in Europe on a regular basis, and has set up the Kanzeon Sangha to support his work here.

Influential in British Zen but not a figure to seek the limelight or promote himself as a teacher of any sort is Trevor Leggett. For many years Head of the Japanese Service of the BBC, Mr. Leggett not only knows Japanese (and also Sanskrit) thoroughly but has received Zen training at Daitoku-ji as well as having studied with Dr. Hari Prashad Shastri, a Vedantist sage. In recent years Trevor Leggett has brought out a series of books on Zen and translations of Zen texts which have added greatly to general understanding. A consummate story-teller, his lectures at the Buddhist Society's annual Summer School and elsewhere have long been greatly appreciated.

All the foregoing of course represent developments from Japanese forms of Zen. There has in fact been little Chinese Zen (Ch'an) activity in Europe, though Richard Hunn of Norwich, who was once a student of Charles Luk (Lü K'uan Yü; 1898–1978) of Hong Kong, is busy translating texts and occasionally holds Ch'an retreats. John Blofeld (Chu Ch'an 1913–87), a longterm English expatriate latterly domiciled in Bangkok, also provided useful texts (*Huang Po*, *Hui Hai*, etc.) as well as producing highly readable accounts of his adventures, spiritual and otherwise, in pre-Communist China. He went there as a young man and lived there intermittently for many years, formally becoming a pupil of the legendary Master Hsü Yün (1840–1959), though in fact he received his actual training in Ch'an meditation from Master Hsü Yün's pupils at Hua T'ing monastery, near Kunming in Yunnan province.

Stephen Batchelor (b. 1953) and his wife Martine run what they call 'Radical Questioning' retreats in Britain based on the Korean Zen training that they received under Kusan Sunim (1909–83) at Songgwang Sa, a monastery in Cholla Namdo province, south-west Korea. Strangely, Korean Zen seems to have taken on most strongly in Poland, where Ven. Sōen Sunim of the Providence Zen Center (Rhode Island, USA) has many devotees; he also has others in West Germany. Genpo Merzel Sensei also teaches in Poland, as does Rōshi Philip Kapleau of the Rochester Zen Center (New York State, USA).

A new innovation in recent years have been the *Western Zen Retreats* organized by John Crook, Reader in Psychology at Bristol University. These usually take place in a secluded farmhouse in mid-Wales and employ a varying combination of *zazen* and other methods, notably the 'Communication Exercise' of Charles Berner. They also incorporate the so-called 'Enlightenment Intensive' brought to Europe by Jeff Love in the 1970s. The Communication Exercise substitutes for the traditional *sanzen* interview. Instead of confronting the *rōshi*, participants break up into pairs and confront each other with the question of self-identity. John Crook says: 'The outcome may be profound insight into the "ground of being" – an event known in Zen as an "enlightenment experience". Whether or not this realization happens, participants share a profound experience in new knowledge of self and others.'

The West also produces the occasional spiritual original, someone who is able to come up with an entirely new approach to the central enigma of who we are. Douglas Harding (b. 1909) is just such a person. The product of an extremely narrow Plymouth Brethren sectarian upbringing, Harding broke away while at London University and began a personal search for spiritual truth. His father and the rest of his family, deeming him utterly Hell-bent, promptly turned their backs on him once and for all. Later, while working as an architect in India, he went on a walking tour in the Himalayas. Unexpectedly he saw something at once extremely profound and extremely obvious: from a purely subjective point of view he had no 'meatball head' on his shoulders, just pure unbounded space in which the world was happening. Long afterwards, delving into the writings of Dr. Suzuki and the Zen Masters, he realized that this experience had correlatives in that tradition. At last finding his affinities, he began to write and teach. His book, *On Having No Head*, is a classic of its type: short, lucid, passionate and original. He has also developed various direct experimental techniques for helping people to 'see who they really are'. His unconventional approach has, however, hindered his reception in Britain and, though he continues to live in his native county of Suffolk, he now teaches mainly in the United States.

The production costs of *On Having No Head* were borne by another rather remarkable fringe member of the British Buddhist scene, who can really only be placed in this category – though he himself would undoubtedly have heartily rejected any attempt at pigeon-holing. This was Terence Gray (1895–1986). He was an immensely wealthy man of Anglo-Irish ancestry who kept a string of racehorses and is reputed to have won the Ascot Gold Cup. Latterly he lived in Monte Carlo and would send gifts of wine from his vinyard in the Rhône valley to Christmas Humphreys in London. Privately, however, he addressed himself to the perennial questions and, under the nom-de-plume of Wei Wu Wei, wrote a number of fascinating, impossible books – *Ask the Awakened, All Else is Bondage, Why Lazarus Laughed* – that seemed designed to precipitate the reader into confrontation with essential nature by so piling paradox upon paradox as to induce a kind of brain seizure.

Mainstream Mahāyāna

The chance discovery around 1937 of one of Dr. Suzuki's books in a bookshop near the British Museum by a scholarly German refugee named Edward Conze (1904–79) was to have a highly stimulative effect on Mahāyāna studies in the West. It revivified an earlier interest in Buddhism, and Conze, an irascible but energetic man with a massive intellect, went on to dedicate the remainder of his life to the study and translation of Mahāyāna texts. He also produced more popular works – his *Buddhism: Its Essence & Development*, a spirited little monograph, is still probably the best introduction to Buddhism for the general reader – as well as anthologies, all of which helped make the fruits of his scholarship available to a wider, less specialist readership. The other, darker side of his nature, meanwhile, asserted itself in his *Memoirs of a Modern Gnostic*, where he indulged a minor talent for character assassination at the expense of a few luminaries of the Western Buddhist scene.

The tradition of Mahāyāna studies inaugurated by Edward Conze has been continued in Britain to the present by Eric Cheetham and his colleagues in the Mahāyāna Study Group. This group dates back to the early 1950s, when several Buddhists began to meet in London under the guidance of Professor Richard H. Robinson, who later went on to found the Buddhist Studies Program at the University of Wisconsin. Whereas so many Buddhists gain their knowledge of the Dharma from popular interpretations, this group is concerned to seek it out at first hand through the close and careful study of (mainly) Indian Mahāyāna *sūtras*:

> From the beginning we wanted to know what Mahāyāna Buddhists were supposed to do – and why. The teachings of the Pali texts and the monk exponents of that teaching were much in evidence. Somehow the Mahāyāna was different but just how and for what purpose we did not know. And we needed to know for the very practical purpose of exercising choice, if there were any, in adopting the Way. Now, many years later, this writer (Eric Cheetham) feels that those early concerns are still valid.[49]

Tibetan Buddhism

Down to 1959, Tibet remained the 'Forbidden Land' from which Westerners were rigidly debarred. But there were a few notable exceptions, among them the eminent Italian Tibet-ologist, Professor Giuseppe Tucci (1894–1984), an aristocratic and immensely wealthy man who established the Istituto Italiano per il Medio ed Estremo Oriente (IsMEO) in Rome in 1933. Between 1927 and 1949, Tucci made a number of well-financed expeditions to Tibet to obtain the manuscripts, books, artefacts and first-hand data that he required for his studies. How exactly he contrived to obtain the necessary official permits, which were notoriously hard to come by, remains something of a mystery, though it does appear that he was a convinced and, to some extent, a practising Buddhist and this may have cut some ice with the Lhasa authorities. He also apparently believed that he had been a Tibetan in a previous incarnation.

Another privileged visitor was E.L. Hoffmann (1898–1985), better known by his Buddhist name of Lama Anagarika Govinda. Of Bolivian and German extraction, Govinda studied architecture and archaeology as well as philosophy in Europe; he was also rather a good artist, and lived for a time in an artistic colony on Capri. Having developed an interest in burial mounds, he went to Sri Lanka in 1928 to study the local *stūpas* and was bitten by the Buddhist bug. At first he was drawn to Theravāda Buddhism, ordained as an *anagārika* and occupied himself with Pali studies. In 1931, however, he encountered Tibetan Buddhism while at a Buddhist conference in Darjeeling. He also met his guru, Tomo Geshe Rinpoche there, and when he died Govinda set up the Arya Maitreya Mandala in his memory. During the 1930s, Govinda pursued his Buddhist studies in Ladakh, Sikkim and Tibet, and between 1947 and 1949 made two important forays into Tibet. The second took him to western Tibet, where he visited the sacred Mount Kailas as well as Tsaparang and Thöling, the lost cities of the ancient kingdom of Gu-gé in the upper Sutlej valley. His experiences in these wonderful places are recounted in his *The Way of the White Clouds*. His most important book, however, was *Foundations of Tibetan Mysticism*, which was the first comprehensive account of Tibetan Buddhism written from within, so to speak, by a Western practitioner. As a writer, Govinda was always lucid and highly readable – but then there was a strong salting of the artist in his nature.

In 1947 two Englishmen were allowed to cross the high passes and seek Buddhist teaching in Tibet. One was Marco Pallis (1895–1989), a professional musician with an interest in mountaineering who had been born in Liverpool of Greek parentage in 1895. His companion was Ronald Nicholson. They went to Sakya, the great monastic centre in southern Tibet about three days travel west of Shigatse. There they located a qualified guru:

> We had to walk a long way to find him. He himself was a recluse: he lived in a little hut. The first time we met, he said, 'Well, now, it's best that you should have the bases', and he produced this large loose-leaved book. 'Now, you learn that by heart and when you know it we'll start.' Well, I conveyed to him that for us this was something very difficult. 'Oh, it's not difficult at all', he said; so I said, 'We'll try. . . . And the next time we went, he said, 'I've thought about what you've said and so I've found another book which is really the same book reduced to a small formula – a few pages. This you must at all costs learn by heart.' We *did* learn it and after a few days we recited it to him correctly. He said, 'That's a good beginning.'[50]

But soon things were to change drastically. 1959 was the crucial year. The great diaspora of Tibetan lamas following the Lhasa Uprising and the subsequent flight of the Dalai Lama made generally available to the West for the first time the rich tantric heritage of the Vajrayāna.

European Buddhists were quick to help the army of Tibetan refugees that spilled over the Himalayas into northern India, Sikkim and Bhutan, many of them in a very sorry condition. One person who responded with particular wholeheartedness was Freda Bedi (1911–77), an English lady who had married a Sikh, lived for many years in India and had been given high public office by Prime Minister Pandit Nehru. She was eventually ordained as a Karma Kagyu nun, taking the name Sister Karma Kechog Palmo. As principal of a school for young lamas in Dalhousie, one of her protégés was a young Karma Kagyu *tulku* from Eastern Tibet, onetime Abbot of the Surmang group of monasteries. His name was Chögyam Trungpa (1939–87).

In 1963, Trungpa Rinpoche sailed to England on a P&O liner to study at St. Anthony's College, Oxford. He was accompanied by a fellow Karma Kagyu *tulku* from eastern Tibet: Chujé Akong Rinpoche, the former Abbot of Drolma Lhakhang monastery, who went to do medical work at the Radcliffe Infirmary in Oxford.

No Tibetan lama who has come to the West has quite possessed Trungpa's unique blend of qualities. He was certainly charismatic; he also had a wonderful talent for presenting Dharma to Westerners clearly, lucidly and creatively. Some of his books, like *Meditation in Action* and *Cutting through Spiritual Materialism*, remain lasting classics. Yet Trungpa soon became a controversial figure. His lifestyle, running to excess, disquieted and alienated many; yet at the same time he always retained the loyalty of a vast following, who staunchly maintained to the end that behind the surface problems lurked the true *bodhisattva* nature: compassionate, wise and capable of giving out profound teachings.

Back in the early 60s, Trungpa soon gathered an entourage of devoted followers in many parts of Europe. It was no doubt quite a strain for him. He was still very young himself, in his early 20s, and here were so many confused people, a lot of them casualties of the permissive society and the hippie era, looking to him to sort out their problems. Still, he galvanized himself to rise to this particular challenge. In 1967, he and Akong Rinpoche were able to establish the first Tibetan Buddhist centre in the West at Johnstone House in Dumfriesshire, amid the windy hills of the southern uplands of Scotland. Appropriately it was named Samyé Ling after the first monastery of Tibet. Trungpa himself has written that, for him, Samyé Ling was not 'entirely satisfying', for 'the scale of activity was small, and the people who did come to participate seemed to be slightly missing the point'.[51]

The early history of Samyé Ling was almost as dramatic as that of its namesake in Tibet, where, it will be remembered, demonic forces frustrated the completion of the building work and had eventually to be subdued by Padmasambhava. Trungpa himself suffered a serious car-crash, which left him partially paralyzed; he also shocked some of his followers by deciding to disrobe and marry. Tensions, conflict and paranoia began to build up and in 1970 he departed to the United States with his new wife, Diana. There he established various highly successful centres and organizations, and more books appeared. He still retained the loyalty of many of his European followers, notably Michael Hookham, who in 1975 founded the Longchen Foundation, of which Trungpa Rinpoche became Director and Dilgo Khyentse Rinpoche, Patron; also the Nitartha School, which exists to promote contemplative study and practice within a systematic matrix. Meanwhile, Dr. Karl Springer has latterly headed the European arm of Trungpa's Vajradhatu organization (founded 1970), which maintains Dharmadhatu centres in London and other important European cities. Samyé Ling has also raised funds and purchased a small island off the Scottish coast. Renamed Holy Island it is in the process of becoming a residential retreat centre.

Samyé Ling has successfully outlived its early upheavals and continues to the present time under the guidance of Akong Rinpoche, now its Abbot and the spiritual head of associated centres in Spain, South Africa and elsewhere. It has indeed grown and presently ambitious plans are afoot for its future development. The Samyé Project, now virtually completed, aims at building a splendid Tibetan-style temple with an ancillary college facility endowed with library, lecture halls, translation room and so forth.

Back in 1975 Samyé Ling was graced with a visit from His Holiness the Sixteenth Gyalwa Karmapa (1923–81), late supreme head of the Karma Kagyu order, who performed the famous Vajra Crown Ceremony there. That year the Karmapa also visited Kham Tibetan House, a second Karma Kagyu centre established in 1973 in the village of Ashdon near Saffron Waldon in Essex by Lama Chime Rinpoche, also a native of Kham, where he was identified as one of the four *tulkus* of Benchen monastery. Lama Chime, who came to England around 1972, also resigned monk status in order to marry. He now combines his Dharma work with a full-time career in the Tibetan section of the British Library. He is also spiritual director of a London Centre: Karma Kagyu Chö Khor Ling.

A highly respected Karma Kagyu *tulku* who has stayed away from the limelight and avoided groups and centres is Ato Rinpoche (b. 1933). He also hails from eastern Tibet, and in his formative years received Gelugpa and Nyingmapa as well as Kagyupa teachings. In the early 1960s he was the Karma Kagyu representative on HH the Dalai Lama's Council for Religious & Cultural Affairs, and later Sister Palmo's assistant at the Young Lamas' School in Dalhousie. Ato Rinpoche married Alethea Martineau in 1967 and came to live in Cambridge, where he worked as a male nurse at Fulbourn Mental Hospital until his early retirement in 1981. He teaches privately or by invitation to groups, though in 1986 he departed from his usual practice to begin a monthly meditation group in Cambridge.

The Kagyu School, incorporating as it does the tradition established by Naropa, Marpa and Milarepa, leans towards the attainment of direct mystical experience. Famous Kagyupa lamas have visited Europe from time to time in recent years, notably Kalu Rinpoche (1905–89) – 'a modern Milarepa' – who has established centres for Westerners in France where three-year retreats are conducted; also Tai Situ Rinpoche, Pawo Rinpoche, Khenpo Tsultrim Gyamtso, et al.

The leaders of the 'established church' of Tibetan Buddhism, the Gelug School, were rather slower in sending lamas to the West than the pioneering Kagyupas. Being in the tradition of Atisha and Tsongkhapa, they also represent a rather more strict tradition that emphasizes monasticism, intensive study of texts and methodical practice according to a carefully graduated system. (Lam.rim). The seminal figure in their work among Westerners was another charismatic lama with great warmth, humour and a talent both for inspiring people and of making Dharma accessible to them as a living teaching. This was Lama Thubten Yeshe (1935–84), a monk trained at the great monastic university of Sera (Jé College), near Lhasa. He began teaching Westerners in Darjeeling and later in Nepal, where in 1971 he founded a centre at Kopan, near Bodh Nath in the Kathmandu valley. His colleague in this enterprise was his chief disciple, Lama Zopa Rinpoche, (b. 1946) who, though a native of Nepal, was also trained at Sera. In 1971, Lamas Yeshe and Zopa founded the Foundation for the Preservation of the Mahāyāna Tradition (FPMT), which has spawned centres in many countries as well as ancillary ventures like Wisdom Publications, a successful publishing concern now based in London, and Wisdom Books in America.

Two of Lama Yeshe's students, Harvey Horrocks and Peter Kedge, managed in 1976 to obtain a vast, rambling but exceedingly dilapidated mediaeval-monastery-cum-Victorian-hospital in the north of England named Conishead Priory. Here they established the Manjushri Institute, the first major centre in Europe geared to giving Westerners traditional Gelugpa training right up to the level of the geshe degree, the Gelugpa equivalent of Doctor of Divinity. In common with its precursors in old Tibet, it was envisaged that, once the necessary renovation work had been accomplished – a vast task in itself – Manjushri would become a monastic university accommodating both ordained Sangha-members and lay students.

Sadly, Lama Yeshe's health was not good and he died prematurely in Los Angeles in 1984, to the great grief of his devoted followers. While his disciple, Lama Zopa, continued his good work around the world, his *tulku* was sought and eventually found among his Spanish devotees. The diminutive Lama Ösel, born to Maria Torres and Paco Hita in 1985, has now been confirmed by the Dalai Lama as Lama Yeshe's new incarnation and duly enthroned. After Lama Yeshe's death, Geshe Kelsang Gyatso (b. 1932), another graduate of Sera, took over as Spiritual Director at the Manjushri Institute. He has since founded the New Kadampa Tradition, with the headquarters at Manjushri and numerous other centres worldwide.

In 1983 a metropolitan Gelugpa centre was established in a town house in the Finsbury Park area of London. Originally called Manjushri London but renamed Jamyang Meditation Centre after formally dissociating with Manjushri Institute when this became the headquarters of the New Kadampa Tradition, it is under the spiritual direction of Lama Zopa Rinpoche. The resident teacher was Geshe Namgyal Wangchen (b. mid-1930s), a lama with a large smiling face and warm personality, and a graduate of Drepung. Ill health eventually forced him to return to India, but another Gelugpa Lama, Geshe Tashi, eventually took his place. As the centre expanded larger premises were needed, and Jamyang now occupies The Old Courthouse at Kennington, South London.

Lam Rim is a Gelugpa centre in South Wales. It is accommodated at Pentwyn Manor near Raglan in Gwent. The Resident Lama there is Geshe Damchö Yonten (b. 1930), yet another product of Drepung, who after leaving Tibet in 1959 was for a time Abbot of Samtenling monastery in Ladakh (North India). Geshe Damcho was brought to the West by another pioneering spirit, Tsunma Tsultem Zangmo (Connie Bolton; 1929–84), at one time an art student lecturer, who, like Freda Bedi, responded to the plight of Tibetan refugees in 1959, and in 1971, with her mother, ordained as a nun. Their original home in Bromley was consecrated by Geshe Rabten (see below) and used as a base by Harvey Horrocks while he was planning the creation of the Manjushri Institute.

Gelugpa activity has not been confined to Britain by any means. In recent years centres have proliferated all over Europe, even in traditionally Catholic countries like Italy, Spain and France, not to mention Germany, Austria, Switzerland and elsewhere. Notable among the many learned lamas that have lived and taught in this part of the world was Geshe Rabten (1920–86), a monk from Kham in eastern Tibet, trained at Sera monastery (Jé College), who in 1975 came to Rikon in Switzerland and two years later established Tharpa Choeling Centre for Higher Tibetan Studies now known as Rabten Choeling. An austere figure, strict in his adherence to the Vinaya and systematic *Lam.rim* training, Geshe Rabten in many ways epitomized the classic Gelugpa lama.

One of Geshe Rabten's ex-students, Stephen Batchelor (formerly Gelong Jhampa Thabkay), is a member of the new generation of European Buddhists who have undergone traditional training and, having become conversant with the Tibetan language in the process, have contributed useful translations of basic texts as well as original works of their own. Keith Dowman and Martin Willson are others. In the USA there are many more: Jeffrey Hopkins, Robert Thurman, Matthew Kapstein, Alexander Berzin, *et al*.

Always a very special event, of course, is a visit to Europe by the Dalai Lama, such as that which took place in 1984. In London that year, as highlights of a strenuous programme that took him all over Britain, His Holiness gave a three-day teaching on Buddhism and a special teaching on Dzogchen at the Camden Centre in King's Cross. The sumptuous brocades and *thangkas* (scroll paintings), the robes and ritual, the aroma of incense, the sounds of low chanting, the presence of numerous distinguished lamas and scholars as well as crowds of devoted Western monks, nuns and laity, all conspired to create a rich atmosphere that was at once deeply spiritual and brightly festive. With apparently inexhaustible energy, patience and good humour, His Holiness taught and performed ceremonial for hour after hour. He wore his high status and profound wisdom lightly, constantly smiling and breaking into laughter; and he put on no airs and graces but was throughout 'the

humble monk Tenzin Gyatso'. Then at a great public meeting at
the Albert Hall, accompanied by the Dean of Westminster, he
talked to a more general audience and showed himself to be the
spiritual leader of world rank that he has undoubtedly become.

A third Tibetan Buddhist tradition, the Sakya, has also
established itself in Europe. In 1977, Ven. Ngakpa Jampa
Thaye (Dr. David Stott, b. 1952) was inspired by his teacher,
Karma Thinley Rinpoche, a learned *tulku* from Kham, to found
Thinley Rinchen Ling in Bristol. Other Sakyapa centres have
since been founded in other parts of Britain. Ngakpa Jampa, a
lecturer by profession, gained his PhD from Manchester
University with a thesis on the History and Teachings of the
Dagpo Kagyu tradition. He received his qualification as a
Dharma-teacher from H.H. Sakya Trizin (b. 1945), the head of
the order, who left Tibet in 1959 and is currently based in India.
Meanwhile, Phendé Rinpoche (b. 1934), the head of the Ngor
sub-school of the Sakya order, came to France in 1969. A
'personality of great wisdom and exemplary faith', he married
a French lady and has established two centres, Ewam Phendé
Ling at Les Ventes-Evereux in Normandy and Ewam Kunzang
Ling in Paris.

Traditionally less worldly and well organized than the
followers of the other schools, the Nyingmapas have not been
so energetic and efficient in founding centres in Europe.
Nevertheless, they have not been inactive either. The late
supreme head of the order, Dudjom Rinpoche (1904–87),
latterly settled in the Dordogne area of France, where he finally
passed away. He had founded two centres in that country:
Dorje Nyingpo and Orgyen Samyé Choeling, where he
conducted a number of summer retreats. He is succeeded by his
son and Dharma heir, Shenphen Rinpoche.

Dudjom Rinpoche visited London three times at the
invitation of Sogyal Rinpoche, a young *tulku* born in Kham in
the mid-1940s and raised as a son by Jamyang Khyentse Chökyi
Lodrö (1896–1959), one of the luminaries of the non-partisan
Ri-mé movement that sprang up among Nyingma lamas in
eastern Tibet towards the end of the last century. True to the
Rimé tradition, Sogyal Rinpoche has received teaching and
transmissions in all the schools of Tibetan Buddhism, and his
Rigpa centres in London, Paris and Santa Cruz (California)

likewise host visits by important lamas of all traditions. After his escape from Tibet in 1958, Sogyal Rinpoche himself was educated at Delhi and Cambridge universities, so he is completely fluent in English and thoroughly adept at dealing with Westerners on their own terms. He is in fact one of a new and thoroughly modern generation of jet-setting lamas who are as conversant with the electronic gadgetry of the communications age as their forebears were with loose-leaved books printed from hand-cut woodblocks. He has given many appearances on the mass media, and attended conferences on psychotherapy, healing, meditation and peace; also death and dying, a subject in which he has lately specialized.

In recent times an ex-art student born in Farnham, Surrey in 1952, who has taken the name Ngakpa Chögyam Ögyen Pogden, has begun teaching as a shamanistic tantric adept (*ngakpa*) of the ancient 'white' lineage of Tibet. Certainly creative and endowed with infectious enthusiasm, Ngakpa Chögyam has also accurately homed in on a glaring deficiency in Western culture: the lack of a spiritually authentic magical dimension. He no doubt aims to fill it.

Finally, Dzogchen. Though this exists as a teaching in the Nyingma school, it is propagated as an independent and self-contained teaching in the tradition of Adjom Drukpa (early 20th century) by Namkhai Norbu Rinpoche, a married lama born in 1938 in the Dergé district of eastern Tibet. Norbu was brought to Europe in 1960 by Professor Tucci and worked for Tucci's IsMEO organization in Rome until becoming a professor in the Oriental Institute of Naples University in 1965. Lately he has guided the Dzogchen Community, an informal association of students scattered through various countries, including Italy, France, Austria, Britain, Denmark, Norway and the USA.

Pure Land Buddhism

Dr. Suzuki is generally associated with the Zen School, so it is often a matter of surprise to hear that he translated many Pure Land Buddhist texts into English and nourished a belief that Pure Land rather than Zen might be the form of Buddhism most suitable for Westerners.

Pure Land Buddhism, which developed from the cult of Amitabha, represents a flowering of the devotional tendency that arose within the Mahāyāna in answer to the demand by lay people for a more substantial spiritual role than had been afforded them within the Hinayana schools. It was passed to China and thence to Japan, where during the 13th century it divided into two main branches:

1. The Pure Land School (Jap. *Jōdo Shū*) of Hōnen; and
2. The True Pure Land School (Jap. *Jōdo Shinshū*) of Shinran.

Both Jōdo Shū and Jōdo Shinshū subscribe to the notion of *mappo*: that we are in a degenerate age when it is hopeless (and arrogant) to think that we can be saved by our own efforts alone. We must therefore surrender ourselves to the infinite mercy of Amitābha (or Amida) Buddha, whose 'other power' (Jap. *tariki*) can achieve what we ourselves, alone and unaided, cannot hope to achieve. The salvation projected is rebirth in Amida's Western Paradise of *Sukhāvatī*, though this may also be discovered here, in the world, while still occupying a human body. Trevor Leggett has retold a forceful story of a great Zen Master who one day met an old lady devoted to Pure Land walking along the road.

'On your way to the Pure Land then, Granny?' the Zen man quipped rather condescendingly.

The old lady nodded.

'Amida Buddha will be waiting for you, I suppose?'

The old lady shook her head vigorously.

'What – Amida Buddha not in his Pure Land! Where is he, then?'

Gently the old lady tapped her heart twice, then continued on her way.

The Zen Master was deeply impressed. 'There's a real Pure Lander!' he said to himself.

The difference between the Jōdo Shū and Jōdo Shinshū is more one of emphasis than of fundamentals. The central practice in both is the recitation of the *Nembutsu* – the *mantra*, (*Namu-Amida-butsu*). However, what little faith in 'self power' (Jap. *jiriki*) remained in Hōnen's thought was completely discarded in that of Shinran, who called for a more total surrender to Amida's mercy. Shinran also married and thereby set a strong non-monastic tradition which has remained to the present. Shinran's Jōdo Shinshū (often called simply Shin) has been most influential in the West.

There was very little Shin in Britain and the rest of Europe down to World War II, though an Englishman born Ernest Hunt in Hoddesden, Hertfordshire (incidentally the home for many years of the Buddhist Society Summer School), was ordained a Jōdo Shinshū priest in Hawaii in 1924. For many years Rev. Shinkaku Hunt (1876–1967) did energetic good work among the expatriate Japanese or *nisei*, many of them Pure Land followers, who form a sizeable community on the Hawaiian Isles. On a return visit to his native land in 1929, he was entertained at the Buddhist Lodge. 'The Lodge welcomed back to England on a well-earned holiday one of its noted Buddhist sons', wrote Christmas Humphreys of the occasion. Hunt gravitated to the Sōtō Zen school towards the end of his life.

A pioneering figure in Britain since World War II was Rev. Jack Austin (1917–93), though his activities were in no way limited to this school alone.[52] In 1976 he co-founded the Shin Buddhist Association in London under the patronage of Abbot Kōshō Ohtani of Nishi (West) Hongwan-ji, one of the twin head-temples of Shin in Kyōto. With Abbot Ohtani's help, Rev. Austin went to Japan in 1977 and was ordained a Hongwan-ji priest. He also stayed at the Kobe home of his Shin teacher of some 25 years, Rev. Zuiken Saizo Inagaki, who arranged visits and meetings in various parts of Japan.

The son of Sensei Inagaki, Professor Hisao Inagaki, also a Shin priest, spent some time in London during the 1970s as a lecturer at the School of Oriental & African Studies. He was co-founder with Jack Austin of the Shin Buddhist Association. He also established a Pure Land Buddhist Fellowship in his home in 1977, and this continues to the present as an informal, non-sectarian 'network of communicants' that seeks to do without leaders, authorities, chairpersons, presidents, secretaries, constitutions, rules and principles (apart from this one).' Max Flisher, one of its members, has written:

For us, our Buddha's Enlightenment is sufficient for all. We are, I suppose, compassion-orientated and hope that our reliance on the Great Compassion is increasing our own and that the promise of the Pure Land (Nirvana) specified in the Primal Vow of Amita (sic) Buddha is being fulfilled in us. All the Buddhas continually say and praise his Name, which we hear as *Namoamitabuddha* (called *Nembutsu* in Japanese). We rely totally on that. The Buddha does everything, including helping us to rely on him. 'Namoamita-buddha' is his voice teaching us the Dharma through our blood, heart, body, nervous system and every fibre of our being. It is calling us to the Pure Land and acculturing us to it. We merely listen (overhear rather). Sometimes it bursts from us in joy and thanksgiving. Who needs an organization? Communication is the name of the game.[53]

Notable in Shin on the Continent is Adriaan Peel, who was initiated as Shaku Shitoku by Abbot Kōshō Ohtani in London in 1977. More recently a property was purchased in Antwerp and consecrated as the first Pure Land temple in Europe. 'The opening was a splendid affair', Rev. Jack Austin reported. 'The Chief Abbot conducted it, and all European Shin leaders were present.'[54]

There is also a Jōdo Shin group in Austria, which has its headquarters in Salzburg. This was set up by Friedrich Fenzl, who was converted to Jōdo Shinshū in 1960 through the influence of Harry Pieper (1902–78), the original leader of the German Shin movement. In 1966, Pieper founded the first Pure Land Association in Europe (Buddhistische Gemeinschaft Jōdo-Shin). His good work is currently carried on by Gerhard Kell (b. 1948). Rev. Jean Eracle and Rev. Jōdo Chevrier, meanwhile, are Shin leaders in Switzerland.

Nichiren School

The success of some of the new Japanese Nichiren societies in Britain and other parts of Europe in recent years has been striking, and parallels a similar success on the other side of the Atlantic. Their lay orientation, unascetic character and simpler approach to practice tend to widen the base of their appeal.

Sōka Gakkai was founded in 1930 by Tsunesaburo Makiguchi (1871–1944). It came to Europe where it is known as Sōka Gakkai International in the 1970s. Its headquarters are in Taplow Court, near Maidenhead, Berkshire, and the first Chairman was Richard Causton (1920–95), a former professional soldier and businessman who came across Sōka Gakkai – an 'electrifying experience' – while working for the Alfred Dunhill organization in Japan. The present chairman is Richard Baynes. Sōka Gakkai International has taken on remarkably, noticeably among many younger people, but later attracting all age groups, whom in the usual course would not be expected to be attracted to Buddhism, such as stars of show business. Part of its appeal may lie in the fact that it does not disparage this-worldly success. Newcomers are encouraged to chant for what they want in terms of money, material goods, job success, and the fulfilment of other personal desires. On the face of it this looks a very un-Buddhist approach, more likely to strengthen than to diminish *tanhā*. However, within the movement things are viewed differently. There desire is recognized as having positive uses; in particular it can be used to demonstrate the power of spiritual practice, and this in itself can have a profoundly transformative effect.

Nichiren Shōshū practice breaks down into three parts:

1 *Faith* – in the power of the *Gōhōnzon*, which is a scroll on which the *mantra*, *Namu-myōhō-renge-kyō* is written in the form of a *mandala*. The original, or *Dai Gōhōnzon*, of which each member has a copy, was written by the 13th century priest Nichiren Daishōnin, and is presently enshrined at the Nichiren Shoshu head temple, Taiseki-ji, at the foot of Mount Fuji in Japan.

2 *Study* – of Buddhist teaching as restated by Nichiren and his successors within the movement, notably Daisaku Ikeda (b. 1928), the current President of Sōka Gakkai International.

3 *Intensive practice* – to perform *Gongyō* twice daily: i.e. chant *Namu-myōhō-renge-kyō* in front of the *Gōhōnzon* and recite part of the second and the whole of the sixteenth chapter of the *Lotus Sūtra*.

Discussion and guidance is also offered and members are now encouraged to share the teachings with others, rather than proselytize or *shakubuku* non-members, as they once did.

The Reiyukai was founded in Japan in 1919 and registered in 1930 by Kakutaro Kubo (1892–1944) and Kimi Kotani (1901–71). The current President is Dr. Tsugunari Kubo, the founder's son. A British branch was set up in 1976 by a Japanese educationalist named Hiromi Hasegawa (b. 1947), who had come to Norfolk some years before to study. Beginnings were modest. A small office was established in a semi-detached house in a Norwich backwater. By 1984, however, sufficient funds had been gathered to open the more ambitious Oriental Arts Centre (current Secretary, Julian Wilde). Another branch of the movement has also been set up in Liverpool, while in Europe there are centres in Italy and Spain; also in France, where it has taken off very strongly thanks to the efforts of Mr. and Mrs. Shinuda.

Reiyukai practice is simple. A typical meeting begins with recitation of portions of the so-called 'Blue Sūtra' (the original copies were bound in blue), a compilation derived from the *Lotus Sūtra*. Afterwards there may be a period of meditation or chanting. (*Namu-myōhō-renge-kyō*), then open discussion. Emphasis is laid on spiritual friendship and on followers positively opening themselves to each other. At one time a form of 'ancestor remembrance' was practised when in true Confucian style family and forebears were remembered, but latterly it has declined in popularity. This is accepted, for, by the very tenets of Buddhism, all things must change.

Rissho⁻ Ko⁻sei-kai was founded in 1938 by Rev. Nikkyo Niwano and Mrs. M. Nakaguma. Its central practices include the *Ho⁻za* (Circle of Compassion) and the Discipline of Veneration. At present there is only one small RKK group in London organized by Jill Sullivan and not more than one or two more in the rest of Europe, though the worldwide membership is said to top 5 million.

Entirely different in character are the monks and nuns of the Nipponzan Myōhōji order, who are strictly ascetic and celibate, and practise frequent ablution rites. Their founder, Ven. Nichidatsu Fujii (1885–1985), who was profoundly influenced by Mahātma Gandhi, saw the world being hustled recklessly towards total destruction by the 'power of machines'. The remedy he proposed was the ideal of *risshō-ankoku*: the establishment of true religion and the realization of peace on earth. From this developed the radical pacifism of the order. Its monks and nuns march for peace, speak out for peace and have built beautiful peace pagodas in many parts of the world. There are two in Britain: one at Milton Keynes and another in Battersea Park on the banks of the Thames in London. Another is to be found in Austria, on the banks of the Danube. The central religious practice of Nippozan Myōhōji is again the chanting of *Namu-myōhō-renge-kyō* (the *Odaimoku*), to the accompaniment of the beating of a hand-drum. Ven. Fujii wrote: 'Just chant *Odaimoku* loudly and beat your drum when you are fearful. Nothing is required. Depend on nothing else. Solely chant *Odaimoku* as long as you can, and die when you can chant no longer. That is all. That is all'.[55]

Theravāda

The remarkable rise of the Māhāyana schools in Europe has not meant that the Theravāda has been totally eclipsed by any means. It still remains a highly significant presence – and indeed, with the unexpected explosion of interest in Buddhism in the 1960s and after, very impressive new developments have taken place within this tradition too.

Basically one can detect two strands within the Theravāda in the West: an ethnic strand and a native Western one. The former consists of activities, notably the founding of temples and centres by expatriate communities from traditional Theravāda countries, mainly Sri Lankans, Thais and Burmese, but also more recently Indian Buddhist followers of Dr. Ambedkar – the former so-called 'Untouchables'. The other strand meanwhile is centrally concerned with the foundation of a Sangha of native-born (or more precisely, Western-born) monks and nuns.

As we have noted, the British Mahābodhi Society was established by Anagārika Dharmapāla in London as far back as 1926, and a Sri Lankan *vihāra* materialized soon afterwards and ran until World War II (1940). After the War, in 1948, a group was formed with the intention of founding a new *vihāra* where *bhikkhus* might reside. The prominent English-educated

Sri Lankan *bhikkhu*, Ven. Nārada Mahā Thera (1898–1983), played an important role in this Buddhist Vihāra Society in England, and he himself visited and lectured extensively in Britain in 1949. Eventually a group of wealthy Sri Lankans headed by Cyril de Zoysa obtained the lease of a house in Ovington Gardens, Knightsbridge, and this was opened as the new London Buddhist Vihāra with all due pomp and ceremony on Vesak Day, 1954. The Thai Ambassador unfurled the flag and speeches were delivered by Nārada Thera himself, the ubiquitous Christmas Humphreys, Miss Grace Constant Lounsbery of Les Amis du Bouddhisme in Paris and others.

Ven. Nārada led the small group of *bhikkhus* resident at the Vihāra until 1955. Then in 1957, Ven. Dr. Hammalawa Saddhatissa Thera (1914–90) came to take over, and remained in London, off and on, until he died. Dr. Saddhatissa was a distinguished scholar who held academic posts at the Universities of London and Toronto; he also lectured widely in Europe, the USA and Japan, as well as writing, editing and translating numerous works. In 1964, the Vihāra moved to new premises in a modestly sized house in Heathfield Gardens, Chiswick, where it has remained ever since. Two years later Ven. Dr. Saddhatissa revived the British Maha Bodhi Society. The present Head of the Vihāra is Ven. Medagama Vajiragnana (b. 1928), a very practically-minded *bhikkhu*, who previously established himself in London in 1967 and in 1974 became Religious Director of the British Buddhist Association, a group founded in the same year by A. Haviland-Nye (a professional silversmith), with the aim of:

1 Providing systematic instruction in the Dhamma, primarily based on Pali sources.
2 Promoting textual, canonical and linguistic studies.
3 Advising on matters relating to the Dhamma, its practice, study and literature.
4 Maintaining close contact with individuals and groups in the West interested in promoting and supporting the foregoing aims.

A Thai *vihāra*, the Buddhapadipa Temple, backed with Thai government funding, was meanwhile opened in London in 1966 by the King and Queen of Thailand. The first incumbent was

Phra Mahā Vichit Tissadatto (b. 1934), who was later promoted to Chao Khun and renamed Sobhana Dhammasudhi. 'Chao Khun' is a title that roughly means 'Noble Lord' and is conferred along with a new name when a *bhikkhu* is elevated to a status virtually equivalent to bishophood. Sobhana Dhammasudhi was a young monk with a great deal of charm and flair, who soon gathered an entourage of enthusiastic Western followers. He caused a few eyebrows to raise, however, when around 1971 he left the robe. Afterwards he worked as a lay meditation master under the name Dhiravamsa, establishing a centre, Chapter House, at Wisbech in Cambridgeshire. Later he crossed the Atlantic and began to experiment with combining traditional *samatha-vipassanā* meditation with modern Western psychotherapeutic techniques. For instance, a certain amount of expression might be permissible within the structure of formal silent sitting practice in the interests of releasing repressed emotional energies. Latest information is that he has reverted to more traditional approaches.

In 1975, the Buddhapadipa Temple moved to the more spacious environs of Barrogill House, Calonne Road, Wimbledon Parkside. In the 4-acre grounds, a beautiful gilded Uposatha Hall[56] has been built in traditional Thai architectural style, with shining white walls, pillars and balustrades, steeply-pitched roof of red tile, and intricately carved eaves and doorways. Inside, the walls have been decorated with vibrantly colourful murals, the work of gifted Thai artists, depicting traditional scenes from the life of the Buddha and from Buddhist mythology. The Hall was opened in 1987.

The Buddhapadipa Temple is occupied by five missionary (*dhammadūta*) monks, who are assisted in running the place by various lay groups. The monks, who come under the authority of a Senior Incumbent, are selected and sent over by the Sangha Supreme Council of Thailand. It offers a very comprehensive full programme of activities, including Pali and Abhidhamma classes, meditation and all the traditional reciprocal activities involving Sangha and laity.

The expatriate Burmese community in Britain did not open a *viharā* until 1978. This enjoys the dual title of West Midlands Buddhist Centre/Birmingham Buddhist Vihāra. For the first four years of its existence it shared a house with the local Karma

Kagyu group and was honoured by the patronage of the late
Gyalwa Karmapa, who appointed Dr. U Rewata Dhamma (b.
1929) as Spiritual Director. Now the Theravāda *vihāra* has its
own premises. Dr. Rewata Dhamma, who first came to Britain
in 1975, is a remarkable Burmese *bhikkhu* who has not only
developed the scholarly side of his vocation but has also trained
in *vipassanā* meditation with S.N. Goenka and been appointed
a teacher by no less a luminary than Mahāsi Sayadaw. At
present he has one resident British *bhikkhu* and together they
operate the *vihāra* on the lines of a small town temple in Burma,
giving Abhidhamma classes, meditation instruction and
retreats, celebrating the feast days and giving those short-term
ordinations that are traditional in the East (see p 130; these are
also given at the Buddhapadipa Temple). More recently, in
1984, a Burmese temple was opened in north London, near
Wembley Stadium. The *sayadaw* here is U Nyanika, an
Abhidhamma scholar, and he presently has three *bhikkhus* with
him, one of them of British birth.

British Buddhist connections with Burma, now Myanmar, go
back a long way, however, due to the old Imperial link. Many
British *bhikkhus*, from the time of the very first, Ananada
Metteyya, have gone to Burma for training, though present visa
restrictions make this no longer feasible. Burmese *bhikkhus*
have also come to Britain from time to time, some of them, like
Mahāsi Sayadaw (1904–82) on brief visits, others, like
Sayadaw U Thittila (1896–1997), for longer stays. During
World War II, U Thittila worked as a stretcher-bearer in
London during the Blitz; he also lectured widely both then and
later, notably on Abhidhamma, and for a while was Librarian
at the Buddhist Society. In 1952, he returned to Burma to take
up the post of Professor of Pali at Rangoon University, though
he returned several times since. Nor should the good work of U
Myat Saw (1918–84) be overlooked. A successful businessman,
he came to Britain in 1965 and in 1971 established a Buddhist
Centre at 'Oaken Holt', a large house just outside Oxford,
where meditation courses and retreats were held until his death.

British-born Buddhists continued to go East for training and
ordination after World War II – indeed, the traumas of the War
encouraged many to do so. Osbert Moore (1905–60), for
instance, discovered a copy of Julius Evola's *The Doctrine of*

Awakening while serving in the Army in wartime Italy. In 1949 he went to Sri Lanka and was ordained the following year as Nāṇamoli Bhikkhu. Thereafter, until his premature death, he did important translation work. Lawrence Mills (b. 1932) also discovered Buddhism through books while with the Army in the Suez Canal Zone after the war. He later received novice ordination in Britain from Ven. Dr. Saddhatissa before going to the East. He was ordained Phra Khantipalo and lived for some 11 years in Thailand before departing for Australia, where he taught for a while at Wat Buddha-Dhamma in rural New South Wales. He later disrobed and married, and is currently trying to set up a Buddhist community in a former hippie area in New South Wales.

But the great saga at the heart of all Theravāda activity in Britain and Europe since World War II has been the ongoing endeavour to establish a native Western Sangha. This holds great symbolic significance for all those Western Buddhists who would like the satisfaction of knowing that Buddhism has taken firm root on their native ground. The key lies in words spoken during the first Buddhist missionary efforts on the island of Sri Lanka. The convert King Devanampiyatissa was also eager to be assured that the Buddha's Way had taken root in Sri Lankan soil; when he asked Ven. Mahinda for confirmation of this, he was told:

> Only when a *Sīmā* (consecrated space for ordinations, etc.) has been built and when a son, born in Sri Lanka of Sri Lankan parents studies the Vinaya in Sri Lanka and recites them in Sri Lanka – only then will it be true to say that the Buddha's Way has taken root here. . . .

The man who carried on the torch first lit by Ananda Metteyya into the post-War era was William Purfurst (1906–71), a small, intense man of many talents. In the War, during the Blitz on London, his duties as a fireman put him in contact with Sayadaw U Thittila, whose pupil he became and with whom he continued his Buddhist studies into the post-War era. His dedication deepened, and eventually he was given permission by his wife to ordain. He became first an *anagārika* and then a *sāmanera* (novice). He worked vigorously for Buddhism, setting up provincial groups, lecturing, writing and even establishing the Buddhist Summer School, which survives to the present day under the auspices of the Buddhist Society, for which he also worked. Full ordination was the next obvious step. He therefore took a job as a barman at a hotel in Surrey to obtain the finance to travel to Thailand, where in 1954, at a ceremony at Wat Paknam, Thonburi, he received novice ordination as Kapilavaddho, the name being based on that of the Buddha's 'home town' of Kapilavatthu, signifying – appropriately – 'he who spreads the *Dhamma*'. Full *bhikkhu* ordination followed a month later at Vesak.

Having applied himself to an intensive course of *vipassanā* meditation, Kapilavaddho returned to London later in the same year with full authority to teach Buddhist subjects. Taking up residence at the Sri Lankan Vihāra in Chiswick, he threw himself into the self-appointed task of founding an English branch of the Bhikkhu Sangha. To this end he established the English Sangha Trust; then, later in 1955, he returned to Thailand with three recently ordained novice *bhikkhus*: Robert Albison, George Blake and Peter Morgan - an Englishman, a West Indian and a Welshman respectively. They were fully ordained early in 1956 and returned to London as a seminal English Sangha, taking up residence at 50 Alexandra Road, St. John's Wood.

But the enormous workload that Kapilavaddho had carried in recent years – and continued to carry with unabated vigour – now began to take its toll. Finally in 1957 his health broke down and he was obliged to disrobe and return to lay life. Happily, the grim prognosis his doctor had given that he had only a month to live was not realized, though as far as the Buddhist world was concerned it might have been. Changing his name to Richard Randall for the sake of anonymity, he remarried and for more than ten years dropped out of sight. Those ten years were a lean period for the English Sangha, for two of the other three *bhikkhus* also left the robe, leaving Ven. Paññavaddho to struggle on for long periods alone. Eventually Ven. Paññavaddho left for Thailand, where he has remained ever since as a disciple of Ajahn Mahā Boowa, apart from a brief visit to England in 1974.

In 1962 new premises were obtained at 131 Haverstock Hill in Hampstead; also a meditation centre at Biddulph in Staffordshire. These were ably run for two years by the

Canadian-born *bhikkhu*, Ananda Bodhi (Leslie Dawson). In 1967, after ten years in the wilderness, Ven. Kapilavaddho returned to the robe and took over the new *vihāra*. As Maurice Walshe, then Chairman of the English Sangha Trust, has written:

> Soon the Hampstead Vihāra was bursting with activity. The *bhikkhu*, with seemingly his old energy restored, was at work. Meditation cells were built at the back, classes were re-established, plans for a Sangha were again formulated. Some young men came forward and received their lower ordination, among them Alan James, who was ordained as Dipadhammo Bhikkhu. Once again, all seemed set fair for the establishing of an English branch of the ancient order of *bhikkhus*.[57]

However, setbacks struck yet again. Alan James returned to lay life and soon after Ven. Kapilavaddho followed suit. He married for a third time, but less than 3 months later his health gave way completely and in 1971 he succumbed to a combination of maladies. Meanwhile, with no *bhikkhus* resident, the house in Hampstead could no longer be called a *vihāra*, just a Buddhist centre in search of a Sangha.

In 1974, Ajahn Mahā Boowa visited Hampstead. Shortly afterwards, an American-born *bhikkhu*, Ven. Sumedho, stopped over briefly on his way back from the United States to Thailand, where for some ten years he had been a disciple of Ajahn Cha, a meditation master of the north-east Thai Forest Tradition who had attracted a number of Western disciples. As a result of this meeting, the Chairman of the English Sangha Trust, George Sharp, flew to Thailand to meet with Ajahn Cha, an auspicious event for in 1977 Ajahn Cha came to Hampstead with several of his Western disciples, including Ven. Sumedho and the English-born Ven. Khemadhammo. Ajahn Cha later returned to Thailand but Ven. Sumedho and his fellow Western *bhikkhus* stayed on at the *vihāra*.

This turned out to be a highly fortunate turn of events. Ajahn Sumedho, as he has become, has proved himself possessed of leadership qualities of an exceptionally high order, with spiritual qualities to match. He also has the ability to put the *Dhamma* across to Westerners in their own terms, and with humour, lightness and lucidity. He has attracted a vast following of lay disciples and many have been inspired by his noble teaching to join the Sangha as monks or nuns.

An important development was the gift of a 108-acre tract of woodland in rural West Sussex, Hammer Wood, which has its own lake – a perfect environment for a forest Sangha. The old Hampstead Vihāra was therefore sold off, and a large derelict mansion, Chithurst House, situated just a stone's throw away from Hammer Wood, was purchased in 1979 and renovated. Later a nearby cottage was purchased to house the growing community of nuns. In 1981, both houses and forest were officially designated for monastic use, and in the same year a simā or 'specially defined area in which acts of the Bhikkhu Sangha may take place' was established with the guidance of Ven. Ananda Maitreya. In July that year three anagārikas received bhikkhu ordination within the new simā, thus broadly fulfilling the terms that Ven. Mahinda stipulated to King Devanampiyatissa.

The growth and spread of this new Sangha has been remarkable. In 1981 a branch monastery, Harnham Vihāra, was opened up in the north of England, in 1983 a Devon Vihāra was opened in the West Country, and in 1997 became the first ever community of western Theravadan nuns. In 1984 a vast complex near Hemel Hempstead in Hertfordshire that had once served as a residential school for handicapped children was acquired and opened in 1985 as Amarāvati: the Deathless. Thus an English Sangha – or more accurately an International Western Sangha – has now been firmly established on British soil – and is sending out tendrils into Europe, America, the Antipodes and other parts of the English-speaking world. In 1985, two bhikkhus were sent to establish a branch monastery in New Zealand, and another is soon to be established in Berne, Switzerland. Ven. Khemadhammo has meanwhile established separate vihāra, firstly on the Isle of Wight and more recently near Warwick in the Midlands. He has also been very energetic in developing a Buddhist Prison Chaplaincy Service (Angulimāla).

A number of people who have received formal Theravāda training, sometimes as ordained Sangha members but not necessarily so, have gone on to establish themselves as lay meditation teachers. Jack Kornfield, once one of Ajahn Cha's *bhikkhus*, is a notable American example. His colleague at the Insight Meditation Society at Barre in Massachusetts, Joseph Goldstein, meanwhile, trained with Anagarika Munindra in Bodh Gāya. In Britain, on the other hand, there are Christopher Titmuss and Christina Feldman, who were two of the founding inspirations behind Gaia House, a retreat centre in South Devon that offers a very full programme of events that includes regular *vipassanā* retreats. These are occasionally led by Anagārika Vimalo (Walter Kulbarz), who was ordained at the old Thai Embassy in London with his twin brother and later spent many years in Thailand before finally giving up the robe.

Vimalo also taught at and later became a member of the Sharpham North Community, situated not far from Gaia House in South Devon. This was an experimental community of non-sectarian meditators, who were concerned to develop a lifestyle in which religious practice is properly integrated but without the encumbrance of all the usual monastic and institutional religious trappings. The community wound down in 1996, but the premises are now used for the Sharpham College of Buddhist Studies and Contemporary Enquiry.

Alan James, who was Ven. Kapilavaddho's right hand man for a time at Hampstead, married his late teacher's widow, Jacqui (1946–89), and together they established the House of Inner Tranquillity at Bradford-on-Avon in Wiltshire, where lectures, classes and courses in *vipassanā* take place. Furthermore, centres have also been set up where the intensive meditation methods developed by Sayagyi U Ba Khin and S.N. Goenka are taught.

Western Buddhism

From the early days of the Buddhist movement there was talk of the development of a distinctly Western form of Buddhism. The arguments are by now classic. The core of Buddhism is timeless and universal, they run, but around this all manner of secondary accretions have built up: the incidental trappings inherited from the various cultures in which Buddhism has developed. These are not only inessential but often distracting or confusing and so prevent Buddhism from becoming readily assimilable in modern Western contexts. What needs to be done, therefore, is to strip away the inessential and reconcile the essential with modern Western culture: the prevailing religious, artistic and intellectual traditions, modern science and psychology – and so forth.

More than half a century ago now, Captain J.E. Ellam, the Hon. Secretary of the original Buddhist Society of Gt. Britain and Ireland, coined the term *Navayāna* – 'New *yāna* (or vehicle)' – and wrote a book on the subject. Later, in 1951, a Western Buddhist Order was set up in the United States by Ven. Sumangalo (Robert Clifton; 1903–63). This was 'an organization dedicated to interpreting the Dharma to the West and establishing groups where none existed.' It was represented in this country by Rev. Jack Austin. More recently, we have seen the emergence in Britain of a Scientific Buddhist Association (founded by Gerald du Pré and Paul Ingram) and also of a movement calling itself the Friends of the Western Buddhist Order (FWBO) – or simply, the Western Buddhist Order (WBO).

The inspiration behind the FWBO is Ven. Mahā Sthavira Sangharakshita (D.P.E. Lingwood; b. 1925). Having discovered his natural affinities with Buddhism, Sangharakshita joined the Buddhist Society at the age of 18. During World War II, he saw service in the East and afterwards remained out there, living the homeless life. He took *sāmanera* ordination in 1949 and *bhikkhu* ordination the following year. He studied Abhidhamma, Pali and Logic at Benares (Varanasi) University with Ven. Jagdish Kashyap, and later settled in the well-known hill station of Kalimpong, where he set up the Triyāna Vardhāna Vihāra ('Monastery of the Three Vehicles'), a title which indicates his interest in *all* schools of Buddhism. When the lamas began to leave Tibet in the 1950s, many passed through Kalimpong and this allowed Sangharakshita to meet and study with several, notably Jamyang Khyentse Rinpoche and Dhardo Rinpoche. The latter gave him Mahāyāna ordination. During this period he put his considerable scholarly and literary skills to good use, writing *A Survey of Buddhism* – many other books followed – and either contributing to or editing a number of journals. He also became active in Dr. B.R. Ambedkar's movement and is said to have officiated at a mass conversion of some 500,000 so-called 'Untouchables' (*Harijans*).

In 1964, Sangharakshita returned to Britain and took up residence at the old Hampstead Buddhist Vihara. For a time his impressive learning made him the idol of the British Buddhist scene, and he in his turn was apparently impressed that 'there was great potential for the Dharma in the West'. But problems arose and there was a parting of the ways. In 1967 he founded the FWBO. Its first meetings were held in a small room beneath a shop selling Orientalia in central London. Soon, however, the Order blossomed and obtained its own premises; then as its numbers grew it was able to branch out in many directions. It now has many city centres scattered right across Britain as well as abroad, each offering a full programme of classes and meditation sessions. Many of these centres are supported by Right Livelihood Co-operatives based on, for example, wholefood shops, vegetarian restaurants, building teams and gardening businesses. There are also retreat and arts centres, and many of the members (though not all) live in single-sex communities with other members. Books and magazines are published too, and a charity, Aid to India, has been set up to support medical, educational and Buddhist missionary work among the Untouchables.

What characterizes the brand of 'Western Buddhism' propagated by the FWBO? In the first place, it disfavours the monastic orientation of traditional Eastern Buddhism but recognizes the advantages to be derived from close association with spiritual friends within the matrix of community. The term '*Sangha*' has a special use within the FWBO: it does not merely denote the monastic segment of the Buddhist community but the whole community. Those who live and work together within the Order are encouraged to develop 'positive and direct communication'[58] with each other, and to generally strive to co-exist in an 'ethical, harmonious and altruistic way'. Begging as a means of livelihood is regarded as not viable within a Western cultural context, hence the development of Right Livelihood Co-operatives. In terms of study and practice, the approach is essentially eclectic: Pali texts, Mahāyāna *sūtras* and Tibetan works are all studied, but intellectual activity is always balanced with meditation, devotional *pūjā* and often some kind of physical discipline like *T'ai Chi* or *karate*. In terms of practice, each individual is encouraged to search for those particular techniques that work in their individual case and then commit themselves to them: a matter of 'more and more of less and less':

> All newcomers are taught Mindfulness of Breathing and the Mettā Bhāvāna (Development of Loving Kindness) meditation practices, and anyone at all seriously involved practises meditation at least once a day. Order Members at their ordination receive a visualization practice and often take up other insight practices as well. Devotional practices are also regularly performed, especially a Sevenfold Pūjā derived from Shantideva's *Bodhicāryāvatāra*. Sangharakshita has said on occasions that many Western Buddhists probably *know* all that they need to know intellectually in order to gain enlightenment. The next step is regular practice of Mettā and of Pūjā so that people can engage their emotions fully in their spiritual lives and create the positive emotional basis necessary for the transformation of Right Views into Perfect Vision.[59]

FWBO writings talk much about *commitment*. Indeed, one of their strongest criticisms of most other Western lay Buddhist societies is what they regard as their lack of serious commitment to practice of the Dharma. Dharmachari Subhuti, a vigorous FWBO theoretician and organizer, claims in one of his books that these societies 'cater for little more than a mild and amateurish interest and . . . their organization is often fraught with intrigue'.[60]

Membership of the FWBO therefore evolves an ever-deepening process of commitment to the Order and to Buddhist practice. Those who merely gravitate to the Order and frequent its centres informally are known as 'friends'. Later they may apply to be ordained as *Mitras*, and later still as Order Members. The last stage is preceded by a period of intensive training, at the end of which the readiness of the various candidates for ordination will be judged. If they make the grade, then they undergo an ordination ceremony based on the traditional *upāsaka* or lay follower ordination, though within the Order the old monk-layman dichotomy has been abolished. The ceremony itself centres around the act of Going for Refuge to the Three Jewels of Buddha, Dharma and Sangha; a new name is also given. Finally, if at any stage an Order Member feels that his spiritual development would benefit from a spell of voluntary celibacy, he may take *anagārika* ordination.

While there is much that is entirely laudable in the FWBO's work and it has certainly been very successful in terms of attracting followers and establishing centres, neither the more conventional lay societies nor the monastic based groups imported from the East have turned out to be as moribund as Dharmachari Subhuti has intimated. Many if not most have done very useful work, not least in encouraging serious practice. So it is as yet unclear what the future shape of 'Western Buddhism' will be: whether that prefigured by the FWBO or something else. Certainly the process of westernization will take time – after all, Buddhism took centuries to become fully sinicized in China – and in all probability the process will very largely take care of itself. There are after all distinct dangers in trying to force the pace: in trying to adapt and modify too fast, and on the basis of insufficient knowledge and understanding. The proverbial baby may be thrown out with the bathwater. Many years ago, when as now these matters were being hotly debated, one wise pundit remarked, 'Perhaps before we begin changing Buddhism to suit ourselves we should know what Buddhism really is' – and the logical corollary was to study the religion in its traditional Eastern forms.

Conclusion

The Buddhist Society has continued to the present discharging its traditional function as a kind of shop-window in which all forms of Buddhism are, without partiality, displayed for the newcomer. Of course the balance has faltered on occasion, and in 1983 it received a grave set-back when its Founder-President, Christmas Humphreys, passed away. For a time, with that towering personality gone, it inevitably drifted for want of definite leadership and direction, but now that its new President, Ajahn Sumedho, has more time at his disposal, there is every hope that a new and positive phase in its history will begin. It continues to offer a full programme of lectures and classes; it publishes a journal, *The Middle Way*, runs a Correspondence Course and holds a two-week Summer School every year. The General Week of the Summer School provides an excellent opportunity for the newcomer to come in contact with most if not all of the different schools of Buddhism.

Besides the important centres that we have described here and the ones in the major cities, small local centres are springing up in smaller towns and villages right across Britain and the rest of Europe. Specialist Buddhist groups are also beginning to emerge: ones concerned with issues like peace, social action and animal rights. The issue of women in Buddhism is a frequent talking point too, not least because women are accorded a distinctly secondary place in traditional Eastern Buddhism and, in addition, the order of nuns has very largely died out, thus denying to half the Buddhist population the advantages inherent in higher ordination. At the same time, Buddhist studies are also beginning to be offered as part of university courses, and the volume of Buddhist books currently being produced in the West, both original works, translations and editions, has reached the proportions of a major industry. Surveying all this, it would certainly seem that Christmas Humphreys' optimistic view that Buddhism is a spiritual movement whose time has come has been amply borne out.

Battersea Peace Pagoda

20 Useful Addresses

After international and national organizations, individual monasteries, centres and groups are listed according to the school or tradition of Buddhism to which they are affiliated. Firstly British addresses are given, then ones in Europe, finally the rest of the world. We end with miscellaneous specialist listings – 'Women and Buddhism', 'Engaged Buddhism', etc.

Those who need more comprehensive listings are recommended to consult:

❑ For Britain: *The Buddhist Directory* (The Buddhist Society, London, 7th edition 1997).
❑ For North America: The US edition of this book (Inner Traditions International, Rochester, Vermont, 1992) and *Buddhist America*, edited by Don Morreale (John Muir Publications, Santa Fé, New Mexico, 1988).
❑ For Japan: *Zen Guide* by Martin Roth and John Stevens (Weatherhill, New York and Tokyo, 1985), which has descriptions and details of the major Zen temples.
❑ For any other country – contact the national organization.

Due to reasons of space, this is necessarily a very brief listing.

International Organizations

Council for the Preservation of the Maháyáa Tradition, Paula de Wys-Koolkin, W.S. de Zwann, Ouderkerkerdijk, 40, NL 1096 CS, Amsterdam, Holland

European Buddhist Union, via Pio Rolla 71, I-10094 Giaveno, Torino, Italy ☎ (011) 93 78 331

International Network of Engaged Buddhists, Box No. 1, Onkgharak, Nakhorn Nayok 26120, Thailand ☎ (66) 37 391 494

World Fellowship of Buddhists, 616 Benchasiri Park, Soi Medhinevet
  Off Soi Sukhumvit 24, Sukhumvit Rd., Bangkok 10110, Thailand
  ☎ 66 11 284-89. Fax (662) 661-0555

National and Umbrella Organizations

AUSTRALIA

Buddhist Federation of Australia, 2nd Floor, Box 161,
  Holme Building, University of Sydney, NSW 2006

Buddhist Society of New South Wales, The Karuna Foundation,
  PO Box 89, North Sydney, NSW 2059 ☎ (02) 9929 8643.
  Fax (02) 9955 6183

Buddhist Society of Queensland, PO Box 536, Toowong,
  Queensland 4066

Buddhist Society of Western Australia, 18/20 Nanson Way,
  Nollamara, WA 6061

AUSTRIA

**Austrian Buddhist Religious Union (Österreichische Buddistische
  Religionsgesellschaft),** Fleischmarkt 16, A-1010 Wien
  ☎ + Fax (01043) 1 512 37 19

BELGIUM

**Federation of Buddhist Associations in Belgium(Fédération des
  associations Bouddhiques en Belgique),** c/o Frans Goetghebeur,
  Kruispadstraat 33, 2900 Schoten ☎ (010 32) 3 685 09 19.
  Fax (010 32) 3 685 09 91

CZECHOSLOVAKIA

Buddhist Society of Czechoslovakia, Richard Susta, Box 439,
  11121 Prague 1

ESTONIA

Estonian Buddhist Society and the Institute of Mahāyān,
  c/o Linnert Mäll, Laboratory of History & Semiotics,
  Tartu State University, Uus 57-24, Tartu ☎ 3 69 49

Estonian Oriental Society, c/o Sven Grünberg, Trummi põik 5a-29,
  Tallinn

FRANCE

French Buddhist Community (Commaunité Bouddhique de France),
  Taikan Jyoji Roshi, La Rialle, St. Laurent du Pape, F-07800

GREAT BRITAIN
The Buddhist Society, 58 Eccleston Sq., London SW1V 1PH
☎ (0171) 834 5858. Fax 0171 976 5238

HUNGARY
Buddhist Mission of Hungary, Rev. Dr. Jozsef Horvath,
Alkotmany u. 83, Budapest XX11, H-1221

ITALY
Italian Buddhist Union (Unione Buddhista Italiana), Ven. Fausto
Taiten Guareschi, c/o Instituto Lama Tzong Khapa,
I-56040 Pomala (Pisa)

LATVIA
Latvian Buddhist Community of Dharma, check address with USSR:
Centre for Coordinating Buddhist Groups (below)

SWITZERLAND
Swiss Buddhist Union (Union Bouddhique de Suisse), Rev. Dr.
Andreü Chevrier, Chainettes 25, CH-1400 Yverdon

Dr. Urs Oberlin, Hofwiessenstr. 330, CH-8050 Zurich

RUSSIAN FEDERATION
Central Buddhist Board of Russia, Tom Rabdanov, 49 Ostozhenka
Street, Moscow 119034 ☎ 245 21 92 and 245 09 39

Centre for Coordinating Buddhist Groups, c/o Aleksandr Breslavetz,
Kuntsechoinei Datsan, 91, Primorsky Prospekt, Russia – 197228
St. Petersburg ☎ (812) 239 0341

The Major Schools and Traditions

Theravāda Buddhism

Amarāvatī Buddhist Centre, Great Gaddesden, Hemel Hempstead,
Herts HP1 3BZ ☎ (01442) 842 455. Fax (01442) 843721

Cittaviveka Chithurst Buddhist Monastery, Chithurst, Petersfield,
Hants GU31 5EU ☎ (01730) 814 986. Fax (01730) 817334

Devon Buddhist Vihāra, Odle Cottage, Upottery, Honiton,
Devon EX14 9QE ☎ (01404) 891 251

Ratnagiri: Harnham Buddhist Monastery, 2 Harnham Hall Cottages,
Harnham, Belsay, Northumberland NE20 0HF
☎ (01661) 881 612. Fax (01661) 881019

Forest Hermitage, Lower Fulbrook, nr. Sherbourne, Warwick CV35
8AS ☎ (01926) 624 564. Fax (01926) 624385

Buddhapadipa Temple, 14 Calonne Rd., Wimbledon Parkside,
London SW19 5JH ☎ (0181) 946 1357. Fax (0181) 944 5788

Birmingham Buddhist Vihara, 47 Carlyle Rd., Edgbaston,
Birmingham B16 9BH ☎ (0121) 454 6591. Fax (0121) 454 6591

Britain Myanmar Buddhist Trust, 1 Old Church Lane,
London NW9 8TG ☎ (0181) 200 6898

London Buddhist Vihāra, Dharmapala Building, The Avenue, Bedford
Park, Chiswick, London W4 1UD ☎ (0181) 995 9493.
Fax (0181) 994 8130

AUSTRALIA
Bodhinyana Buddhist Monastery, Lot 1, Kingsbury Drive,
Serpentine 6205, WA ☎ + Fax (61) 08 95 25 24 20

Wat Buddha Dhamma, Ten Mile Hollow, Wisemans Ferry,
NSW 2775 ☎ (043) 233 193

Dhammaloka Buddhist Centre (Perth), 18-20 Nanson Way,
Nollamara 6061, WA ☎ (09) 345 1711

GERMANY
Buddha Haus, Uttenbühl 5, D-87466 Oy-Mittelberg ☎ 08376 502.
Fax 08376 592

Buddhistisches Haus, Edelhofdamm 54, D-13465 Berlin
☎ (030) 401 55 80. Fax (030) 401 55 80

ITALY
Santacittarama Monastero Buddhista, via dei Casali, Terzo Tratto,
I-04018 Sezze Romano, (LT) Latina ☎ + Fax (0039) 773 88 032.

NEW ZEALAND
Bodhinyanarama Monastery, 17 Rakau Grove, Stokes Valley,
Wellington ☎ (04) 637 193

Auckland Theravāda Buddhist Association, 29 Harris Rd.,
Mt. Wellington, Auckland ☎ (09) 579 5443

SRI LANKA
Island Hermitage, Polgasduwa, Dodanduwa ☎ 583716

SWITZERLAND
Dhammapala Buddhistisches Kloster, Am Waldrand,
CH-3718 Kandersteg ☎ 033/75 21 00

THAILAND
Wat Pa Nanachat, Bahn Bung Wai, Amper Warin, Ubon 34310

Vipassanā Meditation

Gaia House, West Ogwell, Newton Abbot, Devon TQ12 6EN
☎ (01626) 333613

House of Inner Tranquility, 9 Masons Lane, Bradford-on-Avon,
Wilts BA15 1QN ☎ (01225) 866821. Fax (01225) 865262

Samatha Association, The Samatha Centre, Greenstreete, Llangunllo,
nr. Knighton, Powys LD7 1SP ☎ (0151) 722 0893

Sayagyi U Ba Khin Memorial Trust, International Meditation Centre,
Splatts House, Heddington, Wilts SN11 OPE
☎ (01380) 850 238. Fax (01380) 850 833

NEW ZEALAND
Vipassanā Group (Sayangyi U Ba Khin tradition), PO Box 41-185,
St. Luke, Auckland ☎ 810-9097

MYANMAR
Buddha Sasana Nuggaha Organization, Mahasi Meditation Centre,
16 Sasana Yeiktha Rd., Yangon ☎ 541971/552501.
Fax 289960/289961

USA
Insight Meditation Society, Pleasant St., Barre, MA 01005
☎ (617) 355 4378

Insight Meditation West, Spirit Rock Center, 5000 Sir Francis Drake
Boulevard, PO Box 909, Woodacre, CA 94973 ☎ (415) 488 0164

Tibetan Buddhism

Karma Kagyu Tradition
Kagyu Samyé-Ling Tibetan Centre (Ven. Akong Rinpoche),
Eskdalemuir, Langholm, Dumfries, Scotland DG13 0QL
☎ Office (0138 73) 73232, Guests (0138 73) 03873.
Fax (0138 73) 73223

Nezang Buddhist Meditation Group (Ven. Ato Rinpoche), 5 Sedley
Taylor Rd,. Cambridge CB2 2PW ☎ (01223) 240 090

Chos Khor Ling, Marpa House (Ven. Chime Rinpoche), Rectory
Lane, Ashdon, Saffron Walden, Essex CB10 2HM
☎ + Fax (01799) 584415.

Amrita Dzong (Ven. Chime Rinpoche), 38 Kingsland Rd., London E2
☎ (0171) 226 3339

London Shambhala Centre (Chögyam Trungpa organization),
27 Belmont Close, London SW4 6AY ☎ (0171) 720 3207

EUROPE
Shambhala Europe, Wilhelmstrasse 20 D-35037, Marburg, Germany
☎ (49) 6421 17020. Fax (49) 6421 170222

FRANCE
Dhagpo Kagyu Ling, Siege Européan du Gyalwa Karmapa,
24290 St. Léon-sur-Vezère, France ☎ 53 50 70 75.
Fax 53 50 80 54

Fédération Dachang Kaguy, Chatreuse de St. Hugon, Arvillard,
F-73110 La Rechette

GREECE
Karma-Drub-Gyü Chö-Khor-Ling, 15b Sonieru St., 10438 Athens

NEW ZEALAND
Karma Kagyu Thigsum Chokhorling, Karma Chöling Buddhist
Temple, Bodhisattva Rd., Rural Delivery 1, Kaukapakapa,
nr. Auckland ☎ + Fax 09 420 5428

SOUTH AFRICA
Nieu Bethesda Samyé Ling, PO Box 15, New Bethesda 6286,
Cape Province

USA
Karma Do Nga Choeling, 12021 Willshire Boulevard, Suite 667,
West Los Angeles, California 90025

Gelug Tradition
Jamyang Meditation Centre, 10 Finsbury Park Rd., London N4 2JZ
☎ (0171) 359 1394

Lam Rim Buddhist Centre, Pentwyn Manor, Penrhos, Raglan,
Monmouthshire NP5 2LE, South Wales ☎ (01600) 780 383

Tashi Khyil Tibetan Buddhist Centre (Lama Panchen Yudol
Rinpoche), 54 Derryboye Rd., Crossgar, Co. Down,
N. Ireland BT30 9LJ ☎ (01238) 541 581

Jampa Ling Tibetan Buddhist Centre, Owendoon House, Bawnboy,
  Co. Cavan, Eire ☎ (00353) 492 3448

FRANCE
Institut Vajra Yogini, Chateau d'en Clausen, Marzens, F-81500
  Lavaur

GERMANY
Tibetisches Zentrum e. V. Hamburg (Geshe Thubten Ngawang),
  Hermann-Balkstr 106, D-2000 Hamburg 73

INDIA
Drepung Monastic University, Lama Camp No. 2, Tibetan Colony
  581411, Mundgod, Distt. N. Kanara, Karnataka State

Office of H.H. the Dalai Lama of Tibet, Thekchen Chöeling, McLeod
  Ganj, Dharamsala, Distt. Kangra, Himachal Pradesh

Library of Tibetan Works and Archives, Ganchen Kyishong,
  Dharamsala 176215, Disst. Kangra, Himachal Pradesh

ITALY
Instituto Lama Tzong Khapa, via Poggiberna 5, I-56040 Pomaia
  (Pisa)

MONGOLIA
Gandan Monastery, Ulan Bator, MPR

SPAIN
Ösel Ling, Bubión, E-18412 Granada

SWITZERLAND
Tharpa Chöeling, CH-1801 Mont Pélérin ZE1

USA
The Deer Park (Geshe Sopa), 4548 Schneider Drive, Oregon,
  Wisconsin 93575

Rashi Gempil Ling (founded by Geshe Wangyal), First Kalmyk
  Buddhist Temple, R.R.3, Box Howell, New Jersey 07731

RUSSIAN FEDERATION
Kuntsechoinei Datsan, 91 Primorsky Prospeckt, Russia-197228
  St. Petersburg ☎ (812) 239 03 41

Datsan, Ivolginsk, Buryat AR, Russian Federation-671210

Aginsky Datsan, Aginskoe Village, Chita Region, Russian Federation-674460

New Kadampa Tradition
Mañjushri Institute (Geshe Kelsang Gyatso), Conishead Priory, Ulverston, Cumbria LA12 9QQ
☎ (01229) 584029. Fax (01229) 580080

Sakya Tradition
Dechen Community, 15 Parkfield Rd., Aigburth, Liverpool L17 8UG
☎ (0151) 727 0108

FRANCE
Ngor Ewam Phendé Ling (Phendé Rinpoche), 3 rue du Bout de la Ville, 27180 Les Ventes ☎ 32 67 80 63. Fax: 32 67 42 05

INDIA
Sakya Centre, 187 Rajpur Rd., 248 009 Rajpur, Dehra Dun, UP

USA
Sankya Puntsok Ling, 8715 First Ave., # 1510 D. Silver Springs, Maryland 20910

Nyingma Tradition
Longchen Foundation, 30 Beechley Ave., Old Marston, Oxford OX3 OPU ☎ (01865) 725 569

FRANCE
Orgyen Samye Chöling, Langerol, St. Léon-sur-Vezère, F-24290 Montignac

GERMANY
Arya Maitreya Mandala (founded by Lama Govinda), Rev. Rose Kasper, Weissdorngweg 4, 72 076 Tuebingen, Germany
☎ 0049 07071 63280

USA
Nyingma Institute (Tarthang Tulku), 1815 Highland Place, Berkeley, California 94709 ☎ (510) 843 6812. Fax (510) 486 1679

Rimé Tradition
Rigpa Fellowship (Ven. Sogyal Rinpoche), 330 Caledonia Rd., London N1 1BB ☎ (0171) 700 0185. Fax (0171) 609 6068

FRANCE
Rigpa, 11 rue Denis Poisson, F-75017 Paris

USA
Rigpa Fellowship, PO Box 7362, Santa Cruz, California 95061

Dzogchen Tradition (Ven. Namkhai Norbu Rinpoche)
Dzogchen Community U.K., 14d, Chesterton Rd., London W10 5LX
☎ (0181) 964 1176

ITALY
Communità Dzogchen, Merigar, I-58031 Arcidosso, GR

Miscellaneous Tibetan Offices, Centres, Groups, etc.
Tibet Foundation, Phuntsok Wangyal, 10, Bloomsbury Way, London
WC1A 2SH ☎ (0171) 404 2889. Fax (0171) 404 2366

Office of Tibet, Migyur Dorgee, Tibet House, 1 Culworth Street,
London NW8 7AF ☎ (0171) 722 5378. Fax (0171) 722 0362

The Tibet Society, 114/115 Tottenham Court Rd., London W1P 9HL
☎ (0171) 383 7533. Fax (0171) 383 7563

Zen Buddhism

Sótó Zen School
Throssel Hole Priory (Order of Buddhist Comtemplatives),
Carrshield, Hexham, Northumberland NE47 8AL
☎ (01434) 345 204. Fax (01434) 345216

FRANCE
L'Association Zen d'Europe (Deshimaru organization), 14 rue des
Cinq-Diamants, F-75013 Paris

ITALY
Instituto Italiano Zen Soto, Tempio Zen Sôtô Shôbôzan Fudenji,
Bargone 113, 43039 Salsomaggiore Terme, (Parma)
☎ 0524 565667

JAPAN
Sótó Zen Headquarters, 2-5-2 Shiba, Minato-ku. Tokyo 105
☎ (03) 454 5411

USA
Zen Center of San Francisco (founded by Shunryū Suzuki Rōshi,
present abbot Reb Anderson), 300 Page St., San Francisco,
CA 94102 ☎ (415) 863 3136

Rinzai Zen School
Hannya Temple, 10 Belmont St., Chalk Farm, London NW1 8HH
☎ (0171) 485 9576

London Shogendojo Zen Group, 8 South Hill Park Gardens, Hampstead, London NW3 2TG ☎ (0171) 431 0737

JAPAN
Daitokuji, 53 Daitokujicho, Murasakino, Kita-ku, Kyoto 603 ☎ (075) 491 0543

Ryutakuji, Mishima-shi, Shizuoka-ken 411 ☎ (0559) 86-2206

USA
First Zen Institute of America, 113 East 30th St., New York, NY 10016 ☎ (212) 686 2520

Zen Studies Society/Dai Bosatsu Zendo Kongoji, Ven. Eido Shimano Roshi, HCR 1, Box 171, Livingston Manor, New York 12758 ☎ (914) 439 4566. Fax (914) 439 3119

Rinzai-Sōtō Synthesis
Kanzeon Sangha (Dennis Gempo Merzel Sensei), Zen Practice Centre Trust, Barbara Tetsuzen Hussong, 26 Salisbury Rd., Maidstone, Kent ME14 2TX ☎ (01622) 670587

USA
Zen Center of Los Angeles, (Taizan Maezumi Róshi), 905 South Normandie Ave., Los Angeles, California 90006

Diamond Sangha (Robert Aitken Róshi), 2119 Kaloa Way, Honolulu, Hawaii 96822 ☎ (808) 946 0666

Ch'an (Chinese Zen) Tradition
Western Ch'an Fellowship, Dr. John Crook, Winterhead Hill Farm, Shipham, Winscombe, N. Somerset BS25 IRS ☎ (01934) 842231. Fax (01934) 842231

USA
City of Ten Thousand Buddhas (Master Hsuan Hua), Talmage, California 95481-0217 ☎ (707) 0939

Korean Zen Tradition
Yon-Haw-Sa (Lotus House -Ven. Jisu Sunim), 5 Waters Rd., Kingston-on-Thames, Surrey KT1 3LN ☎ (0181) 549 6092

Korean Zen Retreats, Stephen and Martine Batchelor, Gaia House, West Ogwell, near Newton Abbot, Devon TQ12 6EN ☎ (01626) 33613

SOUTH KOREA
Songgwang-Sa, Songgwangmyon, Seungjukun, Cholla Namdo
  Province

USA

Providence Zen Center/Diamond Hill Zen Monastery (Seung Sahn
  Sunim) 528 Pound Rd., Cumberland, Rhode Island 02864
  ☎ (401) 769 6464

Zen Umbrella Organizations
POLAND

Buddhist Zen Sangha, Ven. Ji Boep Sa Do Am (Andrej Czarneki),
  Malowiejska 24, Warsaw

NEW ZEALAND
Zen Society of New Zealand, PO Box 2812, Auckland

SPAIN
Zen Association of Spain (Association Zen de España), Ven. Francisco
  Dokusho Villalba, c/o Titania 55, E-28043 Madrid

Pure Land Tradition

Pure Land Buddhist Fellowship, Jim Pym, 3 Field Rd., Kingham,
  Chipping Norton, Oxfordshire OX7 6XR ☎ + Fax (01608)
  658425

AUSTRIA
Buddhistische Gemeinschaft Jōdo Shinshū, Shaku Friedrich Fenzi,
  Merianstrasse 29/4/52, A-5020 Salzburg

BELGIUM
Rev. Dr. Adriaan Shitoku Peel, Zitaart 21, B-2419, Poederiee,
  Antwerp

CANADA
Buddhist Churches of Canada, 918 Bathurst St., Toronto, Canada
  M5R 3G5

GERMANY
Buddhistische Gemeinschaft Jōdo Shinshū, Shaku Jyoji Kell, La
  Rialle, St. Laurent du Pape, D-1000 Berlin 30

POLAND
Jōdo Shinshū Community, Jack Kozlowski, u. Wandy 4/5/ PL-03-949
  Warsaw

JAPAN
Hongwanji International Center, Higashi-nakasuji, Rokujo Sagaru, Shimogyo-ku, Kyoto 600

SWITZERLAND
Rev. Dr. André Chevrier, Chainettes 25, CH-1400 Yverdon

Dr. Jean Éracle, 14 chemin Pallud, CH-1292 Geneva

USA
Buddhist Churches of America, National Headquarters, 1710 Octavia St., San Francisco, California 94109 ☎ (415) 776 5600

Nichiren Tradition

Soka Gakkai International – U.K., Taplow Court, Taplow, near Maidenhead, Berkshire SL6 0ER ☎ (01628) 773163

Nipponzan Myōhōji, London Peace Pagoda, c/o The Park Office, Albert Bridge Rd., Battersea, London SW11 4NJ ☎ (0171) 228 9620

USA
Nichiren Shōshū USA (NSU), Headquarters, 525 Willshire Boulevard, Santa Monica, CA 90401 ☎ (213) 451 8811

Vietnamese Buddhism

Vietnamese Buddhist Society in UK, Linh-Son Temple, 89 Bromley Rd., Catford, London SE6 2UF ☎ (0181) 461 1887

FRANCE
Thich Nhat Hanh, Plum Village, Meyrac, Loubes, Bernac, F-47120 Duras

NEW ZEALAND
Vietnamese Buddhist Association, 11 Panama Rd., Mt. Wellington, Auckland ☎ 276 9921

USA
Vietnamese Buddhist Association, 3119 Alta Arden Expressway, Sacramento, California 95825

Western Buddhism

Friends of the Western Buddhist Order, London Buddhist Centre, 51 Roman Rd., Bethnal Green, London E2 OHV ☎ (0181) 981 1225. Fax (0181) 980 1960

(There are numerous other FWBO centres in Britain as well as branches abroad. For further information, contact the Office of the Western Buddhist Order – address and telephone number above.)

Non-Sectarian Centres & Organizations

The Buddhist Society, 58 Eccleston Sq., London SW1V 1PH
☎ (0171) 834 5858

Sharpham College of Buddhist Studies and Contemporary Enquiry, Sharpham House, Ashprington, Totnes, S. Devon TQ9 7UT
☎ (01803) 732 542. Fax (01803) 732037

GERMANY
Haus der Stille, Mühlenweg 20, D-2059 Roseburg über Büchen
☎ 0 41 58 214

SOUTH AFRICA
Buddhist Retreat Centre, PO Box 131, Ixopo, 4630 Natal

USA
Springwater Center, 7179 Mill St., Springwater, NY 14560

Women & Buddhism

Sakhyadita International Association of Buddhist Women, 928 South New Hampshire, Los Angeles, California 90006, USA

Newsletter on International Buddhist Women's Activities, c/o Dr. Chatsumarn Kabilsingh, Faculty of Liberal Arts, Thammasat University, Bangkok 10200, Thailand

Dorje Pamo Monastery, Chateau d'en Clausade, Marzens, F-81500 Lavaur, France

Pappaduwa Nuns' Island, Dodanduwa, Sri Lanka

Engaged Buddhism

Network of Engaged Buddhists, Ken Jones, Plas Plwca, Cwmrheidol, Aberystwyth, Wales SY23 3NB ☎ (01970) 880 603

International Network of Engaged Buddhists, Box No. 1, Onkgharak, Nakorn Nayok 26120, Thailand ☎ (66) 37 391 494

Miscellaneous

Angulimala: Buddhist Prison Chaplaincy Organization, The Forest
Hermitage, Lower Fulbrook, Warwick, CV35 8AS
☎ + Fax (01926) 624 385

Buddhist Hospice Trust, c/o Ray Wills, 5 Grayswood Point, Norley
Vale, London SW15 4BT ☎ (0181) 789 6170

The Dharma School, White House, Ladies Mile Rd., Patcham,
Brighton BN1 8TB ☎ (01273) 502055. Fax (01273) 556580

The Meridian Trust, The Buddhist Film & Video Archive, 5 Torrens
St., London EC1V 1NQ. ☎ (0171) 278 2576.
Fax (0171) 837 2800

Network of Buddhist Organisations, c/o The Old Courthouse, 43
Renfrew Rd., Kennington, London SE11 4NA ☎ + Fax (0171) 582
5797

21 The North American Connection

Like the Roman god of new beginnings, Janus, the North American continent has two faces. One looks towards Europe, the other directly across the Pacific to the Orient itself: to China, Japan and Korea.

The very same influences that brought Buddhism to Europe, notably the trading connection with India, washed Buddhist ideas to the eastern seaboard of the United States during the latter part of the 19th century. They were picked up and relayed to a wider audience (though in transmuted form) by a genteel group of New England philosophers, the *Transcendentalists*, who felt a Taoist-like distaste for the artificialities of the social world and a preference for the uncorrupted world of nature. One of them, H.D. Thoreau (1817–62), went to live for a time in a lonely cabin in the Massachusetts woods and out of this experience came his classic work, *Walden*. A simple life with few possessions, a patch of ground on which to grow some vegetables, trees to chop for wood, and the time and space for quiet reflection seemed infinitely preferably to the vexed go-getting of the conventional world. There was a deep strand of Buddhism in all this, for Thoreau drank deeply at the well of Eastern mysticism and, among other things, translated Eugène Burnouf's French version of the *Lotus Sūtra* into English.

Meanwhile, on the other coast, thousands of native Chinese poured in to supply the demand for cheap labour triggered by the great Californian Gold Rush, the laying of the Union Pacific railway line and other great developments. Chinatowns sprang up in many a rapidly growing American city, and they all had temples where Confucian, Taoist and Buddhist deities were venerated. The Buddhist inclinations of these early Chinese immigrants tended mostly towards the Pure Land school, though there were elements of Ch'an too. Meanwhile, on the islands of Hawaii, which were soon to be annexed by the United States, Japanese workers came to labour on contract in the fruit plantations, and before long they too began to spill over onto the mainland. The Buddhists among them were also mainly devotees of Amitābha and the Pure Land. This ethnic Pure Land tradition, over 100 years old now, has flourished in North America to the present day.

The crucial catalyst to the advance and acceptance of Buddhism in North America came in 1893. That year the Columbian Exposition was planned to take place in Chicago and be a great celebration of America's material achievement. Some thought that the spiritual side of things should be represented too, so a World Parliament of Religions was convened. Among those who spoke for Buddhism were Anagārika Dharmapāla – and, more significantly, the Rinzai Zen Master, Sōyen Shaku (1859–1919), who had trained with Imagita Kōsen Rōshi (1816–92) at the famous Engaku-ji temple in Kamakura and, on Kōsen Rōshi's death, succeeded to the abbacy there.

At the Parliament, Sōyen Shaku made a connection with Paul Carus, who ran a comparative religious publishing house called the Open Court Publishing Co. in the Illinois zinc town of LaSalle. Carus needed someone to help him translate texts. Conveniently Sōyen Shaku had a young student who possessed some knowledge of English, D.T. Suzuki (1870–1966), and arrangements were made for him to go to LaSalle. On the very last *sesshin* at Engaku-ji before catching the boat, Suzuki galvanized himself to the full and managed to 'break through', so among his 'hidden imports' to the USA was a degree of authenticated Zen insight. He spent some 11 years there on his first visit, but later, in the 1950s, advanced in years and equally advanced in wisdom, a new phase began when he undertook a strenuous series of teaching engagements at Columbia University (New York City) and elsewhere.

Down to the great Tibetan diaspora of the post-1959 era, Zen was undoubtedly the tradition of Buddhism most popular among Caucasian Americans, thanks in no small measure to D.T. Suzuki's pioneering work. Two other Rinzai teachers also made substantial contributions, both vowing to 'bury their bones' in the soil of America, Nyogen Senzaki (1876–1958) and

Sokei-an Sasaki (1882–1945). Senzaki went to the USA around 1905 to join his teacher, Sōyen Shaku, at the home of Mr and Mrs Alexander Russell in San Francisco. Something went wrong and Senzaki had to leave the house. As he parted from his teacher in Golden Gate Park, Sōyen Shaku laid the stern injunction upon him that he should work with Americans and not 'utter the *B* of Buddhism' for 17 years. Senzaki was obedient to this, but when the stipulated time was up he started his 'floating *zendo*' on the West Coast. Robert Aitken Rōshi (b. 1917), who currently guides the Diamond Sangha in Hawaii, and the poet Gary Snyder, were among his students. He was also responsible for bringing Nakagawa Sōen Rōshi (1907–84) across the Pacific.... Sokei-an Sasaki, on the other hand, also a pupil of Sōyen Shaku, worked latterly on the East Coast and established the First Zen Institute in New York City. In 1944 he married Ruth Fuller Everett (1883–1967), and she carried on his good work after his death a year later. Eleanor, Ruth's daughter by a first marriage to a Chicago attorney, married Alan Watts (1915–73) in 1938, and it was this connection that brought Watts to the USA, where he made a great name for himself as a writer and talker on Zen and related matters.

Today Zen is still very strongly represented in the USA particularly on the West Coast, where there are several very large groupings. The San Francisco Zen Center owes its existence to a very remarkable Sōtō master, Shūnryu Suzuki (1904–71), author of the classic *Zen Mind, Beginner's Mind*. It was under SFZC's auspices that the Zen Mountain Center at Tassajara Springs, the first Zen monastery in the USA with facilities for long-term practice, was set up. Suzuki Rōshi's good work was carried on by his Dharma Heir, Richard Baker, until Baker fell from grace in one of the series of crises that swept American Zen centres in the early 1980s. These also touched the extensive Zen Center of Los Angeles, founded in 1967 by Taizen Maezumi Rōshi (b. 1931), a pupil of Hakujun Kuroda Rōshi and Hakūun Yasutani Rōshi. Maezumi Rōshi, whose lineage combines both the Rinzai and Sōtō traditions, has two Dharma Heirs: Dennis Genpo Merzel Sensei (b. 1944), who now works extensively in Europe, and Bernard Tetsugen Glassman Sensei (b. 1939), who is based in New York. Philip Kapleau Rōshi (b. 1912), a former journalist who trained in various Rinzai and

Sōtō Zen monasteries in Japan, also works on the East Coast, being based in Rochester, New York State. Other Zen teachers currently active include Dainin Katagiri Rōshi (b. 1928), Eido Shimano Rōshi (b. 1932) and Joshu Sasaki Rōshi (b. 1907).

The Chinese Ch'an tradition is currently represented on the West Coast by Dhyāna Master Hsüan Hua (b. 1908), Chairman of the Sino-American Buddhist Association and founder of Gold Mountain Dhyāna Monastery and City of 10,000 Buddhas. Master Hua has a reputation for dispensing tough practice. Some of his students are said to sleep in the lotus position.

Korean Zen, meanwhile, was pioneered by Sōen Sunim (alt. Seung Sahn; b. 1927), who went to the USA in 1972 and set up in Providence, Rhode Island. He now heads the Kwan Um Zen School. Another teacher, Samu Sunim (b. 1941), came to the USA in 1967 but latterly his Zen Lotus Society has been based in Toronto, Canada.

As for Tibetan Buddhism, the Gelugpas were uncharacteristically the first in the field. In 1951, the far-wandering Kamuks were allowed to settle in Freewood Acres, New Jersey, and the following year they opened the First Kalmuk Buddhist Temple in a remodelled garage. The equally far-wandering Geshe Wangyal (1901–83) came to minister to them in 1955, and other lamas followed, notably Geshe Sopa (b. 1923). In 1967, he was invited by Professor Richard Robinson, one of the pioneers of Mahāyāna studies in Britain, to join the Buddhist Studies Program at the University of Wisconsin. In 1981, Geshe Sopa requested HH the Dalai Lama, who has visited the USA several times, to perform a Kālachakra Initiation at his centre, the Deer Park; 12,000 people are said to have attended.

But as in Britain, the great star of the Tibetan transmission was the copiously gifted Karma Kagyu/Nyingma *tulku*, Chögyam Trungpa Rinpoche (1939–87). He left Britain for the USA in around 1970, trailing clouds of controversy behind him. He established important centres in Vermont, Colorado and in Nova Scotia, and set up the international Vajradhatu organization with headquarters in Boulder. He apparently responded to the openness and enthusiasm of the Americans, but still retained a nostalgia for Britain, which he felt would be the place where the Dharma would really blossom in the West.

Since his untimely death, Trungpa's mantle has fallen upon his former Vajra Regent, Ösel Tendzin, who was born Thomas Rich in Passaic, New Jersey.

Other important Karma Kagyu lamas have paid visits to the USA, among them the famous yogi Kalu Rinpoche (b. 1905), who is often compared to Milarepa. He too has performed Kālachakra Initiations at large open gatherings. HH the late Karmapa (1923–81) also came to see the American centres falling under the aegis of his tradition. He made three visits and came to the USA a fourth time for medical attention; sadly he passed away in a Zion, Illinois hospital.

The Nyingma torch was borne to the USA by Tarthang Tulku, a disciple of the great Ri-mé Master Jamyang Khyentse Chökyi Lodrö (1896–1959), who arrived on the West Coast in 1969 and established the Tibetan Nyingma Meditation Centre in Berkeley, California. Dodrupchen Rinpoche (b. 1927) and Sonam Kazi, a Sikkimese layman, are two other teachers active in North America, but many others have paid visits, notably Dingo Khyentse Rinpoche (b. 1910) and the late supreme head of the order, HH Dudjom Rinpoche (1904–87), who established several centres, notably Örgyen Chö Dzong in New York City.

Finally, the Sakyapas: they gained a foothold in the Pacific North-West through the good offices of Dr. Turrell V. Wylie (1927–84), the originator of the Wylie system of Tibetan transcription. From about 1960 onwards he brought Dezhung Rinpoche and other Sakyapa scholars to the University of Washington at Seattle.

Perhaps because the North American countries never enjoyed the same colonial connections with the traditional Theravāda countries of south-east Asia that Britain, for instance, enjoyed and were furthermore not geographically aligned with those areas, this major tradition has not developed as strongly in the USA and Canada as the others. Nor has a monastic Sangha arisen; paradoxically, most of the outstanding North American Theravādins who have stayed in the robe have either gravitated to Britain, like Ajahn Sumedho (b. 1920), or stayed in the East, like Bhikkhu Bodhi (b. 1944), who currently directs the Buddhist Publication Society in Kandy, Sri Lanka. Few *vihāras* have been set up in North America, the most important development being the activities of a number of freelance lay *vipassanā* meditation teachers, most of whom trained in the East, some in the robe. Notable among these are Jack Kornfield, Joseph Goldstein and Sharon Salzberg. The Insight Meditation Society (IMS) at Barre, Massachusetts, is the most important centre for their activities. This now has a new offshoot on the West Coast, Insight Meditation West, in the San Geronimo Valley some 45 minutes drive from San Francisco.

In terms of sheer numbers – though sheer numerical size was never a good index of spiritual quality – the Nichiren Shōshū organization has taken off amazingly in recent years, attracting headlines like 'The Fastest Growing Religion in the West'. Its rise can be traced back to the arrival of one Massayasu Sadanaga, who came to the Los Angeles campus of the University of California to study politics in the 1950s. Changing his name to George Williams, he used his skills to create Nichiren Shōshū America (NSA). His early converts were mainly Japanese war brides and their American ex-serviceman husbands. Growth was rapid through the 1960s and 1970s, then tapered off slightly, but is definitely back on the upswing again. NSA now claims more than 500,000 members in the USA as well as chapters in all the 50 states. In greater Los Angeles alone, one person in every hundred is said to be a member.

22 Buddhism and Psychotherapy

Many of those who have undertaken the study and practice of Buddhism have also taken an interest in the Western psychotherapies that developed from the pioneering work of Sigmund Freud. As well as Freudian psychoanalysis and its derivatives, this includes the analytical psychology of Freud's great but errant pupil, Carl Gustav Jung, as well as subsequent developments right down to the present time, where we find Buddhism and Western psychology coming together in a remarkable synthesis.

These modern Western psychotherapies and the theories underpinning them arose towards the end of the last century and in the early part of the present one partly as a response to the dilemma caused by the decline of conventional religion in the West. The great discovery made by the pioneers of this movement was of the existence of the *unconscious*: an area, or perhaps more accurately, a range of aspects of the human psyche falling outside the normal range of conscious awareness. William James, the psychologist brother of the novelist Henry James and author of *Varieties of Religious Experience* wrote:

> Our normal waking consciousness is but one special type of consciousness, while all about it, parted from it by the flimsiest of screens, there lie potential forms of consciousness entirely different. We may go through life without suspecting their existence, but apply the requisite stimulus and at a touch they are there in all their completeness. . . .

Sigmund Freud (1856–1939), the great 'nerve doctor of Vienna', was basically interested in the therapeutic aspects of this unconscious: what bearing it might have on the cure of his patient's neurotic symptoms. His tendency, therefore, was to view the unconscious as a kind of cellar containing, in Erich

Fromm's phrase, 'mainly man's vices', that is, all those aspects of himself that a person does not wish to confront – unacceptable desires, aggressive impulses, painful memories and so forth. Cure consisted in reclaiming this exiled material from the abyss of unknowing and restoring it to the province of consciousness – or in Freudian terminology: restoring it to the Ego from the Id, a process that Freud compared to reclaiming land from the sea, as in the case of the Zuyder Zee in Holland.

Carl Gustav Jung (1875–1961) of Zürich, on the other hand, tended to take a wider and less negative view of the unconscious. Certainly it had its 'lumber-room of dirty secrets' but this was but a tiny fragment of the full picture. The unconscious was a vast 'unglimpsable completeness of all subliminal psychic factors, a 'total exhibition' of potential nature,' he wrote in his Foreword to *An Introduction to Zen Buddhism*, by D.T. Suzuki (London: Rider. 1957. p. 22). 'It constitutes the entire disposition from which consciousness takes fragments all the time'. It embraces not only personal elements, but collective and even cosmic possibilities as well. It could be a source of profound wisdom too – if only we could become sensitive to its signals: for instance, by learning how to interpret dreams.

If Freud's tendency had been essentially secular (his negative attitude to religion is wellknown), Jung's ideas brought the new psychology into the area once regarded as the preserve of religion. Indeed, he began to see the role of analysis not merely as directed towards curing neurotic symptoms but of assisting harmonious development, the flowering of individual potential, and ultimately towards securing a transformation that would take the individual beyond himself:

> The fact is that the approach to the numinous is the real therapy and inasmuch as you attain to the numinous experiences you are released from the curse of pathology.[62]

In the Freudian view, the psychoanalyst was a sort of medical doctor; in Jungian terms, he was that and more as well – a kind of priest. Jung's analytical psychology still operated on the basic Freudian principle of 'making the darkness conscious'; however, there were differences too, for instance, of method.

Jung had a keen appreciation of the significance of the

burgeoning interest in Eastern spirituality that he saw taking place in his own time. As he wrote in his essay, The 'Spiritual Problem of Modern Man' (1928/31):

> Let us beware of underestimating it! So far, indeed, there is little of it to be seen on the intellectual surface: a handful of orientalists, one or two Buddhist enthusiasts, and a few sombre celebrities like Madame Blavatsky and Annie Besant with her Krishnamurti. These tiny manifestations are like tiny scattered islands in the ocean of mankind; in reality they are the peaks of submarine mountain ranges.[63]

But for Jung, the East was ultimately not a 'Tibetan monastery full of Mahātmas' but a reality that 'in a sense lies within us'. This reality consisted precisely of those spiritual potentials that once Western religion had sought to foster, but, sadly, no more, leaving Western man in his deep dilemma. He did not, however, see salvation in abandoning one's native cultural heritage and recklessly adopting ideas, symbols and practices that had developed in an alien milieu. Indeed, he thought this particularly risky and branded those who did it – the Theosophists were the worst offenders in his book – as 'pitiable imitators'. In particular he warned against the dangers of any Westerner jettisoning reason and its brainchild, science. If one were going to explore the undiscovered country of psyche and spirit, which was fraught with all manner of perils and pitfalls, it would be quixotic and foolhardy to do without this 'one safe foundation of the Western mind'.

The challenge Jung posed, then, was not merely one of self development; one's own native traditions had to be revitalized at the same time:

> It is not a question of our imitating, or worse still, becoming missionaries for what is organically foreign, but rather a question of building up our own Western culture, which sickens with a thousand ills. This has to be done on the spot, and by the real European as he is in his Western commonplaces, with his marriage problems, his neuroses, his social and political delusions, and his whole philosophical disorientation.[64]

These general caveats aside, Jung investigated the 'Wisdom

of the East' fairly extensively and wrote 'psychological commentaries' to the W.Y. Evans-Wentz/Kazi Dawa Samdup renderings of *The Tibetan Book of the Dead* (1939/53) and *The Tibetan Book of the Great Liberation* (1939/54); also a Foreword to D.T. Suzuki's *Introduction to Zen Buddhism* (1939). Important too are his commentaries on the Richard Wilhelm translations from the Chinese of the classic *I Ching* (1950) and *The Secret of the Golden Flower* (1929). Generally speaking he found little to disagree with and much to celebrate in these writings, but always he was cautious about any venture into actual practice. Zen Buddhism, for instance, had great value 'for the understanding of the religious transformation process'; however, 'Its use among Western people is very improbable. The spiritual conditions necessary to Zen are missing in the West'.

Was Jung unnecessarily cautious? Certainly there is sound sense in most of what he has to say; but he was writing in and for a particular time and developments have proceeded apace since then. There is an enormous amount of cross-cultural traffic in our contemporary 'Global Village' – far more perhaps than Jung could have envisaged. In this climate people *do* practice various forms of Buddhism and at the same time hold down executive jobs in business in Western cities like London and New York – nor do they have to be pseudo-Japanese or Tibetan or abandon Western rationality and science in order to do so.

In fact, the wheel has almost now turned full circle and Eastern mysticism is becoming quite respectable in certain forward-thinking scientific quarters. Dr. Fritjof Capra, author of *The Tao of Physics* and *The Turning Point*, has written of the fascinating correspondences between modern theories of atomic and sub-atomic physics and the insights of the Eastern mystics; and Professor David Bohm, a leading theoretical physicist, has had illuminating conversations with the sage, J. Krishnamurti, some of which have been published.

To accord due credit to Jung, however, it must be said that many Western Buddhists have found that his ideas represent a useful bridge into the exotic world of Eastern spirituality. Some have gone so far as to undertake Jungian analysis and have found it helpful, particularly in dealing with specifically psychological problems. (Freudian analysis might be equally helpful in this regard, especially in dealing with problems that have their origin in early life.) It is open to question, however, whether Jungian analysis can offer any contribution towards higher spiritual development that could not equally well be found in Buddhism itself – and, as is often said, at considerably less cost, analysis being strictly for the well-heeled.

In England during the 1930s, the Harley Street psychiatrist, Eric Graham Howe, author of *She and Me* and *War Dance*, was also an early appreciator of the Wisdom of the East and a supporter of the Buddhist Lodge which Christmas Humphreys had started in 1924. Howe was a formative influence upon the young Alan Watts, who was quick to see the fruitful cross-connections that could be made between the Eastern religious traditions (including of course Buddhism) and psychotherapy. By his own account, Watts had been reading the works of Jung while still at school; other, slightly later, influences upon him in this direction were a Dutch psychiatrist named Philip Metman and Dimitrije Mitrinovic, a 'rascal guru' who had studied the psychotherapeutic techniques of Alfred Adler and Trigant Burrow and evolved an early form of encounter group.

As a powerful communicator, Alan Watts was able to express these cross-connections lucidly and persuasively in his books, pamphlets and magazine articles. His first major work which brought his psychotherapeutic interests into primary focus was the pamphlet *Seven Symbols of Life* (1936). Here, in dealing with the symbol of the lotus, Watts points out that the pristine flower has its roots sunk into the 'primaeval slime', from which it also draws sustenance. Although Watts talks of the racial and cosmic dimensions of the unconscious, he does rather tend to dwell upon its 'dark' or shadow aspects, thus making it smack more of Freud's cellarfull of vices than Jung's repository of higher things. Then in 1937 Watts published his second full-length book, *The Legacy of Asia and Western Man,* in which he sought to relate Eastern thought and mysticism to Christianity and 'that young but swiftly-growing science – Psychology' (Christmas Humphreys). Watts went on to develop these themes in his later writings, including *Psychotherapy East and West* (1961). At one stage he propounded the idea that Buddhism has more in common with psychotherapy than with religion as the term is currently understood in the West.

The interest in Buddhism generally and in Zen Buddhism in particular became more widespread among psychotherapists, especially in the United States, following World War II. This interest was no doubt stimulated by Dr. D.T. Suzuki (1870–1966). In the early 1950s, Suzuki began lecturing at Columbia University in New York, and his lectures were attended by psychoanalysts and therapists like Karen Horney and Erich Fromm (neo-Freudians both), and Richard De-Martino. In 1957, Suzuki spent the summer months in Mexico with Fromm and participated in a workshop on Zen Buddhism and Psychoanalysis held under the auspices of the Department of Psychoanalysis of the Medical School of the Autonomous University of Mexico. Nearly 50 psychologists and psychiatrists from both Mexico and the United States took part, and a book resulted, *Zen Buddhism and Psychoanalysis*, (New York, 1960), with contributions from Suzuki, Fromm and DeMartino.

In re-examining this record of what was undoubtedly the first major encounter between Buddhism and Western psychotherapy, one cannot help wondering to what extent the two parties understood – or misunderstood – each other. Suzuki's use of the term 'unconscious' was, for one thing, very particular[65] and he himself gave voice to the thought that psychoanalysts might mean something entirely different. Fromm, on the other hand, had never practised Zen and, as he readily admitted, what he knew about it was derived entirely at second hand, mainly from Suzuki – and presumably this went for just about all the Western participants, barring perhaps DeMartino.[66] Nevertheless, the encounter does seem to have been stimulating – and perhaps set the scene for fruitful future developments.

In his contribution to the resulting book, *Psychoanalysis and Zen Buddhism*, Fromm follows in Jung's footsteps in proposing that psychoanalysis might have altogether more radical aims than those defined by Freud. Instead of being basically concerned with securing the absence of sickness, positive well-being might become the goal – a view given added force by the admittedly 'disappointing results of character analysis (which have never been expressed more honestly than by Freud in his "Analysis, Terminable or Interminable?")'. No fundamental departures from basic Freudian theory or practice were being advocated, however; rather Fromm was calling for a logical extension of them – and, if 'one carries Freud's principle of the transformation of unconsciousness into consciousness to its ultimate consequences, one approaches the concept of enlightenment'. In other words, in ultimate terms the aims of Zen Buddhism and psychoanalysis are identical. Suzuki meanwhile had expressed the aims of Zen Buddhism thus:

> Zen in its essence is the art of seeing into the nature of one's being, and it points the way from bondage to freedom.... We can say that Zen liberates all the energies properly and naturally stored in each of us, which are in ordinary circumstances cramped and distorted so that they find no adequate channel of activity.... It is the object of Zen, therefore, to save us from going crazy or being crippled. This is what I mean by freedom, giving free play to all the creative and benevolent impulses inherently lying in our hearts. Generally, we are blind to this fact, that we are in possession of all the necessary faculties that will make us happy and loving towards one another.[67]

'This description of Zen's aim could be applied without change as a description of what psychoanalysis aspires to achieve,' Fromm declared. Their methods remained entirely different, however. The method of Zen consisted of a 'frontal attack on the alienated way of perception' by means of *zazen*, *kòan* and 'the authority of the Master'; psychoanalysis, on the other hand, was 'psychoempirical' in method and 'trains consciousness to get hold of the unconscious in a different way'. And from there on seemingly never the twain shall meet; for, like Jung, Fromm does not go so far as to suggest that any Westerner, psychoanalyst or layman, should actually experiment with the Zen method. He does, however, concede that students of Zen Buddhism might derive benefits from psychoanalysis.

Logically, the next phase had to be that a significant number of heroic pioneers from the Western world would venture across the dread abyss and actually embark upon Buddhist spiritual practice in earnest. Only then would the true nature of the higher spiritual development that had hitherto been contemplated only intellectually be known at first hand; also the effects and effectiveness of the various practices involved (e.g.

meditation) gauged. This process began to get under way in earnest during that great era of innovative energy, the Sixties. There was a tremendous upsurge in interest in Eastern religion at that time and tens of thousands of Westerners, mostly young and long-haired, journeyed to the East. Most perhaps were moved by collective forces whose true nature they only dimly discerned – or totally misconceived. This was after all the age of 'Make Love Not War' – and the love proclaimed was of a distinctly carnal variety. Sexual orgasm was the *summum bonum* and, through the writings of D.H. Lawrence, Wilhelm Reich, Norman Mailer and others, it had become imbued with quasi-spiritual connotations. Alternative – and better – orgasms were also sought in other spheres. Drugs, for instance, were considered a source of alternative orgasmic highs – and then the word got about that spiritual practices could engineer even better and more durable highs than drugs. It may seem ironic now, but many Westerners who at this time undertook serious spiritual discipline in the East, and to their lasting credit saw the process through (or at least to advanced stages), were led to do so by these kinds of very mixed motives.

With the hippie horde went a few psychotherapists. R.D. Laing, for instance, who had pioneered new approaches to schizophrenia; he spent a time at a temple in Sri Lanka. And Richard Alpert, a former psychology professor at Harvard University who, with Timothy Leary, had attained some notoriety as luminaries of the fashionable psychedelic drug culture that had arisen in the Sixties. Alpert returned to the West gloriously reborn as Baba Ram Dass after having spent some months in India with Neem Karoli Baba. Lately he has also been studying *vipassanā* meditation with, among others, U Pandita, a Burmese teacher. At the same time trained teachers and meditation masters from Tibet, Japan, Thailand, Burma, Korea, China, Sri Lanka – even from Mongolia – have come to the West and numerous centres have been established. Thus no longer did one have to go to the East to study its wisdom and to find facilities for practice.

All this activity inevitably spilled over into psychology, where great changes were afoot anyway. A new 'humanistic' psychology had been evolving which was rather more preoccupied with promoting 'growth' than with specifically curing psychological ills. Growth was very much about liberating energies, bringing potentialities to maximum fulfilment and generally securing optimum well-being – but it only reached as far as the outer limits of the ego stage.

A 'fourth force'[68] in Western psychology was also emerging that was explicitly concerned with extending the parameters to encompass the upper reaches of psychospiritual development. As such, it aspired beyond ego, or beyond the personal, hence its name: *Transpersonal Psychology*. Insofar as these mysterious shores, which were virtually blanks on most Western maps of the psyche, had been more thoroughly charted in the East, Eastern maps were given serious study by researchers. At the same time, it became clear that the practical methods – meditation, yoga and so forth; the transpersonal term for them is *consciousness disclipines* – that had been shown in the East to provide access to a 'broad range of states of consciousness' would have to be studied as well. This could only be done if they were actually practised – and here of course the innovators ran up against the classic prejudice of the Western scholarly orthodoxy that any researcher getting actively and sympathetically involved in his field of research would jeopardize his precious objectivity. Investigations into 'altered states of consciousness' were also begun using LSD and other substances – a direct inheritance of the Sixties, it would seem.

The book, *Beyond Ego* gives a fair idea of the range of interests encompassed by transpersonal psychology; it also includes contributions from many of the leading researchers in the area; Roger Walsh, Daniel Goleman, Duane Elgin, Frances Vaughan, Stanislav Grof, Charles Tart, Ram Dass – and the doyen of them all, Ken Wilber.

To conclude, we will briefly look at the work of Ken Wilber, which in a sense is a consummation of the ever deepening relationship between Buddhism (and the Eastern spiritual traditions generally) and Western psychotherapy. In his various writings, Wilber has charted a panoramic 'spectrum of consciousness' stretching from the most primitive level of undifferentiated embeddedness in Nature (the blissful ignorance of Eden), right up through various expanding levels to the ego stage, and then on beyond up to the most exalted state of spiritual realization (the bliss of conscious unity). This is a process through which the human race itself is collectively evolving and which its most advanced members (such as the Buddha) have completed. Each one of us also recapitulates the process in our own lives, from birth on up to . . . however far we want or are able to take it. Simply put, it is a progress from prepersonal (or pre-egoic) to personal (or egoic) to transpersonal (or trans-egoic). It can also be graphically represented as a Great Chain of Being.

The Great Chain of Being

Wilber's map is compounded of elements drawn from both East and West. In general, the phases up to and including the ego stage have been well charted by Western developmental psychologists, while the upper reaches have been charted in the spiritual psychologists of the East, though also to a lesser extent in Western mysticism. What we have here then is a massive work of synthesis or integration: a marriage of East and West.

As regards the dynamics of the Great Chain of Being, they may be described as follows. All there really is is primal Unity or Brahman (Wilber likes the Hindu term) but 'for the sport and play of it all' Brahman throws itself out, as it has done untold times, and loses itself in its myriad manifestations. Once cast into this bitter exile, each fragment longs to return to the Unity whence it came. This is Atman Project in its positive form, and it is the drive that keeps the Great Chain of Being in motion. Everything might work like clockwork and the multiplicity be smoothly restored to the One, but there are complicating factors. Progress from each stage of development to the next implies self-overcoming, which is a kind of death, hence fears, resistances and other symptoms arise. On the human level, for instance, we all intuit the truth: that our proper evolutionary function is to transcend ourselves and attain conscious unity. But we baulk at this and so instead of working towards *transformation* – i.e. progress to the next stage in the Great Chain – we syphon off the reintegrative energy and dissipate it in the pursuit of substitute goals (e.g. power, pleasure, fame, etc.). This Wilber calls *translation*: false Atman Project: in Buddhist terms it is dilly-dallying around in *Samsāra* instead of getting on with the task of seeking the Deathless.

Basically all the different stages in the Great Chain of Being result from the drawing of boundaries. Boundaries are all basically battlelines because they create pairs of warring opposites (self *versus* not-self, the conscious *vs* the unconscious persona *vs* shadow). Hence problems – or in Buddhist terms, *dukkha* – inevitably arise. Problems are transcended by tearing down the boundaries that created the particular dualism from which they arose in the first place. As boundaries are basically illusory anyway, this just involves *seeing through* them. What was once disowned, cast 'out there', is accepted and embraced. This 'converts enemies into friends, wars into dances, battles into plays'; and so therapy and growth go hand in hand as the boundaries are pushed further and further back until ultimately a state of no boundary is attained, which is conscious unity with the Totality.

As well as defining the various stages of psychospiritual development, Wilber also defines the 'therapy' or method of transformation appropriate to each. His book, *No Boundary* lays out his views in this regard. And here arguably he makes his most important contribution, for, as he himself points out, disagreement and often conflict have arisen as a result of a

failure to understand that therapies and methods are strictly
phase-specific; that is, each is designed to work on a *particular*
developmental phase and is not only unworkable but
potentially harmful if applied to another.

Wilber isolates a particularly regrettable example of this in
'In Praise of Ego'[69], an article that he wrote for *The Middle Way*
in 1983. Here he particularly laments the abyss of misunder-
standing that has arisen between many Buddhists and
psychologists. 'After working with neurotics – who don't have
enough ego-strength – and psychotics – who have no ego-
strength at all – the average psychologist is dumbfounded to
find us Buddhists recommending, indeed actively encouraging,
"no-ego" states', Wilber writes (*ibid.* p. 152). Both the
Buddhist and the 'average psychologist' are right when they
speak in the context of the particular phase with which they are
appropriately concerned, wrong when they generalize what
maintains there to other phases. Thus there is due season for
working to strengthen ego, for ego is a valid phase-specific
structure on the road to Nirvana. In fact one cannot develop
beyond ego until one has developed a firm ego to transcend: a
'self strong enough to die in nirvānic release'. This is precisely a
point emphasized by Jung:

> You cannot destroy a rationalist intellect that was never
> present.... Hence even with us it happens not infrequently that a
> conscious ego and a conscious, cultivated understanding must be
> produced by therapy before one can even think of abolishing I-ness
> or rationalism.[70]

Wilber sees the problem for Buddhists as lying with the
anatta doctrine, which he strongly emphasizes should be treated
as trans-egoic rather than pre-egoic. And hence only those with
a 'more-or-less intact ego' should undertake full Buddhist
training, for applying methods like intensive meditation to
subjects lacking the necessary ego strength can be disasterous:

> ... meditation, far from being a cure-all, can be *extremely
> detrimental* to borderline and narcissistic disorders (simply because
> the person is desperately attempting to create a strong and viable
> ego structure, and intensive meditation tends to dissolve what little
> structure the borderline has).[71]

Clearly, then, meditation should be approached with a certain amount of caution and with proper guidance. Even with the most gentle basic forms, the mind is being opened and material will enter consciousness, for in a sense meditation operates on the classic Freudian principle of making the unconscious conscious. If all goes well, what arises will be observed choicelessly and in due course will pass away. In this way the practitioner will see that problems are vagrant and incidental visitors, not an indissoluble part of the self. In other words, identification will cease. There is great relief and release in this, which is very real therapy. If the process becomes disturbing, however, it is wise to abandon, at least temporarily, whatever meditation practice has been undertaken and seek wise guidance. Another approach might be indicated.

Ken Wilber is also very cautious about optmistic predictions of a 'New Age' and a general raising of the level of consciousness, for 'the vast majority of humanity ... has not yet stably reached the rational egoic level' let alone placed itself in any position to transcend that level. Even in Western societies where the New Age is most vociferously vaunted, social conditions are generally inimical to proper personal development and the resulting stresses cause many promising people to regress to prepersonal phases while masquerading as progressing towards transpersonal ones:

> This was perfectly prefigured in the 'Dharma Bum' period of the Sixties, when an influential number of otherwise highly intellectual people, incapable of supporting rational and egoic responsibility in a culture clearly stressful and drifting, began championing typhonic, narcissistic, regressive freedom from the ego level, through pre-egoic license, while intellectually claiming to be actually pursuing the trans-egoic Zen of spontaneous freedom.... They often took as their heroes a handful of truly trans-egoic souls, pointed to Krishnamurti and Ramana and Zen, and thus managed to front an otherwise undeniable rationalization for their regress to Eden.[72]

There is absolutely no going back to the blissful ignorance of the prepersonal unity of Eden, then. Transpersonal unity is the only valid goal for human beings who wish to fulfil their potential; and it differs from its prepersonal counterpart in that it is fully *conscious*. Psychotherapy and Buddhism both point in this direction and each has its part to play in assisting in its full realization, psychotherapy in helping to develop a sound ego, Buddhism in taking the process on from there.

Part 7

Who's Who in Buddhism:
A Modern Western Perspective

Compiled with the Assistance of
Russell Webb
(Editor of *Buddhist Studies Review*)

Foreword

The following represents a highly selective listing of those Buddhist writers, teachers and practitioners with whom the contemporary Westerner is likely, directly or indirectly, to come in contact. Biographical and bibliographical details are necessarily brief. Neither inclusion nor exclusion in any way represent a value judgement on the relative importance, spiritual attainments, etc., of any particular figure.

There are chapters on each of the traditions: Theravāda, Tibetan, Zen, Pure Land and Nichiren, with an additional Miscellaneous section. This is not a perfect solution to the problem of arrangement as there is inevitably overlap, some figures having been involved with more than one tradition. However, one long homogenized listing would also, it was felt, present other and potentially greater disadvantages.

Some of the details included here were obtained at source, others obliquely. In particular the following books were of considerable help:

How the Swans Came to the Lake. (1986) Rick Fields. Boston & London: Shambhala. (Rev. Ed.)
Buddhism in Britain. (1979) Ian P. Oliver. London: Rider.
Sixty Years of Buddhism in England. (1968) Christmas Humphreys. London: The Buddhist Society.
The Sixteen Karmapas of Tibet. (1981) Karma Thinley Rinpoche. Boulder: Shambhala.
Zen Buddhism in North America: A History & A Directory. (1986) Toronto: Zen Lotus Society.
Living Buddhist Masters. (1984) Jack Kornfield. Boulder: Shambhala. (Repr.)
The Way of Korean Zen. (1985) Kusan Sunim. Translated by Martine Fages. Ed. with an Introduction by Stephen Batchelor. New York & Tokyo: John Weatherhill.

Among individuals, many helped us but the following were astonishingly kind: Patrick Gaffney (RIGPA) and John Stevens (Tohoku Fukushi University). Rosie Warwick (Sakya Thinley Rinchen Ling), Marcia Seymour (ZCLA), Philip Kapleau Rōshi (Rochester Zen Center), Maurice O'C Walshe, Nick Ribush (Wisdom Publications), Rev. Chushin Passmore (Throssel Hole Priory) James Y. Nagahiro (Buddhist Churches of America), Alan James (House of Inner Tranquillity) and Jim Belither (Manjushri Institute).

To simplify matters, even though before 1972 Sri Lanka was known as Ceylon, references are given as 'Sri Lanka', except where proper names are cited, e.g. Ceylon High Commissioner.

To save space, we have minimized accents, cut italicization and both used abbreviations extensively and also reduced titles and honorifics to a minimum (no disrespect implied!). Most of the abbreviations are obvious, viz.:

aka — also known as
assn — Association
b — born
BA — Bachelor's degree
Bdsm — Buddhism
Bdst — Buddhist
C — Central
d — died, death
devt — development
E — East or Eastern
ed — educated, edited by, or edition/s
esp — especially
1st — first
govt — government
HH — His Holiness
imp — important
incl — including
intl — international
Jap — Japanese
Kor — Korean
loc cit — at the place cited
m — married
MA — Master's degree
mths — months
mvt — movement
N — North

NE — North East
op cit — in the work cited
(qv) — quod vide (see reference elsewhere)
S — South
Soc — Society
SE — South East
Tib — Tibetan
tr/s — translation/s, translated by
U — University
UK — United Kingdom
U's or u's — universities
UK — United Kingdom
US — American
USA — United States of America
v — very
Ven — The Venerable
W — West, the West, Western
wk — work
Wstnrs — Westerners
WW I — World War I
WW II — World War II
yrs — years.

23   Theravada Buddhism

NOTE ON TITLES, etc.:

Ajahn (also Achaan): Thai pronunciation of the Sanskrit Acharya ('teacher'). In lay contexts can denote a senior school- or college teacher; in the Thai Sangha a meditation master.

Anagarika: lit, 'Homeless One'; one who enters the homeless life without formally ordaining as a monk.

Bhikkhu: fully ordained Buddhist monk.

Bhikkhuni: fully ordained Buddhist nun (this order has technically died out within the Theravada tradition).

Chao Khun: roughly 'noble lord'; a title granted to important Thai bhikkhus, broadly equivalent to an honorary bishophood, with which a new name also goes.

Dasa Sila Mata: woman who has become a 'homeless one' and adheres to Ten Precepts (a nun in all but name).

Dhammaduta: Bdst missionary work.

Dhutanga: ascetic practice.

Mahanayaka: patriarch or high-ranking Thera.

Mahathera (or Maha Thera): bhikkhu of 20 years' standing. Mahatheras generally just call themselves 'Thera'. The prefixed title 'Maha' when used in Thailand also denotes having passed a certain examination in Pali.

Phra: Thai equivalent of Thera; also prefixed to names of successful Pali examination candidates.

Samanera: postulant or novice who adheres to the Precepts but has not as yet received full ordination.

Sayadaw: Burmese equivalent of 'Maha Thera'; also given to highly respected Burmese bhikkhus.

Tan: (properly **Than**): Thai title roughly equivalent to 'Venerable'.

Thera: 'Elder'; a bhikkhu of 10 years' standing. Sthavira is the rather less used Sanskrit equivalent

Tudong: Pali equivalent for dhutanga. Tudong monk = wandering ascetic.

Amritananda Thera: *Senior Nepalese bhikkhu.* (1918–90), Nepal. Entered Sangha at age 18. Ordained in Sri Lanka; returned to Nepal; 1944: F. Dharmodaya Sabhā (pre-eminent Theravāda organization) at Svayambhunath, nr Kathmandu. 1951: F. All-Nepal Bhikkhu Assocn. 1956: organized 4th WFB (World Fellowship of Bdsts) Conference, Kathmandu. Has travelled in W, USSR, Japan, etc. In his last years he translated Pāli texts into Newari and Nepali and wrote in both languages and English, notably 'A Short History of Theravāda Buddhism in Modern Nepal'.

Ananda Maitreya Mahanayaka Thera: *Senior Sri Lankan monk and scholar active in W.* b 1896, Sri Lanka; 1911: initial ordination. *c* 1911–20: studied Pali, Sanskrit, Bdst philosophy; also Sutta and Vinaya Pitakas. 1916: higher ordination. 1920: joined Ananda College. 1924: first missionary tour of India. 1924–26: lecturer in Pali and Sinhalese at Nalanda College, Colombo. 1926–35: lecturer in Pali, Sanskrit, Sinhalese and Bdsm at Ananda College. 1935: opened Sri Dharmananda Pirivena, an institute for Bdst monks, at Balangoda. 1956: appointed President of Sri Lankan contingent at 6th Sangha Council held in Rangoon. 1954: appointed Mahanayaka Thera of Suddharma school of Sri Lanka. 1959: appointed Professor of

Mahayana Bdsm in Vidyodaya U. (now Sri Jayewardhenapura U. 1963: appointed Dean of t he Faculty of Bdsm in same U. 1966: appointed Acting Vice Chancellor of same. 1967: appointed President and Mahanayaka of the United Amarapura school. 1960: to Manila (Philippines) for Pax Romana Conference as representative of Vidyodaya U. 1973: stayed 3 mths in UK. 1967: to Mahabodhi Centre, Sarnath (nr. Benares) to teach Bdsm. 1980: to England, then to Moscow and Ulan Ude (Mongolia) with other Sri Lankan monks of the World Peace movement. 1981–6: visited England, Scotland, France, Sweden, Canada and USA. Publications include numerous wks in Sinhalese: complete trans of *Digha Nikaya*; abridgement of *Digha Nikaya*; *Life of the Buddha* (for children); *Life of the Buddha* (in pictures); *Khuddakapatha*; ed and tr *Dhammapada*; tr *Udana: Buddhism*; *Sanskrit Grammar and Composition*; *Pali Grammar and Composition*; *Easy Steps to English*; *English Grammar*. In English: versified tr of *Dhammapada*, 1975–8 revised ed., New York 1988, ed Bdst newspaper in Sinhalese (*Buddha Rasmi*).

Ananda Metteyya (Charles Henry Allan Bennett, 1872–1923): *First British bhikkhu and Bdsts missionary*, b London, son of electrical engineer. Trained as analytical chemist. Involved in Golden Dawn (magic) mvt, with W.B. Yeats *et al.* 1890: Arnold's *Light of Asia* kindled an interest in Bdsm. 1898: 'Ill-health drove me from England to the East'. Initially studied Dhamma in Sri Lanka and determined to lead Bdst mission to Europe. 1901: samanera ordination in Akyab (Burma), 1902: bhikkhu ordination. 1903: founded International Bdst, Society (Buddhasasana Samagama) in Rangoon. 1908: led 1st Mission to England; returned to Burma after 6 mths. 1914: ill-health compelled him to disrobe and return to UK; continued Bdst propaganda work, which he attempted to finance by his inventions. Books include *An Outline of Bdsm* and *The Wisdom of the Aryas*.

Ba Khin, Sayaji U Ba Khin (1899–1971): *Lay Burmese meditation master*. 1937: began practising vipassana under Saya Thet Gyi. Mastered several types of concentration meditation and developed powerful vipassana technique. 'This . . . involves sweeping the mind through the body, giving special attention to the ever-changing play of sensations. . . .' (Jack Kornfield). 1941: began teaching individuals and small groups; at the same time held down various important posts in lay life, having entered Accountant General's office and achieved promotion. 1948–53: Accountant General of Burma; offered vipassana instruction to staff. 1952: founded and taught at International Meditation Centre, Rangoon, where intensive 10-day courses given on regular basis. After retirement (1953), was active as a meditation teacher, developed his centre and was also acting head of several govt. depts. Married young and raised 6 children. His style, which emphasizes intensive practice rather than theoretical understanding, is taught elsewhere in the world by his disciples, e.g. S.N. Goenka (qv), Ruth Dennison, Robert Hover. For further information see, *Tranquillity & Insight* (1986). A. Solé-Leris, London: Rider, pp. 136–41.

Bodhi, Bhikkhu (Thera), (Jeffrey Block): *American-born bhikkhu*. b 1944. New York City, of Jewish parentage, ed. Brooklyn College. 1972: PhD in Philosophy from Claremont Graduate School. 1967: formally took Three Refuges. 1972: left for Sri Lanka, intending to enter Sangha. 1972: received samanera ordination, 1973: bhikkhu ordination. 1977: returned to USA and spent nearly 2 yrs at Lamaist Bdst Monastery of Geshe Wangyal (qv) and 3 yrs at Washington Bdst Vihara. 1982: returned to Sri Lanka. 1984: after periods of meditation training at Mitirigala Nissarana Vanaya, accepted the editorship of the Bdst Publication Society upon the retirement of Ven Nyanaponika Mahathera (qv). Now lives together with Ven Nyanaponika at the Forest Hermitage, Kandy. Publications incl *Nourishing the Roots*; *Transcendental Dependent Arising*; *The Noble Eightfold Path*; *The Discourse on the All-embracing Net of Views*; *The Brahmajala Sutta and its Commentarial Exegesis*; *The Discourse on the Root of Existence*; *The Mulapariyaya Sutta and its Commentarial Exegesis*; *The Great Discourse on Causation*; *The Mahanidana Sutta and its Commentarial Exegesis*.

Boowa: see Maha Boowa, Ajahn.

Buddhadasa Bhikkhu (1906–93): '. . . *perhaps the best-known Dharma master in Thailand at this time*,' (Jack Kornfield). b Chaiya, son of well-to-do merchant; ordained at 21. Having completed Bdst studies, taught for some yrs and then lived alone as tudong monk in the forest for 6 yrs, studying Pali etc., avoiding all human contact. Then became Abbot of Wat Phra Data at Chaiya; later moved to Wat Suanmokkhabalarama, 2½ miles outside Chaiya. Influenced by Zen, Christianity, etc. '- teaches a more active outlook towards life and maintains that Nibbana can be attained "here and now"' (*Bdst Forum*, London). Books incl *Anapanasati, Buddha Dhamma for Students, Towards Buddha-dhamma, The Right Approach to Dhamma, Exchanging Dhamma while Fighting, Dhamma – the World Saviour, In Samsara Exists Nirvana, Why Were We Born?, Two Kinds of Language, No Religion, Handbook of Mankind, Christianity & Bdsm (Sinclaire Thompson Memorial Lecture, Bangkok, 1967), Emancipation of the World* and *Toward the Truth*. qv. Louis Gabaude "Une Hermeneutique – Bouddhique Contemporaire de Thailand: Buddhadasa Bhikkhu" (EFEO CL, Paris 1988).

Buddharakkhita Bhikkhu: *Founder of numerous social welfare organizations.* b 1922, Imphal, Manipur State, India, ed Institute of Engineering Technology, Calcutta. World War II: service as Officer. 1946–48: Ramakrishna monk. 1949: bhikkhu ordination. 1949–52: Bdst studies in Sri Lanka. 1952–55: Bdst studies in Burma under Mahasi Sayadaw (qv) et al. Editorial board, Tipitaka Translation, 6th Bdst Synod, Burma. 1955–6: taught at Nalanda Postgraduate Institute. 1956: founded Maha Bodhi Soc, Bangalore. Later founded: International Meditation Centre, school for indigent Bdst boys, Buddha Vachana Publishers and Tripitaka Press, Maitri Mandala, Mahabodhi Burns & Casualty Centre (Bangalore), Institute of Buddhology & Pali Studies (Mysore), Artificial Limb Centre (Bangalore), Arogya Centre, etc., etc. 1980 #aa: has taught and conducted retreats in UK and USA. Publications incl over 50 books.

Chah, Ajahn, (also spelt Cha, Chaa): (See note on name below.) *Meditation master of the Thai forest tradition.* b in rural village in Lao part of NE Thailand. Ordained as a novice in early youth; at 20 took bhikkhu ordination. Studied basic Dhamma, discipline and scriptures as a young monk; later practised meditation under several masters of the forest tradition. Lived ascetic life for several yrs, wandering, sleeping in forests, caves, cremation grounds, then spent a short but enlightening period with Ajahn Mun (q.v.). Eventually settled in a thick forest grove nr. birthplace; a large monastery grew up around him there (Wat Pah Pong) from which numerous branch temples have sprung in NE Thailand and elsewhere. 1975: Wat Pah Nanachat established as special training monastery for Wstnrs. 1977 and 79: visited UK. 1979: visited USA. *(Note on Name: Cha was his first lay name. Original bhikkhu name – Subhatto. Was later appointed Chao Khun with new name, Bodhinyana; does not use Chao Khun title but keeps name that goes with it.)* Books incl *A Taste of Freedom, A Still Forest Pool* and *Bodhinyana.* Died in 1992.

Coleman, John: *Vipassana teacher trained by U Ba Khin.*

Dharmapala, Anagarika (David Hewavitarne, 1864–1933): *Bdst propagandist.* b Colombo, Sri Lanka; joined Theosophical Soc. at early age; met Mme. Blavatsky and Col. Olcott. Studied Pali. 1888: visited Japan with the Theosophists. 1891: founded Maha Bodhi Society; became v. vigorous re the restoration of Bodh Gaya to Bdst hands (this not achieved until 1949). 1893: attended World Parliament of Religions in Chicago. 1896–7: again in USA 1926: founded British Maha Bodhi Soc. in London, then went on to USA. 1928: established Bdst Mission (later London Bdst Vihara). 1931: ordained a *bhikkhu* as Sri Devamitta Dhammapala. (Biography in 'Wheel' Series, BPS, Sri Lanka).

Dhiravamsa: *Thai-born lay meditation teacher.* b NE Thailand c 1934; became samanera at 13 and a bhikkhu (Tissadatto) at 21. 1964: arrived London. 1966: became head of Buddhapadipa Temple as Chao Khun Sobhana Dhammasudhi. 1971: disrobed and established himself as a lay teacher. Had a centre in UK (The Chapter House, Wisbech, Cambs), but later departed for USA. 1977: settled in N California. Runs courses in meditation and Abhidhamma. In recent yrs has experimented with combining meditation with modern psychotherapeutic techniques. Books incl *The Real Way to Awakening, The Beneficial Factors for Meditation Practice, Insight Meditation, A New Approach to Bdsm* and *The Dynamic Way of Meditation*, etc.

Feldman, Christina: *Western vipassana teacher.* 1970–5: study and practice under various Bdst. teachers in India, incl Geshe Rabten (qv). 1975–7: participated in various intensive vipassana retreats and personal retreats for development of insight meditation practice. 1974–86: has guided meditation retreats in Europe, USA, England and Australia. Now lives in Devon where she teaches and is a guiding teacher at Gaia House, Devon, which she also helped to found. In recent yrs has also led retreats which focus upon communication skills, womens' spirituality and family retreats. Books include *Women Awake*.

Goenka, Satya Narayan: *Vipassana meditation teacher.* b 1924, Burma. For many yrs a high-powered businessman with family responsibilities; also performed social good works. 1955: experimented with U Ba Khin's vipassana method hoping to gain migraine relief: was completely cured and achieved deep spiritual insight as well. For next 14 yrs an energetic student of U Ba Khin. 1969: returned to India; conducted own 1st vipassana course in Bombay; others followed in many parts of India; his 'camps' attended by all sorts of people. 1976: Vipassana International Academy (VIA) established at Igatpuri (Maharashtra state); other centres later established at Hyderabad and Jaipur, smaller ones at Dharamsala, Barachakia and in Nepal. In W, Vipassana Meditation centre inaugurated at Shelburne Falls, Mass, USA in 1982; other centres planned for GB and Australia. Has lately retired from business to devote himself to teaching meditation and now holds courses every year in Europe, USA, Canada, Japan, Australia and New Zealand.

Goldstein, Joseph: *American vipassana teacher.* Ex-Peace Corps, trained with Anagarika Munindra (qv) in Bodh Gaya. Invited to teach by Ram Dass (Richard Alpert) in Boulder. Met Jack Kornfield there. The two were peripatetic teachers for a few years until they became involved in the establishment of the Insight Meditation Society at Barre, Mass. Has also trained with S.N. Goenka in India. Books incl *The Experience of Insight*.

Horner, I.B. (Isaline Blew, 1896–1981): *English Pali scholar.* Met the Rhys Davids (qv) when young. 1936: commenced Pali studies when the American scholar Kenneth J. Saunders introduced her to the *Dhammapada*. 1923–36: Librarian of Newnham College, Cambridge; was also a Fellow of the College. 1942–59: Secretary of Pali Text Society; afterwards President. Also Vice-President of Bdst Society. 1980: OBE. Books include *Women Under Primitive Bdsm*, *The Early Bdst Theory of Man Perfected* and *Gotama the Buddha* (with Ananda K. Coomaraswamy). Also many translations from Pali, incl *Vinaya Pitaka, Majjhima Nikaya, Milindapanha, Buddhavamsa, Cariyapitaka* and *Vimanavatthu*. Biography by R.E. and C.W. Iggleden in *Bdst Studies in Honour of I.B. Horner*, D. Reidel, Dordrecht, 1974.

James, Alan: *Vipassana teacher.* b 1940. Read Physics at London U; became dissatisfied with pure science and began studying philosophy and psychology. 1962–3 and 67: to India to study Oriental philosophy and meditation. 1968: ordained at Wat Buddhapadipa (London) as Dipadhammo Bhikkhu. 1967–70: trained under guidance of Ven Kapilavaddho (qv) at Wat Dhammapadipa, Hampstead (London). 1971–3: took over as teacher-in-residence at Dhammapadipa after d of Ven Kapilavaddho. 1972: m Jacqueline Randall. 1975–85: worked as Lecturer in Computer Programming in London and Bristol. 1980: with Jacqui James (qv) founded House of Inner Tranquillity Meditation Centre, Wilts (UK); 1985: The Aukana Trust, a registered charity; 1986: Monastery of Absolute Harmony, Wilts (UK). Co-author with Jacqui James of *A Meditation Retreat, Modern Buddhism*, etc.

James, Jacqui: *Vipassana teacher.* (1946–89) 1968: attended Wat Dhammapadipa, Hampstead (London) and practised intensive samatha and vipassana meditation under Ven Kapilavaddho (qv); conducted meditation classes and assisted with gen admin. 1970–3: took up residence at Dhammapadipa; became Secretary and helped edit bi-monthly journal, *Sangha*. 1971: m Kapilavaddho, then Richard Randall. 1971–3: after d of Kapilavaddho, taught and helped administer Dhammapadipa. 1972: m Alan James (qv); with him co-founded House of Inner Tranquillity (1980), Aukana Trust (1985) and The Monastery of Absolute Harmony (1986). Co-author with Alan James of *A Meditation Retreat, Modern Buddhism*, etc.

Kapilavaddho, Ven (Wm Purfurst, 1906–71): *Founder of English Sangha Trust.* b Hanwell, Middx (UK). Dissatisfied with business life, began studying psychology, philosophy, etc; went to London (on foot) and became photographer in Fleet St; found a teacher to instruct him in Yoga and Vedanta; developed a colour printing process; took up sculpture. 1939: official War photographer, then fireman during Blitz; met U Thittila whose pupil he became; got married; finally photographer with RAF. After War began serious Bdst studies with U Thittila at Bdst Soc (then in Gt Russell St) covering Sutta, Vinaya and Abhidhamma. Began lecturing on Bdsm; founded Manchester Bdst Soc. 1952: adopted anagarika status (with permission of wife); later became Samanera Dhammananada under U Thittila; worked for Bdst Soc; continued lecturing etc., and founded socs in Oxford and Cambridge, also Bdst Summer School. Later resigned samanera status and took job in Surrey hotel as barman to raise finance to go to Thailand. 1954: receiver lower and higher ordinations (single ceremony) in Thailand (name based on 'Kapilavatthu', Buddha's home town; means 'he who spreads the Dhamma'); surprised Thai Sangha with his knowledge, esp of Abhidhamma and Pali lang; successfully practised intensive samatha and vipassana meditation. Returned to UK, to London Bdst Vihara, Knightsbridge, with intention of establishing English Sangha. 1955: to Thailand with 3 British samaneras (Rbt Albison, Geo Blake & Peter Morgan). 1956: triple ordination at Wat Paknam under Ven Chao Khun Bhavanakosol – the core of an English Sangha. Returned UK; acquired house in Alexandra Rd, London NW8; English Sangha Trust founded; period of gt activity. 1957: due to ill-health, disrobed; changed name to Richard Randall; m Ruth Lester; remained 10 yrs in obscurity. 1967: returned to robe at Wat Buddhapadipa under Ven Chao Khun Sobhana Dhammasudhi; took over Hampstead Bdst Vihara (then renamed Wat Dhammapadipa). Again disrobed. 1971: m Jacqueline Gray.

Khantipalo, Phra (Lawrence Mills): *Pioneer British bhikkhu and Pali scholar.* b 1932, nr London. At Suez Canal with British Army, received book on Bdsm. Later joined Bdst Society in London; 3 yrs later took samanera ordination under Ven Dr H. Saddhatissa (qv) at London Bdst Vihara. After 1 yr in the robe in UK, left for 3 yrs in India, studying Pali, travelling and teaching Dr Ambedkar's new Bdsts. Took bhikkhu ordination under Abbot of Wat Cakkapat, Bangkok; studied at Wat Bovoranives; also practised meditation under various distinguished teachers. After 11 yrs in Thailand went to Australia with senior Thai bhikkhu to set up wat (temple) in Sydney. Later moved to Sri Lanka; worked at Bdst Publication Society (Kandy). Subsequently returned to Australia and taught at Wat Buddha-Dhamma, Wiseman's Ferry, NSW 2255. Disrobed after 30 years in the Sangha, married a young Sinhalese woman and lives in Cairns, Queensland, trying to create a Buddhist community in former hippie area. Books incl *Banner of the Arahants, A Life of the Buddha, Calm & Insight, Nanamoli, Tolerance* and *What is Bdsm?*; also tr of *Dhammapada* and ed of Nanamoli's tr of *Majjhima Nikaya.*

Khema, Sister (Ilse Ledermann): *Pioneering Theravada nun.* b 1923, Berlin. 1938: obliged to leave Germany due to Jewish origins. After long spiritual search, trained in vipassana under Robert Hover; subsequently led courses in USA, Australasia and W Germany. 1978: became assistant to Ven Khantipalo (qv) at Wat Buddha-Dhamma, New South Wales, Australia (founded on land purchased by herself). 1979: ordained a nun by Narada Mahathera at Vajirarama, Colombo, Sri Lanka. Founder of Parappuduwa Nun's Island, Dodanduwa, Sri Lanka. Patron of planned Int'l Bdst Womens' Centre. Tours Europe, Australia, etc., teaching and lecturing on Bdsm. 1989: Returned to Germany and F. Buddha-Haus nr. Munich and conducts residential courses. Books incl *Buddha Ohne Geheimnis*, etc.

Khemadhammo Bhikkhu: *British thera and teacher.* b 1944, Portsmouth. 1967: became interested in Bdsm; began to attend Hampstead Vihara (instruction from Ruth Walshe and Ven Kapilavaddho). Also small involvement with FWBO. Took up training seriously under Ven Maha Boonchuay, a Thai bhikkhu resident at Hampstead. At Wat Buddhapadipa, co-founded Lay Bdst Assn and Hon. Secretary until 1971. 1971: to Thailand; began vipassana training under Ven Chao Khun Thep Siddhimuni at Wat Mahadhatu, Bangkok. 1971: samanera ordination. 1972: went to stay with Ven Ajahn Cha (qv); for next few yrs either resident at Wat Pah Pong or various branch wats. 1972: bhikkhu ordination. 1977: to England with Ajahn Cha and Ven Sumedho Bhikkhu; stayed at Hampstead Vihara. 1977: began visiting prisons. 1978: moved to Birmingham Vihara. 1979: established vihara on Isle of Wight, first at Little Duxmore, later at Newport (Naradipa Vihara). 1984: established Buddha-Dhamma Vihara at Kenilworth. 1985: launched Angulimala, the Bdst Prison Chaplaincy (with Yann Lovelock); became its Spiritual Director. 1985: moved to The Forest Hermitage, Lower Fulbrook, Warwick, and became resident Ajahn; also Spiritual Adviser to Buddha-Dhamma Fellowship; lectures at Warwick U in Open Studies programme and occasionally to trainee teachers; in addition teaches Herefordshire Bdst Group and still travels extensively to many prisons.

Kornfield, Jack: *American lay vipassana teacher, writer and editor.* Began Asian & Bdst Studies at Dartmouth College. 1963–9: in Asia, studying and practising Bdsm; Ven Ajahn Cha one of his main tchrs; has also trained with S.N. Goenka (qv) in India. 1969: returned to US and disrobed. Drove taxi for a time, then returned to clinical psychology studies. Invited by Trungpa Rinpoche (qv) to teach Theravada meditation at Naropa Institute. Also taught at Esalen Inst. Peripatetic teacher for some yrs. Co-founder, Insight Meditation Society, Barre, Mass (USA). Publications incl *Living Bdst Masters*; *A Guild to the Meditation Temples of Thailand*; *Dharma Talks* (with Joseph Goldstein), etc.; also comp and ed selection of Ajahn Cha's discourses, *A Still Forest Pool*.

Maha Boowa, Ajahn: (b.c. 1914) *Meditation master of the forest tradition of NE Thailand*. Studied basic Dhamma and mastered Pali before embarking upon meditation training. Spent many yrs practising meditation as a forest monk; received much instruction from Ajahn Mun (qv), who sternly lectured him on the difference between bliss states (jhanas) and the wisdom of Enlightenment. He 'emphasizes the development of strong and steady concentration in practice as a forerunner to the arising of wisdom' (Kornfield). For further information see *Living Bdst Masters*, by Jack Kornfield, ch. 9.

Mahasi Sayadaw (U Sobhana Mahathera, 1904–82): *Burmese meditation master*. At age 6 began studying at monastic school. Became samanera at 12 and bhikkhu at age 20. At Thaton, studied with U Narada (Mungun Sayadaw); after intensive meditation course returned to Moulmein and resumed working as tchr of Bdst scriptures. Later passed govt sponsored Pali and scholastic exams with flying colours. 1949: requested to give meditation instruction in Rangoon by Prime Minister of Burma, U Nu, and Sir U Thwin, both of Buddha Sasananuggaha Assn. Held intensive training courses at Thathana Yeiktha, HQ Buddha Sasananuggaha Assn. Thousands received training (est. 45,000 at centre, 600,000 in all Burma); many ancillary centres set up in Burma and method also spread abroad to Thailand, Bangladesh, India, Sri Lanka, Europe, S. Africa, Australia and USA 1954–6: Questioner (Pucchaka) at 6th Bdst Council in Rangoon to celebrate Buddha Jayanti. d. Rangoon. Books incl *Guide to the Practice of Meditation*, *Progress of Insight* and *Practical Insight Meditation*. *For further information see* Living Bdst Masters, Jack Kornfield, ch. 5.

Malalasekera, Dr Gunapala Piyasena (1899–1973): *One of the most brilliant Bdst savants produced by Ceylon and a warm friend of the Bdst cause throughout the world* (Buddhist Quarterly). ed St Johns College, Panadura and London U. where he gained MA, PhD and DLitt degrees. Taught at Ananda College and Nalanda Vidyalaya, Colombo. 1927–57: Dean of Faculty of Oriental Studies at U of Ceylon; also Prof of Pali. 1950: Founding President of World Fellowship of Bdsts (WFB). Also President, Ceylon Bdst Congress; Hon Secretary and Treasurer of Pali Text Soc (PTS) in Sri Lanka. Participated in UNESCO projects worldwide. 1957: appointed Ambassador for Ceylon to USSR; also represented his country at UN and was High Commissioner for London for 3 yrs. Magnum opus – *Dictionary of Pali Proper Names*; also 1st Editor-in-Chief of *The Encyclopaedia of Bdsm* (1966–). Other publications incl *Pali Literature of Ceylon*.

Mun, Ajahn (Phra Mun Bhuridatta Thera, 1870–1949): *Meditation master of the Thai forest tradition*. b into Kankaew family in Ubol Rajadhani, NE Thailand. Took samanera ordination in Khasmbong at age 15. Disrobed after 2 yrs for family reasons but returned to robe at age 22, taking bhikkhu ordination at Wat Liab. Afterwards trained with Phra Ajahn Sao Kantisilo of Wat Liab. 'Under his guidance the Ascetic Forest Tradition became a very important tradition in the revival of Bdst meditation practice. The vast majority of recently deceased and presently living meditation masters in Thailand are either direct disciples of . . . (his) . . . or were substantially influenced by his Teachings' (footnote in *Bodhinyana*). 'One of the most renowned of the Thai-Lao forest teachers of this century, known for his mastery of concentration and insight practices, for his great powers, and for the fierceness of his teaching style' (Jack Kornfield). Biography: *The Venerable Phra Achaan Mun Bhuridatta*, compiled by Achaan Maha Boowa (English tr Siri Buddhasukh).

Munindra, Anagarika: *Indian mediation teacher*. Bengali active in Maha Bodhi Society, who in 1949 was requested by the new govt of India to take charge of the Bdst Temple at Bodh Gaya. 1957: 6 mths leave to study with Mahasi Sayadaw (qv) in Burma; remained Burma 7 yrs reading entire Pali Canon and training as monk-teacher with Mahasi Sayadaw. Afterwards returned to Bodh Gaya; ordained as anagarika; set up international meditation centre. Occasionally teaches at Insight Meditation center, Barre (Mass., USA).

Nanamoli Bhikkhu (Osbert Moore, 1905–60): *Pioneer British bhikkhu and Pali scholar.* ed Exeter College, Oxford. Discovered Bdsm via Julius Evola's *The Doctrine of Awakening* while serving in Italy during WW II. Joined BBC after War. 1949: went to Sri Lanka and ordained samanera with friend, Harold Musson. 1950: bhikkhu ordination at Vajirarama Temple (Colombo), then studied with Nyanatiloka Mahathera (qv) at Island Hermitage, Dodanduwa. By 1960: had translated *Visuddhimagga* into English as *The Path of Purification*; also translated *Nettippakarana ('The Guide')* and *Patisambhidamagga ('Path of Discrimination')*, most of the suttas of the *Majjhima Nikaya* and several from the *Samyutta Nikaya*. d suddenly while on pilgrimage at Majo; cremated at Vajirarama Temple. Other books incl *The Life of the Buddha* and *A Thinker's Note Book.*

Narada Mahathera (Sumanapala Perera, 1898–1983): *Prominent English-educated Sinhalese bhikkhu.* b Colombo suburb; ed SPCK School, St. Benedict's College (RC) and Paramananda Vihara Sunday School. Entered Sangha at 18; teacher Pelene Vajirañana Mahanayaka Thera; received traditional monastic education but also studied philosophy, logic and ethics at U College (Colombo). Gained experience of Dhammaduta work with Servants of the Buddha Society. 1929: 1st journey abroad (to India); later travelled widely in SE Asia and developed closest ties with Indonesia and Vietnam; also promoted Theravada Bdsm in W Europe. Was elected President of the Bdst Vihara Soc (founded London 1948). A few short stays in London. Also visited Australia. Publications incl *Buddhism in a Nutshell, The Buddha and His Teachings, The Bdst Conception of Mind or Consciousness, The Bdst Doctrine of Kamma and Rebirth, Brahma Viharas or The Sublime States, The Way to Nibbana, The Life of the Buddha, The Bodhisatta Ideal* and *An Elementary Pali Course.* Translations incl *The Dhammapada* and *Abhidhammatthasangaha – A Manual of Abhidhamma.*

Nyanaponika Mahathera (Siegmund Feniger): *Pioneer European bhikkhu.* (1901–94) Hanau-am-Main, W Germany of Jewish parents. Converted to Bdsm via books while living in Upper Silesia. 1922: moved to Berlin and met other German Bdsts. Later formed a Bdst study circle in Königsberg (E Prussia). 1936: to Sri Lanka; samanera ordination at Island Hermitage Dodanduwa. 1937: bhikkhu ordination. WW II – interned as enemy alien in Dehra Dun (N India). 1951: went to Burma with Nyanatiloka Mahathera for 6th Bdst Council. Has served as delegate to World Fellowship of Bdsts (WFB) conferences at Rangoon, Bangkok and Phnom Penh; has also served as one of the Vice-Presidents of WFB, for a term. 1952 and after: resident at Forest Hermitage, Kandy. 1958–84: Founder-Editor of the Bdst Publication Society (BPS); President till 1988. Books in English incl *The Heart of Bdst Meditation* and *Abhidhamma Studies*, and "The Vision of Dhamma".

Nyanatiloka Mahathera (Anton Gueth, 1878–1957): *Pioneer European bhikkhu and notable Pali scholar.* b Wiesbaden (Germany). After high school devoted himself to music in Frankfurt and Paris, then journeyed to India via Greece, Middle East and Ceylon. 1903: samanera ordination in Rangoon; bhikkhu ordination the following yr (the 1st non-British Western one). 1910–11: left Sri Lanka and travelled to Europe; stayed mainly in Switzerland (Lausanne area) and brought many to Bdsm; ordained 1st samanera on European soil. 1911: returned to Sri Lanka; thereafter lived at the Island Hermitage in Ratgama Lake, Dodanduwa. Interned during WW I as enemy alien. 1916: given passport to return to Germany via USA; travelled to Honolulu and then went to China but was arrested in Chungking and imprisoned in Hankow until 1919, then exchanged by the International Red Cross and sent back to Germany. Unable to return to Sri Lanka in 1920, so went on to Japan, became professor at Komazawa U. 1926: finally got back to Sri Lanka. WW II: again interned. 1946: returned to Dodanduwa. Nyanaponika Thera one of his disciples. Books incl *A Bdst Dictionary, Guide Through the Abhidhamma, Path to Deliverance* and *The Word of the Buddha.*

Paññavaddho, Ven (Peter Morgan): *Senior British-born bhikkhu.* b 1925, Mysore, S India. 1955: samanera ordination at London Bdst Vihara (Knightsbridge). 1956: bhikkhu ordination at Wat Paknam, Thailand, under Ven Chao Khun Bhavanakosol; returned to London; helped found English Sangha Trust (also 1956). 1957: took over leadership of vihara at Alexandra Rd, London NW8, from Ven Kapilavaddho (qv). c 1961: left for Thailand and has since trained with Ajahn Maha Boowa (qv) at Wat Pa Barn Tard.

Rahula, Ven Walpola: *Sri Lankan scholar monk,* b 1907, Galle dist, Sri Lanka. ed privately. At

13 or 14, entered Sangha; studied Sinhalese, Pali, Sanskrit, Bdsm. and Bdst History according to traditional monastic curriculum. 1936: entered Ceylon U College; then to Calcutta U; later returned to U of Ceylon and gained PhD. in 1950; also worked with G.P. Malalasekera (qv) on History of Bdsm in Ceylon. 1930s: well-known preacher criticizing some popular Bdst practices and publishing pamphlets; took special interest in social and economic matters; entered struggle for political freedom. 1940s: supported working class mvt and was jailed for 3 days in 1947. 1947: attended Inter-Asian Relations Conference, New Delhi; met many Indian political leaders (Nehru, et al). Sometime Senior Teacher at Vidyalankara Pirivena; also held other posts there. 1950: to Sorbonne (Paris) on French govt fellowship to do research on Mahayana Bdsm (esp wks of Asanga). Worked with Paul Demiéville of Collège de France; met André Bareau et al; tr *Abhidharmasamuccaya* into French as *Le Compendium de la Super-Doctrine (Philosophie) (Abhidharmasamuccaya) d'Asanga*. 1958: member of Ceylon Delegation to UNESCO General Conference; met the future Pope John XXIII. 1964: 1st Bishop Brashares Prof of History and Literature of Religions at Northwestern U, Evanston, Illinois, USA. 1965: made *Tripitakavagisvaracarya* (Supreme Master of the Bdst Scriptures). 1966: became Vice-Chancellor of Vidyodaya U of Sri Lanka. 1969: resigned to resume studies in Paris. 1970: Hon Membership of Sri Lanka Academy of Letters. 1974: left Paris for London; worked with Miss I.B. Horner (qv) for Pali Text Society. 1977: Cornell Visiting Prof, Swarthmore College, Penn., USA. 1978: Hon DLitt. degrees from U's of Sri Lanka, Nava Nalanda Mahavihara (Bihar, India) and Los Angeles (Oriental Studies). 1979: Regent's Lecturer and Visiting Prof of Anthropology, U of California, Los Angeles. Has lectured widely elsewhere, incl Japan. Latterly Chancellor of Kelaniya U and President of Paramadhamma Bdst Institute of Sri Lanka. 1980: Hon DLitt, U. of Kelaniya. Other books incl *The Heritage of the Bhikkhu*, *What the Buddha Taught* and *Zen and the Taming of the Bull*. Festschrift: *Bdst Studies in Honour of W.R.*

Rewata Dhamma Mahathera, Ven Dr: *Senior Burmese bhikkhu teaching in UK.* b 1929, Thamangone, Henzada dist, Burma. Joined local monastery at 5 and studied under various teachers. Age 11: samanera ordination. Age 20: bhikkhu ordination; preceptor – Myint Kwet Sayadaw of Henzada. Studied Pali and Theravada Bdsm at Aung Mingala Thidthi monastery, Rangoon; passed all exams to final Dhammacariya grade. Later went to Dakkhi Narama monastery, Mandalay, to study canon and commentaries under various eminent teachers. Afterwards appointed a teacher at Aung Mingala Thidthi. Age 23: awarded title of Sasanadhaja Siripavaradhammacariya by President of Burma. 1956#aa: studied at Banaras Hindu and Varanasi U's. 1964: obtained MA in Sanskrit. 1967: PhD from Banaras Hindu U. Hon lecturer at both u's. 1972: resigned to develop vipassana meditation under S.N. Goenka (qv); had previously practised with, and been appointed a teacher by, Mahasi Sayadaw. 1975: came to England at invitation of W Midlands Bdst Centre (Birmingham); appointed Spiritual Director by Gyalwa Karmapa (qv). Helped set up other Bdst centres in Birmingham, London and I o Man. Since 1975: has travelled widely in UK, Europe, USSR, Far E and USA, teaching, lecturing, etc. 1982: appointed member of University Court of Birmingham U. Publications incl ed of *Abhidhammatthasangaha* (with commentary), a 3 vol ed of *Visuddhimagga* (with commentary), ed of First Sermon of the Buddha (in Hindi), etc. To 1975: Chief Editor of *Parami* (English/Hindi periodical). 1969: appointed Chief Editor of *Encyclopaedia of Buddhist Technical Terms* by Sanskrit U. Varanasi.

Rhys Davids, Caroline (née Foley, 1858–1942): *Pioneer Pali scholar.* ed U C London; MA and DLitt degrees; also became Fellow. Later Reader in Pali at School of Oriental & African Studies and Lecturer in Indian Philosophy at Manchester U. 1894: m T.W. Rhys Davids (qv); issue – 2 daughters, 1 son. Collaborated with husband in Pali Text Society (PTS); succeeded him as President. 'Interested in isolating in the Pali Canon the actual teaching of the Buddha . . .' (Christmas Humphreys). Numerous trans and eds; books incl *Gotama the Man*, *Sakya or Bdst Origins* and *Wayfarer's Words*.

Rhys Davids, Dr T.W. (Thomas William, 1843–1922): *Pioneer Pali scholar.* b. Colchester, son of Congregationalist minister. ed Brighton and U. of Breslau (Germany), where he gained PhD 1864: entered Ceylon Civil Service. Drawn to Pali studies when work as magistrate produced a case involving a point of Bdst ecclesiastical law; learnt Pali from Sumangala Thera (Yatramulle Unnanse). 1872: resigned from CCS; returned to London and studied Law. 1977: called to Bar; law practice did not flourish, so concentrated upon Pali and Bdst studies. 1881: delivered Hibbert Trust Lectures; also announced the formation of the Pali Text Society. 1894:

m. Caroline Augusta Foley, who had similar academic interests. 1882: Professor of Pali at London U. 1885–1904: Secretary and Librarian of Royal Asiatic Soc; also a founder of School of Oriental & African Studies (London U). 1894: lectured at Cornell U. 1889–1900: visited Bodh Gaya and other Bdst holy places in India. 1904–10: Prof of Comparative Religion, Victoria U. Manchester. 1907: President of Bdst Society of Gt Britain & Ireland. 1910: elected President of India Society. Retired to Chipstead, Surrey. Numerous eds and trans; books incl *The Ancient Coins & Measures of Ceylon*, *Manual of Buddhism*; *Buddhism, its History & Literature* and *Bdst India*. Co-author with Dr Wm Stede of *Pali-English Dictionary*.

Saddhatissa, Ven Dr Hammalawa Mahanayaka Thera, MA PhD DLitt: *Senior Sri Lankan born bhikkhu and scholar*. (1914–90), Hammalawa, Satkorale province, Sri Lanka. 1926: bhikkhu ordination. Undergraduate studies at Vidyodaya Pirivena and Prachina Bhasopakara Samagama (Sri Lanka); also studied Banaras, London (SOAS, 1958–61) and Edinburgh (PhD 1965). Proficient in Pali, Sanskrit, Prakrit, Sinhala and Hindi. 1940–73: held various academic posts, incl Prof of Pali, Banaras Hindu U (1956–7); Lecturer in Sinhala at SOAS, London (1958–60); Professor of Buddhism & Pali at Toronto U (1966–69); visiting lecturer at Oxford (1973). Has also conducted lecture tours in Europe, USA and Japan. 1956: at Nagpur (India) as adviser to Dr Amdedkar (qv) during mass conversions of former 'untouchables' to Bsm. 1957: Head of London Bdst Vihara until 1985. 1966: revived British Mahabodhi Soc (defunct since WW II); became its President. Has helped establish other centres, incl new London Bdst Vihara (1964); Bdst Centre, Oakenholt, Oxford (1971); Bdst Research Library, Nugegoda, Sri Lanka (1984); Buddha Vihara, Handsworth, Birmingham (1986). Current appointments incl President, Sangha Council of Great Britain (1966). Sanghanayaka Thera (Bdst Primate) of UK (1980); Vice-President, Pali Text Society (1984). Books in English incl *The Buddha's Way*; *Bdst Ethics*; *Essence of Buddhism*; *Handbook for Bdsts*; *Introduction to Buddhism* and *The Life of the Buddha*. Various eds of Pali texts.

Silacara Bhikkhu (J.F. McKechnie, 1871–1950): *Pioneer British bhikkhu*. b Hull; worked in garment industry, then emigrated to USA and worked on farms. Later went to Rangoon, Burma to help Ananda Metteyya (qv) edit journal *Buddhism*. 1906: ordained by U Kumara Thera at Kyundagon temple. 1925: health broke; disrobed and returned to UK. Worked with Anagarika Dharmapala at Mahabodi Soc. 1932: health broke again; left London for Surrey. During WW II: retreat at Wisborough Green sold; entered old folks home at Bury until d. Publications incl *The Four Noble Truths*, *The Noble Eightfold Path*, *Kamma*, *Lotus Blossoms*, *Young People's Life of the Buddha*, etc.

Sircar, Réné: *Vipassana teacher*. Former Burmese nun, disciple of Taungpulu Sayadaw, who teaches vipassana and Bdst psychology at the California Institute for Asian Studies.

Story, Francis (1910–71): *Influential English writer*. b Croydon, Surrey (UK) and became Bdst at 16. Qualified in medicine and served in RAMC in WWII. 1948 became Anagoriak Sugotananda at Bodh Gaya, India. 1950: helped form Burma Bdst World Mission, Rangoon, Burma. 1954: Director-in-Chief and joined English Editorial Board of *The Light of the Dhamma* (foremost Theravada periodical 1952–63). 1957: 10 years in Sri Lanka lecturing and broadcasting. Specialized in researching doctrine of rebirth with Prof. Ian Stevenson (Virginia U., USA). 1968: lecture tour of USA on same theme. Books incl. *The Four Noble Truths*, *Dialogues on the Dhamma*, *The Bdst Doctrine of Nibbana* (with P. Vajirañana), *The Case for Rebirth*, *Rebirth as Doctrine and Experience* & 2 vols of collected essays, *The Bdst Outlook* & *Dimensions of Bdst Thought*.

Sumedho, Ajahn: *American-born Theravada meditation master; founder of various W. monasteries*. b 1934. Began Far E Studies at U of Washington; studies interrupted by spell of service in US Navy during Korean War; visited Japan and encountered Bdsm. Later returned to U of Washington to complete degree; then to U of California for MA in Asian Studies; this completed 1963. 1964: to Borneo with Peace Corps; then to Thailand; taught English part-time at Thammasat U, Bangkok and practised meditation. On vacation in Laos recommended to ordain in temple in Nong Kai (NE Thailand); practised solo for 1 yr; later became a disciple of Ajahn Cha (qv) at Wat Pah Pong in Ubon province. 1973: after 7 Vassa (Rains Retreats) allowed to visit India as dhutanga monk. 1974: established and became Abbot of the international Wat Pah Nanachat at Bung Wai. 1976: 1st return visit to USA; visited UK and contacted English Sangha Trust. 1977: came to UK with Ajahn Cha at invitation of English Sangha Trust; resided at Hampstead Bdst Vihara. 1979: established Chithurst Forest Monastery (Wat Pah Cittaviveka) with 108 acres of forest in rural W Sussex (UK) and became 1st Abbot. Various other centres have sprung from this: Amaravati (Hemel Hempstead), Harnham Vihara (Northumberland) and the Devon Vihara. Presently Abbot of Amaravati, but teaches elsewhere and goes on regular world tours. Hon President of the Bdst Society (London). Books incl *Cittaviveka (Teachings from the Silent Mind)*, *The Path to the Deathless*, *The Way It Is* and *The Mind and the Way*.

Sunlun Sayadaw (1878–1952): *Burmese meditation master.* b U Kyaw Din in Myingyan, middle Burma. At 15 became office boy in District Commissioner's office, Myingyan. m Ma Shew Yi. At 30, resigned job; became farmer. Disturbed by intimations of imminent death; interested in vipassana meditation by a mill clerk; began to practise. After certain insights, wished to become monk; obtained wife's permission to do so. Afterwards practised diligently until Oct 1920, when he is reputed to have achieved arahantship. Though barely literate, won gt respect; many disciples. His practices, which emphasize intense effort are taught by a number of meditation masters and in several centres in or nr Rangoon, Burma (e.g. Sunlun Monastery). Further information: see *Living Buddhist Masters*, Jack Kornfield, ch. 6.

Taungpulu Sayadaw (Taungpulu Tawya Kaba Aye Sayadaw): *Burmese meditation master.* Trained with Mahasi Sayadaw's teacher and spent many yrs in austere practice. 1978: invited to USA; set up temporary forest monastery in Palo Alto. 1981: again returned to USA to found permanent vihara on W Coast. Main monastery is in the Meiktila District of Burma.

Tiradhammo, Ajahn: *Canadian-born bhikkhu active in UK.* b 1949, New Westminster, Vancouver, British Columbia, Canada. 1967–69 and 1971–2: attended U of British Columbia (studying engineering, geology, geography). 1970: travelled in Europe and Middle East. 1970–71: to India and Sri Lanka; meditation retreat at Kanduboda. 1972–3: to Thailand. 1973: novice ordination. 1974: bhikkhu ordination. 1975–82: practised with Ajahn Cha (qv) at Wat Pah Pong. 1982: to Chithurst Forest Monastery. 1984: senior incumbent at Harnham Vihara. 1987: established forest monastery nr Berne, Switzerland.

Titmuss, Christopher: *British meditation teacher, spiritual counsellor and social activist.* b 1944, 1962–69: reporter and photojournalist in London, Turkey, Thailand, Laos and Australia. 1970–76: a monk in Thailand and India; studied and practised under Ajahn Dhammadaro at Wat Chai Na and with Ajahn Buddhadasa (qv) at Wat Chaiya; 8-month period of solitary meditation practice at Ko Pha Nga, Thailand. Meditation teacher and lecturer in India, incl 6-month intensive at Dalhousie. 1977–present: international meditation teacher, lecturer, psychological and spiritual counsellor, etc in England, USA, Australia, India and Europe. Co-founder of various spiritual communities and centres; Founder and Editor of *Reality* (newspaper). 'Presently, meditation practice and teaching emphasizes complete integration of awareness into daily life. In the silence and stillness of intensive practice, the emergence of transcendent understanding and the true significance of the nature of reality is experienced.' Active in various engaged organizations, incl Bdst Peace Fellowship. Green Party candidate in S. Devon. Published 100 taped lectures: *Let All Things Be New* (pub Germany). Books incl *The Profound and the Profane* and *The Green Buddha*.

Thittila, Sayadaw U: *Senior Burmese bhikkhu.* (1896–97), Pyawbwe, C Burma. Samanera at 15 under U Kavinda; bhikkhu ordination at 20 under Ashin Adicca Vamsa. At 25 passed doctoral exams with highest hons; taught and lectured in Rangoon for 12 yrs. 1938–52: in UK; spent war yrs there; worked as stretcher bearer in Blitz. Onetime Librarian at Bdst Soc. Lectured widely, esp. on Abhidhamma. 1952: returned to Burma; became Prof of Pali at Rangoon U. Has again visited UK and USA. Tr incl *Vibhanga* (Book of Analysis).

Vajiragnana, Ven Medagama: *Head of London Bdst Vihara.* b 1928, Maha-Medagama, Sri Lanka. 1943: ordained and received traditional bhikkhu training. Also studied at Vidyodaya (BA 1961), Banaras (Diploma 1962) and Jadaipur (Calcutta, MA 1965) U's; subsequently awarded DLitt in Bdst Literature by Sangha Council of Sri Lanka for contribution to Bdst education in UK. After completing studies, worked in education and was principal of a monastic college and later of a Bhikkhu Teacher Training College in Sri Lanka; has since lectured in Asia, Europe and America. 1966: appointed *Kammacariya* (Master of Acts of Vinaya) by Sangha Council of Sri Lanka. 1967: established himself in London; was Religious Director of the British Bdst Assn. Is a Vice President of World Sangha Council and Bdst Patron of UK & Ireland Group of World Conference of Religions for Peace. In Sri Lanka was Joint Secretary of United Religions Organization and a Committee Member of Standing Conference of Inter-Faith Dialogue in Education. Is currently head of London Bdst Vihara and author of a number of publications.

Vimalo, Anagarika (Walter Kulbarz): *German-born meditation teacher.* b 1931. 1958: samanera ordination at former Thai Embassy, London with twin brother (Dhammiko) by Chao Khun Vimaladhammo, Abbot of Wat Mahathat, Bangkok. Both trained as samaneras under Ven Paññavaddho (qv). Bhikkhu ordination in Rangoon. 1967–76: resident in Thailand. Returned to Germany, disrobed and was attached to Haus der Stille, Rosebürg, nr Hamburg. Spent some years at Sharpham North Community in Devon, currently in Germany.

Viradhammo, Ajahn: *Canadian bhikkhu now active in New Zealand.* b 1948 (Vitauts Akers) of Latvian parents in W. Germany. 1952: family emigrated to Toronto, Canada. 1971: met 1st teacher – American bhikkhu in India. 1973: samanera in Bangkok. 1975: bhikkhu at Wat Ba Pong, NE Thailand, under Ajahn Cha (qv). After training, resided in Forest Monastery, Chithurst, Sussex (UK), was Abbot of Wat Bodhinyanatama, New Zealand, currently Abbot of Amaravati Buddhist Monastery, successor to Ajahn Sumedho (qv).

Walshe, Maurice O'Connell: *British scholar and translator of Pali texts.* b 1911, London, ed London U; also Berlin, Göttingen, Vienna. Twice m: (1) Ruth Meisel (b Vienna) 1941, (2) Florence Knight. 1973. Reader in German and Deputy Director, Institute of Germanic Studies, U of London; retired 1979. Sometime Vice-President, The Bdst Soc; also Chairman, English Sangha Trust. Author of *Bdsm for Today*; tr incl 3 vols of sermons by Meister Eckhart; also *Digha Nikaya.*

Webb, Russell: *Editor.* b 1941, Worthing, Sussex (UK). Profession: Lloyd's insurance broker, 1964–6: Hon Secretary and Librarian, London Bdst Assn. 1966–84: Hon Secretary and Librarian, London Bdst Vihara (LBV). 1984–86: Dhammaduta Secretary, LBV. 1964–8: Editor, *Bdst News.* 1968–83: Joint Editor, *Bdst Quarterly.* 1976–82: Editor, *Pali Bdst Review.* 1983–: Editor, *Bdst Studies Review.* Publications incl *An Analysis of the Pali Canon, A Bdst's Manual* (with H. Saddhatissa), etc.; Joint Secretary and Editor of *Bdst Studies in Honour of Hammalava Saddhatissa.*

Woodward, F.L. (Frank Lee, 1871–1952): *Pioneer English Pali scholar.* b Saham, Norfolk. ed Christ Hospital and Sidney Sussex College, Cambridge. Became schoolmaster; began to study Pali and Sanskrit, also E and W philosophy and comparative religion. 1902: joined Theosophical Society, 1903–c 1919: headmaster, Mahinda College, Galle, Sri Lanka. 1919: left for Tasmania and dedicated remainder of life to producing translations for Pali Text Society. Best remembered for anthology, *Some Sayings of the Buddha.*

24   Tibetan Buddhism

NOTE ON TITLES, etc.:

Chögyal: lit. 'Dharma Raja': Religious King. Or 'Protector of the Bdst Religion'.
Chujé: lit. 'Lord of Dharma'.
Gelong: monk.
Getsül: novice (samanera).
Geshe: Gelugpa title corresponding to Doctor of Divinity.
Gyalwa: lit. 'Conqueror' (over delusion); i.e. one who has become a buddha. As a title is used only for the highest spiritual leaders, viz. the Dalai Lama (often called 'Gyalwa Rinpoche') and the Karmapa.
Kazi: a high-ranking Sikkimese.
Khamtrul: title given to a tulku from Kham district of Tibet.
Khenpo: generally 'Abbot'; title indicating high scholarship in Nyingma, Sakya and Kagyu schools.
Khyentse: lit. 'One in whom Wisdom and Compassion are perfectly combined'; a name carried by a number of exceptional Nyingma lamas during the last 200 yrs.
Kongtrul: title given to a tulku from the Konpo district of Tibet.
Kyabje: lit. 'Protector' or 'Lord of Refuges'; a lofty title equivalent to 'His Holiness'.
Lama: important religious teacher or guru; not necessarily a monk.
Lharampa: First Class Honours in the Geshe degree examinations. See *Tibet Journal*, vol 2, No 3, 1977, p. 67 – 'The Structure of the Gelug Monastic Order'.
Ngakpa: lit. 'a practitioner of mantras'; shamanistic practitioner of the Nyingma school, adept at exorcising spirits, making rain, etc.
Rinpoche: lit. 'Precious One'; honorific suffixed to the name of a high lama.
Tertön: Nyingma lama who discovers a terma or (hidden) 'treasure' teaching.
Tulku: voluntary re-incarnation of a religious figure of some distinction.
Yeshe: Wisdom (= ad Jñana).

Akong Rinpoche, Ven. Chujé: *Tulku of Karma Kagyu and Nyingma lineages; Spiritual Director of Samyé Ling Tibetan Centre.* Former Abbot of Drolma Lhakhang monastery and retreat complex, Tsawa Gang, E Tibet. Received teachings from Jamgön Kongtrül of Shechen and other gt teachers. Came to Britain in 1960s. 1967: with Trungpa Rinpoche (qv) established Kagyu Samyé Ling Tibetan Centre in Johnstone House, Langholm, Dumfries-shire, Scotland. After departure of Trungpa Rinpoche for USA (c. 1970), took charge of the centre; has since founded centres in other parts of the world (Spain, S. Africa, etc.).

Atto Rinpoche, (Tendzin Tulku): *Karma Kagyu lama; 7th Incarnation of the Tendzin Tulku of Nehzang monastery, Kham, E. Tibet; currently residing in UK.* b 1933 at Ato Shokha, Gatöd, Kham; son of VIIth Tendzin Tulku. Claimed as tulku by both Jontang monastery (Gelug school) as well as by Nehzang; status confirmed by VIth Panchen Lama. Formally enthroned at age 8 yrs; received usual exhaustive religious training; received initiations and teachings from Dingo Khyentse Rinpoche (qv) et al and underwent various retreats practising Vajra Yogini, Chakrasamvara, Mahakala, and the Six Doctrines of Naropa. 1957: spent 1 yr at Tsurphu serving Gyalwa Karmapa, with whom he took novice vows; also received various teaching and initiations from both Karmapa and Dingo Khyentse. 1958: attended Sera monastery. 1959: sought refuge in India. 1960–63: Kagyupa representative in Dharamsala on Dalai Lama's Council for Religious & Cultural Affairs. 1963–66: assistant to Sister Palmo (Freda Bedi-qv) at Young Lama's School, Dalhousie. 1966: put in charge by Dalai Lama of new monastery created out of Young Lama's School. 1967: m Alethea Martineau; settled in Cambridge (UK). 1967–date: taught privately; also Visiting Teacher at various groups in UK. 1986: began a monthly meditation group in Cambridge. 1970–81; nursing assistant at Fulbourne Mental Hospital, Cambridge.

Ayang Rinpoche: *Tulku of the Drigung Kagyu lineage; a mind emanation of Chögyal Dorje.* b 1941, Gaba province, Kham, E Tibet. Many termas of Chögyal Dorje are preserved in his family. 1949–59: lived in the main Drigung monastery nr Lhasa. 1959: sought refuge in India. Founded monastery at Byalkuppe, S India. A specialist in Phowa (Transmission of Consciousness) practices; carries blessings of the three Phowa lineages: Nyingma, Drigung and Namchö Phowa. At request of HH the Dalai Lama, taught Phowa in Japan; also a frequent visitor to Europe and USA, where he conducts Phowa courses and teaches in his various centres.

Bedi, Freda (Sister Karma Khechog Palmö – 1911–77): *Late English Tib Bdst nun and refugee worker.* ed Oxford etc.; m Baba Bedi and lived many yrs in India; active in Indian Independence mvt and later fought for womens' rights in Punjab. Appointed head of Social Welfare Board by Nehru; responded wholeheartedly to plight of Tibetans post 1959; became Principal of Young Lama's School, Dalhousie. Studied with Sayadaw U Thittila and Mahasi Sayadaw (both qv) in Rangoon. 1966: sramaneri ordination by Gyalwa Karmapa. 1972: bhikshuni ordination in Hong Kong. 1976: (Intl Womens' Yr) National Award from Indira Gandhi. Resided at Rumtek, Sikkim until d.

Beer, Robert: *Western thangka painter.* b 1947, Cardiff (UK). Studied thangka painting in India in 1970 and Nepal with Jhampa, thangka-painter to HH the Dalai Lama, and with Khamtrul Rinpoche. His work has featured in many illustrated publications. Currently working on an encyclopedia on Tibetan symbolism. Lives in London.

Beru, Sherapalden: *Resident thangka painter at Samyé Ling Tibetan Centre, Scotland.* Main lineage holder of Karma Gadri tradition of fine art and temple decoration.

Berzin, Dr. Alexander: *Translator and teacher.* b 1944, New Jersey, USA. 1972: PhD, Harvard. 1969: to India, initially as Fulbright scholar. 1972: joined Lib of Tib Wks & Archives, Dharamasala; studied with various Tib masters. Since 1975 has translated for various Tib masters, incl Dalai Lama and his late tutors. Teaches particularly in South America and Eastern Europe, currently living in Dharamsala. Trs incl *An Anthology of Well-spoken Advice*; *Mahamudra*; *Eliminating the Darkness of Ignorance*; *Dzogchen, the Four-themed Precious Garland*; *The Wheel of Sharp Weapons, a Compendium of Ways of Knowing*; etc.

Chime Youndong Rinpoche, Lama: *Karma Kagyu Lama active in UK.* b Kham; recognized as a tulku of Benchen monastery. From his abbot, Nyentrul Rinpoche, received instruction in Mahamudra; and in Dzogchen from Dingo Khyentse Rinpoche (qv). Sent to W by Gyalwa Karmapa. 1972: resigned monk status and m Celia Jane Pertwee. 1973: set up Kham Tibetan House, Saffron Walden, Essex (UK); and 1987, Karma Kagyu Chö Khor Ling, London. Works for the British Library with their Tb MSs.

Chögyam, Ngakpa Chögyam ögyen Pogden: *British Nyingma shaman.* b 1952, Farnham, Surrey (UK). Trained as illustrator in Bristol. Travelled in E to study and practise under several Tib Tantric masters, incl Chhimed Rigdzin Rinpoche; completed number of retreats; has also studied Tib art. 1983: initiated as a ngakpa. 1985: with wife founded Sang-ngak-chö-dzong (Tibetan Tantric Periphery) in Cardiff. Professional counsellor and healer, works with psychologists and people in the caring professions. Books incl *Rainbow of Liberated Energy*.

Csoma de Körös, Alexander (1784–1842): *Hungarian pioneer of Tib studies.* b Transylvania; son of Calvinist border guard. Inspired to look for 'racial homeland' of Magyars. 1816–18: studied Arabic, Turkish, English and Ethnology at Göttingen. 1819: set out for E on foot; never reached Tibet but travelled and researched in frontier regions (e.g. Ladakh). Obtained modest

British Govt sponsorship; compiled 1st Tib-English dictionary and a Tib Grammar (both published 1834). 1837–42: Librarian of Asiatic Society, Calcutta. 1842: set out again on quest for Magyar racial home; d Darjeeling of malaria. His analysis of the Kanjur and Tanjur was incld in Waddell, L.A., *The Buddhism of Tibet or Lamaism* (1894). Various contributions to *Journal of the Asiatic Society of Bengal*. Dictionary, Grammar and Coll Writings repr Budapest 1984. 1920: Körösi Csoma Tarsasag [*Society*] founded, Budapest.

Dalai Lama: 'Dalai' – 'Ocean'. Title conferred by the Mongol Altan Khan upon Sönam Gyatso (1543–88) in 1578 and retrospectively on his two predecessors. The 1st DL therefore became (posthumously) Gendun-drup (1391–1474), a principal disciple of Jé Tsongkhapa. The title has passed on by the tulku system to the present. Until 1959, the DLs were at apex of Tib religio-political hierarchy.

Dalai Lama, HH the XIVth, (Gyalwa Tenzin Gyatso): *Exiled spiritual and temporal leader of the Tibetan people.* b 1935, Taktser, Amdo, E Tibet of humble origins. Located and recognized as Dalai Lama incarnation 2 yrs later via portents discerned at the oracle lake (Lhama Lhatsö). 1939: brought to Lhasa. 1940: formally enthroned. Began education at 6 yrs; at 24 yrs took preliminary exams at Sera, Drepung and Ganden monastic u's; final exams held at Jokhang ('Cathedral' of Lhasa) during Mönlam Festival; awarded Geshe Lharampa degree with honours at age 25. At age 16 assumed full temporal powers early because of Chinese Communist threat. 1954: went to Peking to hold discussions with Chinese Communist leaders. 1956: visited India for 2500 Buddha Jayanti celebrations; held political discussions with Pandit Nehru and Chou En-lai. 1959: left Tibet following the Lhasa Uprising. Made unsuccessful appeals to United Nations on behalf of Tib people. 1963: promulgated draft democratic constitution for Tibet; since then has conducted government-in-exile at Dharamsala, N India, in accordance with this. Has also v successfully worked to resettled 100,000 Tibetan refugees and to preserve Tib religion, culture, etc. In 1989 he was awarded the Nobel Peace Prize. Widely travelled in both E and W (though has never returned to his native Tibet), has met political and spiritual leaders (incl two Popes, an Archbishop of Canterbury, etc.), scientists, doctors, writers, philosophers – and ordinary people. Visited UK 1973, 81, 84, 91, 93 and 96. Has impressed people everywhere with his (very Buddhist) message of peace and kindness: 'My religion is very simple – my religion is kindness.' A spiritual leader of world rank. Books incl *Opening the Eye of New Awareness*; *Kindness, Clarity & Insight*; *My Land and My People* (autobiographical) and *Freedom In Exile*. Biographies: *Great Ocean*, by Roger Hicks and Ngakpa Chögyam and *The Last Dalai Lama*, by Michael Harris Goodman.

Damcho Yonten, Geshe:: *Gelugpa Lama active in UK.* b 1930, Lhasa. Entered Drepung monastery at age 6. For next 23 yrs studied Bdst philosophy, psychology, logic, debate, scriptural subjects, etc. Also practised meditation under guidance of distinguished lamas. Received Geshe degree whilst still at Drepung. 1959: left Tibet; continued studies in India and Ladakh; became abbot of Samtenling Gompa (Ladakh). 1966: began teaching W students. 1976: came to W. 1978: founded Lam Rim Buddhist Centre, S Wales.

David-Neel, Alexandra (1868–1969): *Pioneering French mystic, traveller and author.* b Saint-Mandé (E suburb of Paris). Discovered E religion and philosophy at Musée Guimet (Paris) at age 23: 'My vocation was born there and then'. Became singer with Opéra Comique; later turned to journalism. 1894: m Philippe Neel (pron. *Nale*) in Tunis; soon separated. In E for next 20 yrs. Met exiled XIIIth Dalai Lama in Darjeeling. In Sikkim met Lama Yongden, her future travelling companion and adopted son. Went into retreat in Himalayan cave-hermitage; met Tib teachers who taught her Tib language and Bdst philosophy. Ventured 3 times into Tibet, once reaching Shigatse before being turned back. Subsequently left for Burma, Sri Lanka and Japan, accompanied by Yongden; then to Korea, China and Mongolia. Studied at Kumbum monastery (E Tibet). 1924: became 1st European woman to enter Lhasa (in disguise). 1925: returned to Europe; bought house in Digne (Haute Provence). 1937: returned to Asia, travelling via Transiberian Railway to China. Japanese invasion of Manchuria forced her westwards to Tatsienlu; spent most of WW II there. Later returned to France via India; subsequently engaged in study and writing at Digne until d at age 100#aa. 1964: Made Commandeur de la Légion d'Honneur. Bks in English incl *With Mystics & Magicians*, *My Journey to Lhasa*, *Tibetan Journey*, *A Tibetan Tale of Love & Magic*, *Secret Oral Traditions of Tib Bdsm* and *Initiations & Initiates in Tibet*.

Dhargyey, Geshe: *Gelugpa Lama with W students.* (1925–95), Kham, E Tibet. Entered local monastery at 7 yrs; at 16 yrs entered Sera Monastery and remained until 1959. Completed studies in India and appointed resident teacher in Library of Tib Wks & Archives (Dharamsala) 1971. In his last years he moved to New Zealand and opened a centre where he taught until his death. Has taught many Wstnrs. Books incl *Advice from a Spiritual Friend* (with Geshe Rabten).

Dilgo Khyentse Rinpoche: *Important Nyingma Master and exponent of Dzogchen Meditation.* (1910–91), from Kham, E Tibet. Recognized as mind incarnation of Jamyang Khyentse Wangpo (1820–92). Studied under many distinguished lamas of all four schools, notably Jamyang Khyentse Chökyi Lodrö, and spent 20 yrs in retreat. A Tertön, has also written many meditation texts and commentaries notable for their poetic beauty. Travels extensively giving teachings in Bhutan, Nepal, India and the W. 1976: to USA on invitation of Trungpa Rinpoche (qv), his pupil. 1983: to London at invitation of Sogyal Rinpoche (qv). Has also visited France, where he supervises students undergoing long retreat. Has transmitted teachings to Dalai Lama. Is rebuilding Shechen Monastic University (formerly one of the great Nyingma centres in Tibet) at Bodh Nath, Nepal.

Dodrupchen Rinpoche (Thubten Trinley Pal Zangpo): *The Holder of the Dzogchen teachings of Longchen Nyingthig.* b 1927, Golok, E Tibet; 4th incarnation of Jigme Trinley Ozer (1745–1821), chief disciple of Jigme Lingpa (1729–98). Studied with Khomey Khenpo, Khenpo Kangnam, Khenpo Chochog and Khenpo Thubnyen. Received transmissions from Jamyang Khyentse Chökyi Lödro, Khenpo Kunpal. Sechen Kongtrul and Dzogchen Rinpoche; received final teachings on Dzogchen monastery; printed and distributed the *Seven Treasuries* and Gangtok, Sikkim, his home; again subsidized the printing of Longchenpa's *Seven Treasuries* and his *Trilogy of Finding Comfort & Ease.* 1973: to USA; established Mahasiddha Nyingma Centre in Massachusetts; has since visited USA a number of times. 1975: taught in London and France.

Donden, Dr. Yeshe: *Notable Tibetan medical practitioner,* b 1929, Lhoga district of C Tibet, nr Lhasa. At 6 yrs entered a monastery. At 11 went to Chakpori Medical College, Lhasa; exhibited considerable ability in memorization and memorized four medical tantras; entered training with Kyenrab Norbu, Director of the College. At 20 yrs came out top of his exams. 1951: began practice in home district. 1959: left Tibet for India. 1960–80: Physician to Dalai Lama. Founded Tib Medical Centre, Dharamsala. 1969–: engaged in private practice in addition to other duties; frequently travels to W to teach; has given a series of lectures at U of Virginia. Books in English incl *Health Through Balance.*

Dorji, Gyurmé: *British Nyingma scholar.* Tr *History of the Nyingma School,* by Dudjom Rinpoche (qv).

Dorjiev, Khampo Agvan Lovsan (1853–1938): *Buryat Mongol Lama of some political notoriety.* b Baikal region of E Russia. 1880: went to Lhasa; settled at Drepung monastery and acquired a reputation for scholarship. Became tutor to XIIIth Dalai Lama and gained influence with him. 1889: went on a journey to Russia to collect funds for his college. 1901: visit to St Petersburg: returned to Lhasa laden with gifts and political overtures. News of this exacerbated existing British fears of Russian designs on Tibet and led directly to the Younghusband Expedition (1904). Before British troops reached Lhasa, fled with Dalai Lama to Mongolia. Was again seen in Lhasa after Dalai Lama's return from 2nd period of exile (1913). 1920s: worked among Mongolian Bdsts. d during Stalinist purges. Root guru of Geshe Wangyal (qv).

Dowman, Keith: *British translator.* From c 1979 at Varanasi and in Himalayan region studying and practising Tb Bdsm. Trs incl *Divine Madman* (The Life and Teachings of Drukpa Kunley), *The Legend of the Great Stupa; Sky Dancer: The Secret Life & Songs of the Lady Yeshe Tsogyel* and *Masters of Mahamudra – Songs & Histories of the 84 Bdst Siddhas.*

Dudjom Rinpoche (HH Jigdral Yeshe Dorje: 1904–87): *Late Supreme Head of the Nyingma order of Tib Bdsm. Outstanding yogi, tertön and meditation master.* b Pemakö, SE Tibet. Recognized as incarnation of Dudjom Lingpa (1835–1904), yogi and tertön. Studied initially at Pemakö with Khenpo Aten, later in gt monastic u's of C Tibet (Mindroling, Dorje Drak and

Tarjé Tingpoling) and E Tibet (e.g. Kathok and Dzogchen); principal teachers incl Phungong Tulku Gyurmé Ngedön Wangpo, Jedrung Trinlé Jampa Jungne, Gyurmé Phendei özer and Minling Dordzin Namdrol Gyatso. A meticulous scholar and prolific writer of 40#aa volumes elucidating the teachings and practice of the Nyingma lineage; writings acknowledged by all schools to be unsurpassed in their knowledge of traditional poetics, history, medicine, astrology, philosophy, etc. A married lama, settled in Darjeeling after leaving Tibet; later lived in Kathmandu, Nepal. 1972: invited to USA by Sonam Kazi; visited Berkeley and New York and conducted refuge and bodhisattva ceremonies and gave public talks. 1976: longer visit to USA on invitation of poet John Giorno; established Orgyen Cho Dzong in New York City. Has also established centres in Hong Kong and France, where European seat of Nyinmapas (Orgyen Samyé Chöling) established 1975. Visited London 1972, 76 and 79. Books incl a History of the Nyingmapas and a complete survey of Buddhadharma; also a History of Tibet written at request of Dalai Lama. Revised canonical teachings (kama) of Nyingmapas, d at home in France. Extended bio-obituary, *The Middle Way*, Vol. 62, p 25ff, 1987.

Dzogchen Rinpoche (Jigme Losel Wangpo): *Young Nyingma tulku; incarnation of Dzogchen Pema Rigdzin.* b 1964, Sikkim. Recognized by Dodrupchen Rinpoche (qv) as VIIth incarnation of Dzogchen Pema Rigdzin (1625–97). 1972: enthroned. Has received teachings from Dudjom Rinpoche, Dingo Khyentse Rinpoche, etc.; education closely supervised by Dalai Lama. Has completed a course at the Bdst School of Dialectics, Dharamsala. Currently rebuilding Dzogchen Monastery (formerly foremost centre of Nyingma study and practice in Tibet) in Mysore, S India. 1985: visited Europe and USA on invitation of Sogyal Rinpoche (qv); bestowed empowerments. Thought to have great potential as a future Nyingma teacher.

Dzongsar Khyentse Rinpoche (Jamyang Thubten Chökyi Gyatso): *Nyingma tulku; incarnation of Jamyang Khyentse Chökyi Lodrö.* b 1960; recognized by Dalai Lama. Received training in all lineages of Tib Bdsm under over 12 gt masters, incl Dalai Lama, Karmapa, Sakya Trizin, Dudjom Rinpoche and Dingo Khyentse Rinpoche. 1986: 1st visit to Europe and USA. Has thriving centre in Australia.

Evans-Wentz, Dr. Walter Yeeling (1878–1965): *Pioneer translator of Tib Bdst texts.* b USA, ed Us of Stanford, Oxford and Rennes, specializing in folk-lore; met W.B. Yeats. 1911: 1st book: *Fairy Faith in Celtic Countries.* An interest in the rebirth doctrine took him to E. 1919: met Kazi Dawa-Samdup in Sikkim; collaborated on translation of several texts, incl *The Tibetan Book of the Dead, The Tibetan Book of the Great Liberation, Tibetan Yoga and Secret Doctrines* and *Tibet's Great Yogi Milarepa.* d. nr. Encinitas, California at age 88 yrs. Biography: *Pilgrim of the Clear Light,* by Ken Winkler.

Fletcher, Frederic (Lama Dorje Prajñananda; 1879–1950): *1st Westerner to be ordained in Tib Bdsm.* b London, ed Oxford, read *Light of Asia*; travelled in E. WW I: Major in Army; sickened by carnage; decided to enter Sangha after war. 1922–3: with McGovern, Ellam and Knight on British Buddhist Mission to Tibet. Reached Shigatse; novice ordination (Gelug); obliged to leave Tibet. 1924: bhikkhu ordination in Sri Lanka. Travelled in India; once returned UK; lived out life in Burma.

Ganden Tripa – or Tri Rinpoche of Ganden (Supreme Head of Gelug Order): see Ling Rinpoche and Jampäl Shenpen.

Govinda, Lama Anagarika (Anagarika Khamsum-Wangchuk; E.L. Hoffmann; 1898–1985): *Pioneer Western exponent and expositor of Tibetan Buddhism.* b Waldheim (old kingdom of Saxony) of German father and Bolivian mother (family had mining interests in Bolivia). Invalided out of WW I. Studied Philosophy and Architecture at U of Freiburg, later Archaeology; research in Mediterranean area and N. Africa. 1928: to Sri Lanka. 1929: anagarika ordination in Burma. 1929–31: studied Pali. 1931: decisive turning point – encountered Tib Bdsm in Darjeeling and met main guru, Tomo Geshe Rinpoche. When TGR d, founded Arya Maitreya Mandala in his memory. 1930s: pursued Bdst studies in Sikkim, Ladakh and Tibet; also taught, lectured and practised art (was gifted artist). During WW II: interned. 1947: m. British-educated Parsi photographer Li Gotami; took Indian nationality. 1947–9: travelled to C Provinces and W Tibet; visited mt Kailas and Gu-gé, as described in his *Way of the White Clouds.* Subsequently devoted himself to *magnum opus: The Foundations of*

Tibetan Mysticism. As his reputation grew, travelled and lectured in USA, Japan and Europe. Latterly based at Kasar Devi Ashram, nr Almora (N India). 1980–1: went to USA for medical treatment; lived until death in Mill Valley. Other books incl *The Psychological Attitude of Early Buddhist Philosophy, Creative Meditation and Multidimensional Consciousness, the Psycho-Cosmic Symbolism of the Buddhist Stupa* and *The Inner Structure of the I-Ching.*

Guenther, Prof. Herbert: *Academic Tibetologist.* b 1917, Bremen (W Germany) of Austrian parents. Holds PhD's of Munich and Vienna U's. Virtuoso linguist, is said to have learnt Chinese at age 9 and later embarked on Sanskrit. Originally learnt Tibet in order to study Tib translations of lost Sanskrit texts; became acknowledged expert. 1959: Appointed to teach Russian at Lucknow U, India. 1958: made Head of Dept of Philosophy and Bdst Studies at Sanskrit U, Varanasi (India). Became interested especially in literature and philosophy of Nyingma school. 1954: became Head of Far E Studies at U of Saskatchewan (Canada). Has also taught at Tarthang Tulku's Nyingma Institute and Trungpa Rinpoche's Naropa Institute. Often criticized for obscurity and for confusingly mingling jargon of various disparate disciplines; has nevertheless been described as 'a true fortress of Tibetan Buddhism – so large it seems unassailable' (Hugh Richardson). Publications incl *The Life & Teachings of Naropa, Buddhist Philosophy in Theory and Practice, The Tantric View of Life, Tibetan Mysticism in a Western Perspective, Treasures of the Tibetan Middle Way, The Dawn of Tantra* (with Trungpa Rinpoche), and *Matrix of Mystery (Scientific and Humanistic Aspects of Dzogs-chen Thought).*

Hookham, Michael: *British Nyingma teacher.* b 1935, London. Mathematician by profession; interested in possible relationships between Bdsm, and W science and psychotherapy. Studied Theravada Bdsm for 9 yrs before meeting his Tib guru, Trungpa Rinpoche (qv), in 1965. 1975: asked by Trungpa Rinpoche to begin teaching. Established Longchen Foundation under Trungpa Rinpoche's overall direction; also established Nitartha School. Currently resides Oxford. Publications incl *On Freeing the Heart.*

Hookham, Shenpen (Shenpen Zangmo): *British Karma Kagyu/Nyingma teacher.* b 1946, Essex. Studied and practised as a nun of the Kagyu school for 9 yrs. Spent over 5 yrs in India before being requested by Gyalwa Karmapa to return to W to teach. 1977: met principal guru, Khenpo Tsultrim Gyamtso Rinpoche. Has acted as interpreter to various eminent lamas while continuing to undertake retreat and pursue studies. Obtained DPhil at Oxford with diss on Tathagatagarbha Doctrine according to Shentong interpretation of Ratnagotravibhaga.

Hopkins, Professor Jeffrey: *American scholar, writer and translator; interpreter to Dalai Lama.* b 1940. 1963: graduated Harvard. Studied for 6 yrs at Lamaist Bdst. Monastery of America (Freewood Acres, New Jersey); entered Bdst Studies Program at U of Wisconsin. 1966: received PhD. 1973: began teaching at U of Virginia; founded a graduate program in Bdst Studies. Has accompanied HH the Dalai Lama as official interpreter since 1979, touring N America, Europe, Australia and SE Asia. Publications incl *The Tantric Distinction; Meditation on Emptiness; Death, Intermediate State and Rebirth in Tibetan Buddhism; The Buddhism of Tibet & the Key to the Middle Way* and *The Precious Garland & the Song of the Four Mindfulness* (both with Lati Rinbochay); *Tantra in Tibet; Yoga of Tibet*, etc., etc.

Jamgön Kongtrül Rinpoche (Karma Lodrö Chökyi Senge): *High Karma Kagyu Tulku.* b 1954, C Tibet. Recognized as incarnation of Jamgön Kongtrül the Great via Jamgön Kongtrül of Palpung by Gyalwa Karmapa; taken under Karmapa's special care from early age. Received education and complete transmission of Karma Kagyu lineage from Karmapa et al. Left Tibet with Karmapa, Dingo Khyentse Rinpoche and Tai Situ Rinpoche (all qv) in face of Chinese invasion. Has travelled extensively and been instrumental in bringing the Dharma to W. At present one of the four Regents for absent Karmapa.

Jampäl Shenpen, HH: *Current Tri Rinpoche of Ganden Monastery; Supreme Head of Gelug School.* b 1921, Kham, E Tibet. At age 12 became monk; studied at Ganden Monastery (Thangtse College); gained Geshe Lharampa degree at age 35. Later became Abbot of Gyüme Tantric College. 1984: appointed by Dalai Lama to succeed Kyabje Ling Rinpoche (qv) as Ganden Tripa.

Jamyang Khyentse Chökyi Lodrö. (1896–1969): *Authority and master of all the schools of Tibetan Buddhism.* Recognized as activity incarnation of Jamyang Khyentse Wangpo (1820–92), notable pioneer of Ri-mé movement. 1st teacher: Kathuk Situ Chökyi Gyatso. Assumed throne at Dzongsar monastery, seat of Khyentses. Studied and practised teachings of all schools of Tib Bdsm under 80#aa masters. A leading light in Ri-mé movement, opened Dzongsar Khamje U and Karmo Tagtsang Retreat Centre, as well as restoring other monasteries, constructing images, printing books and teaching extensively. Two pilgrimages to C Tibet. 1958: settled in Sikkim; became Chaplain to Maharaja; died there. Master of many notable Tibetan lamas (Dingo Khyentse Rinpoche, Dezhung Rinpoche, Kalu Rinpoche, Sogyal Rinpoche, Trungpa Rinpoche, Tarthang Tulku, *et al.*).

Kalu Rinpoche. (Karma Rangjung Kunkyab) (1905–89): *'A modern Milarepa',* Hor region of Kham, E Tibet. Both parents students of Jangön Kongtrül Lodrö Thaye, Jamyang Khyentse Wangpo and Mipham Rinpoche (all prominent in Ri-mé movement). Recognized as tulku but not ordained, instead wandered freely; education supervised by father. At 13 yrs began formal studies at Palpung monastery. Received getsül ordination from 11th Tai Situpa (Karma Rangjung Kunchap). At Palpung and elsewhere studied sutra and tantra teachings; received instruction and empowerments from many great lamas. At age 16 undertook 3 yr retreat at Kunzang Dechen ösel Ling under the direction of root lama, Norbu Tondrup, from whom he received complete transmission of teachings of Karma Kagyu and Shangba Kagyu traditions. At age 25 embarked on 12 yr solitary retreat in mts of Kham. At request of Tai Situpa, returned to Palpung to become Director of 3 yr retreats. Recognized by 16th Gyalwa Karmapa as incarnation of Jamgön Kontrül Lodrö Thaye. 1940s: toured Tibet; in Lhasa, gave teachings to Regent (Reting Rinpoche). 1955: asked to leave Tibet by Karmapa; established 2 centres in Bhutan and ordained 300 monks. Made pilgrimage to Bdst holy places in India. 1965: established Samdrup Tarjay Ling at Sonada nr Darjeeling (now his HQ); at once embarked on another 3-yr retreat. 1971: visited France and N America; founded several centres for practice of Chenrezi Sadhana. 1974, 77/8: 2nd and 3rd US visits. Gave Kalachakra Empowerments in New York City, San Francisco and Boulder. 1976: began 3-yr retreats for Wstnrs in France, where he had established 2 centres. 1983: gave Rinchen Ter Dzö empowerments at Sonada to the 'Four Great Heart-sons' of late Gyalwa Karmapa and others. Publications incl *The Writings of Kalu Rinpoche* (with Kenneth McLeod), *The Chariot for Travelling the Path to Freedom* and *The Dharma that Illuminates all Beings like the Light of the Sun and Moon.*

Karma Thinley Rinpoche: *Sakyapa lama active in the West.* b 1931, Nangchen, Kham, E Tibet. Recognized as incarnation of Beru Kunrik at age 21/2 yrs. Teachers: Khen Rinpoche, Tashi Chopel, Tenpai Nyingpo and Chogay Trichen Rinpoche. Special initiations: Hevarjra, Vajarayogini, Vajrapani and Chakrasamvara. Has made a special study of basic Sakya text known as lam-dre ('The Path and its Fruit'). Specialization: tshogs-shay transmission of Sakya Lam-dre teachings and Kagyu Mahamudra teachings. Holds Khenpo degree. 1959: left Tibet. 1973: founded Kampo Gangra Drubgyud Ling in Toronto, Canada. 1977: inspired establishment of Sakya Rinchen Ling in Bristol (UK). Books incl *A History of the Sixteen Karmapas of Tibet.*

Karmapa, HH the 16th Gyalwa. (Rangjung Rigpe Dorje; 1923–1981): *Late supreme head of the Karma Kagyu subschool of Tib Bdsm.* b Denkhok, Derge dist, Kham, E Tibet. Speedily recognized as new incarnation on evidence left in a letter by previous Karmapa. At age 7 yrs received ordination from Tai Situpa and Jamgön Kongtrül of Palpung; 1 yr later Vajra Crown and Karmapa robes brought to him from Tsurphu (Karmapa seat). Enthroned by Situ Rinpoche at Palpung. In 1931, set out with grand entourage (Karmapa Garchen) for Tsurphu; en route performed Vajra Crown (Black Hat) Ceremony for 1st time at Nangchen. Afterwards visited XIIIth Dalai Lama in Lhasa; underwent hair cutting ceremony; then returned to Tsurphu and underwent 2nd Golden Throne Ceremony. For next 4 yrs studied with Beru Khyentse Rinpoche and Bo Kangkar Mahapandita. 1937: visited Situ Rinpoche at Derge and received empowerments, transmissions, etc. 1940–1: returned to Tsurphu. 1941–4: intensive practice. 1944: pilgrimage to Samyé and Lhodrak; also visited Bhutan at invitation of Maharaja. 1945: given further teachings by Situ Rinpoche and received full monk ordination. 1947–8: travelled in W Tibet, Sikkim, Nepal and India. 1948: teachings from Jamgön Kongrül of Palpung; became master of Mahamudra. Early 1950s: occupied with teaching and administrative duties. 1954: visited Beijing with Dalai Lama. On return to Tibet, enthroned new Situ Rinpoche and tried to improve morale in Kham, then being occupied by Chinese communists. Entertained XIVth Dalai Lama at Tsurphu; Dalai Lama gave him empowerment of 1000-armed Avalokiteshvara; Karmapa performed Vajra Crown Ceremony in return. 1956: visited Druk Dechen Chokhor Ling (principal Drukpa Kagyu monastery), gave teachings and performed purification rite; visited Sikkim and Nepal, and India for Buddha Jayanti Celebrations. 1957: began to send lamas out of Tibet. 1959: left Tibet himself and found refuge in Bhutan, then in Sikkim. HQ set up at Rumtek (monastery completed 1966). 1974: world tour; visited centres established in W. (e.g. Samyé Ling in Scotland and Trungpa Rinpoche's centres in Vermont and Colorado). Performed Vajra Crown Ceremony in London, New York, Boulder, etc. Subsequently established number of centres, notably in 1977 Dhagpo Kagyu Ling (Montignac, France). 1981: dedicated main US centre, Karma Triyana Dharmachakra. d. Chicago after illness. Further biodata available in *Karmapa, The Black Hat Lama of Tibet*, by Nik Douglas and Meryl White; and *The History of the Sixteen Karmapas of Tibet*, by Karma Thinley Rinpoche.

Kelsang Gyatso, Geshe: *New Kadampa Lama active in UK.* b 1932, W Tibet. 1940: ordained and entered Jampa Ling monastery; later graduated to Sera monastery, Lhasa (Jé College). 1959: left Tibet. 1959–77: intensive meditation retreats in Nepal and N India. 1972: awarded Geshe degree at New Sera monastery, S. India. 1977: became Director of General Studies at Manjushri Institute, Cumbria, UK. Established other centres in UK and Spain: Madhyamaka (York), Vajravarahi (Preston), Tara (Buxton & Macclesfield), Chenrezig (Lancaster), Tharpa Retreat Centre (Dumfriesshire), Instituto Dharma (Menorca, Spain). Spiritual Director, Instituto Vajra Dharma, Spain. Founded New Kadampa Tradition, headquarters at Manjushri, with many other centres internationally. Publications incl *Meaningful to Behold* (A Commentary on Shantideva's *Bodhicaryavatara*), *Clear Light of Bliss (Mahamudra in Vajrayana Buddhism)*, *The Heart of Wisdom*, and *Buddhism in the Tibetan Tradition: A Guide*.

Khambo Lama: Title accorded to most senior lamas in Mongolia and Buryatia (E Siberia). The Head of Mongolian Bdsts is The Most Ven. Khambo Lama K1. Ganden (sic), whose seat is at Gandentheckchenling monastery, Ulan Bator. He is President of Asian Bdsts' Conference for Peace (periodical – *Buddhists for Peace*). Buddhist patriarch of Buryatia – Bandido Khambo Lama; he is also titular head of all Soviet Bdsts. Chief Buryat monastery is Ivolginsky Datsan, nr Buryat capital of Ulan Ude.

Konchog Tsewang, Geshe: *Gelugpa lama active in UK.* b 1928, U Lam, E Tibet. 1940: ordained a monk at Zer Dru monastery, E Tibet. Later went to Drepung monastery, Lhasa (Loseling College). Studied Du-ra ('Collected Topics') and Lo-rig ('Mind and Cognition'); *The Ornament for Clear Realisations*, a text by Conqueror Maitreya, and Candrakirti's *Guide to the Middle Way*; also logic by Jam Yang Gun Cho; finally passed on to Vinaya studies and a commentary thereon by Gunaprabha. 1959: left Tibet. 1970: entered Gyutö Tantric College; received Geshe Ngagrampa degree. 1974: Geshe Lharampa degree. Principal teachers: Khensur Yeshe Thubten, the late Khensur Pema Gyaltsen, and Nyima Gyaltsen, all former Abbots of Drepung Loseling College; and Shargön Khen Rinpoche. 1982: came to UK to become Resident Teacher and Director of Philosophical Studies (Geshe Training Programme) at Manjushri Institute, Cumbria, UK.

Landaw, Jonathan: *Writer, translator, teacher.* b New Jersey, USA. 1970 and after: extensive travels in E and elsewhere, studying and teaching Bdsm. Has written and edited several bks for Lib of Tib Wks & Archives, Dharamsala. Other bks incl *Prince Siddhartha*, etc. Currently lives in California.

Lhalungpa, Lobsang: *Tibetan scholar.* b 1924, Lhasa. Studied Bdsm under various Tib masters. Took refuge in India after Chinese Invasion; has since lived there and in W. Onetime teacher of Tib Bdst Classics at U of British Columbia (Canada). Publications incl *The Life of Milarepa* and *Mahamudra: The Quintessence of Mind & Meditation*.

Ling Rinpoche, Kyabje (97th Ganden Tripa; 1903–83): *Late Senior Tutor Dalai Lama; Head of the Gelug Order.* b nr Lhasa; ed Drepung monastery. After obtaining Geshe Lharampa degree, became Abbot of Upper Tantric College, Lhasa. Later became debating partner

(Tsenshab) of present Dalai Lama; accompanied him to China (1954) and to India for Buddha Jayanti Celebrations (1956). 1965: enthroned as Ganden Tripa (Abbot of Ganden Monastery and Head of Gelug School) in exile. Visited and taught in W countries. Succeeded by HH Jamphäl Shenpen (qv).

Lobsang Tenzin, Geshe: *Abbot of Gyumé Tantric College.*

Lodö, Lama: *Karma Kagyu lama active in the West.* b 1941, Sikkim. At age 8 entered monastery. At age 15, met guru, Drupon Tenzin Rinpoche, meditation master of Deyak monastery and a teacher of 16th Gyalwa Karmapa. Began 3-yr retreat in cave but contracted TB and had to discontinue; later recovered and resumed retreat under direction of Kalu Rinpoche (qv), his master having died of same disease in the interim; contracted TB again but persevered and recovered; completed retreat. Afterwards taught in Ladakh; also spent 7 yrs as Meditation Master at Sonada. 1974: sent by Kalu Rinpoche to Europe; guided several students on 3-yr retreat at Plaige (France). 1976: became resident lama at Kagyu Droden Kunchab in San Francisco. Travels extensively in Bay area and elsewhere. Publications incl *Bardo Teachings*; *Quintessence of the Animate & the Inanimate*; *Attaining Enlightenment*; *Maintaining the Bodhisattva Vow*, *Prayers for Generating Guru Devotion* and *Radiant Wisdom*.

Losang Pende, Geshe: *Gelugpa Lama active in UK.* b 1941, Trognang, nr Lhasa. 1953: ordained and entered Ganden monastery (Shartse College). 1959: left Tibet; went to refugee camp at Buxaduar; later moved to Ganden Shartse monastery, Mungod, S India. 1985: received Geshe degree. Has studied all aspects of Bdst philosophy; also Tib culture, chanting, and ritual music. Principal teacher: Lungrig Namgyal Rinpoche, Abbot of Gyutö Tantric College.

Mullin, Glenn H. *Canadian writer, editor and translator.* b 1949, Gaspe, Quebec. 1972–6: joined Bdst Studies Programme at Tib Library, Dharamsala. Later studied at the Dialectic School for 6 yrs. Tutors incl Geshes Ngawang Dhargyey and Rabten (both qv) and both later tutors of Dalai Lama. Worked on a 10-volume series of collections of the writings of the 14 Dalai Lamas for Snow Lion Publications, Ithaca, New York, of which four have appeared to date: *Selected Wks of Dalai Lama 1: Bridging the Sutras & the Tantras*; *Selected Wks of Dalai Lama III: The Tantric Yogas of Sister Niguma*; *Selected Wks of Dalai Lama II: Essence of Refined Gold*; *Selected Wks of Dalai Lama IV: Songs of Spiritual Change*. Other books incl *Death & Dying: The Tibetan Tradition* and *Atisha and Buddhism in Tibet* (with Doboom Tulku).

Namkhai Norbu Rinpoche: *Dzogchen master and scholar.* b 1938, Derge dist, E Tibet. At 2 yrs. recognized as reincarnation of Adjom Drukpa, a gt Dzogchen master of early 20th C. Later also recognized by the 16th Gyalwa Karmapa and Situ Rinpoche as mind reincarnation of Shabdung Ngawang Namgyal, founder of line of Dharma Rajas (monk-kings) of Bhutan. Received initiations from two uncles, both Dzogchen masters, and from others. Age 5–9, educated at Derge Gonchen monastery, and later went on to Dzongsar monastic college for c 6 yrs. At 14 received Vajrayogini initiations according to the Sakya school and later received transmissions from 113-yr-old woman teacher. At 16 went to China as representative of Tib youth; became instructor at SW U of Minor Nationalities, Chengdu (Szechuan, China). Back in Tibet, at 17 met Root Master, Chanchub Dorje (1826–1978). Afterwards went on long pilgrimage to C Tibet, Nepal, India and Bhutan. Returning to Tibet, forced to flee the country due to violent political upheavals. 1958–60 lived in Gangtok, Sikkim; employed as author and editor of Tibetan text bks by govt. 1960: invited to Italy by G. Tucci (qv). 1960–64: research associate at IsMEO, Rome. 1965: Professor in Oriental Institute of U of Naples. 1983: hosted 1st Int'l Convention on Tib Medicine in Venice. For past 10 yrs has been active informally teaching in various countries, incl Italy, France, UK, Austria, Denmark, Norway and, since 1979, USA. The Dzogchen Community, an informal association of students practising under his guidance, has arisen. Speaks English though prefers Italian. Married with two children. Books incl: *The Crystal & the Way of Light*, *The Necklace of Gzi (A Cultural History of Tibet)*, *Dzog.chen and Zen*, *The Cycle of Day and Night*, *The Mirror (Advice on Presence and Awareness)*, *On Birth and Life (A Treatise on Tibetan Medicine)*, *Primordial Experience (Manjushrimitra's Treatise on the Meaning of Bodhicitta in rDozgsChen)* and *Zer-Nga: The Five Principal Points (A Dzog.chen Upadesha Practice)*.

Nyoshul Khen Rinpoche (Jamyang Dorje): *One of the foremost Khenpos of the Nyingma school and a leading exponent of Dzogchen.* Studied with c 25 main teachers, Dudjom Rinpoche and Dingo Khyentse Rinpoche; holds special lineage of Patrul Rinpoche (1808–87). 1960: sought refuge in India; taught large numbers of monks; lived for a time in Bhutan. 1980: came to Europe; spent much time guiding retreat practitioners. Also visited USA. 1985–6: visited UK at invitation of Sogyal Rinpoche. Notable for his remarkable poetry.

Palden Sherab, Khenpo: *One of the most qualified scholars and meditation masters in the Nyingma tradition.* b E Tibet. Joined Gonchen monastery and studied there; also at Riwoche, where he was invested with rank of Khenpo. Teachers include: Dudjom Rinpoche, Khenpo Acho, Kontrol Rinpoche and Jedrung Rinpoche. 1967–80: Abbot in charge of Nyingma Dept of C Institute of Higher Studies, Sarnath, India. Has spent much time teaching at Dudjom Rinpoche's New York center, Yeshe Nyingpo. Has written books on poetry and Tib language; also a notable scholar. Has taught in London at request of Sogyal Rinpoche; also in Paris.

Pallis, Marco: *Writer.* (1895–1989) b Liverpool (GB) of Greek parents. After serving in WWI, became professional musician; also engaged in mountaineering. 1933: 1st came in contact with Bdsm in Sikkim; studied it and Tibetan in Ladakh with Konchog Gyaltsen of Phiyang. 1937: invited Geshe Wangyal (qv) to England for private tuition. 1947: studied with a Tibetan teacher in S Tibet (Sakya region); accompanied by Ronald Nicholson. 1970s: active as a member of the Shin Bdst Assn in London. Books incl *Peaks and Lamas* (1939 – a classic), *The Way and the Mountain* (1960) and *A Buddhist Spectrum* (1980).

Panchen Lamas: *High-ranking Tib Bdst patriarchs.* Title an abbreviation of *Pandita Chenpo*: 'Great Scholar'; given to abbots of Tashilhunpo monastery, nr Shigatse, S Tibet (hence sometimes called Tashi Lamas). Lineage transmitted by tulku system from Chökyi Gyaltsen (1570–1662), tutor to 5th Dalai Lama. Used by Chinese as foil to power of Dalai Lamas. 1728: Emperor made PLs rulers of Tsang province. 1923: VIth PL fled to China; never returned; d 1937, Jyekundo. 1943: tulku (VIIth) discovered Litang, Sikiang; m and lived in China, till he died.

Pawo Rinpoche, H.E. (Tsuglag Mawai Wangchuj): *Kagyupa lama; an Emanation of Amitabha and Vairocana.* 10th incarnation. b 1912, C Tibet. 1917: from age 6 resided at Tsurphu Monastery with Gyalwa Karmapa Khakhyab Dorje and received empowerments, transmissions, explanations of sutra, tantra and terma of Kagyu and Nyingma lineages, etc. 1925: met XIIIth Dalai Lama who performed hair-cutting ceremony and gave him name Tsuglag Thubten Kunsel. Then went into long retreat. 1940: began 4-year residence at Palpung Monastery; received by Tai Situ Rinpoche, Padma Wangchuk Gyalpo, Jamgön Kongtrül Rinpoche of Sechen, etc. 1959: left Tibet; settled in India (Kalimpong). 1962–66: instructor in Bdst philosophy at Sanskrit U., Varanasi. 1966: retired due to illness and settled in Bhutan. 1975: to France for treatment and settled in Dordogne. Is sponsoring the construction of a new monastery, Nehnang Pungtsog Chodar Ling, at Bodh Nath, Nepal.

Phendé Rinpoche (Jamyang Kunzang Chö-chi Gyamtso): *Head of the Ngor subschool of the Sakya order; a teacher active in France.* 'A personality of great wisdom and exemplary faith'. b 1934. 1974: founded Evam Phendé Ling at Les Ventes, Normandy. 1975: founded Pratique du Bouddhisme Mahanaya at Fresnes. m Marie-Hélène Ahni, who administers main residential centre. Tr *L'histoire des Enseignements Sakyapa*.

Rabten, Geshe (1920–86): *Gelugpa lama with many Western students.* b Kham (E Tibet) into farming family. At age 18 entered Sera Monastery (Jé College); teacher was Geshe Jhampa Khedup. Became adept at rigorous philosophical debate; also went into frequent meditation retreat. Suffered poverty and undernourishment until appointed tutor to Gonsar Tulku. 1959: fled Tibet, settled first at Buxaduar; instrumental in setting up courses of study. 1963: awarded geshe Lharampa; shortly afterwards moved to Dharamsala to become personal assistant to Dalai Lama; lived in Namgyal Monastery and began to instruct Wstnrs. c 1970: into retreat nr Dharamsala to contemplate meaning of *sunyata*. 1974: invited to Europe. 1975: returned to Switzerland as Abbot of Tibetan Monastic Institute at Rikon. 1977: founded Tharpa Choeling Centre for Higher Tib Studies at Mont Pèlerin, nr Lausanne; also taught in USA and other European countries; established centres in Germany, Italy, Austria. 'He adhered strictly to the

Vinaya and placed great emphasis on a systematic and gradual training in the Gelugpa tradition . . .' (Stephen Batchelor). Books incl *The Preliminary Practises*, *Advice from a Spiritual Friend* (with Geshe Dhargyey), *The Life & Teaching of Geshe Rabten*, *Echoes of Voidness* and *The Essential Nectar*.

Rampa, T. Lobsang (pseudonym of Cyril Henry Hoskins; 1911–81): *Novelist.* Plumber from Cornwall who had only visited Tibet in the pages of books; enjoyed great vogue for a while with a series of nearly 20 novels on Tibet (e.g. the bestselling *The Third Eye*), which catered to the public's perennial hunger for magic and mystery.

Richardson, Hugh Edward: *British authority on Tibet.* b 1905; ed Oxford. Last British (and 1st Indian) representative in Lhasa. Was present when XIVth Dalai Lama brought to Lhasa. A Tibetan speaker and scholar, studied the culture of Tibet closely, esp various ancient inscriptions. Presently retired to St Andrews, Scotland (also his birthplace). Books incl *Tibetan Précis*, *Tibet & Its History*, *Ancient Historical Edicts at Lhasa*, *A Cultural History of Tibet* (with David Snellgrove).

Sakya, HE Jigdal Dagchen: *Head of Phuntsog Phodrang Palace of royal Sakya lineage.* Seat is at Sakya Tegchen Chöling in Seattle (Washington, USA).

Sakya Trizin, HH: *41st Patriarch of Sakya order.* A married lama, considered an incarnation of Manjushri and Padmasambhava. b 1945, Tsedong, S Tibet. 1953: enthroned. Teachers; Ngawang Lodro Shenpen Nyingpo, Jamyang Khyentse Chökyi Lodrö (qv), Chogay Trichen and Khenpo Appey. Special initiations: Hevajra, Chakrasamvara, Vajrayogini and Vajrakilaya. Studies of special texts: *lam-dre*, ('The Path and Its Fruit'). Specializations: *tsog-shay* and *lob-shay* transmissions of the Sakya *lam-dre* teachings and the Khön lineage Vajrakilaya meditation and rituals. 1959: escaped to Sikkim. Began to learn English; went to Darjeeling to continue religious studies (Madhyamika, Prajnaparamita and Abhidharma philosophy, logic, etc.). Spent 1 yr. in Mussoorie recovering from TB. 1964: founded Sakya centre in Mussoorie. Has also since founded Sakya centres at Rajpur and Puruwala, and is head of all Sakya centres throughout the world. 1967: gave *lam-dre* teaching for 1st time to c 400 monks and 100 lay people. Now fluent in English, has taught in Europe, incl UK.

Serkong Rinpoche (Kyabje Tsenshab Tserkong Tugse Rinpoche: 1914–83): *Late Tutor to Dalai Lama.* b Loka region, S Tibet; recognized as incarnation of Marpa's son, Darmadodey. Studied with masters of all four traditions. Trained at Ganden (Jagtze College); received Geshe Lharampa degree after 14 yrs of study. Spent 9 yrs at Gyüme Tantric College; passed all exams; appointed Master of Discipline. 1948: appointed Debating Partner to HH the Dalai Lama (qv); continued in this capacity t/out life; imparted many lineages, oral transmissions and initiations to Dalai Lama. 1954: to China with Dalai Lama. 1959: to India (and exile). Helped to establish Office of Religious & Cultural Affairs; continued as tutor and close advisor to Dalai Lama. Travelled extensively; made 2 tours of Europe and N America.

Shamar ('Red Hat') Rinpoche (The Shamarpa): Has often acted as Regent and lineage-holder during the minority of a Karmapa.

Shechen Rabjam Rinpoche: *Young Nyingma Lama.* Recognized by Gyalwa Karmapa and other Heads of the Tib Bdst Schools as VIIth Incarnation of the Founder of Sechen Monastery, Kham, E Tibet. Since age 5 yrs with Dingo Khyentse Rinpoche, receiving teachings and empowerments.

Shenphen Dawa Rinpoche: *Youngest son and Dharma-heir of late Dudjom Rinpoche.* b Tibet. Studies closely supervised by father; has received empowerments and transmissions of all the Nyingma lineages from an early age. Has played a major role in establishing centres and in the spread of the Dharma worldwide; in particular will ensure continuance of Dudjom Lingpa's lineage.

Snellgrove, David R. *British academic Buddhologist.* b 1920, c 1950–82, Lecturer/Reader/ Professor of Tibetan at SOAS (London U). Widely travelled in India and Himalayas. Overseas University posts and consultancy at Vatican. Fellow of British Academy. Bks incl *Buddhist*

Himalaya, Himalayan Pilgrimage, The Hevajra Tantra (2 vols), *Four Lamas of Dolpo* (2 vols), *A Cultural History of Tibet* (with Hugh Richardson (qv)), *A Cultural History of Tibet* (with T. Skorupski), and *Indo-Tibetan Bdsm*. Ed *The Image of the Buddha*.

Sogyal Rinpoche, Lama: *Incarnate lama of Ri-mé tradition based in London.* b. mid-1940s, Kham, E Tibet; recognized as tulku of famous lama and mystic, Tertön Sogyal; also of Do Khyentse, gt Dzogchen master. Raised as a son by Jamyang Khyentse Chökyi Lodrö (qv) at Dzongsar Monastic U (E Tibet); received complete training in surtras and tantras with transmissions and empowerments of all four schools of Tib Bdsm (esp Nyingma) from Khyentse and other gt masters. Mid-1950s: with Khyentse on long pilgrimage to C Tibet; visited inter alia Lhasa, Samyé and Sakya. 1958: accompanied Khyentse to Sikkim; later attended school in India; continued to receive spiritual teachings from Dingo Khyentse Rinpoche and Dudjom Ripoche. Then undertook BA students in Philosophy aT St Stephen's College, Delhi U; from there won scholarship toTrinity College, Cambridge. 1973: accompanied Dalai Lama on 1st European tour; also accompanied Dudjom Rinpoche on US tour as translator and aide. 1974: began to teach in London. 1975: established Dzogchen Orgyen Chöling in London. 1976–7: began to teach in Paris, later in USA. 1981: founded Rigpa Fellowship in London. Currently directs Rigpa centres in London, Paris and Santa Cruz (California, USA). Teaches widely with special emphasis on Dzogchen. Has made death and dying a speciality, working with hospices and nr death researchers.

Sonam Kazi: *Sikkimese Dzogchen teacher (Nyingma school) active in USA.* A layman, received a Roman Catholic education; later studied psychology in Delhi. Suffered from depression in early life; this led to an interest in meditation. Posted to Lhasa with Sikkimese diplomatic legation; studied with various gurus; referred to Dudjom Rinpoche (his root guru); became devoted follower of Dzogchen. 1970: arrived in USA. Later invited to New York, where the Longchen Nyingthig Bdst Soc developed around him.

Sopa, Geshe Lhundup: *Gelugpa lama working in USA.* b 1923, Tsang province, Tibet. At 9 yrs began monastic training locally. At 18 joined Sera monastery. Lhasa, and studied for Geshe degree. One of the examiners when Dalai Lama took Geshe exams in 1959. 1959: sought refuge in India. 1961: completed studies and attained Geshe Lharampa degree. 1963: to Lamaist Bdst Monastery of America, New Jersey; became President. 1967: invited by Prof. Richard Robinson, founder of Bdst Studies Program at U of Wisconsin, to teach at the Madison campus; became Prof in SE Asian Studies Dept. 1978, 1987: awarded Fulbright scholarships to study in India and Tibet. Is currently Abbot of Evam monastery and main teacher at Deer Park, Wisconsin. Travels widely on teaching engagements. Publications incl *The Theory & Practice of Tibetan Buddhism, The Wheel of Time*, etc.

Stott, David (Ngakpa Jampa Thaye): *English Sakyapa teacher.* b 1952, Bolton, Lancs. 1971: began training. Teachers: Karma Thinley Rinpoche. Ngor Phende Rinpoche and Sakya Trizin. Special initiations: Hevajra, Vajrayogini, Chakrasamvara and Amitabha. Studies of special texts: *Lam-dre* ('The Path & Its Fruit). Specializations: Vajrayogini meditation. 1977: appointed Dharma Regent of Karma Thinley Rinpoche. 1985: further qualifications bestowed by Sakya Trizin. 1986: PhD U of Manchester on History & Teachings of the Dagpo Kagyu Tradition. 1977: founded Sakya Thinley Rinchen Ling (centre) in Bristol, UK under inspiration of Karma Thinley.

Tai Situ Ripoche, H.H.: *Notable Karma Kagyu tulku.* b 1954, Kham, E Tibet. Recognized as 12th incarnation of Tai Situpa by 16th Gyalwa Karmapa. (First of line, who are regarded as emanations of Maitreya, received honorific title Kenting Tai Situ Rinpoche from Emperor of China in 1407). At age 18 mths enthroned at Palpung monastery, the traditional seat of the Situpas and HQ of a monastic grouping comprising some 180 major monasteries and numerous smaller ones. 1954: left Tibet; went first to Bhutan and then to Rumtek monastery, Sikkim; completed training, receiving transmissions from Gyalwa Karmapa et al. Has since travelled widely. Presently engaged in building Sherab Ling ('Land of Wisdom'), a religious and educational centre in Himalayan foothills, N India.

Tara Tulku: *Gelugpa Lama; former Abbot of Gyutö Tantric College.* b 1927, E. Tibet. Studied for nearly 30 yrs at Sendru and Drepung monasteries. 1959: sought refuge in India. Has now retired as Abbot of Gyutö Tantric Monastery. Among other things, currently teache Westerners at Bodh Gaya, India.

Tarthang Tulku: *Nyingma Lama active in USA.* b 1935, Golok, E Tibet. Left home at 17 to travel in Kham; studied with many famous teachers of all schools but mainly Nyingma. 1958: left Tibet for Bhutan and India; later to Sikkim to study with root guru Jamyang Khyentse Chökyi Lodrö (qv). c 1962: appointed to represent Nyingma trad at Sanskrit U, Varanasi; founded Dharma Publishing. 1968: to USA; established Tibetan Nyingma Meditation Center (Berkeley, Cal), Nyingma Institute and Odiyan Retreat Center. m to French—Egyptian lady. Bks incl *Gesture of Balance, Oppenness Mind, Hidden Mind of Freedom, Skillful Means, Kum Nye Relaxation I and II, Sacred Art of Tibet; Time, Space and Knowledge; Lnowledge of Freedom, Love of Knowledge,* and *Copper Mountain Mandala.* Trs incl *Calm and Clear, Mother of Knowledge.* Gen Ed of *Crystal Mirror* series, *Ancient Tibet,* and of new Nyingma Ed of *kangyur* and *Tangyur.*

Tendzin, Ösel (Thomas Rich): *Vajra Regent of Chögyam Trungpa Rinpoche.* From Passaic, New Jersey. Former student of Swami Satchidananda. 1976: became first Westerner to be empowered as a holder of the Kagyu Lineage. As the foremost student of Chögyam Trungpa, lectures widely in America and Europe. Book: *Buddha in the Palm of Your Hand.*

Thondup, Tulka: *Incarnation of Komey Khenpo, one of the principal teachers at Dodrupchem monastery.* Studied under Khenpo Chochog at Dodrupchen monastery; subsequently travelled to USA where, 1stly as Visiting Scholar and later as Research Fellow, was attached to the Center for the Study of World Religions at Harvard U.

Thrangu Rinpoche: *Karma Kagyu lama active in W.* b 1933, Kham, E Tibet. Recognized as 9th tulku of his lineage of Gyalwa Karmapa and Situ Rinpoche. Traditional ed at Thrangu monastery. At 16, began to study 'inner wisdom' (incl Abhidharma, Madhyamika, religious dialectics, *Bodhicaryavatara, Prajñaparamita, Uttara Tantra, Hevajra Tanta,* etc) under Khenpo Lodro Rapsel. At 23, given monk ordination by Karmapa with Surmang Gawang Rinpoche and Trungpa Rinpoche (qv). Many retreats, initiations, etc followed; also introduced to absolute nature by Khenpo Gangshar Wangpo. 1959: from Tibet to Rumtrek, Sikkim; further teachings incl Six Yogas of Naropa and Mahamudra, 1967: after exams, awarded degree of Geshe Rabjam; praised by Dalai Lama; made khenpo by Karmapa and has since taught Shamar Rinpoche, Situ Rinpoche, Jamgön Kongtrül Rinpoche and Gyaltsap Rinpoche; became Yarnay Khenpo(director of rainy season retreats) and published many texts. 1976: moved to Nepal; established retreat centre at Namo Buddha and monastery at Boudha nr Kathmandu. 1979: visited UK, Germany, Belgium, Denmark, Norway and USA. 1981 and 84: to Europe again. 1982: pilgrimage and teaching tout of Sri Lanka, Thailand, Indonesia, Malaysia, the Philippines and Hong Kong. 1984: several mths in Tibet; visited Thrangu monastery and ordained 100+ monks and nuns.

Thubten Ngawang. – see Addenda, p. 334

Thurman, Robert Alexander Farrar (Upasaka Tenzin Chotrag): *President, American Institute of Bdst Studies; translator and academic.* After Harvard and Asian travels, studied with Geshe Wangyal (qv) (mainly Tib language and texts), then to Dharamsala (c 1963), was ordained by Dalai Lama and spent time at Namgyal monastery. Became fluent in Tibetan and studied Nagarjuna and Tsongkhapa. Later resigned monk status and returned to academic life. 1972: PhD at Harvard with a tr of a Madhyamika text by Tsongkhapa. Currently Professor of Religion at Amherst College. Trs incl *The Holy Teaching of Vimalakirti; The Life & Teachings of Tsong Khapa,* and *Tsong Khapa's Speech of Gold in the Essence of True Eloquence.*

Trogawa Rinpoche: *Tibetan lama doctor.* b 1931 in Tibet; recognized as tulku of famous lama doctor; underwent traditional medical apprenticeship in Lhasa. 1954: left Tibet. Has since practised Tib medicine throughout Himalayan region; has also taught at School of Tib Medicine and Astrology, Dharamsala. Principal guest speaker at 1st International Conference on Tib Medicine held in Italy. Founder of Chakpori inst of Medicine, USA and France.

Trungpa Rinpoche, Vidyadhara Chögyam. (Karma Ngawang Chökyi Gyatso Künga Zangpo;

1939–87): *One of the first lamas to come to the West; meditation master of the Kagyu and Nyingma lineages and writer.* b Geje, E Tibet. Recognized and enthroned as 11th Trungpa Tulku by Gyalwa Karmapa at 11/2 yrs. Became Abbot of Surmang monasteries. Took sramanera precepts at 8 yrs; also went into 3-month retreat (to meditate on Manjushri). At 9 met principal guru, Jamgön Kongtrül II of Sechen. At 11 yrs, began ngondro (preliminary practices for Vajrayana teachings). At 14, conducted 1st full empowerment (wangkur), which lasted 3 mths. Later left Tibet for India. Became protégé of Freda Bedi (Sister Palmo – qv). 1963: came to W as Spalding Fellow at Oxford U; studied W philosophy, psychology, art and comparative religion. 1967: co-founder with Chujé Akong Rinpoche (qv) of Samyé-Ling Tib Centre in Scotland, the 1st Tib Bdst meditation centre in W. Late 1960s: m Diana Judith Pybus (Lady Diana Mukpo); several children born. 1970: left for USA; established important centres in Vermont (Tail of the Tiger), Colorado (Karma Dzong in Boulder and Rocky Mountain Dharma Center) and Nova Scotia (Gampo Abbey). Numerous other centres (Dharmadhatus) in USA, Europe, etc. Headed Vajradhatu, a world-wide organization. d Halifax, Nova Scotia. Books incl *Meditation in Action, Cutting Through Spiritual Materialism, The Myth of Freedom, Mudra, Shambhala – The Sacred Path of the Warrior* and *Journey Without Goal.* Autobiography: *Born in Tibet* (with Esmé Cramer Roberts).

Tsultrim Gyamtso, Khenpo: *Senior Karma Kagyu Lama.* b c 1937. Ordained young after completing rigorous 9-yr course; took Khenpo degree; afterwards went into 3-yr retreat, practising rituals and meditation practices of the Mahamudra teachings. 1977: at instruction of his main guru, Gyalwa Karmapa, moved to Europe; also, alternating with Thrangu Rinpoche, serves as chief teacher at the monastic college (shedra) at Rumtek monastery, Sikkim, for some mths annually; is also Abbot of Drup di Gon monastery, Bhutan. Books incl *Progressive Stages of Meditation on Emptiness.*

Tucci, Prof. Giuseppe (1894–1984): *Pioneer Italian Tibetologist.* b Macerata. 1919: D.Litt from U. of Rome, where he became a Lecturer, soon rising to Professor of the Religions and Philosophies of India (to 1969). 1929: elected to Italian Academy. 1933: founded IsMEO (Istituto Italiano per il Medio ed Estremo Oriente) in Rome. 1927–48; travelled, researched and collected MSS and artefacts on several expeditions to Tibet. 'A man of outstanding wealth, social position and power', and 'a believing and to some extent even practising Buddhist (E. Conze). Books in English incl *The Religions of Tibet, The Theory & Practice of the Mandala, Tibet, Secrets of Tibet, Transhimalaya, Indo-Tibetica, To Lhasa & Beyond* and *Tibetan Painted Scrolls.*

Urgyen, Tulku: *Senior Nyingma Lama noted for Dzogchen teachings; special holder of Terma lineage of Chogyur Dechen Lingpa.* Lived in Ka-Nying Shedrup Ling monastery, Bodh Nath, Kathmandu, Nepal; spent most of his time in retreat. 1981: visited W to teach with son, Chökyi Nyima Rinpoche. Died 1996.

Wangchen, Geshe Namgyal: *Gelugpa lama teaching in UK.* b mid-1930s. 1948: entered Drepung monastery (Loseling College) at 13. 1959: fled from Tibet; spent next 10 yrs in Indian refugee centre (Buxaduar), continuing Geshe studies. 1972: received Geshe degree. 'Geshe Wangchen studied the vast range of Mahayana Buddhist thought under the guidance of his main Guru, Khensur Pema Gyaltsen Rinpoche, and other special masters of the tradition' (Manjushri London programme). Lived for a time at the new Drepung Loseling in Karnataka, India; later moved to Delhi to work as Librarian at Tibet House. Instructed American students under the auspices of U of Wisconsin at Sarnath. 1981 (April): came to UK and became Resident Teacher at Manjushri London. Fluent in English. Is working on several books. Currently in Drepung, South India.

Wangyal, Geshe. (1901–83): *Late Gelugpa Lama of Kalmuk origin active in USA.* Studied at Drepung. Root guru: the Buryat Lama Agvan Dorjiev. At 19, with Lama Dorjiev in St. Petersburg. In Peking during the 1930s; also travelled with Sir Charles Bell in C Asia. 1937: invited to Britain by Marco Pallis (qv). 1951: when Chinese entered Kham, left Tibet. Visited Paris, Hanoi and Hong Kong. 1955: to Freewood Acres, New Jersey (USA) to minister to community of Kalmuk refugees brought over after WW II by Tolstoy Foundation. Brought over four lamas from India, incl Geshe Sopa (qv) and Lama Kunga. Taught 1-day weekly in Dept of Altaic Languages at Columbia U (New York). Books incl *The Door of Liberation; The Jewelled Staircase,* etc.

Wylie, Turrell V. (1927–1984): *Originator of the Wylie System of Tibetan Transcription.* b Durango, Colorado. Onetime Professor of Tibetan Studies at U. of Washington, Seattle. Studied with G. Tucci (qv) in Rome. Following invasion of Tibet (1959), helped with relief work via Rockefeller Foundation. Travelled in India and met Tibetan scholars, some of whom he brought to Seattle. Books incl *The Geography of Tibet according to 'Dzam-gling-rgyas-bshad.* Many articles, incl 'A Standard System of Tibetan Transcription' (*Harvard Journal of Asiatic Studies,* 22: pp. 261–67. Dec. 1959). Anonymous co-author of Shakabpa's *Tibet: A Political History.*

Yeshe, Lama Thubten (1935–84): *Gelugpa Lama and influential teacher of Westerners.* b nr Lhasa; ed Sera Monastey (Jé College). 1959: to India; settled at Buxaduar. Began teaching Wstnrs with principal disciple, Zopa Rinpoche (qv), in Darjeeling and later Kathmandu. 1971: helped found Kopan Monastery at Bodh Nath in Kathmandu Valley, Nepal. In subsequent yrs he and his students established over 65 centres under auspices of FPMT (Foundation for the Preservation of the Mahayana Tradition). Also instrumental in establishing Wisdom Publications, The Universal Education Association, a couple of monasteries for W monks and nuns as well as supporting leper colony in India, etc., etc. Toured and lectured annually in N America, Asia, Australia and Europe. Books incl *Wisdom Energy* (with Lama Zopa).

Yeshe, Lama (new incarnation: Lama ösel): *b 1985, Granada, Spain, 5th child of Maria Torres and Paco Hita, students of late Lama Yeshe who helped found ösel Ling, retreat centre nr Granada. First met by Lama Zopa at age 6 mths; confirmed by Dalai Lama, 1986.*

Zong Rinpoche, Kyabje. (Zongtrul Jetson Losang Tsondu Thubten Gyaltsen; 1904–84): *Revered Gelug lama.* b Kham, E Tibet; recognized as reincarnation of Zongtrul Tenma Chöphel (1836–99). Came to C Tibet at age 12 and entered Ganden monastery (Shartse College). Late Trijang Rinpoche became 1st mentor. Soon displayed skill in debate and scholarly talents. At 25, passed Geshe exams with honours; passed exams at Gyutö Tantric College similarly well. Appointed Abbot of Ganden Shartse by Regent (Reting Rinpoche) and instituted reforms and useful new developments. Resigned after 9 yrs to go on pilgrimage. Left Tibet; found refuge in India at Buxaduar; became Principal of Tib Teachers' Training Programme. 1969: 1st Principal of new C Institute for Tib Higher Studies at Sarnath (nr. Varanasi). On retirement, devoted himself to practice. Gave teachings to both Tibs and Wstnrs. Visited Europe and USA. d S India following tour of N America and Europe.

Zopa Rinpoche, Lama: *Gelug lama; teacher of Wstnrs.* b 1946 of Sherpa stock at Thami, NE Nepal, nr Everest. At age 5 recognized as tulku of Lawudo Lama, gt Nyingma practitioner, ed Solu Khumbu region (Nepal). Taken on pilgrimage to Tibet by uncle while still young and decided to remain. Studied first at Dungkar monastery, later at Sera (Jé College). 1959: to India; lived in refugee camp at Buxaduar; there met Lama Thubten Yeshe (qv), his guru. Remained several yrs studying under various Tibetan masters. 1965: he and Lama Yeshe met their first W student (Zina Rachevsky). 1969: with LTY and ZR, founded small centre at Kopan in Kathmandu Valley, Nepal; taught intensively there in following yrs. 1971: helped found FPMT with Lama Yeshe. 1974: made 1st visit to W., visiting USA and Australia. Co-author with Lama Thubten Yeshe of *Wisdom Energy.*

ADDENDA:

Chhimed Rigdzin Rinpoche (Khordong Terchen Tulku Chhimed Rigdzin Rinpoche): *Nyingma lama; incarnation of Nuden Dorje Drophang Lingpa.* b 1922; recognized as tulku by various imp lamas. At 4, enthroned at Khardong Gompa; overall charge of 12 gompas. At 10 discovered 2 imp termas; also pilgrimage to Lhasa. c 1932–4: various empowerments, instructions and practice; then returned to Khardong; trained under various lamas. Later given imp instructions and predictions by Tulku Tsurlo: that at 18 he would wander in the mts of Nepal, Bhutan and Sikkim, then 2 yrs solitary retreat, etc. c 1959: to Italy at invitation of G. Tucci (qv). 1984: received requests to return to Tib; accordingly visited Tib and proposes returning. m with issue.

Thubten Ngawang, Geshe: *Gelug lama active in Germany.* b 1931 of nomad family on pilgrimage to Mt Kailas. From age 14, studied at Dhargyey monastery, Tehor-Kham, E Tibet, with Geshe Jampa Khedrup. At 25, to Sera monastery; taught by Geshe Rabten (qv). 1959: from Tibet; in refugee camp at Buxaduar. 1969: to new Sera monastery, Bylakuppe, Mysore, S India. 1975-9: Geshe Lharampa degree. 1979-: spiritual head of Tibetisches Zentrum, Hamburg. Various publications-in German.

25 Zen Buddhism

NOTE ON TITLES, etc.:

Daiosho: (Jap) lit. 'great priest'.
Dharma Heir: disciple to whom a Master has given Dharma Transmission (qv).
Dharma Transmission: the transmission of Truth or the One Mind from master to disciple, heart to heart (i.e. beyond words and concepts).
Dojo: (Jap) training hall.
Inka: (Jap) lit. 'seal'; signifies that the Master has formally certified the disciple's understanding.
Kensho: (Jap) first glimpse of one's true nature.
Osho: (Jap) priest.
Roshi: (Jap) lit. 'old teacher'; signifies a Zen Master.
Sesshin: (Jap) intensive retreat.
Sensei: (Jap) teacher.
Sunim: (Kor) formal title for Korean monks and nuns.
Transmission: see Dharma Transmission.
Zendo: (Jap) Zen training hall.

Aitken Roshi, Robert: *Hawaii-based Zen teacher of the Sanbo Kyodan lineage and writer.* Captured on Guam by Japanese and interned as enemy alien for duration of WW II. Preceding interest in Japanese literature, esp. haiku poetry, given new impetus by encounter with R.H. Blyth (qv) in POW camp (1944); also became interested in zazen, though unable to practise. After War, began Zen practice with Nyogen Senzaki (qv) in California. 1950: returned to Japan to continue haiku studies; also began practice as a lay student at Ryutakuji under Yamamoto Gempo Roshi and Nakagawa Soen Roshi (qv). Later also studied with Yasutani Hakuun Roshi (qv) and Yamada Koun Roshi. 1974: received title roshi from Yamada Koun Roshi. Currently closely associated with the Diamond Sangha, which has zendos on various of the Hawaiian islands as well as in elsewhere in USA and Australia. Wife, Anne Aitken, has been partner in all Zen work. Books incl *A Zen Wave: Basho's Haiku & Zen* (A study of Basho's *haiku*), *Taking the Path of Zen* and *The Mind of Clover: Essays in Zen Bdst Ethics.* Writes regularly in the journal *Blind Donkey.*

Awakawa, Yasuoichi (1902–79): *Scholar of Zen art,* trained as an economist with PhD from Kyoto U; devoted life to collecting and cataloguing Zen art. Books incl the classic *Zen Art.*

Baker Roshi, Richard: *Dharma Heir to Shunryu Suzuki Roshi.* A Harvard graduate and onetime head of San Francisco Zen Centre; now operating independently.

Blyth, Reginald H (1898–1964): *Writer and translator.* b London; went to Korea via India; taught English and studied Zen under Kayama Taigi Roshi. 1940: moved to Japan; taught English; tutored Crown Prince. Interned during WW II as enemy alien. Books incl *Zen & Zen Classics* (5 vols), *Japanese Humour, Japanese Life & Character in Shenryu, Edo Satirical Verse Anthologies, Haiku* (4 vols), *History of Haiku,* (2 vols) etc.

Chisan Zenji (Koho Keido Chisan Zenji; 1879–1968): *Japanese Soto Master.* b Toyama prefacture; ordained by Koho Hakugan of Yoko-ji. 1901: Dharma transmission from Kyoto Hakugan. 1904: graduated from Soto Ken U and entered Soji-ji. 1948: became Chief Abbot of Soji-ji and of Kanto Plains; also received honour of Daikyosei ('Great Teacher') from Emperor. 1950s: 2 world tours; whilst in England met Jiyu Kennett Roshi (qv) and invited her to train with him in Japan. First Founder of Shastazan Chisan-ji (Shasta Abbey) posthumously.

Deshimaru Roshi, Taisen (1914–82): *Japanese Soto Zen teacher active in Europe.* Lived layman's life for many yrs; later trained with Kodo Sawaki; received Dharma transmission. 1967: settled in France; became based in Paris. 1970: founded L'Association Zen d'Europe; dojos and zazen centres established in France, Belgium, W Germany, N America, N Africa and S America. d Tokyo; cremated Soji-ji temple, Yokohama. Books include, *Vrai Zen, Zazen, La Pratique du Zen, Zen-Geist, Zen-Bdsmus und Christentum, Zen im den Kampfkünsten Japans, Zen et Arts Martiaux, La Pratique de la Concentration, Questions à un Maitre Zen,* and *Le Bol et le Baton.* Autobiography: *Autobiographie d'un Moine Zen.*

Dumoulin, Heinrich, S.J.: *Author* b 1905. 1929: PhD, Gregorian U, Rome. 1941: Prof of Philosophy & History of Religions, Sophia U, Tokyo. 1970: Director, Institute of Oriental Religions, (ibid). Books incl *The Development of Chinese Zen after the VIth Patriarch in the Light of the Mumonkan; Ostliche Meditation und Christiche Mystik; Christianity Meets Buddhism; Zen Enlightenment: Origins & Meaning* and *A History of Zen Bdsm* (the definitive wk). Ed *Buddhism in the Modern World* (UK ed *Buddhism Today*).

Eido Tai Shimano Roshi – See Shimano Roshi, Eido.

Freedgood, née Stuart, Roshi, Maurine (1922–90): *Canadian-born Zen Master.* Trained as pianist. Early 1960s; began formal Zen practice with Yasutani Roshi (qv) in New York. 1977: ordained Rinzai priest by Eido Roshi (qv); participated regularly in retreats at Dai Bosatsu Zendo (Catskill Mts). 1982: authorized to teach by Nakagawa Soen Roshi (qv). 1979: resident teacher and president of Cambridge [Massachusetts] Bdst Assn. till died. See Lenore Friedman *Meetings with Remarkable Women: Buddhist Teachers in America* Boston: Shambhala, 1987.

Furukawa Roshi, Gyudo (1872–1961): *Important early 20th C Rinzai Zen Master.* A disciple of Soyen Shaku (qv); while Soyen in USA studied with Nantembo (qv). Succeeded Soyen as Abbot of Engaku-ji. 1930: following retirement, visited US at request of Chisaki Nyogen. 1935: re-elected Abbot of Engaku-ji.

Glassman Sensei, Bernard Tetsugen: *Dharma heir of Maezumi Roshi (ZCLA)* b 1939, Brooklyn, New York. ed Polytechnic Institute of Brooklyn and U of California; PhD in applied maths 1970. Worked as administrator and engineer in US space program for 15 yrs. 1958: began studying Zen. 1963: began zazen practice at Zenshu-ji [Soto] Zen Mission, Los Angeles, guided by Sumi Roshi. 1968: began practising with Maezumi Roshi (qv). 1970: ordained Zen Bdst monk at ZCLA. Undertook and completed koan study with Maezumi. 1977: received Shiho or Dharma transmission from Maezumi Roshi. At present is Abbot of Zen Community of New York (ZCNY), Zenshin-ji, a Soto Zen temple and training centre in Riverdale, New York. Early 1980s: started Greyston Bakery as 'livelihood practice' of ZCNY.

Goto Roshi, Zuigan (?–1965): *Rinzai Zen Master.* Zen master in the lineage of Imagita Kosen Roshi (qv) and Soyen Shaku (qv). Graduated in Philosophy from Imperial U, Tokyo. 1906: accompanied Sokatsu Shaku, Sokei-an Sasaki et al to USA. Later became Abbot of Myoshin-ji (Kamakura), later still of Daitoku-ji (Kyoto). Teacher of Oda Sesso Roshi, Morinaga Soko Roshi, Ruth Fuller Sasaki, Walter Nowock (to whom he gave inka) et al. (all qv). Retired to Daishu-in; succeeded as Abbot of Daitoku-ji by Sesso Oda Roshi (qv). On d succeeded at Daishu-in by Morinaga Soko Roshi (qv).

Harada Roshi, Sogaku (1870–1961): *Japanese Zen Master.* Trained in both Rinzai and Soto traditions, entered Soto temple as novice at age 7. Continued training in Soto temples during primary and high school yrs. At 20 became monk at Shogen-ji, a Rinzai monastery; after 2½ yrs of strenuous training, attained kensho. At age 27 enrolled at Soto-sponsored Komazawa U.

Continued to do research under well-known scholars for 6 yrs after graduation. Then trained with Dokutan Roshi of Nanzen-ji, Kyoto for 2 yrs; later moved into Nanzen-ji as Dokutan's assistant and applied himself wholeheartedly to zazen and koans; completed all koans and received inka from Dokutan Roshi. At this time, recalled to Komazawa U; spent 12 yrs teaching there, part of the time as full professor; combined Zen training with academic work. Afterwards became Abbot of Hosshin-ji; a post he retained for 40 yrs. Until almost age 90, conducted week-long sesshin at Hosshin-ji 6 times a year; also held sesshin elsewhere. 'Nominally of the Soto sect, he welded together the best of Soto and Rinzai and the amalgam was a vibrant Bdsm, which has become one of the great teaching lines in Japan today'; 'His commentary on *Shushogi*, a codification of Dogen's *Shobogenzo*, is recognized as one of the most penetrating of its kind' (Philip Kapleau).

Herrigel, Eugen (1884–1955): *Author and translator.* With August Faust, responsible for introducing Zen to Germany. ed Heidelberg; read Philosophy with Shuei Ohasama (Jap Rinzai Master) and together tr Zen texts based on W philosophical terminology. Books incl *Zen in the Art of Archery*, *The Method of Zen*, etc.

Hisamatsu, Sin'ichi (1889–1980): *Zen philosopher.* Disciple of Nishida Kenji, studied Zen under Ikegami Shozan of Myoshin-ji. Became Prof of Bdsm at Kyoto U; also taught at Harvard and travelled widely abroad. Active as tea master, founded FAS Society in Kyoto to promote philosophical and practical understanding of Zen. Major wk in English: *Zen & the Fine Arts*.

Hsü Yün, Ch'an Master (1840–1959): *'Universally regarded as the most outstanding Bdst of the Chinese Sangha in the modern era' (Richard Hunn).* Dharma successor of all five Ch'an schools; main reformer in Chinese Bdst Revival (1900–50). b Chuan Chou, Fukien prov. Left home at 19; took Refuge at Yung Chuan Ssu on Mt Ku; head shaved there by Master Chang Kai. At 20 took precepts with Master Miao Lien and received Dharma name Ku Yen; remained on Mt Ku 4 yrs. c 1868–71: lived in wilderness on Mt Ku on grass, nettles, etc. At 31 began travelling; given kung-an 'Who is dragging this corpse about?' by Master Yung Ching of Luang Chuan Temple on Mt T'ien T'ai. At 43: extensive pilgrimage on foot carrying incense and prostrating every 3rd step to P'u T'o Shan, Wu T'ai Shan, Omei Shan, Tibet, Bhutan, India, Sri Lanka, Burma, back to China by sea, then visits to more holy sites in Yunnan, Hunan, Anhwe, etc. In 56th yr achieved final awakening at Kao Min Ssu in Yang Chou. Thereafter began revival and teaching work. 1934; while Abbot of Ku Shan Ssu, had visions of 6th Patriarch; eventually invited to yake charge of 6th Patriarch's temple (Ts'ao-Chi'i), then v run down; restored it along with other temples and monasteries; also in his life founded many schools and hospitals. Spent last yrs in cow-shed nr Chen Ju Ssu, Mt Yun Chu, where he died in 120th yr. Had also travelled in Malaysia and Thailand; also taught King of Thailand. Autobiography: *Empty Cloud*, tr Charles Luk. *Ch'an & Zen Teaching*, Series 1, tr Charles Luk contains his 'Discourses & Dharma Words'. Chinese sources incl *Hsu Yun Ho Shang Shih Chi ('Records of Master Hsu Yun')*, *Hsu Yun Ho Shang Nien Pu ('Autobiography of Master Hsu Yun')*.

Hsüan Hua, Tripitaka (or Dhyana) Master (Dharma names An Tz'u and Tu Lun) (1908–95): *Abbot of Gold Mountain Dhyana Monastery (California) and Chairman of Sino-American Bdst Ass'n.* b 1908, Shuang-Ch'eng district, NE China. Trauma at age 11: encountered death; resolved to become a monk right away but delayed by family duties, though did take refuge in 3 Jewels; Ven Master Ch'ang became teacher. Well (though not formally) ed in Chinese classics, Bdst scriptures, medicine, physiognomy and astrology. At age 19 mother died; took sramamera ordination; mourned by mother's grave for 3 yrs; meditation intensive; Hui Neng (6th Patriarch) also appeared, predicting future journey to W. After WW II, travelled 3000 miles to Nan Hua monastery in Canton province to visit Ven. Hsü Yün (qv). Received bhikshu ordination at Mt P'u T'o during journey. Hsü Yün transmitted mind seal; made him 9th patriarch of Wei Yang lineage; asked him to be Director of Nan Hua Institute for the Study of the Vinaya. 1950: resigned post at Nan Hua monastery; travelled to Ta Chiao monastery where Ven. Hsü Yün had become Abbot. Soon after left for Hong Kong; lived in cave in the New Territories until requested by refugees from mainland China to help establish temples; remained in Hong Kong 12 yrs. 1962: to USA (San Francisco). Awaited developments. 1968: declared that the 'flower of Bdsm would bloom that yr. in America with 5 petals'; in summer conducted a Surangama Sutra Dharma Assembly lasting 96 days; 5 people took ordination subsequently. Has delivered lectures on other sutras; more people have ordained. 1971: established Gold

Mountain Monastery; subsequently also set up Bdst Text Translation Soc, Intl Institute for the Trans of Bdst Texts, Instilling Virtue Elementary School, City of 10,000 Buddhas and Dharma Realm Bdst U (both at Talmage, Cal). Has delivered extensive commentaries to canonical texts; published as *The Shurangama Sutra, The Heart Sutra, The Diamond Sutra, The 6th Patriarch's Platform Sutra, The Amitabha Sutra, The Sutra of the Past Vows of Earth Store Bodhisattva [Kstigarbha], The Great Compassion Heart Dharani Sutra, The Sutra in 42 Sections, The Dharma Flower Sutra [Avatamsaka]*; also *The Shramanera Vinaya, The Awakening of Faith in the Mahayana Shastra* and several series of *Ch'an & Pure Land Dharma Talks.*

Hyobong Sunim (1888–1966): *'One of the most remarkable Bdst teachers of this century in Korea'* (Stephen Batchelor). b nr present capital of N Korea. Studied law; became judge during Japanese occupation. Resigned after c 10 yrs, on grounds of conscience, left home and became wandering toffee seller. At 39 yrs commenced intensive monastic meditation practice. At age 43: into solitary retreat; after 1½ yrs achieved insight. For next 30 yrs was widely known and respected teacher at Songgwang-sa, Tonghwa Sa, Haein Sa and other monasteries and hermitages. Became head of the Chogye Order. Conferred Dharma transmission on Kusan Sunim (qv). d in meditation posture while staying at P'yoch'ung monastery.

Imagita Roshi, Kosen (1816–92): *Major 19th C Rinzai Master.* b Osaka; studied to become Confucian scholar; at age 25 decided to become Zen monk; divorced wife and entered Shokukuji (Kyoto). Awarded inka at age 36 by Gisan. As Abbot of Engaku-ji (Kamakura) staunchly defended Bdsm during troubled Meiji yrs. A mentor of D.T. Suzuki (qv), who wrote a biography.

Kapleau Roshi, Philip: *American Zen teacher,* b 1912, New Haven, Connecticut. 1946: Chief Court reporter, Intl Military Tribunal, Nuremberg. 1947: court reporter, Intl Military Tribunal, Tokyo. 1953–66: trained in various Rinzai and Soto Zen monasteries and temples in Japan. Teachers – Harada Roshi, Yasutani Roshi and Nakagawa Soen Roshi (all qv). Also spent 1 yr in SE Asia living at ashrams in India, Burma and Sri Lanka. Centres established: Rochester, New York (1966 – headquarters); Toronto and Montreal, Canada; Evanston, Illinois; Denver, Colorado; Santa Fe, New Mexico; Madison, Wisconsin; Mexico City; San Jose, Costa Rica; Poland (3 centres); Stockholm, Sweden; W. Berlin, Germany. Makes periodic visits to all, conducting sesshin and workshops. Holds two 3-month formal training periods annually at Rochester. Has also for 20 yrs spoken at colleges, universities, growth centres and symposia, etc. Plans to go into semi-retirement in 1987. Books incl *Three Pillars of Zen; Zen Dawn in the West; Wheel of Death; To Cherish all Life (The Bdst Case for Vegetarianism); A Pilgrimage to the Bdst Temples and Caves of China; The Private Encounter with the Roshi: Its Hazards and Rewards,* and *The Passage of the Flame: Practical Guidance in Death, Dying, Karma & Rebirth.*

Katagiri Roshi, Dainin: *Sotto Zen master of the Eihei-ji line who works in the USA.* b 1928. 1963: came to USA to serve at Zenshu-ji Soto Zen Mission, Los Angeles, 1964–71: assisted Shunryu Suzuki Roshi (qv) at Soko-ji Soto Zen Mission, San Francisco; later helped established San Francisco Zen Center and Tassajara Mountain Center. 1972: moved to Minneapolis; founded Minnesota Zen Meditation Center; has since worked all over Mid-West. 1976: helped found Catching-the-Moon Zen Mt Center in SE Minnesota (nr New Albin, Iowa). Has ordained a number of Wstnrs into the Bdst priesthood.

Kennett Roshi, Jiyu. (Peggy Teresa Nancy Kennett) (1924–96): *British-born Soto Zen master working in the USA.* b England. ed Trinity College of Music, London, and Durham U. Early Bdst studies at London Bdst Vihara and Bdst Society. 1962: ordained into the Rinzai Zen tradition by Seck Kim Seng, Abbot of Cheng Hoon Teng Temple in Malacca, Malaysia; then went on to study Soto Zen in Japan at Soji-ji under Chisan Koho Zenji (qv); received transmission from Koho Zenji; installed as Abbess of Unpuku-ji (Mie Prefecture); granted Sanzen license. 1969: to San Francisco on lecture tour. 1970: Zen Mission Soc founded; moved to Mt Shasta and became Abbess and Spiritual Director at Shasta Abbey; also Instructor at U of California Extension in Berkeley since 1972; sat on the faculty of the California Institute of Transpersonal Psychology and lectured at universities worldwide. Also founded numerous Zen temples and meditation groups through USA, Canada and in England (esp Throssel Hole Priory). Shasta Abbey is HQ of her reformed Soto Zen Church and Order of Bdst Contemplatives (OBC). Books incl *Zen is Eternal Life* (1st issued as *Selling Water by the River*);

How to Grow a Lotus Blossom, or *How A Zen Bdst Prepares for Death*; *The Wild White Goose*, *Diaries of Years in Japan* (2 vols); *The Book of Life*, etc.

Kitaro, Nishida (1870–1945): *Japan's premier modern philosopher*. Became Professor at Kyoto Imperial U in his 40s and 50s. 1927: retired early but retained status as Japan's foremost thinker; published a great deal – collected wks run to 19 vols.

Kusan Sunim (1909–83): *Korean Zen Master*. b Namwon, SW Korea of farming stock. Worked as farmer and married; then at 26, severe illness cured by reciting Bdst mantra; 3 yrs later left home to dedicate himself to Bdsm. Became student of Hyobong Sunim (qv) at Songgwang Sa monastery. At 31 bhikshu ordination at T'ongdo Sa. Not interested in sutra study; instead dedicated himself to meditation practice in meditation halls and hermitages. 1st imp experience at Sudo Am hermitage and another major breakthrough at Popwang Dae hermitage in 1946. During Korean War escaped to UN controlled territory; lived in temples in or nr Chungmu. After war accepted number of administrative posts: chief inspector at National Sangha HQ in Seoul and later head of general monastic affairs in Cholla Namdo province. Also founded Milae Sa temple nr Chungmu and was abbot there 1954–7. To deepen meditation practice, resigned and went to small hermitage (Paegun Am); achieved another awakening; then received Dharma transmission from Hyobong Sunim. 1962–6: Abbot of Tonghwa Sa monastery. 1966: visited SE Asia, India and Nepal. 1967: moved to Songgwang Sa and in 1969 became spiritual director with title *Pangjang Sunim*. 1973: founded Bul-il Intl Meditation Centre at Songgwang Sa for foreign monks and nuns. Latterly made several visits to USA and founded centres in Los Angeles and Carmel; also visited Europe and founded centre in Geneva. d in meditation posture after short illness. Books incl *Nine Mountains* and *The Way of Korean Zen*.

Kyungbo Sunim: *First Korean Zen teacher to visit USA*. 1964: visited USA and toured various Bdst groups. 1965–69: studied at Temple U, Philadelphia; PhD for study of early history of Korean Zen. 1969: returned to Korea and became Dean of the Bdst College, Dongguk U, Seoul. Has visited USA regularly since 1973, but set up no teaching organisation, though the Il Bung Zen Bdst Assn is umbrella organization for his groups. His disciple, Gosung Sunim, has also visited the USA. A prolific writer.

Leggett, Trevor Price: *Writer on Zen, the martial arts and Vedanta*. b 1914. LIB degree at London U. Lived and worked for 10 yrs in E (India, Japan); studied traditional Yoga of the Self under Hari Prasad Shastri; studied Japanese language, Bdsm and Judo in Japan. Did Zen training at Daitokuji (Kyoto). Was 1st foreigner to obtain 6th Dan (senior teacher's degree) in Judo from Kodokan. 1946–70: Head of BBC Japanese Service. 1984: Order of the Sacred Treasure (3rd class) for services to Anglo-Japanese relations. 1987: Bukkyo Dendo Kyokai literary prize for trs of Bdst classics. Lives in London. Books incl *A First Zen Reader*, *The Tiger's Cave*, *Zen & the Ways*, *Encounters in Yoga & Zen* and *The Warrior Koans*; also four books on Judo (including *Demonstration of Throws*); and *Shogi* (Japanese chess). From Sanskrit: 1st translations of Shankara's *Chapter of the Self* and the (newly discovered) *Commentary on the Yoga Sutras*. On panel of trs of Prof Nakamura's *The Development of Vedanta Philosophy*.

Luk, Charles. (Upasaka Lu Ku'an Yü; 1898–1978): *Translator and Writer on Ch'an*. b Canton. Studied with Hutuktu (- Tulku) of Sinkang (a Vajrayana teacher of both Kagyu and Gelug lineages) and Master Hsü Yün (qv), who urged him to translate Chinese Bdst texts. Dedicated the last 20 yrs of his life (from 1956) to this cause. Lived in exile in Hong Kong, maintaining a world-wide correspondence. 1st visited Europe in 1930s; visited London and met Christmas Humphreys (qv) in 1935. Publications incl *Ch'an & Zen Teachings* (3 vols); trs of various sutras (*Surangama, Vimalakirti, Diamond, Heart*); *Secrets of Chinese Meditation*; *Taoist Yoga*; *The Transmission of the Mind Outside the Teaching* and *Practical Bdsm*.

Maezumi Roshi, Hakuyu Taizen (1931–95): *Founder of Zen Center of Los Angeles*. b Otawara, Tochigi prefecture, Japan. Age 11: ordained a Zen monk. Received degrees in Oriental literature and philosophy from Komazawa U. Afterwards studied at Soji-ji. 1955: received Dharma transmission from Hakuun Kuroda Roshi. Also received inka from Koryu Osaká Roshi and Hakuun Kuroda Roshi, thus also becoming Dharma successor in two major lines of Rinzai Zen. Holds Sanzen Dojo Shike (Training Master's credentials) too. 1956: came to Los Angeles as priest of Zenshuji temple. 1967: founded Zen Center of Los Angeles (ZCLA).

1976: established Kuroda Institute for Transcultural Studies (now called Kuroda Institute for the Study of Bdsm & Human Values). Also founding influence behind Zen Arts Center, Mt Tremper, New York. Books incl *On Zen Practice* (I and II, both ed. with Glassman, B.T.), *The Hazy Moon of Enlightenment* (with Glassman, B.T.) and *The Way of Everyday Life*.

Merzel Sensei, Dennis Genpo: *Dharma Heir of Maezumi Roshi (ZCLA):* b 1944, Brooklyn, New York. Raised and schooled in S California. Holds undergraduate degree in economics and MS in educational administration. Taught school for 8 yrs before moving to ZCLA. 1972: began studying with Maezumi Roshi (qv). 1973: ordained a Zen monk. 1978: assisted Maezumi Roshi in guiding student practice. 1979: completed koan study and appointed Dharma Holder. 1980: received Dharma Transmission. 1981: travelled to Japan for installation as Zen priest. Resided with wife Hobai at ZCLA until 1984; held post of ZCLA executive vice-president. Since June 1984 has been guiding the Kanzeon Sangha, an international organisation of groups in Holland, England, Poland, Germany and USA. Recently resided Amsterdam, currently Maine.

Morgan, Daishin: *Abbot of Throssel Hole Priory.* b 1951, London. 1974: ordained and began monastic training at Throssel Hole Priory. 1977: to Shasta Abbey, California, to train under Jiyu Kennett Roshi (qv). 1980: received certification as teacher of Bdsm. 1981: certification as Master (Roshi). 1982: appointed Abbot of Throssel Hole Priory; continues as its spiritual director while running retreats and lecturing all over UK.

Morinaga Roshi, Soko (1925–95): *Rinzai Zen Master.* b Uotsu, Toyama prefecture. Conscripted into WW II at c age 19. 1947: graduated Toyama High School. Loss of faith following the Japanese defeat in War pointed him towards Zen; became disciple of Goto Zuigan Roshi (qv). 1948: ordained a monk. 1949: undertook training at Daitoku-ji (Kyoto). On d of Zuigan Roshi, became incumbent of Daishu-in, a sub-temple in the Daitoku-ji complex. Visited London and taught at the Zen Centre and the Bdst Soc. Books incl *Pointers to Insight*.

Myokyo-ni. (Dr Irmgard Schloegl): *Austrian-born Teacher of Rinzai Zen in UK.* b. 1920, Feldbach, nr Graz. Ph.D. in natural sciences; later specialized in mining. 1950: came to England; Asst Lecturer in Geology, Imperial College (London); joined Bdst Soc. Early 1962: to Japan for 10 yrs Rinzai Zen training at Daitoku-ji (Kyoto) under Oda Sesso Roshi and Morinaga Soko Roshi (both qv). Returned to UK and began teaching at Bdst Soc, where she worked for a time as Librarian. Later founded The Zen Centre in Christmas Humphrey's house in N London (house subsequently dedicated as Zen temple, renamed Shobo-an). 1984: ordained a Zen nun by Morinaga Soko Roshi. Books incl *The Zen Way* and *The Wisdom of the Zen Masters*; has also tr the *Rinzairoku* as *The Record of Rinzai*. Numerous contributions to *Zen Traces*, journal of The Zen Centre.

Nantembo (Nakahara Toju; 1839–1925): *One of the most colourful Zen priests of the modern Era.* Famed for giving students a taste of his heavy Nanten-staff whether they 'spoke or not' and for taking on other Zen Masters in 'Dharma combat'. Had over 3,000 students, incl famous generals Nogi and Kodama; bestowed inka on 6 priests and 25 laymen. Wrote many bks and produced large no of Zen paintings and calligraphies.

Nakagawa Soen Roshi – see Soen Roshi, Nakagawa.

Nhat Hahn, Thich: *Exiled Vietnamese monk, peace activist and poet; proponent of 'Engaged Bdsm',* b. 1926. One-time student at Columbia U; recalled to native Vietnam, then at war, to help with 3rd Way of Reconciliation, an attempt at a viable alternative to the corruption of Saigon and the communism of Hanoi. Established Van Hahn U; also School of Youth for Social Service, which went out to help the peasantry in the war-torn rural areas. Coined term 'Engaged Bdsm' in his book *Vietnam: Lotus in a Sea of Fire*. Prolific writer on meditation and translation of Chinese sutras paralleled in the Pali canon, also compiled a text-based biography of the Buddha, *Old Path, White Clouds*. Other books include *The Miracle of Mindfulness*. Presently lives in exile at Plum Village, Meyrac, France.

Nowick Roshi, Walter: *First American to receive full Dharma transmission in orthodox Rinzai Zen lineage.* Studied piano under Henriette Michelson (onetime member of First Zen Institute,

New York) at Juillard School, New York. Later became lay student of Rinzai Zen at Daitoku-ji (Kyoto) under Goto Zuigan Roshi (qv), who eventually conferred inka on him after c 17 yrs training. Supported himself in Japan playing concerts and teaching piano. Later spent 10 yrs working on his farm in Maine (USA) and teaching music before beginning to teach Zen. Life at his isolated and austere centre in Maine described in *A Glimpse of Nothingness* by Janwillen van der Wetering.

Oda Roshi, Sesso (1901?–66): *Rinzai Zen Master*. Brother senior disciple with Morinaga Soko Roshi (qv) under Goto Zuigan Roshi (qv). One time Abbot of Daitoku-ji (Kyoto).

Omori Roshi, Sogen: b 1904, Yamanashi prefecture. Originally a teacher of kendo (swordsmanship), became Zen priest of Tenryu-ji school in his early 40s. 1948: established Tesshu Society in Tokyo. this became influential and attracted a number of foreign trainees. 1970s and early 80s: Professorand later President of Hanazono U (Kyoto). Author of score of bks of Zen theory and practice, incl *Zen & the Art of Calligraphy* (with Terayama Katsujo). Now retired.

Prabasa Roshi, Dhama. (formerly Geshin Myoko): *German-born Zen teacher*. b 1931 nr Frankfurt. Onetime painter. 1967: emigrated to USA. Became disciple of Joshu Sasaki Roshi (qv). 1970:appointed 1st Head, Mt Baldy Zen Training Center. 1972: ordained teacher of Rinzai Zen. Thereafter founded and directed Intl Zen Institute of America (Los Angeles). Often visits Europe.

Samu Sunim: *Korean Zen Master active in USA*. b. 1941. 1967: to USA; stayed New York City until 1968, working as parcel sorter on night-shift and practising meditation in the daytime; started Zen Lotus Society in Manhattan room. 1968: to Montreal, Canada; applied for refugee status; studied French and conducted meditation sessions. 1972: to Montreal. 1974: into 3-year retreat in basement flat following instructions of teacher, Solbong Sunim (1890–1969); afterwards began to teach Zen. 1979: purchase of Toronto property to become Zen Bdst Temple of Toronto (home of Zen Lotus Society); journal *Spring Wind* inaugurated. 1981: branch temple in Ann Arbor, Michigan. 1985; El Centro Zen Loto de Mexico inaugurated.

Sasaki Roshi, Joshu: *Zen Master currenty based in USA*. b 1907; entered Rinzai Zen (Yoshenji line) training at 14. 1962: came to USA having been resident monk of Shoju-an, a small mt temple in Nagano prefecture. Began toteach in the Los Angeles area. 1966: established Cimarron Zen Center. 1970: established mt Baldy Zen Center. 1974: established Jemez Bodhi Mandala in New Mexico. Umbrella organization – Rinzai-ji. Travels extensively each yr teaching and conducting sesshin, etc.; currently visits First Zen Institute of America, New York. Books incl *Zen: Center of Gravity*.

Sasaki, Ruth Fuller. (1883–1967): *Pioneer of Zem Bdsm in USA*. Early 1930s: to Japan; zazen at Nanzenji (Kyoto) for a few mths. 1938: settled New York City; became supporter of Sokei-an Sasaki's Bdst Society of America (later The First Zen Institure of New York, later still of, America). 1994: m Sokei-an Sasaki (d 1945). 1949: returned to Japan with 3-fold purpose: (1) to find a teacher to take over First Zen Institute; (2) to complete transactions of *Rinzairoku* and other Zen texts; (3) to complete her own Zen training. Studied at Daitokuji with Goto Zuigan Roshi (qv). 1956: allowed to build a small zendo and library, Ryosen-an, at Daitoku-ji; this is a branch of First Zen Institute of America; believed that the only authentic way to studt Zen was in Japan. 1958: ordained a Zen priest at Daitoku-ji, sponsored by Sesso Oda Roshi. Books incl *Zen – A Religion; Zen – A Method for Religious Awakening; Zen Dust* and *The Zen Koan* (with Isshu Miura); *The Recorded Sayings of Layman P'ang* (repr as A Man of Zen, with Iriya Yoshitaka and Dana R Fraser); and *Recorded Sayings of Lin-chi* (with Yoshitaka).

Sasaki, Sokei-an. (Sokei-an Shigetsu Osho; 1882–1945): *Pioneer teacher of Zen in USA*. b. Japan and trained as a dragon carver. Served in Manchuria during Russo-Japanese War. Encouraged to 'carve a Buddha statue' (i.e. become a Buddha himself) by Soyen Shaku (qv). 1906; to USA with group aiming to found Rinzai Zen monastery in California and begin teaching Zen to Americans. After mission left, stayed in USA and eventually established himself as a Zen teacher in New York. 1931: Bdst Society of America formed (later First Zen institute of New York, later still of America). Group slowly grew and in 1938 joined by Ruth Fuller Everett.her son-in-law, Alan Watts, also studied with Sokei-an for a short time. 1942: internment camp as enemy alien. 1944: m Ruth Everett.

Schloegel, Dr. Irmhard – see Myokyo-ni.

Senzaki Sensei, Nyogen. **(1876–1958):** *Pioneer teacher of Rinzai Zenin USA* b and orphaned in Siberia; finally came under patronage of Soto Zen priest and kegon scholar who began his ed in Chinese Classics and Bdsm at c age 5. Studied Soto Zen, Shingon snf Vineya School teachings. Met Soyen Shaku. 1896: entered Engaku-ji, despite aving TB. 1901: left Engaku-ji. Influenced by 'kindergarten' ideas of Frobel, set up nursery school (Mentorgarten). c 1905: went to USA; joined Soyen Shaku at home of Mr and Mrs Alexander Russell in San Francisco. Soon discharged; parted from Soyen Shaku in Golden Gate Park; told to work with Americans and not 'utter the B of *Bdsm*' for 17 yrs. To 1992; worked variously mostly in hotel business, then hired a hall in San Francisco and gave first lecture; thus begun his 'floating zendo'. 1927; small financial aid from Japan. 1931: moved to Los Angeles and set up zendo (Mentorgarten Meditation Hall, a.k.a. Tosen Zkutsu). Lived austere monkish lifestyle. 1934: began correspondence with Nakagawa Soen Roshi (qv). 1943: interned as an enemy alien. 1945: took top floor apartment at Miyako Hotel in Little Tokyo, Los Angeles; Mentorgarten meetings took place there; students included Robert Aitken (1947) and Garry Snyder (briefly). 1955: brief return visit to Japan; met Eido Tai Shimano Roshi (qv). BooKs incl *The Iron Flure.* (ed. Ruth McCandless); *Zen Flesh, Zen Bones* (with P. Reps), and *Bdsm and Zen.*

Seung Sahn. **(Soen Sunim – alt. Soen Sa Nim):** *Korean Zen Master based in USA.* b 1927, Korea, as Lee Duk An during Japanese occupation. Parents Christian. Joined underground mvts. After WW II, studied W philosophy at Dongguk U; became disenchanted with both politics and scholarship, 1948: became Bdst monk and embarked upon intensive meditation. At 32 received Dharma Transmission from Zen Master Ko Bong. During Korean warspent 5 yrs in S Korean Army; afterwards returned to monastic life; became abbot of temple in New Seoul. Then spent 9 yrs in Japan and Hong Kong, founding temples and teaching. 1972: went to USA; at first worked in a laundry in providence, Rhode Island; began to gather students from Brown U; Providence Zen Center developed, now head temple for many sub-centres and affiliated groups both in N America and in Europe (Poland, W Germany, etc.). Books incl *Only Don't Know, Dropping Ashes on the Buddha* and *Boe of Space: Zen Poems.*

Shimano Roshi, Eido Tai: *Zen Master active in USA.* b 1932. Responsible for guiding Zen Studies Soc. 1976; International Dai Bosatsu Zendo founded in Catskill Mts, new York State (1st traditional Zen monastery in N America).

Soen Roshi, Nakagawa. **(1907–84):** *Japanese Zen Master and noted poet.* ed. Tokyo U.; majored in Japanese literature; then became Zen monk and trained under Yamamoto Genpo Roshi at Ryutaku-ji. Went with Genpo Roshi to Kyoto; Genpo briefly Abbot of Myoshin-ji; then to Manchuria, where Gempo Abbot of branch monasteryof Myoshin-ji during WW II. 1951: became Abbot of Ryutaku-ji, Mishima. 1974: retired. He was known particularly for his innovative and creative changes in ritual, and for his interest in the development of Zen Bdsm in the West. He was also a nationally known poet . . .' (RobertAitken). Late 1930s: began to correspond with Nyogen Senzaki (qv). 1948: 1st of series of visits to USA; led various sesshin after Senzaki's death. Instrumental in establishment of Diamond Sangha in Hawaii; encouraged other US Zen centersin Los Angeles and anew York, where disciples Eido Tai Shimano Roshi and nakagawa Khudo Roshi continue to teach.

Soen Sunim *(see Seung Sahn)*

Soyen Shaku. **(1895–1919):** 'The first modern Zen masterof Japan'. Pupil of Imagita Kosen Roshi and teacher of D.T. Sezuki. Received inka at 25. Afterwards sent by Kosen Roshi to Keian U to study W subjects, then on to Sir Lanka to study Theravada Bdsm. Returned to Japan after 2 yrs as Theravada bhikkhu (later disrobed); on d of Kosen Roshi (1892) became Master of Engaku-ji. 1893: at World Parliament of Religions in Chicago. Is reputed to have said: 'Following history, it will take 300 yrs for Zen to come to its full flowering in America.' 1905–6: taught in San Francisco and adjacent cities with D.T. Suzuki (qv) translating; talks collected, issued as *Sermons of a Bdst Abbot.* Was a man with a progressive, modern outlook, who wished to evitalize Bdsm and make it relevant for the coming age. 'His attitude was something like that of a free thinker, grounded on Bdst idealism, hopeful of joining with other religious leaders in forging a world class way of mutual benefit for the sentiment beings of the future' (Mary Farkas). Two pupils also taught in SA: Nyogen Senzaki Sensei and Sokei-an Sasaki (both qv).

Stevens, John: *Bdst scholar, translator, calligrapher and Aikido instructor,* b. 1947, Chicago. 1975: ordained a Soto Zen priest. 1978: graduated, Bdst Seminary Tohoku Social Welfare U, Sendai,Japan. 1984: resigned from the priesthood. Holds 5th dan blackc belt in Aikido. Current posting: Professor of Bdst Studies and Aikido Instructor, Tohoku Social Welfare U. Director. Zen Art Soc. Publications incl *One Robe, One Bowl: The Zen Poetry of Ryokan; Mountain Tasting; Zen Haiku by Taneda Santoka; Sacred Calligraphy of the East; Aikido: The Way of Harmony; The Sword of No-Sword: Life of Master Warrior Tesshu; Zen Guide, Where to Meditate in Japan; Shobogenzo:* English translation, with K. Nishiyana et al; *Abundant Peace: The Life of Morihei Ueshiba, Founder of Aikido; Marathon Monks of Mt. Hiei.*

Suzuki, Beatrice Erskine (née Lane): *American pioneer of Bdst studies.* Graduate of Columbia U. 1911: m D.T. Suzuki (qv); collaborated with him in his work – co-Editor of *The Eastern Bdst,* etc. Student of Soyen Shaku (qv); latterly drawn to Shingon. Onetime Professor of English at Otani U (Kyoto). d 1939. Books incl *Bdst Readings, Mahayana Bdsm* etc.

Suzuki, Daisetz Teitara. (1870–1966): 'The Man Who Brought Zen to the West' Also wrote many books and articles about Shin Buddhism. b Kanazawa, Japan. After school, taught English. 1891: entered Tokyo Semmon Gakko (Waseda U.). 1891: began Zen training under Imagita Kosen Roshi and Soyen Shaku (qv) at Engaku-ji (Kamakura). 1897: to USA (LaSalle, Ill.) to work for Open Court Publishing Co. 1909: returned to Japan; became lecturer at Peers' School and at Tokyo Imperial U. 1911: m Beatrice Erskine Lane. 1912: visited England at invitation of Swedenborg Soc. 1921: began publication of *The Eastern Bdst;* also moved to Kyoto to Chair of Bdst Philosophy at Otani U. 1936: attended World Congress of Faiths in London and lectured on Zen and Japanese culture at various British and American u's. 1946: founded Matsugaoka Bunko ('Pine Hill Library') in Kamakura, nr. Engaku-ji; began publication of *The Cultural East.* 1947: lectured on Bdsm to Emperor of Japan. 1950–58: lectured and toured extensively in the W, notably in USA; held posts at Columbia U. Books incl *Essays in Zen Bdms* (3 series), *Studies in the Lankavatara Sutra, Introduction to Zen Bdsm, Manual of Zen Bdsm, Japanese Bdsm, The Essence of Bdsm, The Zen Doctrine of No-Mind, Living by Zen, A Miscellany on the Shin Teaching of Bdsm, Studies in Zen, Mysticism: Christian and Bdst, Zen & Japanese Bdsm, Zen and Japanese Culture, Zen Bdsm & Psychoanalysis, The Field of Zen, Shin Bdsm, What Is Zen?, Sengai the Zen Master* and *Collected Writings on Shin Bdsm.* Translations include *The Lankavatara Sutra, The Awakening of Faith* (Asvaghosha), *Sermons of a Bdst Abbot* (Soyen Shaku), *The Life of Shinran Shonin* and *The Kyogyoshinsho.* Biography by A. Irwin Switzer 111. Memoir: *Suzuki Remembered,* ed. Masao Abe.

Suzuki Roshi, Shunryu. (1904–71): *Eminent teacher of Soto Zen in USA: founder of San Francisco Zen Center.* b Japan; father a Zen Master; at early age began Zen training under Gyokujun Soon-daiosho, a Soto Master, and other teachers. Recognized as a Zen Master c 30; became responsible for many temples and a monastery. During WW II led a pacifist group. 1959: to USA intending only short visit but settled in San Francisco area, where a group formed. 1962: San Francisco Zen Center formally inaugurated; this grew to occupy a number of Californian locations, incl Zen Mountain Center at Tassajara Springs (1st Zen monastery in USA with facilities for long-term practice; established 1967). 1971: installed Richard Baker (qv) as Dharma Heir. Author of the classic *Zen Mind, Beginner's Mind.*

Suzuki Roshi, Sochu: *Soto Zen Master with W connections.* b 1921, Tochigi prefecture. 1931: entered Seitai-ji temple, Mino, Gifu prefecture after d of parents. Stayed for some yrs in Taiwan where his Master established a school of Zen. 1939: entered a Rinzai school; soon drafted into Army; survived WW II at Saipan Island. 1947: entered Hanazono College. 1957: ordained as monk and entered Ryutaku-ji; studied under Genpo Yamamoto Roshi and Soen Nakagawa Roshi (qv). 1977: became Abbot of Ryutaku-ji. Has travelled abroad to W German, Israel and Italy and has visited London on a no of occasions.

Takashina Roshi, Rosen: *Primate of the Soto Zen sect.* One-time President, Japan Bdst Assn. Writings incl *A Tongue-tip Taste of Zen (Zetto Zemmi).*

Terayama, Katsujo. (Tanchu): *b 1938, Saitama prefecture. Studied for many yrs with Omori Sogen (qv), receiving inka in 1971. 1965: pilgrimage to Bdst sites in India. Currently Head of Zen Calligraphy Soc (Hitsuzenkai) and professor at Nishogakusha U (Tokyo). Has instructed many foreign students and given exhibitions and workshops in Europe. Author of several imp studies of Zen art; in English* Zen & the Art of Calligraphy (with Omori Sogen).

Tesshu, Master Warrior. (Yamaoka Tesshu): *Zen Master, Calligrapher and Swordsman.* Widely regarded as saviour of Japanese Bdsm in general and Zen in particular during Meiji period. Founded and restored scores of temples; protected Bdst treasures from thieves and vandals; defended Dharma against anti-Bdst forces; supported a small army of priests and nuns, down-and-out sumarai, beggars and stray animals. Established 'No-Sword' School; was also one of the gtest Zen artists of modern times, producing 1 million + wks, mostly to raise finance for noble causes. Biography: *The Sword of No-Sword*, by John Stevens.

Thien-An, Thich. (1926–80): *Late Vietnamese Zen Master and scholar active in USA.* Trained in Lin-chi (Rinzai) tradition but adopted ecumenical approach. 1966: came to USA; lectured at UCLA. 1967: began to teach in Hollywood. Founded Int'l Bdst Meditation Center and, 1973, College (later U) Oriental Studies, Los Angeles. 1975: after fall of Saigon , active in helping Vietnamese refugees to USA.

Tsuji Somei: *Present-day Master.* b c 1903. Studied at Tokyo U. of Commerce (now Hitotsubashu U); later went into business, working as accountant for a big oil company. 1925: began Zen training at Engakuhi under Furukawa Hyodo Roshi (qv).Currently incumbent at Funi Zendo, Tokyo.

Uchiyama Roshi, Kosho. *Former Abbot of Antai-ji.* has had many foreign students; author of 2 bks in English – Refining Yr Life and Approach to Zen.

van de Wetering, Janwillem: *Dutch-born writer on Zen.* b 1931, The Netherlands. Wrote two books on experience in Zen centres; The Empty Mirror describes 1½ yr stay at Daitoku-ji (Kyoto), and *A Glimpse* [in US *A Touch*] of *Nothingness* represents his participation in an obscure settlement on E Coast of USA. Also writer of thrillers; spent 7 yrs on active duty with Dutch Special Constabulary. Currently resides in Maine, USA.

Yamada Roshi, Mumon: *Japanese Rinzai Zen Master.* b 1900, Aichi prefecture, ordained a Bdst priest at 19 by Kawaguchi Ekai (adventurer-monk-scholar who was 1st Japanese to enter Tibet and spent 3 yrs there prior to dramatic flight). Was president of Hanazono U for 30 yrs; trained many of the current generation of Rinzai priests. Also served as Primate of Myoshin-ji Rinzai school prior to retirement. Several foreign students have trained with him; has also visited main Zen centres overseas. Perhaps the most prolific modern Zen teachers; his huge corpus of wk being published by Zen Culture Institute, Kyoto (which he helped found).

Yamahata Roshi, Hogen Daido: *Japanese Zen Master.* Abbot of Chogenji (Japan). Trained in both Rinzai and Soto schools. Now leads Soto-style sesshin in Europe each yr that incorporate hatha yoga in addition to traditional elements. 'Hogensan's teaching imparts the classic Zen flavour of transcendental understanding coupled with a direct down-to-earth approach to life's realities' (press release). In UK teaches at Gaia House, Devon.

Yasutani Roshi, Hakuun. (1885–1973): *Japanese Zen Master.* At age 5 yrs, head shaven and sent to live in a temple. Remained there until 12. At 13, became novice at large Soto temple; then, after 2 more yrs of primary school, went on to a Soto seminary and later spent 4 yrs in teachers' training school. At age 30, m and begot 5 children; remained nominally a priest but worked as schoolteacher for c 10 yrs and continued zazen practice. At 40 began training with Sogaku Harada Roshi (qv); relinquished principalship of school; became temple priest and began aT5tending sesshin at Hosshin-ji. Attained kensho during 2nd session using koan Mu. Received inka from Harada Roshi at 58 and appointed Dharma Heir. held periodic sesshin at his temple in the suburbs of Tokyo and elsewhere in the vicinity; also in Hokkaido and Kyushu. 1962–9: travelled annually to USA. At 80,undertook extended stay in USA/ 'Husband, father, schoolmaster, and ultimately Zen master, Hakuun Yasutani did not achieve his distinction by avoiding the pains and joys incident tothe life of the ordinary man but in experiencing and then transcending them. In this his life reflects the Mahayana ideal that Self-realisation is for the householder no less than the celibate monk' (Philip Kapleau). Wrote and published 5 vols of commentary on the *Mumonkan*, the *Hekiganroku*, the *Shoyoroku* and the *Denkoroku*; also on the *Five Degrees of Tozan*.

26   Pure Land Buddhism

Austin, Rev Jack (1917–93): *Pioneer of Shin Bdsm in UK*, b Caerleon, Gwent (S Wales, UK). With Richard Robinson, founded Dharma Study Group for studying Mahayana sutras. 1946–52: a member of 1st ad hoc council of Bdst Soc. 1952: with Richard Robinson, ordained by Ven Sumangalo (qv) in London. 1953: launched *Western Bdst* to promote Mahayana Bdsm. 1954: initiated into Arya Maitreya Mandala (founded by Lama Govinda (qv)) in Das Buddhistische Haus, W Berlin. 1966: initiated into Soto Zen by Chisan Koho Zenji (qv) in London. With others founded the Hannyakai to practise zazen under proper tuition for the first time in the UK, inviting Sochu Suzuki Roshi (qv) from Japan (later London Zen Soc). Served as Bdst representative on various committees. 1975: Development Officer of World Congress of Faiths, organizing conferences and interfaith activities; served on several related committees, incl Bdst Religious Adviser, especially in education. Contributed to numerous Bdst and related publications, incl new ed of Dhammapada for the Bdst Soc. 1976: co-founder of Shin Bdst Assn in London (Patron: Chief Abbot Kosho Ohtani). 1977: ordained a Hongwan-ji priest in Kyoto. Has also visited Shin temples in Hawaii, San Francisco and New York.

Bloom, Alfred: *Dean, Institute of Bdst Studies; author.* b 1926, Philadelphia. 1951: Eastern Baptist Theological Seminary, AB and ThB; m; 2 children. 1953: Andover-Newton Theological Seminary, BD and STM. 1963: Harvard, PhD. 1953: ordained Baptist minister. 1957–9: Fulbright scholar. 1970: Prof. Religion, U of Hawaii. Member, American Academy of Religion. Publications incl *Shinran's Gospel of Pue Grace, The Life of Shinran, The Journey of Self-Acceptance, Indian and Far Eastern Religious Traditions, Resource of Modern Living – Tannisho,* and *Shoshinge: The Heart of Shin Bdsm.*

Chevrier, Rev Jodo A: *Swiss Shin leader.* Has produced many Fr trs of imp Shin texts. 1975: ordained as Rev Jodo at Nishi Honganji. Ed. "The Link", newsletter for European Shin Bdsts.

Clifton, Robert: – see Sumangalo.

Eracle, Rev Jean: *Swiss Shin leader and translator.* Curator and researcher in Asiatic Dept, Ethnographical Museum, Geneva. 1970: President, Société Bouddhique Swiss Jodo-Shinshu, with chapel nr Geneva linked to Nishi Hongwan-ji. Publications incl 1st complete tr. of three Pure Land sutras. Also *La Doctrine Bouddhique de la Terre Pure, Un Bouddhisme pour tous: l'Amidisme.*

Fenzl, Friedrich: *Leader of Shin mvt in Austria.* b 1932. Although read Bhikshu Subhadra's *Bdst Catechism* in 1949 did not formally become Bdst until 1955. Became associated with Bdst Soc of Vienna and George Grimm's Old Bdst Community (Bavaria). 1960: under the influence of H. Pieper, converted to Jodo Shinshu; set up Austrian branch in Salzburg (where he works at U). 1965–75: edited newsletter *Mahayana.* Established social welfare body along Bdst lines.

Furukawa, Rev Tariyu. Head priest of the Seimeizan Schweitzer Temple, Kumamoto, Japan. Also recognized as a Zen Roshi and master calligrapher, with exhibitions in Italy and Japan. Publications incl 2 books on the Tannisho (in Japanese). Visited Europe often, in contact with groups in Italy, Poland and UK, also China. Campaigner for prison reform, peace and international friendship.

Hunt, Ernest (Rev Shinkaku Hunt, 1876–1967): *Possibly 1st Western Shin propagator.* b Hoddesden (UK), ed Kensington, Eastbourne; later went to sea. 1915: emigrated to Hawaii;

worked in plantations; joined local Jodo Shin temples. 1924: ordained a priest of the Hongwan-ji by Bishop Imamura; became active in imparting (via English lang) the authentic Bdst teachings to young generation of Japanese immigrants (Nisei); founded and became headmaster of schools and won popularity thru social welfare activities among Bdst community. 1932: Founded Intl Bdst Inst of Hawaii. 1952: joined Soto Zen temple in Honolulu. 1962: 'choro' ordination from Vice Abbot Iwamoto of Sojiji; later received Dharma succession from Zenkyo Komagata, was given name Daiko and later still made daiosho. Books incl *An Outline of Bdsm, The Religion of Wisdom & Compassion; Bdsm in Hawaii* and numerous wks for children.

Inagaki, Rev Prof Hisai: *Executive Secretary of Intl Assn of Shin Bdst Studies (founded 1984).* Currently Prof of English at Ryukoku U. 1970s: lectured at SOAS (London U); the (British) Pure Land Bdst Fellowship initiated in his house at that time. Editor of *The Pure Land.* Member of the English and Portuguese Translation Ctres at Hongwanji International Centre. Editor of Ryokoku Translation series. Publications include *A Dictionary of Japanese Bdst Terms; A Glossary of the Sukhavativyuha Sutras, The Three Pure Land Sutras, The Amida Sutra Mandala, The Way of Nembutsu Faith.*

Inagaki, Rev Zuiken Saizo (1885–1981): *Shin Bdst Priest.* A prime inspirer of the development of Jodoshinu in Europe. Born Himeji, taught English, became student of Riken Katsura and ordained priest of Nishi Hongwanji in 1945. Publications incl over 70 books in Japanese, translated Anjin and Tannisho into English.

Kell, Gerhard: *2nd leader of German Shin mvt.* b 1948, Halle; studied modern langs and law at Free U (W Berlin) and privately E religions. 1978: joined German Jodo Community; confirmed at Nishi Hongwan-ji. 1978: succeeded H. Pieper (qv) a leader. Specializes in tr Shin Bdst texts.

Murakami, Toshio: *Bishop, Bdst Churches of Canada.* b 1931, Kita Kyushu-shi, Fukaoka, Japan. 1959: MA from Ryukoku U, Kyoto; ordained Jodo Shinshu minister, Bdst Churches of America. 1959–60: orientation at Berkeley. 1960–2: Oregon. 1963–8: San Jose. 1964: m Yoko Murakami; 2 daughters. 1968–71: Monterey. 1971–7: Director, BCA Bureau of Education. 1981–3: Exec Asst to Bishop. 1982–3: Executive Director, Inst of Bdst Studies. 1984–6: Oakland.

Ohtani, Lord Kosho: *Chief Abbot Emeritus, Nishi Hongwan-ji, Kyoto.* President of the International Assoc of Bdst Studies. Has visited Europe several times and conducted ordinations, refuge ceremonies, consecrations, etc. Currently oversees the development of Shin Buddhism in Europe.

Peel, Rev Shitoku Adriaan: *Chairman, Federation des Associations Bouddhiques de Belgique/Federatie van de Boeddhistische Verenigingen Belgie; Ed, Dutch Shin journal Eko* 1956–7; ed Theravada oriented periodical *Magga.* 1976: became active in Jodo Shinshu; founded 1st Belgian branch in Antwerp. 1977: initiated as Shaku Shitoku in London by Lord Kosho Ohtani (qv) of Nishi Hongwan-ji. Chairman, Belgian branch of World Congress of Faiths; Belgian representative of Intl Assn of Shin Bdst Studies (Kyoto). Dean, Faculty of Comparative Study of Religions, Antwerp. Publications incl *Shin-Boeddhisme – De Simpele Weg; Problems of Shin Bdsm in Europe & Its Relations to Other Bdst Denominations; Some Fundamental Differences between Bdsm & Christianity,* etc.

Pieper, Rev Harry (1902–78): *Seminal leader of German Shin Mvt.* b Berlin; attended Das Buddhistische Haus. 1946: formed a Mahayana group. 1951: joined Arya Maitreya Mandala; received ordination and became Secretary. Met Prof Osamu Yamada: invited him to lecture on Shin Bdsm. 1954: on visit of Kosho Ohtani (qv), received initiation in Nishi Hongwan-ji lineage; resigned from AMM. 1956: founded 1st Pure Land Assn in Europe (Buddhistische Gemeinschaft Jodo-Shin). 1962: founded 1st Buddhist prison chaplaincy in German-speaking world. Tr many US and Japanese bks on Shin Bdsm.

Pym, Jim: A founder member of the Shin Bdst Assoc and The Pure Land Bdst Fellowship, a non-sectarian network of those interested in Other Power/Pure Land Buddhism. Studied

Jodoshinshu with Rev. Austin, initiated into Jodoshinshu 1976. Currently contact for PLBF and editor of Pure Land Notes.

Sasaki, Rev Prof Esho: Secretary of International Assoc of Bdst Culture, which promotes Shin Buddhism Worldwide, particularly Europe. Professor of Buddhism at Kyoto Women's University.

Snow, Elson: English editor of The Wheel of Dharma, newspaper of Bdst Churches of America. Publications include *Blue Tiles*, *Women at Yoshizaki*, translations of Kisamboge and Ogon-ge.

Sumangalo, Ven (Robert Stuart Clifton, 1903–63): *Pioneering W Shin Priest in USA.* b Birmingham, Alabama, USA as Harold Amos Eugene Newman. Travelled in E. 1st Wstnr to be ordained a priest of Nishi Hongwan-ji by Ven Kosho Ohtani (qv). Returned to USA; performed priestly function while working as probation officer, etc. 1951: founded W Bdst Order, 'an organization dedicated to interpreting the Dharma to the W and to establishing groups where none existed' (*The Western Bdst*). Later moved to Malaya and worked vigorously for Bdsm there until his d.

Tabrah, Rev Ruth: Shin Bdst Minister, author and lecturer. A director of Bdst Study Center Press, Hawaii. Publications include *The Monk Who Dared*, *The Natural Way of Shin Buddhism*, and *Ajatasatru: the story of who we are* (with Shoji Matsumoto).

Tsuji, Kenryu Takashi: *Minister, Bdst Churches of America.* b 1919, Mission City, BC, Canada. 1946: m Sakaye Kawabata; 5 children. 1937: U of BC, Canada. 1942: U of Toronto. 1948: Ryukoku U, Kyoto. 1958: ordained minister, Jodo Shinshu, Bdst Churches of America. 1968: Bishop, Bdst Churches of America. 1941–2: minister, Vancouver Bdst Church. 1942–5: Slocan Bdst Church. 1945–58: Toronto Bdst Church. 1958–68: National Director of Bdst Education, BCA. 1968–81: Bishop, BCA; President of Inst of Bdst Studies. 1981–: Eko-ji Bdst Temple. Editor, Program of Studies of Bdst Sunday Schools. 1960: Publications incl *Three Lectures on Tannisho*. Has made documentary films, incl *In the Footsteps of Shinran*, *The Story of Hongwan-ji*, *A Bdst Pilgrimage*, and *Sri Lanka, Where the Dhamma is Preserved*.

Yamaoka, Seigen Haruo: *Former Bishop, Bdst Churches of America (1981); President, Inst of Bdst Studies.* b 1934, Fresno, California. 1966: m Shigeko Masuyama; 2 children. 1956: BA from California State U, Fresno. 1961: MA from Ryukoku U, Kyoto. 1969: MRE, and 1979, PhD (Ministry in Religious Education) from Pacific School of Religion, Berkeley, Cal. 1964: ordained, Bdst Churches of America: Research Committee, BCA. Minister, Bdst Church of Oakland. 1971–81: Stockton Bdst Temple. 1969–71: Registrar, Inst of Bdst Studies. Berkeley, Cal. 1970–5: member, Research Committee, BCA. 1971–5 and 1979–81: member, IBS Board of Trustees. 1972–5: English Secretary, Ministers Assn. 1977: member, Board of Bdst Education. 1979–81: Chairman, Ministers Assn. Publications incl *Compassion in Encounter*, *Teaching & Practice of Jodo Shinshu*, *Jodo Shinshu – Religion of Human Experience*, *Meditation – Gut Enlightenment . . . The Way of Hara* and *Six Aspects of Jodo Shinshu*. Office; San Francisco.

27 Nichiren Tradition

Causton, Richard (1920–95): *Chairman and Director General of Nichiren Shoshu (UK).* ed Sandhurst. Joined Border Regiment; remained a professional soldier to age 38. WW II: served in Burma. 1958: retired from Army with rank of Lieut. Colonel. Joined Harrods; later became General Sales Manager for Dunhill cigarettes; moved to Far East to set up Dunhill operation there; discovered Soka Gakkai Buddhism. After many yrs of 'trying to be a good Christian', this was 'an electrifying experience'. 1971: committed himself to NS. 1974: returned to UK. 1977: gave up business to join permanent staff of NSUK. 1975: became Ch and DG; also Vice President of Nichiren Shoshu European Institute and Vice President of Soka Gakkai International.

Fujii, The Most Ven Nichidatsu (1884–1985): *Founder and preceptor of the Nipponzan Myohoji order.* 1903: became a monk. 1918: began to preach Bdsm publicly, travelling widely through China, Korea, Manchuria and Japan. Warned of the growing militarism in Japan. Disciples joined him in the practice of beating the hand-drum and chanting the prayer for peace (*Namu myoho renge kyo*). 1924: first Nipponzan Myohoji formed at Tagonoura, nr Mt Fujji. 1931–33: travelled in India to regenerate Bdsm there; met Gandhi. Throughout WW II, prayed and regularly fasted for early peace. After War, began promoting construction of peace pagodas in Japan and later elsewhere. In UK, pagodas built at Milton Keynes and Battersea Park (London). Books incl *Buddhism for World Peace, Beating Celestial Drums, Ichienbudai, The Time Has Come*, etc.

Hasegawa, Hiromi: *Founder of Reiyukai in UK. b 1947, Kyoto. Became a teacher. Mid-1970s: visited UK for study purposes; stayed in Norfolk; later returned to Japan and converted to Reiyukai. 1976: returned to Norfolk to (successfully) establish Reiyukai in England.*

Ikeda, Daisaku: *Current (3rd) President of Soka Gakkai (Nichiren Shoshu).* b 1928, Ormori, Tokyo, 5th son of edible seaweed farmer. Childhood dogged by poverty and ill-health. 1940: left school at age 12; persevered to read in spare time – and later to write. c. 1947: introduced to SG 'and knew instantly that this was a way of life he must follow.' Greatly influenced by Josei Toda (qv), 2nd President of SG, his 'master in life'. 1960: on Toda's d, became 3rd President of SG. Set out to raise membership to 3 million, to erect a large reception hall at Head Temple and 'to arouse an awakening in religious circles'. 1962: 1st goal realized. 1964: 2nd goal realized. 3rd is 'forever in his heart and actions'. 1975: Soka Gakkai International formed; began international activities, holding dialogues with eminent world leaders and leading intellectuals, arranging cultural exchanges, etc. 1972: Sho Hondo, Grand Main Temple, opened at Head Temple (Taiseki-ji). 1983: presented with UN Peace Award by UN Sec Gen Perez de Cuellar. Books include *The Living Buddha, My Recollections, Dialogue on Life (A Buddhist Perspective on Life and the Universe); Life an Enigma, a Precious Jewel; A Lasting Peace; Buddhism: the First Millennium; Choose Life* (with Arnold Toynbee), *The Human Revolution (5 vols)*, etc.

Kotani, Kimi (1901–71): *Co-founder of Reiyukai.* b Miura, Kanagawa prefecture, Japan. 1925: m Yasukichi Kubo, elder brother of Kakutaro Kubo (qv), founder of Reiyukai. Worked with Kubo to expand movement and eventually became its Hon President (1930). After d of Kubo, widened scope of Reiyukai as social welfare organization; created many youth programmes. 1963: Kotani Scholarship established.

Kubo, Kakutaro (1890 or 92–1944): *Founder of Reiyukai.* b Kominato, Japan, the birthplace of Nichiren Daishonin. A carpenter, later in life taken up by Baron Sengaku, a fervent follower of Nichiren. Lived in Tokyo; employer in Imperial Household Ministry. 1919: began formulating own philosphy. 1920s and 30s: worked to attract support for his vision of a lay Bdst society. 1930: installed as Chairman of Board of Directors. 1940: registered his organization with the city of Tokyo. Until d worked with Kimi Kotani (qv). 1958: Kubo Memorial Hall completed in Tokyo and dedicated as social welfare facility.

Kubo, Dr Tsugunari: *Current President of Reiyukai.* Took over Presidency following d of Kimi Kotani (qv) in 1971.

Makiguchi, Tsunesaburo (1871–1944): *Founder & 1st President of Soka Kyoiku Gakkai (forerunner of Soka Gakkai).* b Niigata prefecture, NW Japan. At 14, went to Hokkaido; ed Sapporo Normal School (now Hokkaido University of Education). Later served as teacher and principal of several elementary schools in Sapporo and Tokyo. Formed small organization of educators. 1928: converted to Nichiren Shoshu. 1930: established Soka Kyoiku Gakkai (lit 'Value-creating Education Society'); worked to spread knowledge of Nichiren's teachings. 1943: arrested together with other leaders for opposing Shintoism and criticizing war effort. d in prison at age 73. Publications incl *Soka Kyoikugau Taikei* (The System of Value-Creating Pedagogy) and *Kyodaka Kenkyu* (Research Studies in Folk Culture of Local Communities).

Naganuma, Mrs Myoko (1899–1957): *One of the founding inspirations of Rissho Kosei-Kai.* b of farming stock in Saitama prefecture. Came to Tokyo; worked in factory; married man in ice business. Due to disease, had to drink much milk; met N. Niwano (qv), then in the milk business. Joined Reiyukai. 1938: with Niwano set up Dai Nippon Rissho Kosei-Kai; became 1st Vice-President.

Niwano, Rev Nikkyo: *Founder of Rissho Kosei-Kai.* b 1906, Tokamachi, Niigata prefecture, Japan, of farming stock; named Shikazo. Saw military service in Japanese Navy. No higher education. 1923: went to Tokyo; apprenticed to shopkeeper; studied religion, divination, Chinese classics, etc. Daughter's sickness led him to join Reiyukai. 1934: set up milk shop in order to meet people. 1938: seceded from Reiyukai, not because of doctrinal differences, but due to growing awareness of his own powers of leadership and consequent desire for independence; with Mrs M. Naganuma (qv), established Dai Nippon Rissho Kosei-Kai; became its 1st President. Membership has since grown to c 5 million with branches throughout Japan and overseas. Practices incl Hoza (Circle of Compassion) and the discipline of Veneration. 1979: won Templeton Prize. Books incl *Bdsm for Today.*

Toda, Josei (1900–58): *2nd President of Soka Gakkai.* In 1920s, joined staff of school where Tsunesaburo Makiguchi (qv) headmaster; joined Makiguchi's small organization. c 1928: followed Makiguchi in converting to Nichiren Shoshu, joined M's small embyro organization. Interned with Makiguchi during WW II. Took over Presidency after d of Makiguchi. Had powerful spiritual experience in Sugamo Prison. 1945: 'Toda emerged at the end of the war fired with the determination that he would rebuild and develop the lay society' (Nichiren Shoshu leaflet). Health v poor but began new organization and called it Soka Gakkai. At d membership 750,000 + households.

Wilde, Julian: *Secretary of British branch of Reiyukai.* b 1951, Norwich (UK). Attracted to Bdsm at c 11 yrs; studied Zen, Tibetan Bdsm. 1976: encountered Hiromi Hasegawa (qv); joined Reiyukai; visited Japan. Books incl *The Grimoire of Chaos Magick.*

Williams, George: *General Director of Nichiren Shoshu of America (NSA).* Of Japanese origin, changed his name from Massayasu Sadanaga. Came to UCLA in early 1950s to study politics; set about creating NSA.

28 Miscellaneous

Ambedkar, Dr Bhim Rao (1891–1956): *Founder of the Indian movement for converting harijans (untouchables) from Hinduism to Bdsm.* Movement of Bombay Legislative Assembly, later Law Minister in the Central Government at Indian independence. 1956: at Nagpur, he and his wife along with c 500,000 followers formally renounced the Hindu religion and espoused Bdsm. Work carried on by Indian Bdst Society, which he founded. Book: *The Buddha and His Dhamma*. See *Ambedkar & Buddhism* by Sangharakshita.

Arnold, Sir Edwin (1832–1904): *English poet and journalist.* b 1832, Gravesend, Kent. ed King's School, Rochester; King's College, London and U. C. Oxford. 1852: won Newdigate Prize. 1853: 1st book of poems published. 1854: m Katherine Biddulph. Became master at King Edward VI School, Birmingham; afterwards Principal of Deccan College, Poona (India). Mastered Sanskrit; produced translations. 1861: became Asian Affairs correspondent of *Daily Telegraph*; worked for the paper for c 40 yrs. 1879: *The Light of Asia* appeared – 'the "best seller" of all Bdst books in the West' (Christmas Humphreys). Later drew attention to the poor state of the Bdst holy places in N India; initiated scheme for buying Bodh Gaya from its (then) Hindu owner. Honours: Companion of the (Order of) the Star of India (British), and Order of the White Elephant (Thai); knighted by Queen Victoria.

Batchelor, Stephen: *Writer and translator.* b 1953, Scotland. Travelled in the East. 1971: began Tib Bdst studies. 1974: ordained as Gelugpa monk (Gelong Jhampa Thabkay); studied with Geshe Rabten (qv) in India and Switzerland. 1981–85: ordained at Popch'on Sunim and trained in Korean Zen with Kusan Sunim (qv) at Songgwang Sa Monastery. At Sharpham North Community, S Devon (UK) till 1990 and conducts retreats in UK, Europe and USA. Publications incl *Alone with Others (Outlines for an Existential Approach to Buddhism)*; *Flight (An Existential Conception of Buddhism)*; and *The Jewel in the Lotus (A Survey of the Buddhism of Tibet)*, *The Faith to Doubt*, *The Awakening of the West*, *The Tibet Guide* and *Buddhism Without Beliefs*. Tr include Shantideva's *Bodhicaryavatara* (from the Tib), Geshe Rabten's *Echoes of Voidness*.

Blavatsky, Helena Petrovna (1831–1891): *Co-founder of the Theosophical Society in New York 1875.* 1880: declared herself a Bdst in Galle (Sri Lanka). Credited with inspiring Bdst revival in Sri Lanka. Books incl *Isis Unveiled*, *The Secret Doctrine* and *The Voice of the Silence*.

Blofeld, John (Chu Ch'an; 1913–87): *English writer and translator specializing in Bdsm and Taoism.* ed Haileybury College and Cambridge (Downing College); read natural sciences at latter; did not take degree but left in 2nd yr and went to China. 1933–9: in China; visited many Bdst monasteries; formally became pupil of Master Hsü Yün (qv) but actually received training in Ch'an meditation from his pupils at Hua T'ing Monastery, nr. Kunming, Yunnan; also received Vajrayana teachings. 1939–40: taught at School of Oriental Studies, London U. 1940–2: War service as Army Captain at War Office, London. 1942–5: Cultural Attaché, British Embassy, Chunking. 1947–9: Chinese National Govt. scholarship to study T'ang dynasty Bdsm in Peking; translations of Huang Po and Hui Hai drafted; married Chang Meifang. 1949–61: taught in Hong Kong and Bangkok. Also visited Darjeeling to study with Nyingma teachers incl Dudjom Rinpoche (qv) and Dodrupchen Rinpoche (qv). 1961–74: worked for UN (ECAFE), Bangkok. 1974–9: taught English at Kasetsart and Chulalongkorn Us, Bangkok. 1978–80: Extensive lecture tours of USA and Canada. Latterly engaged in studying Chinese composition and literature. Books incl *The Jewel in the Lotus*, *Red China in Perspective*, *The Wheel of Life* – autobiography, *People of the Sun*, *The Zen Teaching of*

Huang Po, The City of Lingering Splendour, The Zen Teaching of Hui Hai, The Book of Change, The Way of Power – US title: *The Tantric Mysticism of Tibet, Mahayana Bdsm in South-East Asia, The World of Bdsm, King Maha Mongkut of Siam, The Secret and the Sublime, Beyond the Golds, Mantras, Compassion Yoga, Taoism: Quest for Immortality, Gateway to Wisdom, The Chinese Art of Tea,* and a book of reminiscences written in Chinese.

Conze, Dr Edward Julius Dietrich (1904–79): *Pioneer naturalized British Bdst scholar and translator; authority on the Prajnaparamita literature.* b London, son of German Vice-Consul, ed Germany; PhD Cologne 1928. 1933: emigrated to UK due to dislike of Nazis. 1937: chance discovery of book by D.T. Suzuki revivified an earlier interest in Bdsm; thereafter devoted himself tirelessly to Bdst studies and produced a steady flow of books, incl Mahayana translations and anthologies. Held academic posts at Us of Wisconsin, Washington, Lancaster, California, Bonn and at Manchester College, Oxford. Also sometime Vice-President of The Bdst Society and Custodian of C Asian MSc at Indian Office Library. 'In his writings he was that *rara avis* a man deeply versed in technical scholarship yet at the same time both loving and striving to live the religion of which he was such an able exponent' (Christmas Humphreys). 'He was in my view the most important scholar of Bdsm in post-war Britain . . .' (Ninian Smart). Books incl *Bdsm Its Essence & Development, Thirty Years of Bdst Studies, Further Bdst Studies, Selected Sayings from the Perfection of Wisdom, The Buddha's Law Among the Birds, Bdst Meditation, Bdst Wisdom Books, Bdst Scriptures, Bdst Texts through the Ages, A Short History of Bdsm, Bdst Thought in India* and translations of the *Abhisamayalankara* and the *Astasahasrika.* Autobiography: *Memoirs of a Modern Gnostic (2 vols)*.

Dahlke, Dr Paul (1865–1928): *Pioneer German Bdst.* E Prussia; studied medicine and became homoeopath in Berlin. Came to Bdsm via writings of A. Schopenhauer. 1900: to Ceylon; studied with Sumangala Thera, W.O.C. Wagiswara et al. Commuted between E and W for many yrs. Eventually built Das Buddhistische Haus, one of the 1st Bdst vihare in Europe in garden of house at Frohnau, nr Berlin; here he 'lived in ascetic conditions, observing the Rules of the Sangha' (Christmas Humphreys). Books in English incl *Buddhist Essays, Buddhism & Science, Essays and Poems, Buddhist Stories* and *Buddhism & Its Place in the Mental Life of Mankind*; edited and largely wrote *Die Brockensammlung.* Tr *Dhammapada* into German.

Grimm, George (1868–1945): *Pioneer German Bdst.* b Rollh bei Lauf. Destined for priesthood but took to Law instead. Attracted to Schopenhauer's philosophy; became close friend of Dr Paul Deussen (1845–1919); began to study Bdsm. After retirement from Supreme Court Bench, spent remaining 37 yrs of life on study, practice and propagation of Bdsm in Germany. Wrote books and articles and lectured widely (e.g. at U of Munich). 1921: formed Old Buddhist Community at Utting am Ammersee in Bavaria (with Dr Karl Seidenstucker). Books in English incl *The Doctrine of the Buddha (The Religion of Reason & Meditation)*.

Harding, Douglas E.: *Discoverer and proponent of The Headless Way,* b 1909 into an Exclusive Plymouth Brethren family in Lowestoft, Suffolk (UK). Left Brethren while architectural student at London University (Bartlett School). Disowned by family. Later went into architectural practice in India and in England. While walking in the Himalayas had a profound seeing into his own self-nature that is recounted in his book, *On Having No Head.* Has taught his Way, through a variety of skilful means, in Britain (e.g. at The Buddhist Society Summer School) and in the USA (e.g. under the auspices of EST). Other books incl *The Hierarchy of Heaven and Earth* and *Religions of the World.* An occasional journal, *Share it,* is produced by those following his Way. Lives nr Ipswich in Suffolk (UK).

Humphreys, Travers Christmas QC (1901–83): *Great propagator of Bdsm in the West.* b London. ed Malvern and Trinity College, Cambridge. Called to the Bar in London and like his father, Sir Travers Humphreys KC, enjoyed a long and distinguished career in criminal law. As First Treasury Counsel, led for the prosecution in many famous murder trials held in courtrooms of London's Central Criminal Court (Old Bailey); e.g. those of Ruth Ellis and Craig & Bentley. After WW II went to Japan to sit on International War Crimes Tribunal. 1927: m Aileen Faulkner (known as 'Puck'); no issue. Member and in 1956 elected Master of the Worshipful Company of Saddlers. Also a poet and a pundit in the debate over the authorship of the plays ascribed to Wm. Shakespeare. Founded The Bdst Lodge, later The Bdst Society, in 1924. Great public speaker, broadcaster and writer on Bdsm. Books incl: *The Great Pearl*

Robbery of 1913, Bdst Poems, The Mountain Side (poems), Poems of Peace and War, Seagulls & Other Poems, Shadows & Other Poems, Via Tokyo, The Field of Theosophy, Bdsm, The Bdst Students' Manual, The Bdst Way of Life, Concentration & Meditation, Exploring Bdsm, Karma & Rebirth, A Popular Dictionary of Bdsm, The Search Within, Sixty Years of Bdsm in England, Studies in the Middle Way, Teach Yourself Zen (Zen, a Way of Life) Thus Have I Heard, Walk On! The Way of Action (The Bdst Way of Action), A Western Approach to Zen, What is Bdsm?, Zen Bdsm and Zen Comes West. Autobiography: *Both Sides of the Circle.* See also special Christmas Humphreys memorial issue of *The Middle Way, vol. 58, no. 2 (Aug. 1983).*

Huyên-Vi, Thich: *Important Vietnamese Bdst leader in the W, propagator and writer.* b 1924 in Ninh-Thuan, S Vietnam. 1935: entered Sangha, 1940, Srāmanera, 1946 bhiksu, graduated from An-quang Bdst. Inst. Saigon. Lecturer there and in 1955 became Director. 1961 enrolled at Nalanda Pāli Post-Grad Research Inst. Patna. 1967: MA thesis. Magadh University – *The Four Abhidhammic Reals*, 1971: PhD, Magadha U (Patna) for 'A' Critical Study of the Life & Wks of Sariputta Thera'. Directs Monastère Bouddhique Linh-Son (Paris), which is centre of worldwide network of temples. Publications incl *The Four Abdhidhammic Realms, La Vie de Bouddha Sakyamuni, Dharma Talks*, etc. 1973: Prof. at Van-Hanh University, Saigon. 1974: Prof of Bdst Studies, Saigon University. 1975: invited to Paris by Linh-So'n Bdst Assoc. 1977: Abbot. 1978: President. 1986: Vice President for France of World Bdst Sangha Sabhia. Translated Nāgārjuna's Sūtrasamuccaya, ed and translated multi-lingual version of Heart Sutra.

Ling, Trevor (1920–95): Learnt Pali at school of Oriental Studies, London University, PhD *Buddhism and the Mythology of Evil* (Oxford 1977) 1971–84: Chair of Comparative Religion, Manchester University. Publications include *Buddha, Marx and God, Religious Chance in the Secular World, Buddhist Revival in India, The Buddha: Buddhist Civilization in India & Ceylon.* Translated Dīgha Nikāya, called *The Buddha's Philosophy of Man.*

Sangharakshita, Ven Maha Sthavira (D.P.E. Lingwood): *Founder of the Friends of the Western Bdst Order (FWBD); writer and poet.* b 1925, Stockwell, S London. Little formal education but read widely. Joined Bdst Soc at 18. 1943: joined Royal Corps of Signals; served in India, Ceylon and Singapore during WW II. Left the service in India at end of War and pursued the homeless life. 1949: samanera ordination. 1950: bhikkhu ordination. Spent 1 yr at Banaras U studying Pali, Abhidhamma and logic with Ven Jagdish Kashyap. Settled in Kalimpong; founded Young Men's Bdst Assn and established Triyana Vardhana Vihara ('Monastery of the Three Vehicles'). Sat on Edl Board of *Maha Bodhi Journal* and founded journal *Stepping Stones*. 1950s: exodus of lamas from Tibet; received teachings from Dhardo Rinpoche, Jamyang Khyentse Rinpoche (qv) et al; also studied Ch'an. 1957#aa: became active in Bombay area, working among 'Untouchables'; advised Dr Ambedkar (qv) and 'personally officiated at the conversion of 200,000 people' (Subhuti). 1964: returned to UK, to Hampstead Bdst Vihara. 1967: established Friends of the Western Bdst Order (FWBO). 1970: conducted Hall Seminar at Yale. Publications incl *Messengers from Tibet and other Poems, A Survey of Bdsm, The Three Jewels, Peace is A Fire, Flame in Darkness, The Enchanted Heart, Crossing the Stream, The Path of the Inner Life, The Religion of Art, Travel Letters, Mind – Reactive and Creative, Aspects of Bdst Morality, Bdsm, World Peace and Nuclear War, The Bodhisattva, Evolution and Transcendence, The Glory of the Literary World, Going for Refuge, Human Enlightenment, Peace is a Fire, Alternative Traditions, Bdsm & Blasphemy,* and *The Eternal Legacy.* Autobiography: *The Thousand-Petalled Lotus.*

Tennisons, Karlis Alexis (1873–1962): *Onetime Bdst Archbishop of Lithuania, Estonia & Latvia by decree of 13th Dalai Lama.* b North Latvia. Travelled to E Siberia, etc, in search of Bdst teaching. Trained by HH Mahacariya Ratnavajra, a Lithuanian Bdst living in E Russia. Became 'profound Sanskrit scholar and Indologist'. Did Dhammaduta wk beyond Arctic Circle among Yakuts, Samoyeds, etc, and in C Asia. Also studied in China. 1890s: with Friedrich Lustig (a Baltic German) et al, established 1st W Bdst community on European soil. Supervised building of Bdst temple in Leningrad/St Petersburg (opened 1915). During WW I: Bdst chaplain to Russian Army. 1917: went into exile. 1956: with Lustig in Delhi for Jayanti celebrations. d Rangoon, Burma.

Watts, Alan Wilson (1915–73): *Writer and talker on Zen and religion in general.* b Chiselhurst, Kent (UK). ed King's School, Canterbury. 1930: began correspondence with Christmas Humphreys of Bdst Lodge; introduced to writings of D.T. Suzuki. 1931: first article published. 1932: left school; did not go on to university instead took daytime job and pursued spiritual interests in spare time. 1936–8: Editor of *Bdsm in England.* 1936: 1st book: *The Spirit of Zen.* 1938: m Eleanor Everett, daughter of Ruth Fuller Everett (later Sasaki); emigrated to USA. 1944: ordained Episcopalian priest in Chicago; became Chaplain at Northwestern University (Evanston). 1950: left Episcopalian Church. 1951: m Dorothy De Witt. 1951–7: taught at American Academy of Asian Studies, San Francisco; served as Dean 1953–6. Involved in Californian Counterculture (fictionalized as Arthur Whane in Kerouac's *Dharma Bums*). Took part in experiments with LSD in UCLA Dept of Neuropsychology. After 1957 worked independently ('lived by my wits') as lecturer, writer, broadcaster, etc. 1958: Hon DD, U of Vermont; visited Europe; lectured at C.G. Jung Institute and had discussions with D.T. Suzuki. c 1959: m Mary Jane Yates. 1961: went to live on houseboat *Vallejo* in Sausalito. 1960–5: visited Japan, escorting parties to Kyoto. d of heart failure at home at Druids Heights, Mt Tamalpais, California, after exhausting lecture tour of Europe. Books incl *The Spirit of Zen, The Legacy of Asia & Western Man, The Meaning of Happiness, Behold the Spirit, Theologica Mystica of St. Dionysius, The Supreme Identity, Myth & Ritual in Christianity, Nature Man & Woman, The Wisdom of Insecurity, Easter – Its Meaning & Story, The Way of Zen, This Is It, The Book on the Taboo Against Knowing Who You Are, Psychotherapy East and West, The Joyous Cosmology, The Two Hands of God, Cloud-hidden, Whereabouts Unknown, Does It Matter?, Man's Relation to Materiality,* and *Tao: The Watercourse Way.* Autobiography: *In My Own Way.* Biographies: *Alan Watts,* by David Stuart, and *Genuine Fake,* by Monica Furlong.

Wei Wu Wei (Terence Gray, 1895–1986): *Zen/Taoist writer, b of wealthy Anglo-Irish ancestry* at Felixstowe, Suffolk. Completed education at Cambridge and much involved in setting up a theatre in the town. Latterly lived Monte Carlo and owned vinyard in Rhone Valley where produced own wine At one time kept a string of race horses and won Ascot Gold Cup one year. A member of the Carlton Club, he ran a Rolls Royce. married twice. 1960s:travelled in east; visited Lama Govinda (qv) in Almora and Arthur Osborne in Turuvannamalai; met John Blofeld (qv) in Bangkok and visited Taiwan and Hong Kong in search of remnants of the Ch'an tradition; in Japan, stayed with Ogata San and visited D.T. Suzuki (qv) and Nakagawa Soen Roshi (qv). Books incl *All Else is Bondage, Why Lazarus Laughed, Ask the Awakened, OOO, Fingers Pointing at the Moon* and *Posthumous Papers.*

Wilber, Ken: *American scholar and writer on Bdsm, transpersonal psychology, meditation and allied topics.* b 1949, Oklahoma City. Bachelor's degrees (B) in biochemistry; Master's degrees in biochemistry/biophysics (both U of Nebraska). At age 23: left graduate school to wirte first book, Spectrum of Consciousness . . . 'I just kept on writing, basically, and since then have written 10 books and close to 100 articles/reviews'. Co-founder and Editor-in-chief of *ReVision;* Consulting Editor for Journal of *Transpersonal Psychology;* General Editor of New Science Library/Shambhala Publications. 1971: began Zen practice; was particularly influenced by Philip Kapleau, Eido Roshi, Katagiri Roshi, and Maezumi Roshi. Later began to study and practise Vajrayana Bdsm under Trungpa Rinpoche and Kalu Rinpoche. 'My spiritual studies have also been strongly influenced by Krishnamurti, Ramana Maharshi, Aurobindo and Da Free John'. Married to Treya Killam Wilber. Books incl *The Spectrum of Consciousness, The Atman Project, Up from Eden, Eye to Eye, No Boundary, A Sociable God and Transformations of Consciousness.* Edited *The Holographic Paradigm* and *Quantum Questions.*

Notes

[1] *The Life of the Buddha*. (1978) Nanamoli. Kandy: B.P.S. pp. 176–7. My italics.

[2] *Zen and Zen Classics, Vol. 4 – Mumonkan*. (1972) Translated by R.H. Blyth, Tokyo: Hokuseido Press. p. 11.

[3] I say 'the Indian religious outlook at its best' because of course there have been instances when it has manifested at less than its best: for instance during the terrible fighting between Hindus and Muslims following Independence from British Rule.

[4] Strictly speaking, the Vedas consist of three parts: the Samhitas, the Brahmanas and the Upanishads. The Samhitas, consist of the collections of hymns listed in the text. The Brahmanas, on the other hand, are prose texts dealing with brahminical sacrificial rites. Finally, the Upanishads are discourses concerning Brahman (Ultimate Reality) and other lofty philosophical topics – they are discussed later on.

[5] *Early Indian Religious Thought*. (1956). Phiroz Mehta. London: Lusac. pp. 32–3.

[6] *The Life of the Buddha*. (1949) E.J. Thomas. London: Kegan Paul. p. 31.

[7] *Majjhima Nikaya*, 245–6. Quoted in *Reflections on the Life of the Buddha*. (1983) Garry Thomson. London: The Buddhist Society, p. 7.

[8] Bimbisara was the first important king of Magadha and has been described as a man of determination and political foresight. His conquest of Anga extended his power over the trading routes and he was also one of the earliest Indian kings to see the need for efficient administration. In about 493 BC he was murdered by his son, Ajatasattu, who then became king and was determined to continue his father's aggressive expansionist policies.

[9] *Sutta Nipata*, 1074, 1076. Quoted in Thomson (1983), p. 22.

[10] *Buddhism in Translations*. (1896) H.C. Warren. Cambridge, Mass.

[11] *A Still Forest Pool: The Insight Meditation of Achaan Chah*. (1985) Compiled and edited by Jack Kornfield and Paul Breiter. Wheaton, Illinois: Theosophical Publishing House. p. 51,

[12] 'Kamma & Rebirth'. Ajahn Sumedho. In: *The Middle Way*. Vol. 57, p. 17.

[13] Maha-Nidana-Suttanta ('The Great Discourse on Causation'). In: *Dialogues of the Buddha, Pt. 2*. (1977) translated by T.W. Rhys-Davids, London: Pali Text Society. (Reprint) p.50.

[14] The term 'Hinayana', meaning 'Little (or Lesser) Vehicle', was coined by the followers of the Mahayana as a natural contrast to the term they coined for their own 'Greater Vehicle'. Non-Mahayanists sometimes find the term perjorative and object to it, with obvious reason. However, it is the most useful term for the basic tradition of Buddhism that spawned the Eighteen Schools, and in a non-sectarian, non-judgemental spirit it is used here.

[15] *Indian Buddhism* (1970) A.K. Warder. Delhi: Motilal Banarsidas. p. 290.

[16] *A Short History of Buddhism*. E. Conze (1980) London: Allen & Unwin. p. 45ff.

[17] This clearly does not accord with the Buddha's own statement that he did not teach with 'the closed fist': i.e. did not hold anything back, or teach an esoteric set of doctrines.

[18] *The Eternal Legacy*, Sangharakshita. (1985) London: Tharpa Publications. p. 96.

[19] *ibid*. p. 96.

[20] *Buddhism, Its Essence and Development*. (1960) E. Conze, Oxford. p. 122.

[21] *Buddhist Thought in India*. (1962) E. Conze, London. p. 251.

[22] *Essentials of Buddhist Philosophy*. (1975) J. Takakusu, Delhi: Motilal Bandrsidass. p. 104–5.

[23] This sexual union symbolizes the process whereby the passive male aspect of ultimate reality is brought into manifestation by the powerfully creative female aspect.

[24] One kind person who has cast an informed eye over and commented upon this chapter suggests that this highly formalized systematization of Tantra, though the usual one given in books and disseminated by the more orthodox schools, somewhat misrepresents what happens in actual practice in certain cases. There are less formal approaches to Tantra where things proceed in a more intuitive way.

[25] *Tantra in Tibet*. (1977) Tsongkhapa. London: Allan & Unwin. Introduction.

²⁶ A *Sima* is a consecrated area in which ordinations may be performed.
²⁷ *A Short History of Buddhism.* E. Conze (1980) London: George Allen & Unwin. p. 59.
²⁸ 'Some Great Buddhists After Asoka'. (1959) In: *2500 Years of Buddhism.* Ed. P.V. Bapat. Delhi: Govt. of India Publications Division. pp. 199–200.
²⁹ 'Beyond the Jade Gate: Buddhism in China, Vietnam and Korea'. Erik Zürcher. In: *The World of Buddhism.* (1984) Ed. H. Bechert & R. Gombrich, London: Thames & Hudson. p. 201.
³⁰ *D.T. Suzuki: A Biography.* (1985) A. Irwin Switzer III, London: The Buddhist Society. p. 42.
³¹ *A Short History of Buddhism.* E. Conze (1980) London: George Allen & Unwin. p. 85.
³² *Buddhism: History & Diversity of a Great Tradition.* (1985) Elizabeth Lyons and Heather Peters. Philadelphia: The University Museum, University of Pennsylvania. p. 25.
³³ 'Some Thoughts on Buddhism in China'. (Nov, 1986) John Blofeld. In: *The Middle Way.* Vol. 61, No. 3. pp. 146 ff.
³⁴ *Zen & Japanese Buddhism.* (1970) D.T. Suzuki. Tokyo: Japan Travel Bureau. p. 93.
³⁵ *ibid.* p. 93.
³⁶ *ibid.* p. 95.
³⁷ *Zen Master Dogen: An Introduction with Selected Writings.* (1976) Yuho Yokoi, New York & Tokyo: Weatherhill.
³⁸ *Zen & Japanese Buddhism,* p. 103.
³⁹ Anthologized in: *The Tiger's Cave.* (1977) Translated by Trevor Leggett, London: Routledge & Kegan Paul.
⁴⁰ 'Zen & the Common Man: Social Dimensions of Hakuin Zenji's Art'. John Stevens. In: *The Middle Way.* Vol. 60, pp. 32 ff.
⁴¹ HH the Dalai Lama. Introduction to *Atisha, A Biography of the Renowned Buddhist Sage.* (1984) Lama Thubtan Kalsang *et al.*, 2nd Reprint. New Delhi: Mahayana Publications. p. xii.
⁴² Professor Norbu and his followers appear to believe that Zen is more superficial than Dzogchen. See review by Stephen Batchelor of *The Crystal & the Way of Light* by Prof. Norbu in: *The Middle Way.* Vol. 61, p. 183–4, and John Shane's reply in *ibid.* pp. 254–5.
⁴³ *The Middle Way.* Vol. 61, p. 89 (slightly rephrased).
⁴⁴ *The Middle Way.* Vol. 60, pp. 67.
⁴⁵ *ibid.* p. 68.
⁴⁶ 'The Jewel in the Lotus. A Survey of the Buddhism of Tibet' by S. Batchelor. In: *The Middle Way.* Vol. 59, p. 170.
⁴⁷ *The Sea of Faith.* (1984) Don Cupitt. London: BBC Publications, p. 171.
⁴⁸ *Serene Reflection Meditation.* (1987) Carrshield: Throssel Hole Priory. pp. 4–5.
⁴⁹ 'Profile of a Buddhist Study Group'. Eric Cheetham. In: *The Middle Way.* Vol. 60, p. 36.
⁵⁰ Recorded interview with the author, 1984.
⁵¹ *Born in Tibet.* (1981) Chögyam Trungpa. Boulder: Prajña Press. (Revised edition) p. 252.
⁵² For a full listing of his activities and achievements, see entry in Who's Who section.
⁵³ Letter to the author, dated 12th November, 1986.
⁵⁴ Letter to the author, dated 24th January, 1987.
⁵⁵ *Buddhism for World Peace.* (1982) Ven. Nichidatsu Fujii. Translated by Yumiko Miyazaki. Los Angeles: Japan Buddha Sangha. p. 151.
⁵⁶ An Uposatha Hall is where monks and nuns assemble on full moon days to listen to the reading of the Disciplinary Code.
⁵⁷ *Sangha.* (1972) Vol 3, No 5, pp. 1ff.
⁵⁸ The quotes in this passage are taken from 'FWBO for the Middle Way'. Dhammadinna. In: *The Middle Way.* Vol 59, pp. 225ff.
⁵⁹ *ibid.* p. 227.
⁶⁰ *Buddhism for Today.* (1983) Dharmachari Subhuti. Salisbury: Element Books. p. 25.
⁶¹ Quoted in *Beyond Health & Normality.* (1983) ed. Walsh & Shapiro. New York: Van Norstand Rehinholt, p. 45.
⁶² *ibid,* p. 55.
⁶³ Reprinted in *The Portable Jung.* (1978) ed. Joseph Campbell. US Penguin ed. p. 470.
⁶⁴ Commentary to *The Secret of the Golden Flower.* (1962) trans R Wilhelm. London: Routledge & Kegan Paul, p. 84.
⁶⁵ Suzuki preferred the term Cosmic Unconscious. In his view, this is a vast mystery, 'not known in the way relative things are known', which itself gives birth to consciousness and 'once recognized, enters into ordinary consciousness and puts in good order all the complexities there which have been tormenting us to greater or lesser degrees'. This is the source of creativity 'whereby not only artists nourish their inspirations, but even we ordinary beings are enabled,

each according to his natural endowments, to turn his life into something of genuine art'. See *Zen Buddhism and Psychoanalysis.* (1974) London: Souvenir Press. (Paperback ed.) pp. 16 and 17.

[66] DeMartino was in Japan immediately after World War II, working with the International Military Tribunal in Tokyo. In 1947 he visited D.T. Suzuki with Philip Kapleau. See *How the Swans Came to the Lake.* (1986) Rick Fields. Boulder and London: Shambhala Publications. p. 195ff.

[67] *Zen Buddhism.* (1956) D.T. Suzuki. New York: Doubleday Anchor, p.3.

[68] The other three 'forces' in modern Western psychology are (1) psychoanalysis; (2) behaviourism (with which we have not been concerned here); (3) humanistic psychology.

[69] 'In Praise of Ego: An Uncommon Buddhist Sermon'. Ken Wilber. *The Middle Way*, Vol. 58, pp. 151ff.

[70] Foreword to *Introduction to Zen Buddhism*, by D.T. Suzuki. Reprinted in *Psychology & the East.* (1986) London: Ark, p. 154 (trans. slightly different from the one quoted in the text).

[71] 'In Praise of Ego' – p. 152.

[72] *Up From Eden.* (1983) Ken Wilber. London: Routledge & Kegan Paul, pp 323ff.

Further Reading

Part 2   The Buddha

The Indian Background

The Rig Veda. (1981) Translated by Wendy O'Flaherty. Harmondsworth: Penguin.
The Upanishads. (1965) Translated by Joan Mascaró. Harmondsworth: Penguin.
Early Indian Religious Thought. (1965) P.D. Mehta. London: Luzac.
Prehistoric India. (1950) by Stuart Piggott. Harmondsworth: Penguin.
A History of India. Vol. 1. (1966) Romila Thapar. Harmondsworth: Penguin.
Hinduism. (1961) K.M. Sen. Harmondsworth: Penguin.

The Life of the Buddha

Reflections on the Life of the Buddha. (1983) Garry Thomson. London: The Buddhist Society.
The Life of the Buddha. (1976) H. Saddhatissa. London: Unwin Books.
The Life of the Buddha. (1949) Edward J. Thomas. London: Kegan Paul (3rd Ed)
The Life of the Buddha. (1971) Bhikkhu Nanamoli. Kandy: Buddhist Publication Society.
'The Legend of the Buddha Shakyamuni'. In: Chapter 2 of *Buddhist Scriptures.* (1959)
   Translated by Edward Conze. Harmondsworth: Penguin.
The Buddha. (1983) Michael Carrithers. Oxford: OUP.
The Buddha. (1973) Trevor Ling. Harmondsworth: Penguin.

Part 3   The Basic Teachings and Practices

The Buddhist World View

'Buddhist Cosmogony and Cosmology', L. de La Vallée Poussin, and 'Indian Cosmogony and
   Cosmology'. H. Jacobi. In: *The Encyclopaedia of Religion and Ethics.* (1921) Ed. James
   Hastings. Edinburgh: J. Clark.
Buddhist Cosmology. (1983) Randy Kloetzli. Delhi: Motilal Banarsidass.
Fundamentals of Mainstream Buddhism (Booklet No. 1: Samsara and Rebirth). (1985) Eric
   Cheetham. London: The Buddhist Society.

General Books

The Buddha & His Teachings. (1980) Narada Thera. Kandy, Sri Lanka: publisher not stated
   but probably Vajirarama.
The Buddha's Ancient Path. (1974) Piyadassi Thera. Kandy, Sri Lanka: Buddhist Publication
   Society.
Buddhist Dictionary. (1980) Nyanatiloka Thera. Kandy, Sri Lanka: Buddhist Publication
   Society.
Cittaviveka. (1983) Ven. Ajahn Sumedho. Petersfield: Chithurst Forest Monastery.
What the Buddha Taught. (1972) Walpola Rahula. Bedford: Gordon Fraser. (Highly
   recommended.)

Buddhist Ethics

Ethics of Buddhism. (1981) Tachibana, S. London: Curzon Press. (Reprint).
Buddhist Ethics. (1970) Saddhatissa, H. London: Allen & Unwin.

Buddhism and Food

The Buddhist Case for Vegetarianism. (1982) Philip Kapleau. London: Rider.

Buddhism and Sex

Buddhism & Sex. (1972?) Maurice Walshe. Sangha Guide No. 5. London: Wat
Dhammapadipa.

Buddhism and Death

Death & Dying: The Tibetan Perspective. (1986) Glenn H. Mullin. London: Arkana.
Death, Intermediate State & Rebirth. (1979) Lati Rinbochay & Jeffrey Hopkins. London:
Rider.
Rebirth and the Western Buddhist. (1987) Martin Willson. London: Wisdom Publications.
The Tibetan Book of the Dead. (1974) Translated by Francesca Fremantle & Chögyam
Trungpa. Berkeley & London: Shambhala.
Who Dies? (1982) Stephen Levine. New York: Anchor/Doubleday.

Meditation

The Heart of Buddhist Meditation. (1983) Nyanaponika Thera. London: Rider.
Living Buddhist Masters. (1983) Jack Kornfield. Boulder: Shambhala Publications. (Reprint).
Meditation in Action. (1969) Chögyam Trungpa. London: Watkins.
The Path to the Deathless. (undated, probably *c.* 1985) Ven. Ajahn Sumedho. Hemel
Hempstead: Amaravati.
Tranquillity & Insight. (1986) A. Solé-Leris. London: Rider.
Visuddhimagga ('The Path of Purification'). (1979) Bhadantacariya Buddhaghosa, Translated
by Bhikkhu Nanamoli. Kandy: BPS.
See also *The Atman Project.* (1980) Ken Wilber. Wheaton, Illinois: Theosophical
Publishing House, chap. 12.

Part 4 The Development of Buddhism in India

Hinayana

Buddhism, Its Essence and Development. (1960) Conze, E. Oxford: Cassirer. paperback
edition.
Buddhist Thought in India. (1962) Conze, E. London: George Allen & Unwin.
Indian Buddhism. (1970) Warder, A.K. Delhi: Motilal Banarsidass.
An Analysis of the Pali Canon. (1975) Russell Webb. Kandy, Sri Lanka: Buddhist
Publication Society.
The Central Conception of Buddhism, and the Meaning of the Word 'Dharma'. (1974)
Th. Stcherbatsky. Delhi: Motilal Banasidass. (Reprint).
The Manual of Abhidhamma. (1956) Narada Maha Thera. Colombo: Vajirarama.

Mahayana

Indo-Tibetan Buddhism. (1987) David Snellgrove. Boston & London: Shambhala/Serindia.
A Short History of Buddhism. (1980) Conze, E. London: George Allen & Unwin.
The Central Philosophy of Buddhism. A Study of the Madhyamika System. (1955)
Murti, T.R.V. London: George Allen & Unwin.
The Essentials of Buddhist Philosophy. (1975) Takakusu, J. Delhi: Motilal Banarsidas.

Studies in the Lankavatara Sutra. (1930) D.T. Suzuki, London: Routledge & Kegan Paul.

Tantra

Foundations of Tibetan Mysticism. (1960) Lama Anagarika Govinda. London: Rider.
An Introduction to Tantric Buddhism. (1974) S.B. Dasgupta. Berkeley & London: Shambhala. (Reprint).
'The Jewel in the Lotus. A Survey of the Buddhism of Tibet. Part 5: The Tantras'. Stephen Batchelor. In: *The Middle Way.* Vol. 60, pp. 17ff.
Tantra in Tibet: The Great Exposition of Secret Mantra. (1977) Tsong-ka-pa, Translated by Jeffrey Hopkins. Introduction by HH the 14th Dalai Lama. London: Allen & Unwin.
The Tantric View of Life. (1976) Herbert V. Guenther. Boulder: Shambhala.
The Theory & Practice of the Mandala. (1969) Giuseppe Tucci. Translated by A.H. Brodrick. London: Rider.

Part 5   The Spread of Buddhism

Sri Lanka

Two Sinhalese records record the early history of Buddhism in Sri Lanka: The *Mahavamsa* (a translation exists by Wilhelm Geiger) and the *Dipavamsa*.

The Heritage of the Bhikkhu. (1974) Walpola Rahula. New York: Grove Press.
History of Buddhism in Ceylon: the Anuradhapura Period. (1956) Walpola Rahula. Colombo: Gunasena.

Burma

A History of Burma. (1925) G.E. Harvey. (2 vols).
Religion & Politics in Burma. (1968) D.E. Smith. Cambridge, Mass: Princeton UP.
Sanskrit Buddhism in Burma. (1936) N. Ray. Calcutta: U of Culcutta.
A Thousand Lives Away. Buddhism in Contemporary Burma. (1964) Winston L. King. Oxford: Cassirer.

Thailand

Buddhist Monk, Buddhist Layman. A study of Buddhist monastic organization in central Thailand. (1973) Jane Bunnag, Cambridge: CUP.
Sangha, State & Society. (1986) Yoneo Ishii. Honolulu: University of Hawaii Press.
Buddhism in Thailand. (1971) HRH Prince Damrong. London: Information Service of Thailand.

The North-Western Springboard

The Buddhist Art of Gandhara. (1960) Sir John Marshall. Cambridge: The University Press.
A Guide to Taxila. (1960) Sir John Marshall. Cambridge: The University Press.
The Real Tripitaka. (1952) Arthur Waley. London: George Allen & Unwin.
'Expansion to the North: Afghanistan and Central Asia'. Oskar von Hinüber. In: *The World of Buddhism* (1984) Ed. H. Béchert & R. Gombrich. London: Thames & Hudson.
'Evidence of Buddhist Activity in the North Western Provinces of India'. Eric Cheetham. In: *The Middle Way.* Vol. 55, p.7.
'The Kashmiri Bridge'. Eric Cheetham. In: *The Middle Way.* Vol. 56, No. 1. p. 59.

The Silk Road

'Buddhism in Central Asia'. R.E. Emmerick. In: *The Encyclopaedia of Religion.* Ed. Mircea Eliade. New York: Macmillan. Vol. 2, pp. 400ff.

Foreign Devils on the Silk Road. (1980) Peter Hopkirk. London: John Murray.
On Ancient Central Asian Tracks. (1933) Aurel Stein. London: Macmillan. (Reissued Chicago: University of Chicago Press. 1974. Ed. Jeannette Mirsky).
Buddhism in Central Asia. (1970) Kshanika Saha. Calcutta: Mukopadhyay.

China

Buddhism in China. (1964) Kenneth Ch'en. Princeton, New Jersey: Princeton University Press.
Buddhism in Chinese History. (1965) A.F. Wright. Stanford, Cal.: University of California Press. (Reprint).
The Buddhist Conquest of China. (1959) E. Zürcher. Leiden: E.J. Brill.
Chinese Thought: An Introduction. (1985) Ed. Donald H. Bishop. Delhi: Motilal Banarsidass.
The Essentials of Buddhist Philosophy. (1975) Junjiro Takakusu, Delhi: Motilal Banarsidass.
Monkey. (1942) Wu Ch'en-en. Translated by Arthur Waley. London: George Allen & Unwin.
A Record of the Buddhistic Kingdoms (Being an Account by the Chinese Monk Fa-hien of his Travels in India and Ceylon (A.D. 399–414) in Search of the Buddhist Books of Discipline). (1886) Translated by James Legge, Oxford: The Clarendon Press. (Reprint: New York: Paragon Book Reprint Corp./Dover Publications Inc. 1965.)
A Source Book in Chinese Philosophy. (1963) Translated and compiled by Wing-tsit Chan. Princeton, New Jersey: Princeton University Press.
The Wheel of Life. (1959) John Blofeld. London: Rider.

Vietnam and Korea

Buddhism & Zen in Vietnam. (1975) Thich Thien-An. Los Angeles & Toyko.
'Buddhism in Korea'. (1987) Robert Evans Buswell Jnr. In: *The Encyclopaedia of Religion.* Ed. Mircea Eliade. New York: Macmillan.
The Korean Approach to Zen: The Collected Works of Chinul. (1983) R.E. Buswell Jnr. Honolulu: University of Hawaii Press.
The Way of Korean Zen. (1985) Kusan Sunim. Translated by Martine Fages and edited with an Introduction by Stephen Batchelor. New York & Tokyo: Weatherhill.

Japan

A First Zen Reader. (1960) Compiled by Trevor Leggett. Tokyo & Rutland Vermont: Tuttle.
A History of Zen Buddhism. (1968) Heinrich Dumoulin. London: Faber & Faber.
The Religions of Japan. (1984) H. Byron Earhart. San Francisco: Harper & Row.
Sources of Japanese Tradition. (1964) Compiled by R. Tsunoda, ed. Wm. T. de Bary (Editor) and Donald Keene. New York: Columbia University Press. (2 vols).
Taking the Path of Zen. (1982) Robert Aitken. San Francisco: North Point Press.
'This World & the Other Power: Contrasting Paths to Deliverance in Japan'. (1984) Robert K. Heinemann. In *The World of Buddhism.* Ed. H. Bechert and R. Gombrich, London: Thames & Hudson.
Unsui. A Diary of Zen Monastic Life. (1973) Giei Sato & Eshin Nishimura. Honolulu: University of Hawaii Press.
Zen Action, Zen Person. (1981) T.P. Kasulis. Honolulu: University of Hawaii Press.
Zen & Japanese Buddhism. (1970) D.T. Suzuki. Tokyo: Japan Tourist Bureau.
Zen & Japanese Culture. (1959) D.T. Suzuki. New York: Pantheon Books.
The Zen Life. (1977) Sosei Kuzunishi & Koji Sato. New York & Tokyo: Weatherhill/Tankosha.
Zen & the Ways. (1978) Trevor Leggett. London: Routledge & Kegan Paul.

Tibet

Advice from a Spiritual Friend. (1978) Geshe Rabten & Geshe Dhargyey. Translated and edited by Brian Beresford. London: Wisdom Publications. (Revised edition).
A Cultural History of Tibet. (1968) David Snellgrove and Hugh Richardson. Boston &

London: Shambhala. (Revised edition).
Foundations of Tibetan Mysticism. (1960) Lama Anagarika Govinda. London: Rider.
The Jewel in the Lotus. A Guide to the Buddhist Traditions of Tibet. (1987) Stephen Batchelor. London: Wisdom Publications.
The Religions of Tibet. (1980) Giuseppe Tucci. London: Routledge & Kegan Paul.

Mongolia and Russia

'Der Buddhismus in Russland in Vergagenheit und Gegenwart'. (1985) Friedrich Fenzl. In: *Bodhi Baum*. (Austrian Buddhist journal). Vol. 10, No. 2, pp. 91ff.
The Religions of Mongolia. (1980) Walter Heissig. London: Routledge & Kegan Paul.
The Empire of the Steppes: (1970) René Grousset, tr. N. Walfard. New York: Franklin Watts.
The Kalmyk Mongols. (1967). Paula G. Reubel. Bloomington: Indiana U.P.

Part 6   Buddhism Comes West

Slow Beginnings

Both Sides of the Circle. (1978) Christmas Humphreys. London: George Allen & Unwin.
A Buddhist Student's Handbook. (1956) Ed. Christmas Humphreys. London: The Buddhist Society.
The Early Writings of Alan Watts. (1987) Vol. 1. Ed. John Snelling. Los Angeles: Celestial Arts.
Genuine Fake. (1986) Monica Furling. London: Heinemann.
In My Own Way. (1973) Alan Watts. New York: Vintage Books.
Sixty Years of Buddhism in England. (1968) Christmas Humphreys. London: The Buddhist Society.
The Western Contribution to Buddhism. (1974) William Pieris. Delhi etc.: Motilal Banarsidass.

After World War II

Born in Tibet. (1981) Chögyam Trungpa. Boulder: Prajña Press. (Revised edition).
Buddhism in Britain. (1979) Ian P. Oliver. London: Rider.
The Buddhism of the Sun. (1982) Compiled by Jim Cowan. Richmond, Surrey: NSUK.
Buddhism for Today. (1983) Dharmachari Subhuti (Alex Kennedy). Salisbury: Element Books.
Memoirs of a Modern Gnostic. Vol. 1. (1979) Vol. 2. (1979) Vol. 3 not issued. Edward Conze. Sherborne: Samizdat.
On Having No Head. (1986) Douglas Harding. London: Routledge & Kegan Paul (Arkana Books). (Revised and enlarged edition).
The Thousand Petalled Lotus. (1976) Ven. Maha Sthavira Sangharakshita. London: Wm. Heinemann.

Buddhism in North America

How the Swans Came to the Lake. (1986) by Rick Fields. 2nd Revised and updated edition. Boston: Shambhala.*
Nine-headed Dragon River. (1986) by Peter Mathiessen. Boston: Shambhala.
Zen Buddhism in North America, A History and a Directory. Toronto: Zen Lotus Society.

* highly recommended

Buddhism and Psychotherapy

The Awakening of the Heart. (1983). Ed. John Welwood. Boulder & London: Shambhala.
Beyond Ego (Transpersonal Dimensions in psychology). (1980) Ed. Roger Walsh and Frances Vaughan. Los Angeles, California: J.P. Tarcher/HOughton Mifflin.

Beyond Health & Normality. (1983) Ed. Roger Walsh and Deane H. Shapiro. New York: Van Nostrand Reinhold.

Beyond Therapy. (1986) Ed. Guy Claxton. London: Wisdom Publications.

Buddhist and Western Psychology. (1983) Ed. Nathan Katz. Boulder & London: Shambhala.

The Legacy of Asia and Western Man. (1937) Alan W. Watts. London: John Murray.

Psychotherapy East and West. (1961) Alan W. Watts. New York: Ballantine.

The Supreme Doctrine. (1955) Hubert Benoit. London: Routledge & Kegan Paul.

Zen Buddhism and Psychoanalysis. (1974) D. T. Suzuki, Erich Fromm and Richard DeMartino. London: Souvenir Press.

By C.G. Jung:

Psychology & Religion: West and East. (1958) Vol. 11 of the Collected Works. London: Routledge & Kegan Paul. (Second edition, 1969).

Psychology and The East (1986) London: Ark Paperbacks.

see also *Jung and Tibetan Buddhism.* (1987). Radmila Moacanin. London: Wisdom Publications.

By Ken Wilber:

The Atman Project. (1980) Wheaton, Ill.: Theosophical Publishing House.

Eye to Eye. (1983) New York: Anchor/Doubleday.

No Boundary, (Eastern and Western Approaches to Personal Growth). (1981) Boulder & London: Shambhala.

Sprectrum of Consciousness. (1977) Weaton, III: Theosophical Publishing House

Up From Eden. (1983) London: Routledge & Kegan Paul

'In Praise of Ego'. *The Middle Way*, Vol. 58, No. 3. (Nov. 1983).

APPENDIX 1: A Checklist of Major Buddhist Festivals

Buddhist festivals vary from country to country, though the most important ones usually celebrate the major events of the Buddha's life. Mostly they fall on days in the local lunar calendar.

Theravàda Buddhist Festivals

In Theravàda countries, the Birth, Enlightenment and *Parinirvà*na of the Buddha are celebrated on the full moon day of May. This festival is called *Wisakha Pùja* in Thailand, *Wesak* in Sri Lanka. Other festivals in these countries are:

Sri Lanka

Poya, full moon days, are of special importance, five in particular. They are named after the lunar months in which they fall: *Duruthu* (Dec/Jan), *Navam* (usually Feb), *Wesak* (see above), *Poson* (June – celebrating the bringing of the Dhamma to Sri Lanka by Ven. Mahinda) and *Esala* (July/Aug). The distinctive Sri Lankan festivity is a colourful parade-pageant called a *perahera*. At the *Esala Perahera* in Kandy each year the Buddhas's Tooth Relic is paraded through the streets on the back of a magnificently caparisoned elephant. The Sri Lankan New Year falls mid–April.

Thailand

Asàlha Pùja (June/July) celebrates the Buddha's First Sermon. The 3-month Rains Retreat (*Vassa*) starts immediately afterwards. It is followed by *Kathina* (Oct or Nov), a kind of Thanksgiving when the laity donate requisites to the Sangha. *Màgha Pùja* (Jan/Feb) celebrates various minor events in the Buddha's life, including his prediction of his *Parinirvàna*. *Maha Jat* celebrates his past lives. The New Year Festival, *Songkran* (mid-April), includes a Water Festival. Finally, there are special observance days each month.

Mahàyàna Buddhist Festivals

Tibet

The Buddha's Birth is celebrated on the 9th day of the 4th month of the Tibetan calendar, his Enlightenment and Parinirvana on the 15th day of the same month. The New Year ceremonies are spectacular, and were even more so in the old days. *Gutor* is a pre-New Year festival when all the negative accumulations of the Old Year are put to rest. *Losar* is the New Year festival proper; it lasts for 4 days and is followed by a long religious ceremony, *Mönlam Chenmo* (lit. 'Great Prayer Festival'), which goes on for about 3 weeks and culminates in a Butter Festival. *Dzam Ling Chi Sang* (15th day, 5th month) is a day when offerings are made to local deities. Tibet National Uprising Day, commemorating the Lhasa Uprising (1959) has been fixed for March 10 in the Western Calendar, and the Dalai Lama's Birthday for July 6. *Chökhor Düchen* (4th day, 6th month) commemorates the Buddha's First Sermon and *Lha Bab Düchen* (22nd day, 9th month) his ascent into the Tushita Heaven to give teachings to his mother. *Ngachö Chenmo*

(25th day, 10th month) is a festival of lights commemorating the death of Jé Tsongkhapa. There are numerous other festivals and auspicious days every month.

Japan

Hana Matsuri (April 8) celebrates the Buddha's Birth, *Nehan* (Feb 15) his Enlightenment and *Ròhatsu* (Dec 8) his Death. The two equinoxes are celebrated at *Higan* (around March 21 and Sept 20), while *Obon* spans 4 days beginning July 13 and commemorates the release from one of the hells of the mother of one of the Buddha's foremost disciples. The object of *Setsubon* (early Feb) is to drive out evil spirits. Special Zen celebrations include: Bodhidharma Day (Oct 5), and the anniversaries of Rinzai Zenji (Jan 10), Daito Zenji (Nov 22), Dògen Zenji (Aug 28) and Keizan Zenji (Aug 15). The Jòdò Shin school celebrates the birth of Shinran Shònin on May 21; his death commemoration (*Ho On Ko*) varies between Jan 16 and Nov 16 according to the head temple followed.

The West

Now that Buddhism is coming to the West there are moves afoot to bring Buddhists of all schools and traditions together in a single celbration of the Life and Teaching of the Buddha, called Buddha Day, on the full moon day of May.

Index

NOTE: *The Who's Who in Buddhism (Part 7) section is not indexed, nor the individual groups, centres, etc. listed in Chapter 20, 'Useful Addresses'; direct reference should be made to those sections for relevant information. Countries, traditions and themes occurring in Chapter 20 are included, however. Finally, accenting has been minimized in the interests of simplicity.*